THE ANATOMY OF WOOD:

its Diversity and Variability

THE ANATOMY OF WOOD:

its Diversity and Variability

by

K.Wilson, Ph.D., F.I.Biol.
Professor Emeritus in the University of London
and formerly Head of the Department of Botany
at the Royal Holloway College.

and

D.J.B. White, Ph.D., F.I.W.Sc., F.I.Biol.
University College, London.

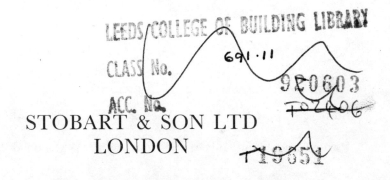
STOBART & SON LTD
LONDON

Published 1986

British Library Cataloguing in Publication Data

Wilson, K.
  The anatomy of wood : its diversity and
  variability.
  1. Wood
  I. Title   II. White, D. J. B.
  620.1'2   TA 419

  ISBN 0–85442–033–9
  ISBN 0–85442–034–7   Pbk

Stobart & Son Ltd, 67–73 Worship Street, London, EC2A 2EL

Printed and bound in Great Britain by A. Wheaton & Co Ltd., Exeter

Preface

THIS book is the outcome of an invitation from our publishers to prepare a work similar in its content and purpose to "The Structure of Wood" by the late F. W. Jane; this is now not only out of print, but in the light of subsequent developments in the subject, has become outdated in its treatment of some topics.

In responding to this invitation, within the smaller compass afforded to us, we have attempted to follow the essential character of Jane's book, and to provide, primarily for students of timber technology, an introduction to the sources, growth and anatomy of wood, and the use of its structural features, both macroscopic and microscopic, in the identification of unknown specimens. While pressure on space has compelled the omission of some topics, which we judge now to be of less relevant interest than they were, variants of timber structure which most commonly have some influence on its properties are outlined and discussed. At the same time we have endeavoured, with more botanically orientated students in mind, to draw attention to the wider aspects of some of these matters, especially those relating to the ultrastructure of wood and those associated with the initiation and formation of reaction wood and its role in the life of the tree.

How the problems of wood identification may be most usefully considered within a limited space must be very much a matter of opinion. The approach we have adopted is to focus attention more on those anatomical features which have been found useful in distinguishing one wood from another, rather than on the whole structure, in wider terms, of an extensive range of timbers each considered individually. We then show how these features may be used in a systematic way for the purposes of identification. Thus we hope that students who have worked through and understood Chapters 4, 5 and 10 will know what kinds of features to look for when they examine a wood sample with a hand-lens or a microscope, how to recognize and describe these features, and so, in short, will have the necessary background to embark on the use of a key.

Chapters 6 and 9, especially, concerned respectively with the ultrastructure of wood, and reaction wood, go further than timber technology students will generally need. However, some appreciation, even in the broadest terms, of the fundamental nature of the wood substance itself, and its bearing on the shrinkage and strength properties of timber, will be of use to them, while students of botany, with some knowledge of cell wall structure in other groups of plants, will recognize universal problems associated with the study of wood cells. Concerning reaction wood also, the timber technology student, who will be interested primarily in its mechanical properties and their bearing on its utilization, should be aware not only that its characteristics have their origins in its aberrant ultrastructure, but also that it is not merely a defect in timber; it is a fundamental feature of the growth of the tree, and is thus always liable to be present. That the stimulus to its formation, and its mode of action, still present unsolved problems, will perhaps not greatly interest him, but these problems will continue to be of special interest to the botanist.

Those of our readers who are acquainted with "The Structure of Wood" will perceive our debt to that work, a debt which we fully acknowledge. While the present volume covers much of the same ground, it is however not simply a third edition of Jane's book, but has been written completely anew, and the great majority of the illustrations are also new. Inevitably it rests widely on the relevant literature of the subject, as the list of references indicates. In a book of this nature the choice of those which should be brought to the reader's notice must be much in the minds of its authors, and those listed here are very much a personal selection; they will however suffice to lead the enquiring mind into further study. At the same time we have aimed to produce a text which can be read as a connected account independently of wider reading.

We are indebted to Messrs A. and C. Black for permission to reproduce Figures 34, 36, 37, 54, 62, 75, 78 and 82 from "The Structure of Wood" by F. W. Jane, and to Her Majesty's Stationery Office for permission to reproduce Figure 136. We are grateful to Dr A. W. Robards for Figures 93, 94, 126*B* and 129; to Dr. P. D. Burggraaf and the Koninklijke Nederlanse Botanische Vereniging for Figure 73; to Dr. D. W. Brett and Dr. M. P. Denne for the loan of slides, and to Mr. C. C. Lorenzen and Messrs Meyer-International PLC for a gift of veneers.

It is a pleasure also to record our thanks to Professor J. D. Dodge, Head of the Department of Botany at the Royal Holloway College, University of London, for the loan of slides and specimens, and for opportunities for photo- and electron-microscopy. We are especially grateful to David Ward and Lynne Etherington, members of the departmental technical staff, for their invaluable assistance in the preparation of the photographs.

Contents

1

Sources of Timber

Wood has evolved, over a period of hundreds of millions of years, to meet the mechanical and physiological needs of the tree; it is, arguably, the most remarkable structural material on earth. In the course of time it has achieved great diversity; there are estimated to be upwards of 20000 different kinds of trees, and thus potentially a similar number of different kinds of timber. Although those of commercial importance number only a few hundreds, the range of anatomical structure and chemical and physical properties that they display is nonetheless most striking.

While later chapters are more specifically concerned with this diversity of wood structure, it is however appropriate, in considering timber in general terms, to identify at the outset the two broad groups of timbers which are distinguished commercially as hardwoods and softwoods. These terms have precise meanings, but must not be interpreted literally, since, for example, the wood of the yew-tree, technically a softwood, is harder (and heavier) than many hardwoods, while the lightweight balsa wood, familiar in its use in model making, is technically a hardwood, even though it is so soft as to be easily indented by the finger-nail.

More fundamentally, the distinction between hardwood and softwood timbers is based on differences in their microscopic structure, and is related closely to the wider botanical differences between the trees from which the two groups of timbers are derived. All timber trees reproduce by seeds, and botanists divide seed-plants into two groups; Angiosperms, which include the broad-leaved trees, the hardwoods of the timber merchant, and Gymnosperms, which include the coniferous trees, the softwoods.

There are certain constant differences between Angiosperms and

Gymnosperms. The principal difference is in the manner in which the seeds are borne. In Angiosperms (and therefore in hardwood trees) the seeds are always produced inside an ovary or fruit of some kind, as for example, the "pips" in an apple, the seeds in a pod in laburnum, or the "conkers" in the fleshy fruit of a horse-chestnut. In Gymnosperms, however, the seeds are naked, not enclosed in this way, though in their development they are usually concealed and protected by the aggregation of the scale-like structures on which they are borne into specialized reproductive shoots. These are, of course the female cones, familiar, for instance, in pine and cedar. Yew, and a few other related coniferous trees, are exceptional in this respect, in that their seeds are borne singly on the young shoots, though they are nevertheless naked and unenclosed. The terms Angiosperm and Gymnosperm, which are of Greek derivation, refer to this basic difference between enclosed and naked seeds. Lest it may seem therefore, to the non-botanist, that an acorn, commonly thought of as the seed of the oak tree (i.e. a hardwood tree) is a naked seed, it may be emphasized that an acorn is in fact a fruit; the seed, properly defined, is enclosed within it. The same is true of the "seeds" of some other trees, for instance, ash and sycamore.

Secondly, associated with this and other important differences in the reproductive structures of the two groups, there are major anatomical differences between them. The most important of these relate to the anatomy of the wood, or secondary xylem; the wood of softwood trees has a simpler, and in general terms, a rather more uniform structure than that of hardwoods (see Chapters 4 and 5). There are also differences between the two groups in their inner bark, or phloem, (the tissue principally concerned in the transport in the tree of sugars and other organic nutrient substances). This however is outside our purview and will not be considered further.

In addition to these fundamental and universal differences between angiosperms and gymnosperms, and thus between hardwood and soft-wood trees, others, though less exclusive, may be recognized. For instance, most softwood trees are evergreen; the leaves persist for several years, and though some are shed every year the tree never has a leafless period. There are however a few exceptions to this general statement, notably, for instance, the European larch, introduced and widely planted in Britain, and the swamp cypress, or bald cypress, of North America, also grown here, although more rarely, as an ornamental tree. Many common softwoods, such as pines, spruces, firs and larches have needle-like leaves such as are rarely found in hardwoods, while in others, such as the cypresses, the leaves are little more than small green scales. In a few, however, for instance the podocarps of the Southern hemisphere, the leaves are relatively large and not unlike those of certain (evergreen) hardwoods.

Among hardwoods there are both deciduous and evergreen trees. Thus the native English oaks shed their leaves annually, while the holm oak, a native of the Mediterranean region, but often seen in Britain as an ornamental tree, is evergreen; so too is holly, which is native in Britain. Temperate hardwoods are in general deciduous, while among tropical trees both types occur; the deciduous habit, though associated in temperate climates with winter cold, may in the tropics be related to the regular occurrence of a dry season.

In considering trees and timber it is feasible, up to a point, as indeed we have done so far in this chapter, to refer to them by their common everyday names. Thus among British native trees, of which there are comparatively few different kinds, such common names as oak, ash, pine, yew and so on are sufficiently unambiguous; even in the wider context of the trees of Europe a similar usage would be adequate for many purposes. However, as it becomes necessary to refer to trees of greater variety, range or distribution, the use of common names proves, for various reasons, quite inadequate. It then becomes increasingly necessary to use the formal botanical Latin names for trees, and thus, by derivation, for the timbers derived from them. At this point therefore it is appropriate to digress from our main theme to explain briefly, for the non-botanist, the nature and use of botanical names. These will be freely used, as may be necessary, throughout this book.

A readily distinguishable kind of tree, or for that matter, any other plant, is referred to as a species (often abbreviated as sp.), and closely similar species (abbreviated, in the plural, as spp.) are grouped into a genus (plural, genera). The botanical name of a species thus consists of two words, the first one being the generic name (which should always have a capital initial letter) and the second one which defines the species (among the others in the genus). Thus the common oak is *Quercus robur*, (Latin names of plants are always printed in italics); *Quercus* refers to oaks in general, and *robur* to this particular species of oak, thus distinguishing it from the sessile oak, *Q. petraea*, the holm oak, *Q. ilex*, the cork oak, *Q. suber*, and the many other species of oak known to science. There are about 300 or so, of which many are commercially important. When the name of a genus occurs repeatedly, as it does in this explanatory sentence, it may be abbreviated to its initial letter, as long as this practice does not give rise to ambiguity. Strictly speaking, the botanical name should also include, for added precision, the name (usually in an abbreviated form) of the botanist who named the plant. Thus the full botanical name of the common oak is *Quercus robur* L., the "L" referring to the Swedish botanist, Linnaeus, to whom this name is due. This practice is necessary because it has often happened, through accidents of discovery, or differences of opinion, that different botanists have given different names to the same species, or even to the same genus, or have used the same name in different senses. Again, as long as ambiguity is avoided, this indication of the authority for a name is however, commonly omitted.

The classification of plants involves the grouping of what are considered to be similar or related species into a genus, as we have already seen, and of related genera into a family. Thus botanists consider that oaks (*Quercus* spp.), chestnuts (*Castanea* spp.) and beeches (*Fagus* spp.) are all sufficiently closely related for them to be put into one family, the Fagaceae; the name of a plant family is usually formed from the name of one of the principal constituent genera by the addition of the ending -aceae to the stem of the generic name, as in this instance. The timber technologist hardly needs to take plant classification any further than this, though botanists group related families into orders, and orders into still larger taxonomic aggregates; see for instance Jane (1970), who also outlines some other aspects of botanical taxonomic practice as they relate to timbers. Reference may also be usefully made to Willis (6th ed., 1931), or 8th ed., (1973). Though the latter, more up-to-date on taxonomic matters, lacks the general information included in the earlier edition, this has been separately collated and extended by Howes (1974).

However, most timbers have common names and sometimes special trade names, derived from the common name of the tree from which the timber is obtained. Such names, while meaningful within a small area, are likely to become unreliable in a wider context for various reasons. Sometimes they arise from apparent, but botanically unacceptable, likenesses between different trees; sycamore (*Acer pseudoplatanus*) and plane (*Platanus hybrida*, formerly *P. acerifolia*), are confused in this way, even within Britain. In Australia, emigrants from Britain found many unfamiliar trees, to which they applied names based on apparent resemblances between the timbers of these trees and those they knew in their home country. Thus there is an Australian timber known variously as Tasmanian oak, Victorian ash and mountain ash, because of its supposed similarities to the oaks, (*Quercus* spp.) and ash, (*Fraxinus excelsior*) of Europe. Yet this tree is neither a *Quercus* nor a *Fraxinus*; it is *Eucalyptus regnans*, a member of another family altogether, the Myrtaceae, and a most excellent timber in its own right.*Eucalyptus* is a large genus, of some 500 species, many of which produce valuable timbers. Some of their common names are however so different from one another as to conceal the fact that they refer to members of the same genus.

Elsewhere also, notably in Africa and the Far East, most trees have native names. These may be very local, so that the same tree may have different names in different parts of its range, or the same name may be applied to different trees in different places. Some names are also unselective in that they refer to a number of broadly similar trees found growing together; for instance, a group of species of *Shorea* (a genus of South East Asia) are known collectively as meranti, lauan and seraya in different parts of their range. In other cases, when unfamiliar timbers, largely unknown to the market, were first imported into the United Kingdom it was a common practice to attach another and more familiar name to them to make them more readily saleable. Thus timber from the tropical African tree, *Lovoa trichilioides* Harms (= *L. klaineana* Pierre ex Sprague), variously known locally, within its natural range, as apopo, sida, bibolo (and other names), came to be sold as African walnut or Nigerian walnut, because of its superficial resemblance to the wood of the well-known European walnut (*Juglans regia*). In this kind of way considerable confusion arose concerning the identity of some of the increasing number of timbers becoming commercially available. Ideally, for maximum precision, the botanical name of the tree from which the timber is obtained should be used (assuming it to be known), but for most commercial purposes it is sufficient to use the standard name as laid down by the British Standards Institution (1974). The botanical and British Standard names of all the timbers to which reference is made in this book are given in the appendix; the more extensive lists given by Jane (1970) follow the previous (1955) edition of the Standards. Standard names are also given by the Building Research Establishment (1972c, 1977, 1978).

In the Northern hemisphere softwood and hardwood trees show certain broadly recognizable geographical distributional differences, as is illustrated by Spurr (1979). In the higher temperate latitudes there is a belt of coniferous forest, which in Europe and Russia comprises principally pine (*Pinus sylvestris*), spruce (*Picea abies*), larch (*Larix decidua*), and fir (*Abies alba*). In North America there are similar associations, but of other species of the same genera, together with trees of other genera, such as Douglas fir (*Pseudotsuga menziesii*) and hemlock (*Tsuga* spp.). At lower latitudes, in situations where available moisture and other environmental factors allow, there are familiar temperate hardwood trees; oak, ash, beech, birch, alder, maple, elm, poplar, walnut, willow (and others), common in Britain and Europe. The same genera are strongly represented in North America, though again, characteristically, by different species.

This distinction of latitudinal distribution must not however be taken too literally. It is much modified by altitude, so that in mountainous or hilly country the areas of hardwood and softwood forest, as shown on a map, often appear to interpenetrate one another, hardwoods tending to occupy the lower levels and softwoods the higher. Moreover, although the only native pine in Britain (*Pinus sylvestris*) is a northern tree, the genus *Pinus* is a large one, of nearly 100 species, and some of

these occur in Europe, as timber trees, as far South as the Mediterranean. Other species, in North America, which form the important
Southern pine forests of the U.S.A., similarly extend to Texas and
Florida. The clearance of natural hardwood forest, and its widespread
sylvicultural replacement by the faster-growing softwoods, has also
tended greatly to modify the general picture. Many of these trees, both
hardwoods and softwoods, though not native to Britain, are to be seen
here in gardens and arboreta, and some in larger plantations (Mitchell,
1974; Phillips, 1978). Students of their timbers should find additional
interest in opportunities to examine the living trees.

In the Southern hemisphere the distribution of softwoods and hardwoods cannot be described simply in similar terms. Softwoods are in
any case rather poorly represented; the principal ones are species of
Podocarpus in East Africa and New Zealand, of *Agathis* (kauri pines) in
Australia and New Zealand, and *Araucaria* in Australia and South
America. One of the latter furnishes Parana pine. The principal hardwoods are also very different from those of the Northern hemisphere;
among them reference may be made to the very numerous species of
Eucalyptus in Australia (some of them widely planted elsewhere), and
the species of *Nothofagus* (Southern beech) in South America, Australia
and New Zealand.

Within the tropics, in areas of high rainfall, hardwood trees provide
a vast assortment of timbers. In a primary tropical rain forest there
will commonly be 40 species of trees, with trunks at least 10 cm in
diameter, in a sample plot of a hectare ($2\frac{1}{2}$ acres), and there may be as
many as 100 (Richards, 1952). Moreover, a second, similar sample is
likely to show one-quarter to one-third as many additional species
which happened not to be represented in the first one. It is to be noted
also that these numbers refer to species, not to individual trees, which
are several times more numerous, and a considerable proportion of
which may grow to heights of 50–60 m (160–200 ft). This wealth and
diversity of timber does however have the corollary that any one
species may be comparatively sparsely scattered; trees which are
especially desirable commercially, e.g. teak (*Tectona grandis*), may be
represented in a natural teak forest by only 2 or 3 individuals per
hectare.

Thus, clearly, the problems, and hence the practices, of the felling
and extraction of timber in the diverse conditions of these various kinds
of forest differ greatly. The older method of clear felling, and (if the
land is not to be used for agriculture) allowing the forest to regenerate
naturally, perhaps from a few trees left standing as seed sources, produces a second growth markedly different from the original. There is
also the likelihood, in many areas, that owing to soil erosion, or for some
other reason, forest regeneration may fail altogether. In the developed

countries the trend has been towards the use of clear felling, followed by replanting with seedling trees of known provenance, sometimes of exotic species, selected for desirable features such as fast growth and early maturity; that is, in effect, tree farming. The widespread planting in Britain of Sitka spruce (*Picea sitchensis*), a species of North West America, is a case in point. In contrast is the practice of the extraction of individual trees, so managed as to maintain a permanently productive forest of trees of mixed age; this involves the limitation of the volume of the recurrent cut of timber (taken as whole trees) to the productivity of those remaining. A variant of this is the widespread practice of coppicing, followed in Britain for hundreds of years, whereby trees were cut to near ground level and allowed to regenerate from the stumps, on a 10–12 year cycle. At the same time, and in the same area, a limited number of others might have been allowed to grow to maturity, as in the oak/hazel or oak/hornbeam coppiced woodlands of Southern England. The coppice provided small wood for fuel and varied agricultural purposes and the mature trees larger constructional timber. Coppicing reaches its logical conclusion in the trials in recent years of techniques of the growth and harvesting of very short rotation crops of *Populus* spp. as possible sources of wood pulp (Isebrands and Parham, 1974; Parham *et al.*, 1977).

In tropical rain forests the scale and complexity of the varied forest ecosystems present special problems for the extraction of timber (Whitmore, 1975). Even though only a relatively small proportion of the larger trees may be felled at any one time, a considerable fraction of what remains is liable to be lost in the extraction process as a result of damage by the falling trees and the extraction machinery. These forests are also being destroyed at an increasing rate by clearance in response to the demands of shifting agriculture, and how long, and to what extent, they may survive as sources of timber is problematical. Yet after the food plants, trees and tree products are the most important of the world's renewable resources.

It is estimated that nearly half the timber cut annually throughout the world is used as fuel, and wood has another major role, especially in the developed countries, in the form of wood-pulp and its derivative products. As worked timber the unique constructional and decorative qualities of wood have been utilized and appreciated since the earliest recorded times. In the last 100 years or so (and more especially since the first world-war) the scope of its uses has been greatly widened by the development of plywood and laminated boards and beams of various kinds; these have made new methods of construction possible, and enabled the more effective use of smaller logs. These trends are being repeated in the present-day development, dating from the second world war, of particle-board in its various forms, thus making structural use

of what would otherwise be largely waste wood and even waste bark
(Kollmann, Kuenzi and Stamm, 1975; Findlay, 1975).

Nevertheless, the demands for wood will inevitably continue to rise,
especially as it seems likely to be of increasing importance in the future
as a source of starting-points for synthetic processes in the chemical
industry; ligno-chemicals could well, in time, as oil becomes scarcer,
substitute in large measure for petro-chemicals. Thus the maintenance
of tree growth, in forests and plantations, sufficient to meet the widening
uses of wood and to ensure a continuing supply of this unique and
indispensable material, is, no less than for wider ecological reasons, a
necessity for the future.

2

The Structural Organization of a Tree

A tree has been defined as a woody plant, usually with only one stem at the base, and more than 30 ft (9 m) high (Willis, 6th ed., 1931, and later reprints). Although the height cannot, obviously, be too precisely insisted upon, this definition, distinguishing it from a shrub — a woody plant, of less than 30 ft, much branched to the ground — is an appropriate one in the context of timber formation. It emphasizes, by implication, the particular value as timber, of a single trunk, of a useful length, compared with the shorter and thinner multiple stems of a shrub. In fact, however, the distinction between trees and shrubs may not be quite so clear cut; for instance, hazel (*Corylus avellana*), which usually grows as a shrub, will sometimes form a small tree.

A tree thus consists of a root system, largely out of sight (but notably, the first part to be initiated when the seed germinates) supporting a trunk which in its upper parts carries a system of branches bearing the leaves and reproductive shoots — the flowers of a hardwood tree or the cones of a softwood. The branches and leaves are sometimes collectively referred to as the crown, or canopy, of the tree, and the trunk, in its lower unbranched parts, as the bole. Near the base it is commonly somewhat irregularly fluted in its junction with the main roots, and in many large tropical tree species the roots may form conspicuous buttresses extending some metres up the trunk. The root system will commonly be similar in its lateral spread to that of the canopy, or it may be even much wider; the proportion of it revealed when a tree is forcibly uprooted is usually a small part of the whole. The depth and spread of the root system is however very variable, depending on the tree species and the nature of the soil and sub-soil (Büsgen and Münch, 1929; Kozlowski, 1971).

9

Of these three principal components of the tree, two, considered physiologically, may be regarded as being especially active. The canopy, by the photosynthetic activity of its green leaves, produces by far the greater part of the dry matter of the tree, and the root system absorbs the remainder, the necessary mineral ions, from the soil. In forest trees this absorption is generally mediated and enhanced by one or other of a number of fungi, which growing in close symbiotic association with the tree, give rise to specialized forms of absorptive minor roots termed mycorrhizae. Mineral matter absorbed from the soil typically comes to comprise a few per cent of the dry weight of the leaves and a fraction of one per cent of that of the wood.

From photosynthetic carbohydrate and mineral ions, together with water, the tree is able to synthesize the multiplicity of organic and inorganic compounds which make up its total structure and enable it to grow; water is of course a vital component in these syntheses and the respiratory activity on which they depend. Further, the tree requires and absorbs very much more water than is immediately involved in this way in its chemical make-up, because the pathways of the diffusion of carbon dioxide from the atmosphere into the leaves (a pre-requisite of photosynthetic assimilation) are also, inevitably, pathways of the escape of water vapour from the leaf tissue. The low concentration of carbon dioxide in the atmosphere imposes a need for its relatively unobstructed diffusion into the leaf, so that the escape of water vapour from the humid interior of turgid photosynthesizing leaves into the (relatively) dry external atmosphere is similarly unobstructed. In consequence the weight of water lost from the leaves of a tree is likely to be some hundreds of times greater than its synthesis of dry matter in the same period. A temperate woodland in high summer may transpire up to about 40 tonnes of water per hectare per day; for an individual tree this may mean a daily loss of water of the order of a few hundred litres, which of course, in the long term, must be made good by absorption from the soil. Those features of wood structure and function especially relevant to the maintenance of this sap flow are outside our purview; they have been authoritatively described and discussed by Zimmermann (1983).

To a first approximation, the trunk of a tree thus has two main functions, as a mechanical support for the canopy, and as a transport system between the canopy and the roots. The latter is, of course, a two-way system, in very general terms upwards in the wood from the roots to the canopy for water and ions, and downwards in the inner bark from the canopy to the lower parts of the tree for organic substances synthesized in the leaves; among these, sucrose (cane sugar) is the most abundant. This does not mean, however, that physiologically the trunk is merely a system of pipes; it has other subsidiary functions, including the storage of food reserves. Furthermore it embodies a means of growth in diameter (the vascular cambium), as the continuing growth of the canopy may require, and also of the production and maintenance of an outermost inert protective layer, the outer bark or periderm, which is derived from one or more cork cambia. Thus, although in everyday usage the term "bark" includes all the tissues external to the wood, its inner and outer zones are entirely different in their structure and functions, and so must be clearly distinguished (see Chapter 3).

If one examines the transverse surface of a freshly cut tree-stump, or the end of a log — an end-grain surface as it is sometimes called — the principal features of its structure can be seen. Ideally it should be smoothed off with a sharp plane, at least in part, to make the details clearer. In the centre is the pith, originally the soft middle part of the young shoot before it became thickened. The greater part of the transverse surface, the wood or secondary xylem, will show, in temperate trees, concentric increments of growth, which may vary markedly in width. Outside the wood is the inner bark or secondary phloem, of which only the innermost part, a band often as little as 0.2–0.3 mm in width, is active in transport. The outer bark is dead tissue; it is always corky, and is very variable in thickness; in some tree species it is scaly or fibrous in nature.

The vascular cambium lies between the wood and the inner bark, but it is not separately identifiable in a log; it calls for microscopical study. In the cambial zone the cells are capable of repeated cell division, and thereby the production of successive increments of xylem and phloem. Those regions of plants, like the cambium, in which the cells regularly divide to produce new cells, are collectively termed meristems, and are described as being meristematic.

Extending radially through the wood and inner bark there are thin strands which are clearly different from the main bulk of these tissues. These are the vascular rays; they will be most easily seen in such timbers as oak, elm and beech, in which a proportion of them are relatively wide, and visible to the unaided eye. In many other hardwoods, for example poplar and willow, and also in softwoods, they are narrow and relatively inconspicuous, and may be barely detectable even with the aid of a lens.

The mode of formation of the wood of the trunk may be visualized in a simple way by considering the growth of a one-year old tree seedling, as follows. Towards the end of the season it will have a terminal bud at its apex, and a few leaves along its length, in the axils of which lateral (axillary) buds will be present. Its stem wood will be found to be in the form of a hollow, open-ended cone, which externally is narrower at the top than at the bottom, as is exemplified in the measurements of a one-year seedling (of sycamore) given in Table I.

Table I Diametral measurements of successive internodes of a one-year seedling of sycamore (*Acer pseudoplatanus*) (mm). The points at which the leaves are borne on the stem are termed the nodes, the internodes being the regions of the stem between them (but see also p. 22).

Internode number	Diameter of stem	Outer diameter of wood	Diameter of pith	Radial width of wood
1 (lowest)	5.80	4.80	0.84	1.98
2	5.72	4.80	0.80	2.00
3	5.20	4.32	1.04	1.64
4	4.80	4.08	1.12	1.48
5	4.56	3.76	1.20	1.28
6	4.32	3.60	1.40	1.10
7	4.12	3.48	1.92	0.78
8	3.96	3.20	2.24	0.48
9	3.88	3.12	2.56	0.28
10	3.68	3.04	2.60	0.22
11		not measured		

The table also shows the diameter of the pith increasing upwards in the course of the year; this follows from the growth in diameter of the apical bud during this period, in its development from its small size in the seed. The form of the wood at the end of the year may thus be represented diagrammatically as in Fig. 1A. In the following spring the terminal bud will grow, producing further extension growth, and then, at the end of the second growing season, forming a new bud for the next winter period. The wood of the second-year extension growth will also be in the shape of a hollow cone, but the formation of this increment of wood will continue downwards over the outer surface of that of the previous year, so that the structure at the end of the second year may be represented as in Fig. 1B. Similarly, in the third year, extension growth and secondary thickening continue (Fig. 1C), and the process is repeated annually in a similar way throughout the life of the shoot. The growth rings of the end-grain surface of a log are thus sections of successive growth cones (Fig. 1D) which have been laid down in this way. They are visibly distinct from each other by virtue of the anatomical differences which they usually show, between the wood produced at the beginning of the growth period, the earlywood, and that produced nearer the end, the latewood. These differences cannot usefully be defined in formal anatomical terms, because their nature differs in different kinds of trees, as Chapters 4 and 5 exemplify, and the one merges into the other during the growing season. Broadly, however, the cells of the latewood, as seen in transverse sections, tend to be smaller than those of the earlywood, and to have thicker cell walls, so that the latewood is denser than the earlywood; the proportionality

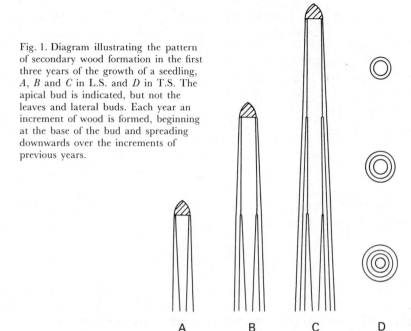

Fig. 1. Diagram illustrating the pattern of secondary wood formation in the first three years of the growth of a seedling, A, B and C in L.S. and D in T.S. The apical bud is indicated, but not the leaves and lateral buds. Each year an increment of wood is formed, beginning at the base of the bud and spreading downwards over the increments of previous years.

A   B   C   D

between them thus influences the density and hence the strength of the timber as a whole (see Chapter 8). There is usually, but not invariably, one growth increment each year, so that the number visible in an end-grain surface near the base of the trunk is a good approximation to the age of the tree. Because of this pattern of growth the trunk as a whole tends to taper upwards, though the regularity of the taper may be obscured by branching; moreover, in some trees, the amount of new wood produced in successive growing seasons gradually becomes less near the base than higher up, so that the trunk may tend more to a cylindrical than to a conical form.

As the trunk increases in diameter the older wood, nearer the centre, gradually ceases to function in conduction and storage. The living cells of the wood die, the moisture content of the wood usually, but not invariably, decreases, and other varied changes may occur (see Chapters 4 and 8). In many species, but by no means universally, these changes include the deposition of dark-coloured substances, so that this inner, older wood becomes readily recognizably different from the outer, younger wood; it is then termed heartwood, in distinction from the still actively functional sapwood surrounding it. Among European trees this is well shown, for instance by oak and elm, and by larch and yew, but not by poplar or spruce. The dark-coloured timbers of the tropics, the mahoganies, teaks and so on, are cut from the heartwood of the tree. The change from sapwood to heartwood is often very regularly related to the growth in diameter of the trunk, so that the sapwood may remain approximately constant in width over long periods, and characteristic differences in this respect, as between species, may be recognizable. For example, the sapwood is relatively narrow in larch and sweet chestnut, and much wider in the maples. On the other hand, the colour change may be irregular or intermittent, as occurs in some ebonies (*Diospyros* spp.), so that patches of pale-coloured wood, which look like sapwood, are to be seen within the heartwood core of the trunk; they are described as included sapwood. Trees which do not show heartwood are sometimes referred to as all-sap trees. This is however, in a sense, a misnomer; in functional terms there is a heartwood, which is not evident as a change of colour, but which in some instances can be revealed by a suitable chemical test.

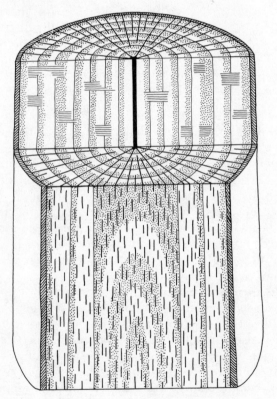

Fig. 2. Diagram representing a log which has been cut to show transverse, radial and tangential surfaces, and the characteristic patterns of the growth rings and rays that they display.

The radial symmetry of the structure of the wood of a log, which arises from the way in which it was formed, and which is evident, as we have seen, on a transverse surface, has the consequence that if the log is cut longitudinally the appearance of the cut surface varies according to the position of the cut. If it passes through the pith, and hence lies along a radius, it exposes a radial longitudinal surface; if on the other hand it has been made nearer the outside of the log, missing the pith altogether, it is said to be tangential longitudinal. In the strict geometrical sense it is of course tangential only in its middle part, where it is at right angles to a radius; elsewhere its direction, as seen in the transverse plane, lies somewhere between the truly tangential and the radial. The interrelationships of the appearances of these cut surfaces are represented diagrammatically in Fig. 2, which shows a short log as it might appear when cut along transverse, radial and tangential planes. The conical growth increments, which appear as concentric circles on the transverse surface, show as a set of near parallel lines on the radial surface, and as a set of inverted V's or U's on the tangential surface. The rays are also indicated, they appear on the transverse surface as thin lines, radiating like the spokes of a wheel, on the radial surface as extensive sheets, limited in height, but extending irregularly across the growth increments, and on the tangential surface as thin vertical lines, where they are cut more or less at right angles to their radial length. This diagram, like the previous one, is of course, greatly simplified. In reality logs are rarely accurately circular, nor is the pith necessarily in the centre. Moreover, the growth increments are not infrequently somewhat undulating in their shape, and the rays are likely to be neither straight nor wholly radial in their orientation. In consequence, it would be rare, in a radial surface, to see a ray throughout its length; more usually, rays appear as patches of variable radial extent, as they intersect the plane of the cut surface. Similarly, irregularities in the basically conical form of the growth increments tend on the tangential surface to produce very marked distortions of the basic patterns of V's and U's which simple theory requires. Nevertheless an understanding of the basic pattern, as displayed in Fig. 2, is an essential background to the interpretation of wood sections prepared for microscopical study, and relates also to the conversion of the log into usable timber (see also Chapter 7).

When a log is sawn into planks it may, in the simplest way, be "plain-sawn" ("slash-sawn" or sawn "through-and-through"), as indicated in Fig. 3A). Here, clearly, most of the planks will be more or less tangentially orientated, and only those few near the diameter will show substantially radial faces. If radial faces are especially desirable, as for instance in the decorative use of oak, when its "silver grain" (due to the rays) is to be displayed, these planks will be selected accordingly.

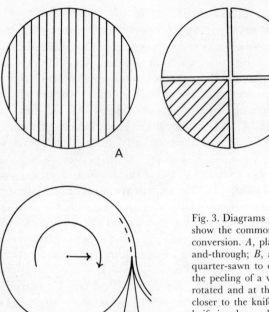

A   B

C

Fig. 3. Diagrams of the end of a log, to show the commoner methods of conversion. *A*, plain-sawn or through-and-through; *B*, a simplified form of quarter-sawn to display radial figure; *C*, the peeling of a veneer. The log is rotated and at the same time moved closer to the knife, or alternatively the knife is advanced towards the rotating log.

Alternatively a different method of conversion of the log may be used. It is hardly practicable to cut up a log entirely radially, as one might cut a cake, but a simpler approximation to this, which is sometimes used, is to cut it into four billets and then to cut each of these in the manner indicated in Fig. 3*B*. A greater proportion of these pieces will then be orientated sufficiently near to the radial direction to show something of the figure it is desired to display. Similar considerations apply, of course, in the cutting of veneers. For plywood, the usual method, of peeling them spirally from a rotating log, as in Fig. 3*C*, clearly produces a continuous truly tangential surface, and where this has been done with a log which has somewhat irregular and strongly marked growth increments, it is an interesting exercise to attempt to interpret the changing but basically repetitive patterns which sometimes appear in the veneer. Again, however, where a radial, or some other specific surface is wanted, the veneer cannot be peeled, but must be sliced in the appropriate direction.

The foregoing discussion of radial and tangential surfaces in wood has, in a somewhat over-simplified way, made no reference to the effects on these surfaces of branching in the tree, and these must now be considered. The extension growth of the shoot bears leaves in its first year, in the axils of which lateral buds are formed. Later, in their second or subsequent years, some of these buds will grow out into branches, which increase also in thickness and so give rise to knots in the wood of the parent shoot which bore them. Thus, although knots are generally regarded as defects in timber, they are inevitable and indeed necessary features of the growth and structure of a tree. A knot, considered in the solid, is a conical or approximately cylindrical

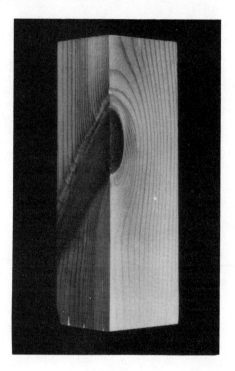

Fig. 4. A knot, cut longitudinally, to show the 'splay' face and half the 'round' face, about 2/3 natural size. This is a live or tight knot; the growth increments of the parent shoot and of the knot are in continuity. Note however the disturbance in the grain of the parent shoot, both radially and tangentially, caused by the knot.

structure, the wood of the base of a branch. It lies radially in the wood of the trunk, often at an angle inclined outwardly upwards. In a radially sawn board it will thus be cut longitudinally, when it is known as a spike knot or a splay knot; in a tangential board it will be cut more or less transversely, so appearing circular or elliptical in shape, and termed a round knot (Fig. 4). In a piece of sawn timber of which the faces are neither truly radial nor tangential, a knot will lie obliquely through it and may emerge on an edge; it is then described as an arris knot.

It need scarcely be emphasized that these different descriptive terms applied to knots refer merely to different aspects of the same kind of structure. Nevertheless, knots do differ among themselves, in a rather more fundamental way. Initially, in the growth of a branch, its vascular cambium is in continuity with that of the trunk which bears it, the growth increments of both are thus also organically united, and as long as the branch continues to grow this continuity will be maintained (Figs. 4 and 5A). A knot originating from a growing branch cannot thus be pushed out of a board in which it may occur, it is a live, or tight, knot. If however a branch dies, as a result perhaps of overshadowing, or of breakage by wind damage or the weight of snow, and its cambium

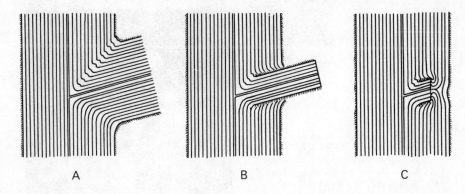

A   B   C

Fig. 5. Diagrams to illustrate the formation of live and dead knots. *A*, the base of a growing branch, of which the growth increments are continuous with those of the trunk; this branch will give rise to a live, tight knot. *B*, a branch has been cut and has died, so that in the subsequent thickening of the parent trunk, its base, no longer growing, will become enclosed in the growing trunk, giving rise to a dead or loose knot. *C*, a branch has been cut off flush with the trunk. Subsequent growth of the trunk produces knot-free timber.

in consequence ceases to function, the erstwhile continuity between the wood and the bark of the base of the branch and those of the trunk will no longer be maintained (Fig. 5B). In a board cut through this part of the base of the branch, therefore, the knot would be a dead, or loose, knot and would be liable to fall out. If however the dead branch had been broken off (as occurs in the forester's procedure of brashing) or better still had been pruned off flush with the trunk, it would eventually be buried by the later growth increments of the trunk, and subsequent growth would be free of it altogether (Fig. 5C). Foreign bodies, such as nails driven into the trunk, and fencing-wire or even iron bands attached to it, may in time become embedded in later-formed wood in a similar way (Fig. 6).

This capacity of trees for the healing of wounds is a very general one. On a small scale it occurs regularly following leaf-fall, a thin bark being formed at or below the exposed surface. On a larger scale it is well exemplified in Fig. 7, which shows a slice through a partially healed wound in an oak. A patch of bark seems to have been lost, and as a result the wood immediately within was invaded by a wood-rotting

Fig. 6. Twin trunks of a European
beech (*Fagus sylvatica*) which had been
strapped together with iron bands many
years before the photograph was taken.
These bands (which are about 5 cm
wide and 1 cm thick) have become more
or less buried in the wood by the
continuing secondary growth. About 1/20
natural size.

Fig. 7. A transverse slice of European
oak (*Quercus* sp.) cut through a partly
healed wound, about 1/2 natural size.
The wound led to the loss of the bark,
which allowed a rot to attack the wood
within. Meanwhile continuing cambial
activity in the surrounding area has
covered the margins of the original
wound.

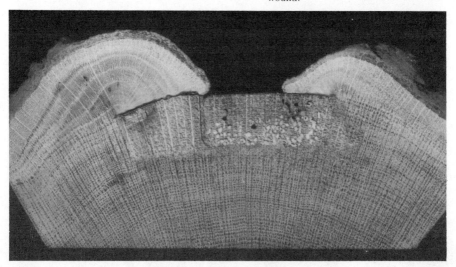

organism; this is the pale, more or less rectangular area in the middle of the figure. Gummy material (wood gum) has been secreted in the surrounding wood (itself a common response to wounding), and in the later growth of the trunk locally re-orientated secondary thickening has given rise to a creeping covering of wood and bark which has more than half sealed over the damaged area.

Many of the axillary buds arising in the young extension growth of a main shoot do not however grow out into lateral branches in the manner outlined above. They remain dormant, or more correctly, perhaps, suppressed, showing only a very low level of activity, perhaps for many years, until they are released, or stimulated, into growth; they are termed epicormic buds. This growth may follow a variety of causes; often it is a consequence of severe pruning or lopping of a tree, or of browsing by animals. Epicormic buds contribute markedly, for instance, to the familiar tightly-packed branching characteristic of a regularly pruned hedge. During their relatively inactive period epicormic buds are carried outwards on the surface of the thickening parent shoot, remaining small and more or less concealed in the bark. Each has a very thin vascular strand, originating, like the bud itself, in the first-year stage of growth of the parent shoot. As the latter thickens, this strand grows slowly in length (but not appreciably in diameter), so keeping pace with the thickening, and maintaining its continuity with the bud. This strand thus extends radially through the secondary xylem, giving rise, on a radial surface, to a very thin spike knot, or, on a tangential surface, to a correspondingly small round knot, termed a pin knot. Epicormic buds may themselves give rise to lateral branches, which originate from them within the bark of the parent shoot, and which bear similar daughter buds at its surface. In this way groups of numerous epicormic buds may be formed, which, in their aggregate growth, build up the somewhat irregular swellings known as burrs; these are frequently to be seen, for instance, on elms and yews (Büsgen and Münch, 1929; Zimmermann and Brown, 1971). In some timber trees the numerous knots of epicormic buds may severely degrade the quality of the trunk wood; in others the burrs are highy valued, since when sliced into veneers they display a decorative figure (see Chapter 7).

Another type of irregular branching derives from the formation of adventitious buds, which, unlike epicormic buds, have no connection with a former apical meristem. They arise *de novo*, commonly in response to wounding of the tree, in tissues near the wound. Adventitious shoots and epicormic shoots are often not readily distinguishable one from the other, and both may contribute to wound responses, as for instance in initiating the new growths of coppiced or pollarded trees, or in the formation of burrs. Internally, however, adventitious shoots lack a

Fig. 8. Part of an almost diametral plank cut from a Scots pine (*Pinus sylvestris*), about 1/5 natural size. The vertical distance between the pairs of large knots represents a year's extension growth, and the distances between the growth rings record the incremental growth in the years following the extension growth. The tiny knots just visible in the middle of the heartwood are the vascular strands of the leaf-bearing short shoots which originally clothed the young stem. The dark flecks in the wood are resin ducts.

vascular strand extending back to the first-year wood of the parent trunk or branch, which is characteristic of the epicormic type.

In everyday usage we refer to the age of a tree, meaning the time elapsed since it emerged as a seedling, and we recognize that this has some real biological significance, since, for instance, trees survive to limited ages, often recognizably different in different species; they do not live for ever. Nevertheless it will be evident that the wood of the trunk of a tree, because of the way it is formed, does not have any one age; the ages of its various parts differ, according to their position in the tree, in a manner which is perhaps not immediately obvious.

Clearly, from what has gone before, wood adjacent to the pith is progressively more recent in origin and younger in years the higher it lies in the tree. The same is true of the wood of any growth increment which is identified as being a given number of rings (counted outwards) from the pith. Branches of the regular system are of course similarly of more recent origin the higher they are in the tree. One consequence of this can be seen in Scots pine (*Pinus sylvestris*). In this species (though not in all pines) only a single whorl of branch buds is formed each year, towards the end of the extension growth of that year, just below the apical winter bud (Fig. 8). Then in the following season, as these buds grow, they give rise to a whorl of branches immediately below the base of the new extension growth of the trunk. Thus the longitudinal distances between the knots of successive branch whorls, as they might appear in a plank cut subsequently from the trunk, form a record of the annual extension growth of the trunk[1]. If the plank happened to be a diametral one (i.e. passing through the pith and so lying at right angles to the growth rings) it would of course embody also a record of the annual thickening of the trunk.

On the other hand, normally the outermost increment of the trunk wood is, at all levels throughout its height, its youngest part, laid down in the same growing season. In a standing tree it is the current year's growth, or perhaps that of the year before. Thus at any level in the trunk, such as may be seen on a transverse surface, the growth rings within, considered sequentially in reverse, from the outside inwards, may be read as going backwards in time from the year of the felling of the tree. Moreover they preserve, in the variability of their width, a record of fluctuation in the growth of the tree back to the year of the innermost ring. This variability is an integrated response to natural variation, from year to year, or over longer periods, in the diverse ecological factors which interact to influence the activity of the vascular cambium; the weather and soil conditions in their various aspects and competition with nearby trees. This competition also may take different forms, for example there may be competition among tree crowns for light, or competition among their root systems for moisture or mineral nutrients.

The effects of the weather have proved to be largely interpretable in terms of the concept of water-stress which they impose on the tree. This may be thought of, simply, as the degree to which the living cells of the tree are less than fully turgid. This condition, if severe or prolonged, may affect their whole physiological activity, and hence the rate of

[1] It is appropriate to note here that foresters refer to the distances along the trunk of a softwood between successive branch whorls as its internodes, thus differing fundamentally from botanists in their use of this term.

growth of the tree. Thus years of severe water-stress are years of narrow growth increments, and close comparative study of the variation in growth increments which have been formed over long periods of time may thus identify sequential patterns of ring width common to the trees of a given area. This is the basis of the science of dendrochronology, which endeavours to make use of these patterns as markers in the time scale of the growth rings, and by matching them with similar patterns in the wood of retrospectively older trees with overlapping life spans, to extend the time scale backwards into the distant past. It thus offers a systematic means of dating past events, in such matters as climatic change and the assessment of its nature, and the dating, in archaeological studies, of artefacts derived from wood. There are, of course a number of possible sources of uncertainty in the establishment of such time scales, such as may arise from the inherent variability of the individuals of a tree species and the variation of the growth increments in the different parts of an individual tree. There is also the well-known occurrence, from time to time, of more than one growth ring in a growing season, or of the formation of a partial ring, or even of the failure of a growth ring to develop at all. However, the effects of such variability in relation to chronology can be minimised and largely eliminated by appropriate methodology and statistical treatment of the data. A general account of tree growth and dendrochronology in relation to climate, based largely on American experience, has been given by Fritss (1976). Dendrochronology has been generally considered to be a much more uncertain matter in Britain on account of our variable maritime climate and the greater local diversity of site factors, but nevertheless Baillie (1982) has found it possible to establish an archaeological tree-ring chronology for Northern Ireland, using oak, and has given a concise account of the principles, practicalities and results of dendrochronology in relation to the development of this work.

3

Tree Growth at the Cellular Level

In this chapter we are concerned with a closer examination and understanding of the anatomical aspects of tree growth which relate most nearly to the formation of wood, and in particular with the structure and activity of the meristems involved in the growth of the aerial parts of the tree. Considerations of the maturation of the products of cell division in the vascular cambium into wood is however deferred to later chapters. Root growth also is not discussed, not thereby to imply that it is in any sense a less essential factor in the life of the tree than the growth of the trunk and branches, but because roots are very minor sources of wood, even though they may, in favourable circumstances, be worth extracting for conversion into wood-fibre products. Moreover, in spite of the differences between the apical meristems of shoots and roots, there are essential similarities in their processes of extension growth, secondary thickening and wood formation.

The production of trunk wood is initiated, fundamentally, in the activity of the apical buds of the shoot, on the growth of which the extension of the trunk and branches and the origin of new leafy shoots depend. This continued extension growth has the functional requirement of an associated growth of the mechanical, conductive and storage functions of the trunk, and thus of an increase in its thickness, by the production of secondary xylem and phloem. The activity of the vascular cambium, to which this thickening is due, is stimulated and largely controlled by the activity of the apical meristems.

Such meristems, when in the dormant state, as for instance in trees of temperate climates during winter, or in tropical trees perhaps in a dry season, are enclosed and protected in most species by a regular array of closely fitting and overlapping bud scales. The bud scales are known also as cataphylls, which means lower leaves, and thus refers to

24

their essentially leafy nature and their position in relation to the younger foliage leaves within them.

The stem apex within the bud has a rounded conical form, and bears leaf primordia on its flanks, thus constituting, in an embryonic state, the new growth to appear in the following season. The whole meristem of the apex, stem and leaf primordia together, forms a unified system, of which the apparent simplicity of structure, at this stage, belies the very high degree of its internal organization. Its cells are all capable of growth and division; these processes begin at bud-break and they go on, in a highly integrated fashion, to form the new shoot. The meristem cells have prominent nuclei and thin primary walls, and as electron microscopy shows, cytoplasm rich in organelles concerned with the metabolic activities of synthesis and growth processes in general. Although their living protoplasts appear, under low magnification, to be isolated in the separate "boxes" of their cell walls, they are in fact in continuity and communication by way of very numerous plasma-desmata, sub-microscopic strands of protoplasm which extend from cell to cell through perforations in the cell walls. In their co-ordinated action the cells collectively maintain the unity of the meristem itself and the pattern of growth which will derive from it.

The leaf primordia, lying within the bud scales, follow them acropetally in the same pattern, the oldest, clearly leaf-like, even in the bud, and the youngest, on the shoulder of the apex itself, often no more than a rounded or crescentic bulge on the surface of the stem. The pattern of their arrangement, a well-defined geometrical sequence, is termed the phyllotaxy. Thus, for example, in oak and elm, as in most trees, the leaf primordia are formed singly, following successively in a spiral (strictly, a helix) round the stem, each being displaced laterally from its predecessor by an approximately constant angle. In other trees, in ash and maple, for example, the leaf primordia arise in opposite pairs, each pair lying at right-angles to the one before; this is termed the decussate arrangement.

Within the meristem there are already discernible the beginnings of a vascular system, consisting at this stage of procambial (or provascular) strands. These arise in close association with the leaf primordia, in a related pattern, and are distinguished, very early in the development of a primordium, by their somewhat elongated cells, among those of the main bulk of the meristems, which are more or less isodiametric. The procambial strands relating to the older leaves are progressively thicker and better developed and show the beginning of the differentiation within themselves of xylem and phloem elements; at the base of the bud they can be seen to be in continuity with the vascular system of the previous year's growth (Esau, 1965a & b).

As the growing season opens, bud break occurs and extension growth

AW–B

begins; various environmental factors may be involved in this resumption of growth. For instance, in some temperate trees a certain minimum period of chilling during the winter months, at temperatures around 6 °C, is necessary for the "release" of the buds from their dormant state. Their subsequent growth is then largely governed by rising spring temperatures, though increasing day-length may also be a factor (Kramer and Kozlowski, 1979).

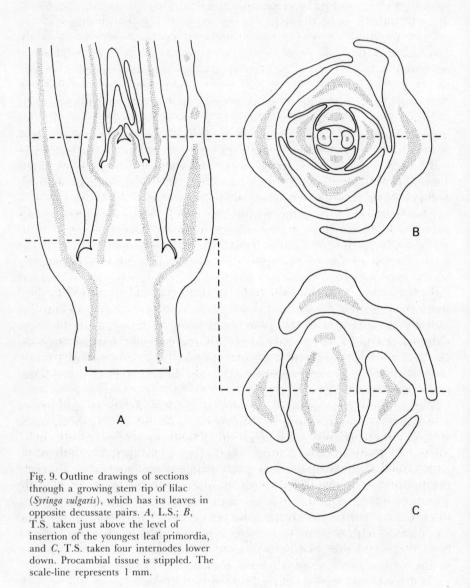

Fig. 9. Outline drawings of sections through a growing stem tip of lilac (*Syringa vulgaris*), which has its leaves in opposite decussate pairs. *A*, L.S.; *B*, T.S. taken just above the level of insertion of the youngest leaf primordia, and *C*, T.S. taken four internodes lower down. Procambial tissue is stippled. The scale-line represents 1 mm.

The drawings of Fig. 9 show median longitudinal and transverse sections of the tip of an apical meristem of *Syringa* shortly after its growth has begun. The sections include a few of the younger leaf primordia; the older primordia and the bud scales are not shown. In this apex the phyllotaxy is decussate; although this pattern is less common than the spiral arrangement, it has been chosen for illustration because its structure, as seen in sections, is easier to understand. In longitudinal sections of apices with spiral phyllotaxy, successive leaves are inevitably cut at different angles to their median planes, and the interpretation of the sections is in consequence complex and difficult. In a decussate apex matters appear simpler, in that a longitudinal section which has been cut medianly through the outermost visible pair of leaves will also cut medianly through every alternate pair of leaves within. It must however be recognized that the leaf pairs intermediate between those which are cut in this way may not appear in such a section at all. In Fig. 9A therefore, pairs of leaves should be visualized as arising on the stem in between those shown, in positions lying above and below the plane of the paper. Reference to the transverse sections, Fig. 9B and C, should make this clear; the inverted V-shaped and strip-like portions of leaf primordia, which appear in Fig. 9A above the stem apex, are parts of the second youngest pair of primordia. Although their attachment to the stem is not shown in this section, for the reasons given above, their upper parts, having in their growth curved somewhat over the tip of the stem, appear in the section in this apparently unattached way.

Lower down in the bud the individual procambial strands of the leaf primordia become joined laterally to form a unified system, as Figs. 9A and B show. This is in the form of a hollow cone or slightly tapering cylinder, which is perforated only in the region of the base of each leaf primordium. These perforations, associated with the outward departure of the procambial strands into the leaf primordia, are termed leaf gaps.

This pattern of growth, whereby an essentially uninterrupted more or less conical or cylindrical procambial system is formed within the young extension growth, is characteristic of a number of tree species; it is found, for instance, in lime (Esau, 1965a) and *Hoheria* (Butterfield, 1976). In many, perhaps most, other trees, however, the individual procambial strands of the leaf primordia of the shoot apices largely retain their individuality throughout the extension phase of growth, forming only an open network among themselves. Only at a later stage, after the end of extension growth, do the largely separate internodal bundles of the young stem, which have developed from them, become fully united into the characteristic conical or tapering cyindrical form of the vascular system of a woody stem (see p. 30).

Anatomical details of the progress of bud growth can be followed by

the study of sections cut from buds at successive stages of their development. Cell enlargement, cell division and cell differentiation continue
in a closely integrated fashion, internodes elongate, bud scales are shed
and the new shoot emerges, ultimately to achieve a length ranging
probably from a few centimetres to a metre or more according to the
species and the circumstances. Concurrently the leaf primordia enlarge,
unfold and expand into their characteristic mature form, and as they
do so new growing points (which were to be seen in embryonic form
at an earlier stage in sections of the bud) become externally evident as
axillary buds. These are, of course, potential points of origin of lateral
branches; thus the basic branching pattern of the young shoot has its
origin in its phyllotaxy.

Later in the season, as extension growth slows and comes to a halt,
a new terminal bud is organized. Leaves are shed (again day length
may be a relevant factor) and the tree passes again into the dormant
stage (Wareing, 1969). The timing and duration of this growth cycle
are varied, and an interesting related structural factor lies in the extent
to which the growth in one season may already have been pre-formed
in the bud laid down in the previous season. In some trees, for example
in some northern pines and other softwoods, and also in beech, the
dormant bud contains within itself, in primordial form, the whole of
the following season's extension growth (Parke, 1959). Thus the extent
of the new growth, in terms of the number of leaves and internodes
which may appear, is pre-determined in the bud, and when these have
reached their full development extension growth ceases; this may occur
even in mid-summer. In other instances, in some tropical pines, in
larch, in *Ginkgo* and in some species of poplar, birch and maple (among
others), the new growth is known not to be limited to the parts pre-
formed in the bud, but in addition to these, extra leaves and internodes
are initiated during the growing season. These later leaves, which have
grown continuously from their initiation to maturity, often differ slightly
in shape or some other feature from the earlier ones, the growth of
which was interrupted during their period of dormancy in the bud
(Critchfield, 1960, 1970; Kozlowski, 1964; Zimmermann and Brown,
1971; Kramer and Kozlowski, 1979). Their formation and growth may
continue until late in the season, when shorter days initiate the formation of new buds and the onset of winter dormancy. In urban areas,
where street lamps may locally maintain long daily illumination (even
though at a low level), their effect in delaying leaf-fall in nearby trees
is often to be seen. The yearly cycle may also be modified by the
occurrence of a second, minor flush of growth in the late summer, in
the form of so-called Lammas shoots. These are common in English
oak and in several other European and North American trees, especially
in moist summers. More rarely, a second flush may also develop after

defoliation of the earlier normal growth, and is sometimes caused in this way in English oak by the activity of caterpillars of the oak roller moth.

Within the young growing meristem, as shoot elongation and leaf expansion proceed, the procambial strands become thicker by predominantly longitudinal cell divisions within them, and they also extend progressively into the enlarging leaves; there they will ultimately become intensively branched to form the leaf-vein systems. As they grow, vascular differentiation follows, protoxylem being formed along their inner and adaxial margins, and protophloem at the outer and abaxial.

The cells of the protoxylem are characteristic. They are smaller than the later-formed conducting elements of the wood, and as their differentiation proceeds they develop a secondary wall which takes the form of annular or spiral bands laid down on the inner surfaces of their thin primary walls. Their secondary walls subsequently become lignified, though often not very strongly so.

As these cells mature their protoplasts die (in Angiosperms their transverse walls will already have been dissolved so that vessels are formed). The longitudinal walls, lacking protoplasts, are in consequence not capable of further growth. However, since these changes take place while the shoot is still in the extension phase of its growth, the continuing growth of the surrounding living tissues causes severe stretching of the protoxylem elements. The rings and spirals of their secondary walls, which had been laid down in close-packed array, are thus pulled apart, to the extent that eventually the earlier protoxylem elements may break down completely and virtually disappear from view; isolated fragments of their thickenings may sometimes be seen among adjacent parenchyma. The remarkable extensibility shown by the primary walls of these cells, before complete breakdown supervenes, derives largely from the enzymic hydrolysis of their hemicelluloses, so that the coherent toughness of their microfibrillar component is greatly reduced (see Chapter 6 and O'Brien, 1981).

Later-maturing protoxylem elements become stretched to a lesser degree, as one might expect, and a sequential series of these elements, with their spiral or annular thickenings progressively less extended, may thus be recognized in radial longitudinal sections. Following on, as extension growth of the new shoot draws to a close, the course of cellular differentiation changes, and metaxylem elements, with thicker and more rigid patterns of secondary wall development, reticulate or pitted, are formed.

Correspondingly, but less obviously, there is a comparable sequence in the phloem. The sieve-tube elements of the protophloem, less easy to recognize in sections than their characteristically thickened protoxylem counterparts, are readily torn and squashed, and tend to disappear from view as elongation and lateral expansion of the vascular strands proceed; they are replaced, in the physiological sense, by the onset of the differentiation of metaphloem. Thus a physiologically functional system of vascular strands is initiated and maintained, even during the period of extension growth, and in spite of the disruptive effects of the latter. It serves to bring water and mineral ions to the new growing shoot, now with transpiring leaves, and to transport away from these, as they become larger, their photosynthetic products.

In the growth and development of the procambial strands, and their differentiation into mature vascular tissues, the longitudinal divisions which take place in them are, as seen in transverse sections, at first rather variably orientated. Subsequently, however, they tend to become more regularly and tangentially aligned; in consequence successive vascular elements which are derived from them come to be formed in radial rows, more especially so in the xylem. This radial pattern of growth and differentiation, centrifugal in the xylem and centripetal in the phloem, does not, however, proceed throughout the procambial strand; there remains a middle zone which retains its meristematic character, in which tangential cell divisions may continue indefinitely, their products as they differentiate thus extending the existing radial rows of xylem and phloem elements. In this way there occurs a gradual transition from primary to secondary growth, a change which, it may be emphasized, cannot be precisely pin-pointed. The meristematic zone which persists across the middle parts of the primary vascular strands has come to behave as a vascular cambium, and is referred to as such, even though it has not, as yet, acquired all the characteristics of the vascular cambium of an older woody stem, but differs from it in certain distinctive features.

Characteristically (with certain exceptions which need not concern us) the woody stems of trees have a vascular cambium of which the form may be idealized as that of a hollow, steep-sided cone or a slightly tapering cylinder. In some species, as we have seen, this may be developed in the growing apex itself, though in many others, as indeed is more usual, its formation is delayed until a somewhat later stage. In these instances the vascular system of the extension growth takes the form of a conical network of discrete strands, which later, as elongation comes to an end, become united laterally into the uninterrupted conical or nearly cylindrical form by a renewed capacity for cell division in the parenchymatous cells of the regions between them. In a single-layered sheet of cells lying within each of these regions, and extending approximately tangentially between adjacent vascular bundles, each cell undergoes two longitudinal cell divisions. Two parallel, tangentially orientated cell walls are laid down, and the new cell so formed between them, becomes a cambial cell, with a capacity for continued meristematic activity. An interfascicular cambium, that is to say one extending between the cambial zones of the original vascular bundles, has thus become established. From this stage onward, therefore, there is a united cambium which is capable of producing a woody stem. A sequence of this kind occurs, for instance, in most conifers, and in sycamore and willows.

Other differences between the cambial zones of these young vascular tissues, and those of the older, thicker parts of the tree, are most evident if the two stages of the meristem are seen in their longitudinal aspects, since as they appear in transverse sections they may look much alike. The cambial cells of the young vascular bundles can be seen in longitudinal section to be a small fraction of a millimetre in length, with more or less transverse end walls, and the cells of the interfascicular cambium are similar.

In contrast, the cells of the vascular cambium further back from the apex, in a part of the shoot where secondary thickening is well established, will be found to be differentiated into two distinct types not evident in the earlier stage. These are most clearly distinguished in their appearance in tangential sections; in this view there appear to be axially elongated cells with tapering pointed ends, which are termed fusiform initials, and scattered among them axial columns or groups of apparently more or less isodiametric cells, which are ray initials (Fig. 10). The development, from the one type of cambium to the other, has been described in specific instances by Esau (1965b), Larson and Isebrands (1974) and Butterfield (1976). It should however be noted that Fig. 10 is in part misleading; in reality the fusiform initials have wedge-shaped ends, but because the planes of the wedges are radially aligned, the cells appear, in a tangential section, to be pointed. Furthermore the ray initials are commonly not isodiametric, but may be markedly elongated in the radial direction; again this is not apparent from their appearance in tangential sections (Wodzicki and Brown, 1973).

The fusiform initials, which are descendants of the cells of the procambium, can readily be seen to be considerably longer than their predecessors, and moreover, they and their successors go on elongating during the first 20–50 years or so of the life of the tree. In mature softwood trees they commonly reach a length of some 3–4 mm (in exceptional instances up to twice this), though in hardwoods their mean maximum length is characteristically much less, of the order of 0.25–1.5 mm (Bailey, 1923, 1954). Elongation of fusiform initials thus continues in regions of the stem which have long-since completed their extension; the cells are elongating individually, though the cambium as a whole is not. Cell extension in these circumstances involves the cells in the

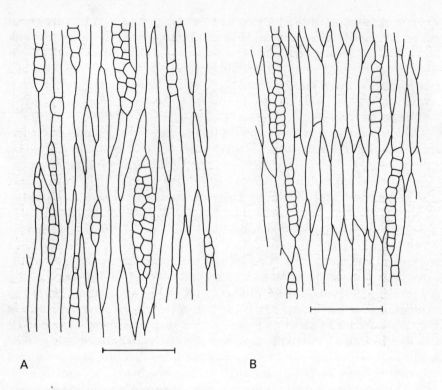

A   B

Fig. 10. Camera lucida drawings of
vascular cambium, as seen in scrapings
from the surface of the growing wood (see
p. 35). Fusiform initials and ray initials
are shown. *A*, ash, a non-storied
cambium; *B*, robinia, a storied cambium.
The scale-line represents 100μm.

phenomenon known as intrusive growth; this is discussed further below
(see p. 40).

In the formation of secondary xylem and phloem the fusiform initials
give rise to the axially elongated cells of these tissues; tracheids, vessel
elements, fibres and parenchyma in the xylem; sieve cells, sieve tube
elements, companion cells, fibres and parenchyma in the phloem. The
ray initials similarly produce, in both xylem and phloem, the radially
orientated cells of the vascular rays; in general these are parenchymatous, but especially in certain softwoods, ray tracheids also occur.
In all this activity more xylem than phloem is produced, as indeed is
fairly obvious from the inspection of transverse sections. There is,
however, a good deal of variability in this respect. Thus Artschwager
(1950) found in pecan (*Carya pecan*) xylem : phloem ratios (expressed
in terms of their radial dimensions) exceeding 5 : 1 in fast-growing
branches and falling to 3 : 1 or less in slower growing, fruiting branches.

In terms of actual cell numbers Bannan (1955) reported a ratio in white cedar (*Thuja occidentalis*) of 15 : 1 in vigorous trees, falling to 2 : 1 with decreasing vigour. Wilson (1963) found 14 : 1 in Colorado fir (*Abies concolor*) and Waisel *et al.* (1966) found 4 : 1 in *Eucalyptus camaldulensis*. In this last instance the ratio was apparently independent of the rate of growth.

In general, the fusiform initials, as seen in tangential longitudinal sections, show no regular pattern in their arrangement; their tapered ends overlap considerably in an apparently irregular and random manner. In many hardwoods, however, cell divisions in the early growth of the cambium take place in such a way that as it matures the fusiform initials come to lie in regular transverse tiers; such a cambium is said to be storied or stratified. In consequence, some degree of storied arrangement is evident in the wood, so that parenchyma, or fibres, or in some instances, whole rays may be storied. Storied cambium occurs in many tropical trees, but is rare among temperate ones. It is also especially frequent in some families, for instance in the Leguminosae; *Robinia pseudoacacia*, which belongs to this family and is also often grown in Britain as an ornamental tree, furnishes a good example (Fig. 10*B*). In ash the cambium shows an intermediate condition; while it is generally non-storied (Fig. 10*A*), localized storied areas may frequently be seen in it. A wide-ranging account of the structure and growth of vascular cambia has been given by Philipson *et al.* (1971).

A vascular cambium, once established from an apical meristem, has the capacity to function throughout the life of the trunk or branch in which it arose; in long-lived trees this may extend to a period of hundreds or even thousands of years. However, not only is the cambium derived from, and dependent on, bud growth for its formation, but in addition its activity during its life-time is still very much subject to apical influences. These are partly nutritional, in the sense that the general growth rate and well-being of the tree, the extent of the leafy canopy and the consequent supply of photosynthetic products available from it, markedly affect the cambial activity in the trunk. There are also, however, very strong hormonal influences, in that growth-regulating substances, principally auxins and gibberellins, but probably also other substances, are produced by growing buds, and are translocated downwards in the phloem and exert a stimulatory and controlling influence on the activity of the cambium below them. Thus the onset of the seasonal activity of the cambium in many temperate trees is well known to be regulated in this way. At or about the time of bud-break in the spring, growth substances are liberated and a "wave" of renewed cambial activity spreads downwards from the buds, reaching the base of the trunk a few days or weeks later (Kozlowski, 1971). The new vascular growth increment is thus initiated progressively, most rapidly so in the ring-porous oak, ash and elm; much more slowly in alder, birch, beech and horsechestnut, which are diffuse-porous. Conifers show an intermediate rate of this downward progression. There is a large literature on the growth-physiology of vascular cambium; recent short accounts have been given by Phillips (1976), Wareing and Phillips (1981) and Kramer and Kozlowski (1979).

Another aspect of this dependence of cambial activity on bud growth is exemplified in pruning practice, where, if part of a pruned shoot is left above the topmost remaining bud, the cambium in that part of the shoot remains inactive and dies; this is for instance particularly evident in the pruning of roses. In trees similarly, the death of branch cambia, leading to the formation of dead knots in the trunk wood, (see Chapter 2) may be caused in this way. Denne and Wilson (1977) found that cambial dormancy in spruce may be induced by disbudding; continued cambial activity depends on auxin from the buds, which cannot be supplied by the mature leaves or tissues of the shoot itself.

Where, as in Britain and the temperate zone generally, markedly seasonal activity is the rule, the growing and dormant phases of the cambium present very different appearances. At the height of the growing season the cambium appears, in transverse section, as a zone of rather delicate, vacuolate, thin-walled cells, which is commonly some 10–20 cells wide, lying between the youngest recognizably differentiating xylem elements on its inner side, and the corresponding youngest phloem elements external to it. The cells of this cambial zone appear approximately rectangular, narrower radially than tangentially, and lie in regular radial files. They have prominent nuclei, and, as electron microscopy has shown, are rich in cytoplasmic organelles (Robards, 1968, 1970; Robards and Kidwai, 1969; Murmanis, 1970, 1977; Evert and Deshpande, 1970). Periclinal (i.e. tangential) cell divisions, giving rise ultimately to new xylem and phloem elements, occur throughout this cambial zone; they are not restricted to a single layer of cells. These tangential divisions in the fusiform initials are remarkable, especially in softwoods, on account of the length of these cells (up to 3–4 mm). After the nucleus, lying in the middle of the cell, has divided, formation of the cell plate begins in the region between the two daughter nuclei in the usual way; it then grows, in asociation with its phragmoplast, up and down the full length of the cell, so completing the division (Bailey, 1920, 1954).

In contrast, in the dormant phase, when cell division has ceased and the great majority of the new cells produced in the growing season have completed their maturation into xylem or phloem elements, as the case may be, the cambial zone presents a very different appearance. It consists only of very few, perhaps only one or two, layers of undifferentiated cells between the new xylem and phloem; moreover, their protoplasts are denser and their cell walls, especially the radial ones, markedly thicker than in the growing season. In short, the cambium looks very different at different times of the year, which has led to some controversy about what is meant by the term cambium, and how it should be used (see p. 39).

In its active phase the cambial zone is mechanically fragile and forms a region of weakness between the wood and the bark (using this term in its general sense); the bark slips readily on the wood. The development of this condition may be made use of as an indicator of the beginning of cambial division and as the basis of a simple means of its study (Priestley *et al.*, 1933). When the cambium is active, it is possible, after making a rectangle of incisions in the bark, to lift off the enclosed portion, so exposing the surface of the wood. If this is then scraped gently the scrapings will consist of the inner part of the cambial zone, together with recently formed xylem elements in the course of differentiation; if the scrapings are plunged immediately into water, or a fixative, they can be studied microscopically. Ash provides favourable material, in which, in particular, stages in vessel differentiation (which precedes that of other cell types) may be readily seen. Sequential sampling by this technique, used on a wider scale, enables the downward extension of cambial activity in the late spring to be followed without serious damage to the tree.

In contrast to trees of markedly seasonal growth, many of those of tropical rain-forests, where annual climatic variation is relatively small, grow more or less continuously throughout the year. There may be several "flushes" of leaves during the year, with corresponding multiple growth increments in the wood, which may be ill-defined or even unidentifiable anatomically (Alvim, 1964; Amobi, 1974; Whitmore, 1975; Detienne and Mariaux, 1977).

The increasing girth of the wood brought about by cambial activity has a range of anatomical consequences in the tree, which arise from the forces of tangential stretching and radial compression which the expanding wood generates in the cambium and all the tissues external to it. The most immediate of these effects relates to the cambium itself. If this is to continue to function as an unbroken cone or cylinder, as the growth of the tree requires, it must itself grow tangentially, and this it does in various ways. Firstly, the cambial cells, considered individually, gradually become somewhat wider tangentially as the tree grows, perhaps by a factor of two or thereabouts. Secondly, as we have already noted, they also become axially longer, especially in conifers, and in a system consisting of tangentially overlapping fusiform cells, a general increase in their length, by increasing the extent of their overlap, will increase their aggregate tangential dimension. Thirdly, the cambial cells, besides initiating the formation of new xylem and phloem tissues by periclinal (i.e. tangential) divisions, also from time to time divide anticlinally (i.e. radially). Such divisions are also known as multiplicative divisions in the cambium, in distinction from those that give rise more immediately to xylem and phloem elements.

In a non-storied cambium (the commoner type) the process of anticlinal cell division is unexpectedly complex; it is illustrated diagrammatically in Fig. 11A–D. When a cambial cell divides in this way the new dividing wall, when first laid down, is markedly oblique to the radial longitudinal direction, often so far as to be nearly transverse; Fig. 11A and B. Subsequently, however, the two daughter cells undergo differentially localized extension growth, their tips intruding between adjacent cells as they do so. At the same time the new wall between them becomes longer and progressively re-orientated towards the longitudinal direction; Fig. 11C and D. In this way the two cells, which initially were one above the other, come to lie, to a substantial degree, side-by-side, so locally displacing adjacent cells laterally, i.e. in the tangential direction (Bailey, 1923, 1954). Cambial cell divisions of this type are often referred to as being pseudotransverse.

In a storied cambium, in which the cells are much shorter than those of a non-storied cambium, the process of multiplicative division is essentially radially longitudinal from the beginning; Fig. 11E and F. It is followed by some localized cell wall growth at the tips of the daughter cells, which, together with some mutual adjustments of cell shape involving nearby non-dividing cells, maintains the storied condition; Fig. 11G and H. Thus here, as in the pseudotransverse divisions in a

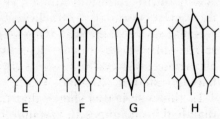

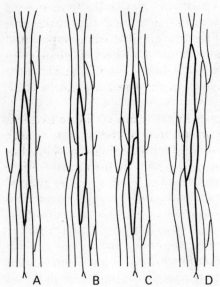

Fig. 11. Diagrams illustrating multiplicative divisions in cells of vascular cambium, as seen in tangential sections. $A - D$, successive stages in a non-storied cambium; $E - H$ in a storied cambium.

non-storied cambium, a localized extension in the tangential direction is achieved.

As Fig. 11 indicates, cambial cells do not undergo multiplicative divisions in unison. The divisions occur singly, and moreover seem to be distributed in the cambium in a random fashion. Thus, considered as a whole, the cambium grows tangentially by the cumulative effects of these scattered, isolated cell divisions and the enlargement of their daughter cells, the plastic nature of cambial cell walls allowing the necessary local adjustments of cell shape to take place. In some conifers which have been studied the divisions are known largely to occur late in the growing season (Bannan, 1967a) and we may perhaps see a possible reason for this timing of them. The tangential expansion of the cambium associated with multiplicative divisions relates not to the cell divisions as such, but to the subsequent growth of the daughter cells produced. Thus the divisions, occurring late in the season, ensure that in the following spring there is in the cambium a maximum proportion of newly formed initials which are ready to expand and so to enable the cambium to maintain its tangential continuity in the circumstances of the new surge of incremental growth of the wood.

The occurrence and role of pseudotransverse divisions in conifer cambium have been extensively studied by Bannan and his co-workers. Their observations and the conclusions drawn from them are based on the following considerations. In conifers the axial elements of the wood are almost entirely tracheidal, and the tracheids are much the same size as the cambial cells from which they arose. It follows therefore that the pattern of tracheids to be seen in a given area of a tangential section of the wood can be regarded as a permanent record approximating closely to the pattern of cambial cells in that area, as it was at the time they gave rise to those tracheids. Thus by detailed examination and comparison of sequential tangential sections of the wood, changes in tracheidal patterns can be detected and followed, and from them the occurrence of pseudotransverse divisions in the cambium can be confidently inferred (Bannan, 1950).

In this way it was shown that these divisions are far more frequent than had been supposed, and indeed occur much oftener than is minimally necessary to maintain the integrity of the expanding cambial cylinder. Of the new cambial cells so formed, which in their turn initiate new files of vascular elements, most cease to divide after a short interval and become themselves differentiated into xylem or phloem cells. In consequence the files of mature elements, which had been produced by their temporary meristematic activity, are also terminated. The increasing girth of the wood is thus accommodated in the cambium by a slowly changing dynamic equilibrium between the formation and death of new cambial cells, which is reflected in the corresponding initiation and termination of files of tracheids derived from them.

It is evident that for a given thickness of growth increment its proportionate effect on the girth of the wood, and therefore of the cambium, will be greatest in the early years of the thickening of a trunk or branch. Furthermore, in any part of the wood, an unusually wide growth increment will call for a corresponding unusually large increase in the girth of the cambium. Thus pseudotransverse divisions in the cambium tend to be more frequent in the growth of young stems and in the formation of wide growth increments. There is, however, no simple proportionality between the growth rate and the frequency of pseudotransverse divisions, because other factors are involved. Nevertheless the proportion of tracheids in the wood which are derivatives of the products of recent pseudotransverse divisions in the cambium, does tend to be higher in young stems and in wide growth rings.

Since a pseudotransverse division of a fusiform cambial cell gives rise to two cells, each of which is not much more than half its length, and both of which take some time to grow to the length of their parent cell, the tracheids which originate from them during this period of their elongation are unusually short. In consequence, in circumstances in which pseudotransverse divisions and their newly derivative files of tracheids are more frequent, the overall average length of the tracheids is correspondingly reduced. There thus tends to be an inverse relationship between the growth rate of the wood and the mean length of its tracheids (Bannan, 1960, 1967b, 1970). This is a factor in the variability of tracheid length throughout the tree (see Chapter 8) and is also exemplified in certain differences between normal wood and compression wood (see Chapter 9).

In the cambium of dicotyledonous trees, as in conifers, frequent pseudotransverse divisions and losses of fusiform initials are known to occur (Philipson et al., 1971). Compared with conifers, however, the wood of dicotyledons is less uniform in structure, its elements are less regularly arranged and the fibres among them undergo intrusive growth to a much greater and more varied degree. For these reasons analysis of the wood structure as an indicator of cambial growth patterns is not practicable. However limited evidence bearing upon them has been inferred in a similar way from comparable studies of the files of phloem cells (Evert, 1961, 1963).

A further response of the cambium to the increasing girth of the wood relates to the fact that as the rays diverge outwards in their courses, the ray initials in the cambium, which maintain their outward radial growth, become further apart tangentially, so that the proportionality of ray initials to fusiform initials in the cambium tends to fall. This tendency is counteracted in the cambium by the formation of new ray initials. Where the rays are uniseriate (one cell wide), as most conifer rays are, this is brought about by the transverse division of a fusiform initial, or part of one, to form a column of ray initials which henceforward give rise to a new ray; this sequence has been followed in detail by Bannan (1934), and others. In many dicotyledons, in which wide multiseriate rays are present, a number of contiguous fusiform initials will be concerned, in a unified way, in the origin of the initials of a ray of this kind. Multiseriate rays may also arise by the fusion of uniseriate rays, and conversely, large multiseriate rays may split up into smaller rays, each of which may then gradually increase in size (Barghoorn, 1940). In trees in which there are aggregate rays, for example alder and hornbeam, (see Chapter 5) the maintenance of the non-divergent, parallel paths of the constituent components of an aggregate ray is a consequence of the lack of effective multiplicative divisions in the cambium within the region of aggregate ray production, so that there is no pressure on the individual rays of the aggregate ray system to diverge from one another (Philipson et al., 1971).

The occurrence of multiplicative divisions in the cambium, whereby new cambial cells arise, and the conversion of fusiform initials to ray initials, whereby new rays arise, have some bearing on the question, already touched upon, concerning the use and meaning of the term cambium. Is it to be regarded strictly as a specialized single layer of cells with uniquely meristematic properties, as (probably) the majority of investigators would hold, or is it, less definitively, a meristematic zone, variable in radial width and in the number of layers of cells comprising it, without any internal specialization, as indeed it may appear at the height of its activity?

If we assume that there is, in the cambial zone, a single layer of cells with special properties, which constitute what we might term a "true" cambium, then though we are most probably not able to indicate precisely which layer it is, we might attempt to narrow down its location by arguing that the periclinal divisions which occur towards the inner side of the cambial zone are taking place in derivatives of the cambium which are already destined as xylem initials; i.e. they are xylem mother cells. Correspondingly, certain divisions which occur near the outer side of the zone might be regarded as occurring in phloem mother cells; see for instance, Wilson, (1964). The cambium itself, however, in giving rise to both xylem and phloem mother cells, must have a wider initiating potential than either of these regions alone. Thus if it were possible to identify some feature of the activity of the cambial zone which is simultaneously reflected in the growth and differentiation of both the xylem and the phloem, this would be evidence for the real existence of the assumed "true" cambium.

The work of Bannan (1955, 1968) involving intensive study of radial cell sequences in conifer cambium, has in fact brought to light two such features and emphasized a third. He found that, in the great majority of instances, when a pseudotransverse division occurs, it initiates a new file of cells in both xylem and phloem. Similarly, if a fusiform initial is lost from the cambium, the corresponding file disappears from both xylem and phloem, or if it gives rise by transverse divisions to a column of ray initials, thus originating a new ray, this also is propagated alike in the xylem and phloem; xylem rays regularly have their counterparts in the phloem, as indeed less specialized everyday observation shows. In short, there seem to be good reasons for the belief that, in conifers, the cambial zone conceals within itself a "true" cambium, a single layer of cells which have attributes of cellular initiation not wholly shared by the cells of the cambial zone at large. Evidence bearing on the possible identification of this layer is brought forward and discussed by Mahmood (1968) and Murmanis (1970) among other investigators. The generally greater production, by the cambial zone, of xylem elements can now be seen as arising from two causes. Firstly, more cells are cut off by the cambium towards the xylem than towards the phloem, and secondly, more numerous divisions occur among these xylem mother cells than among phloem mother cells, which indeed may divide only infrequently before they differentiate into their mature forms. A good case can thus be made for the existence and identification of the cambium, as a single initiating layer, within the cambial zone. It should however be noted that the evidence, and the interpretation of it, derives from studies of conifers. In hardwoods the situation is less clear; a number of investigators have found it impossible to distinguish such a layer. The problem is discussed by Catesson (1974).

Another aspect of cambial activity which calls for further consideration is the matter of intrusive growth, referred to earlier, whereby fusiform initials may continue to elongate individually in regions of a stem in which extension growth has ceased. Intrusive growth is not however restricted to cambial cells; it is widespread in the growth and differentiation of their derivatives as they mature into tracheids or xylem fibres, which are normally longer at maturity than when they were first formed. In softwood tracheids the increase in length is commonly up to about 20%, in hardwood xylem fibres it may be proportionally very much greater, up to 400% or so. It also occurs in other types of fibre cells, besides those of wood, and is thus to be regarded as a general feature of cell growth.

This kind of cell extension, in the circumstances in which it occurs, must seem at first sight to involve the extending cells in sliding past each other as they grow, and at one time it was interpreted in these terms. However, as Sinnott and Bloch (1939) pointed out, if it is postulated that different parts of a cell may grow at different rates, as they found to be the case in grass root meristems, then actual sliding of one cell on another, and the problems that this raises, need not be involved; if a cell grew only at its tips it could be visualized as extending between neighbouring cells without sliding, and they coined the term intrusive growth to describe this concept.

There is a good deal of evidence in support of this idea, and it has been generally accepted. For instance, in macerations of wood the tips of mature fibres may not infrequently be seen to be forked or distorted in ways not shown by their shorter cambial precursors, (Wardrop, 1964a; Süss and Müller-Stoll, 1969; Chalk, 1970); (see also Fig. 12).

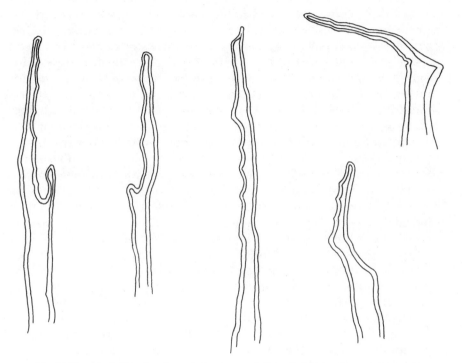

Fig. 12. Camera lucida drawings of the tips of fibres from the wood of an oak, exemplifying the varied shapes that may result from their intrusive growth among other fibres and adjacent rays (× ca. 500).

Furthermore, differentiating fibres may be seen to pass through a stage in which their ends are in an earlier phase of growth than their middle parts; the deposition of the secondary wall thickening begins in the middle of the cell, where extension growth (if any) has ceased, and spreads later to the ends, as their growth, in its turn, is concluded. It may be envisaged that the extending cell tip pushes its way between adjacent cells, probably assisted by enzyme action on the middle lamella into which it is intruding, (Wenham and Cusick, 1975). Tangential tensile stresses existing in the cambial zone might be expected to facilitate this process, (Hejnowicz, 1980).

Outside the cambium the mechanical effects of its activity become progressively greater. Not only does the cambium itself increase in girth, but it also produces new phloem elements outwards. Thus the primary phloem is compressed radially at an early stage in the secondary thickening of the stem, and the secondary phloem, which follows it, laid down initially at a relatively small radius from the centre of the stem, is displaced outwards to a larger one; not only is it subjected to radial compression, but is also put under increasing tangential tensile stress. Furthermore, secondary phloem is a highly differentiated tissue, comprising not only the conducting elements and associated paren-chyma, but commonly also conspicuous strands of thick-walled fibres or sclereides, cells which have lost the capacity for further growth and division, or may even be dead. In consequence the growth potential of the secondary phloem, in relation to tangential tensile stress, is very limited, especially if the fibres or sclereides are grouped in tangential bands, as they often are. Thus what usually happens is that the phloem rays provide the major part of the tangential growth necessary in this part of the stem to maintain tissue continuity; this is especially notice-able in the early stages of secondary thickening. Ray parenchyma cells extend tangentially and divide radially, so that the phloem rays, or some of them, as seen in transverse sections, become wider as they diverge outwards from the cambial zone; they are said to become dilated. Thus they acquire a wedge-shape in section, the inverse of that of the segments of axial phloem tissue lying between them.

As this dilatation proceeds, other changes take place in the phloem. Its translocatory activity is usually of relatively short duration, known in some trees to be only for one or two years, though the annual increments of secondary phloem are, in general, not well-defined like those of secondary wood. Thus not only is less phloem than xylem produced in the first instance, as we have already seen, but only a small proportion of the visible phloem is conductive; active sieve elements are limited to a very narow band, usually only a fraction of a millimetre in width, adjacent to the cambial zone. In older phloem the sieve areas (in conifers) or sieve plates (in dicotyledons) become blocked by the deposition of callose, and the sieve cells or sieve tubes collapse or are squashed by the forces of continued cambial activity. *Tilia* (lime), so often used to demonstrate the anatomy of secondary phloem, is excep-tional in this context, in that its sieve tubes may remain functional for some 5–10 years.

In the cortex and epidermis, as in the phloem rays, some dilatation of the tissues commonly occurs by generalized cellular enlargement and radial cell division. Quite early, however, after the beginning of secondary growth, this phase of generalized cell division is followed by the formation of a specialized meristem, the cork cambium or phellogen, the activity of which gives rise to the cork, or phellem, of the outer bark. The phellogen and its products are collectively known as the periderm.

The cork cambium is usually formed in the first instance in the outer cortex by meristematic activity of cortical parenchyma; its origin may however in some instances be more deeply seated, or alternatively, in some trees, even in the epidermis. It cuts off radial files of cells from its outer side, and in these cells the walls become impregnated with wax and suberin, the protoplasts die and the cell lumens become air-filled; they make up the cork or phellem. In general they are closely adherent, without intercellular spaces, so that they form a physiological barrier ensheathing the stem, a barrier which is relieved only by the presence of lenticels, small circular or elliptical areas in which the cork cells become rounded, with intercellular spaces between them; these enable some degree of gaseous diffusion to continue between the interior of the stem and the atmosphere. The phellem thus effectively replaces the epidermis and cuticle of the young stem, and as the earlier-formed tissues external to it die off and are shed, it becomes visible as a thin bark. In addition, some cork cambia, besides producing cork cells in this way, also cut off, from their inner sides, a number of layers of parenchyma cells, forming what is termed a phelloderm or secondary cortex. These cells do not become suberized.

Continuing activity of the vascular cambium, with consequent increasing girth of the stem, tends of course to rupture the new bark, a tendency which the plant counters in various ways. In some trees the initial phellogen grows tangentially, by cell enlargement and radial cell division, thus maintaining its continuity for many years. As the older, outer layers of cork become torn and shed, new cork is formed within it by the extending phellogen; the bark of the tree thus remains relatively smooth, as in beech. In some trees, as the phellogen grows tangentially in this fashion, the lenticels may also become correspondingly extended, so that from their beginnings as small circular or elliptical areas, two or three millimetres in diameter, they become conspicuous, transversely oriented bands in the bark up to several centimetres long, a feature well shown in cherry and birch. Alternatively, if the first-formed periderm does not grow like this, or after an initial period ceases to do so, then another one is formed inside it. Rarely, this may also be continuous round the stem, but more usually it takes the form of a number of curved scale-like areas, concave outwards, and of limited extent, which are formed within the torn regions of discontinuity of its predecessor. As these new areas of periderm, in their turn, become disrupted, repetition of this "patching" process leads eventually to the formation of a many-layered multiple periderm built up of patches within patches, termed a rhytidome (Esau, 1965a and Fig. 13). If its constituent parts adhere to the tree, and are only slowly eroded away externally, the outer bark formed in this way may become very thick and deeply fissured in various patterns, as is well shown, for instance, in elms and sweet chestnut. In contrast, in some trees the outer layers of the rhytidome are regularly shed, conspicuously so in London plane, and also in Scots pine, in *Arbutus* and in some species of *Eucalyptus* (the stringy barks), among other trees. Schwankl (1956) has given an illustrated description of many different forms of bark.

Fig. 13. Camera lucida drawings of a young rhytidome of Douglas fir (*Pseudotsuga menziesii*). *A*, a transverse surface; *B*, a radial longitudinal surface. Cork is shown in black, and secondary phloem, mostly dead, is stippled. The 'shells' of cork overlap, so maintaining a protective covering over the growing tissues within. The innermost, still living phloem and the vascular cambium are not shown. The scale-line represents 1 cm.

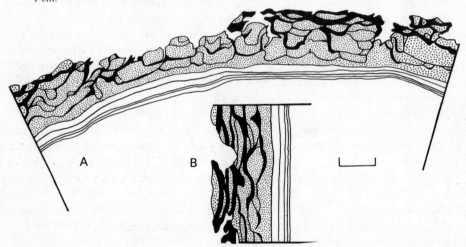

The wide-spread capacity of trees to form successive cork cambia is particularly well-developed in the cork oak (*Quercus suber*), a Mediterranean species, which is the source of commercial cork. The first-formed bark, which is of inferior quality commercially, is stripped off, after which a more deep-seated phellogen arises, producing better quality cork. When this new bark is a few centimetres thick, which may take 10 years or so, it is also stripped for use, and subsequent phellogens, similarly treated, produce successive crops of cork at similar intervals throughout the life of the tree, some 150–200 years.

In the growth of a rhytidome, involving successively deeper cork cambia, the cortex soon disappears as a recognizable region of a trunk or branch, and from this stage onwards cork cambia arise in the still-living parenchyma of the outer parts of the secondary phloem. In this way, old phloem, no longer serving a translocatory function, is gradually incorporated into the rhytidome and is eventually lost to the tree. Its harder tissues, such as fibres and stone cells, may still be recognized among the successive component periderms of the rhytidome (Howard, 1971; Nanko and Côté, 1980). They may influence its mechanical properties and the characteristic pattern of its fissures, and their presence is an important factor in the utilization of bark as a constituent in the manufacture of certain forms of particle board.

The three principal types of meristem of the growing tree, that is to say the many apical meristems of its buds, its vascular cambia and its cork cambia, which appear at first sight to be separate systems, are thus sequentially inter-related, structurally and physiologically. Together with their counterparts in the root system they function in a unified manner to produce the overall growth and structure of the tree.

4

The Anatomy of Secondary Xylem

I. Conifers (Softwoods)

In softwood trees the cells produced towards the inner side of the cambial zone enlarge and differentiate to give rise to timbers which share a considerable degree of uniformity and homogeneity of structure. Although the practised eye may readily recognize some of these timbers at sight, in general the anatomical differences which distinguish those of different kinds (insofar that such distinctions can be made) are rather small and subtle, and can be appreciated in full only by close microscopical study. We turn now, therefore, to consider, in outline terms, the formation of softwood timbers from the cells of the cambial zone, and the mature structure of those of the principal genera. Special attention is given to certain finer features of their anatomy, since an understanding of these features, and the ability to recognize them in wood sections, are necessary for the identification of the different timbers.

As Chapters 2 and 3 have shown, wood, like the vascular cambium from which it arises, may be considered as being built up of two structural components or systems, the axial elements of the wood being derived from the fusiform initials of the cambium, and the radial elements from the ray initials. Nevertheless it must be borne in mind that this division is largely one of convenience of thought; the two systems are but two components of a unified whole. Neither has an existence independent of the other, and neither can be fully comprehended, in structure or in function, without reference to the other. In some conifers there is, in addition, what may be considered as a third system, that of the resin canals. These are in part axial and in part radial in their organization and so emphasize, if emphasis is necessary, the unity of the total wood structure.

As has already been exemplified at the macroscopic level (p. 15),

46

it is necessary for the student of wood anatomy to cultivate the art of visualizing structure in three dimensions. This applies not only in the examination and interpretation of the surface features of a sawn log, but equally in the study of microscopic sections. Here it is more difficult; in general one can see only one aspect of an anatomical feature, e.g. the shape of a cell or the structure of a pit in its wall, at any one time. A real understanding of that structure in the solid comes only from the mental capacity to recognize the same type of structure when it is seen in a different aspect, and to assemble the different two-dimensional images into a three-dimensional picture in the mind's eye. At first, students will often try to remember what they see in transverse and in radial and tangential longitudinal sections as separate unrelated images — a demanding task — then later, as they develop the ability to "see" the whole wood, they find that the structural details begin to fall naturally into place and the effort of memory is greatly reduced. The cultivation of this ability is thus an important aspect of the study of wood anatomy. In recent years the achievement of this level of understanding has been greatly assisted by the application of the scanning electron microscope to the study of wood, in that it produces striking and informative three-dimensional pictures of wood structure (Findlay and Levy, 1970; Meylan and Butterfield, 1972; Butterfield and Meylan, 1980). An example of a scanning electron micrograph of this kind is shown in Fig. 14. However, images such as this, made at magnifications similar to those of ordinary microscopy, rarely reveal anything that cannot be inferred by a competent microscopist using the more familiar methods, and students of wood anatomy should aspire to a comparable level of interpretation of what is to be seen in their sections (compare Fig. 15).

Nevertheless, and in spite of this emphasis on the unity of wood structure and its three-dimensional nature, the student has to begin somewhere; it cannot all be absorbed at once. In this chapter, therefore, we begin by examining the axial and radial elements of softwoods separately, and only then fitting them together into the solid whole. Against this background the resin canals, characteristic of certain genera, will then be considered.

The great majority of the axial elements of softwoods, almost to the exclusion of other types of cell, are tracheids. A tracheid is a cell which at maturity has developed a thick lignified cell wall, with bordered pits, and of which, in its mature functional state in the wood, the protoplast has broken down and disappeared; thus only the non-living cell wall remains.[1] Each tracheid is derived from a single fusiform initial of the

---

[1] A glossary of terms for use in the anatomy of wood has been published by the International Association of Wood Anatomists (1964).

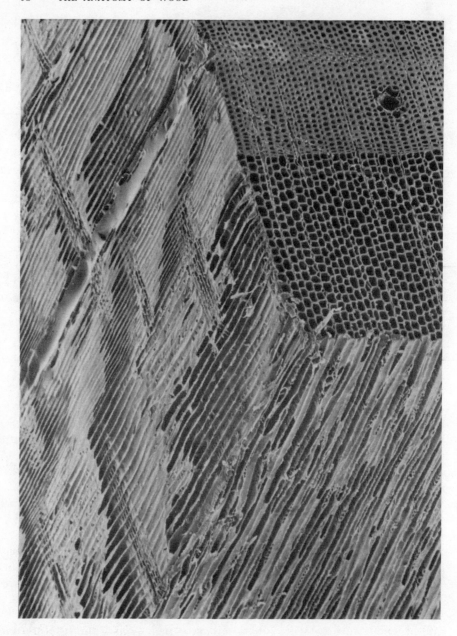

Fig. 14. An oblique scanning electron
microscope view of a small block of the
wood of *Pinus sylvestris*, × ca. 60.
Transverse, radial, and tangential
surfaces, and their structural
interrelationships can be seen. (Compare
Fig. 15).

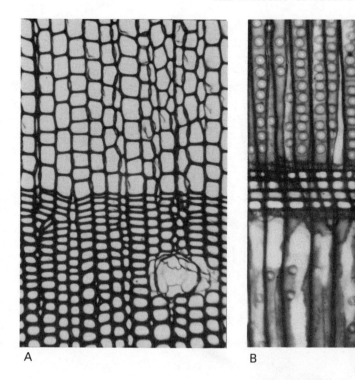

A

B

Fig. 15. *Pinus sylvestris*. *A.*, T.S. × 130.
Note the axial resin canal, with thin-
walled epithelial cells, near the end of a
growth ring. *B*, R.L.S. × 130. Bordered
pits are seen in face view in the axial
tracheids. The ray parenchyma cells
have large window-like pits; the ray
tracheids are dentate. *C*, T.L.S. × 130.
Most of the rays are uniseriate. There is
one fusiform ray containing a resin
canal which has thin-walled epithelial
cells. (Compare Fig. 14).

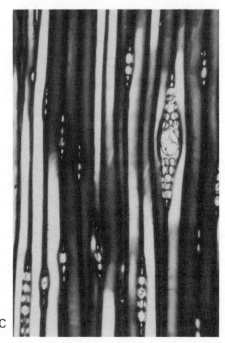

C

cambial zone, and at maturity still largely retains the fusiform shape and wedge-like ends of the latter, the planes of the wedges lying in the radial direction. Thus the ends of a tracheid, as seen in tangential longitudinal sections, appear pointed, whereas in radial sections they show a rounded, more spade-like shape (Figs. 16 and 31).

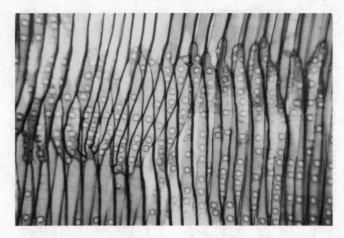

Fig. 16. *Chamaecyparis nootkatensis*. R.L.S.
× 130, showing varied shapes of
tracheid ends, the result of intrusive
growth.

As a fusiform cambial derivative develops into a tracheid it elongates, up to some 15–20%, by the growth of its ends. This is intrusive growth, the cell tips pushing their way among neighbouring cells (see p. 40). It also enlarges radially, to a variable extent, depending largely on its position in the growth increment. There is however virtually no expansion in the tangential direction, so that the regularity of the radial files of cells in the cambial zone persists in the wood. During this period of enlargement the developing tracheid has only a thin primary wall; the cellulosic framework of the secondary wall is deposited within it as its growth comes to an end (Esau, 1965a; Cutter, 1978; Murmanis and Sachs, 1969; Barnett, 1981a). Finally the whole wall structure, beginning in the cell corners and including also the middle lamella, becomes lignified. The protoplast dies and dissolves, and is carried away in the transpiration stream. Thus mature axial tracheids, as they are seen in sections, usually appear empty of contents, though in several softwoods some tracheids may come to contain resin, either as lumps on their walls or as biconcave discs (resin plates) extending right across their cell cavities. The resin originates in living parenchyma cells, from which it is secreted into the tracheids (Fig. 17).

The structure and growth of the tracheid wall are considered in chemical and physical terms in Chapter 6; suffice it here to emphasize that what is commonly rather loosely described as the "wall" between two tracheids, or for that matter between other kinds of wood cell, is in fact a five-fold structure (Fig. 18). It consists of the centrally placed

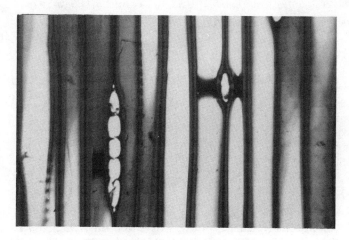

Fig. 17. *Agathis vitiensis.* T.L.S. × 200.
Resin plugs in the axial tracheids. The
resin was secreted by ray cells.

middle lamella, or intercellular substance (which contains no cellulose and cannot be ascribed to either cell), with primary and secondary walls on each side of it, laid down individually by the protoplasts of the two cells. These details of wall structure are not ordinarily fully identifiable in sections of mature wood; the fine line which is commonly visible in the middle of the "wall" between two tracheids represents the

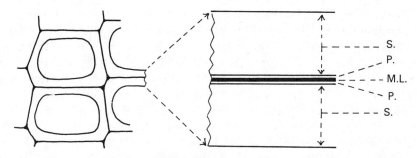

Fig. 18. Diagram to illustrate the 5-fold
'wall' between tracheids. M.L., middle
lamella; P., primary wall; S., secondary
wall.

middle lamella and primary walls together, an aggregate of structures sometimes referred to as the compound middle lamella. Wood tracheids are very strongly adherent, an essential factor in the mechanical strength of wood. They generally fit closely together without intercellular spaces, as is shown, for instance, in Fig. 15*A*, though in a few species, e.g. pencil cedar (*Juniperus virginiana*) and hoop pine (*Araucaria cunninghamii*) they tend to be somewhat rounded in transverse section, so that spaces are present (Fig. 38). This is also one of the features, in softwoods generally, of that type of wood known as compression wood (see Chapter 9).

Mature tracheids are commonly some 1.5–5.0 mm in length, dependent in part on their position in the tree (see Chapter 8). They are usually some 15–80 μm (0.015–0.080 mm) in transverse dimensions, again largely according to their position in the growth ring. Thus they are very tenuous structures, often of the order of 100 times longer than wide. Their wall thickness is also variable, concomitantly with their width. Earlywood tracheids are usually relatively wide radially, with not greatly thickened walls; seen in transverse section they are hexagonal in outline, and those of adjacent radial files tend to alternate in their positions along the radius. In the latewood the tracheids are much narrower in the radial direction, with thicker walls, and those of adjacent files are more nearly opposite; latewood may often be some 3–4 times denser than earlywood. In some trees, such as Douglas fir (*Pseudotsuga menziesii*) and European larch (*Larix decidua*) the change in wall thickness, as earlywood passes into latewood, is abrupt; in the spruces (*Picea* spp.) the transition is more gradual. Similar differences may exist within one genus, as for instance among the pines (*Pinus* spp.). There are also considerable differences in the proportion of thick-walled tracheids in the growth ring, for example it is relatively large in Douglas fir, and very small in pencil cedar. It is also likely to vary appreciably within an individual tree, depending on the rate of growth and the width of the growth ring (Fig. 19).

In addition to this variation of a basic type of tracheid in its size and wall thickness, there is similarly a uniformity, and also a diversity, in some of the much less obvious microscopic features of its structure. It is these which we now have to examine. Tracheids, and other wood cells, in common with plant cells generally which develop secondary cell walls, always show pits in them. Pits are formed over the sites of primary pit-fields in the primary wall; they are well-defined areas in which the primary wall is thinner than elsewhere and where secondary wall deposition does not occur, so that there is a cavity in the secondary wall, at the base of which the primary wall and the protoplast of the living cell are still in contact. Pits in the common "wall" between adjacent cells are, with rare exceptions, opposite to each other, so that

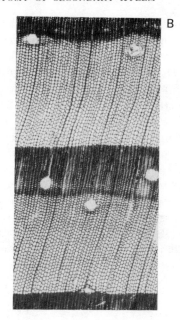

Fig. 19. Transverse sections of A, *Larix* sp.; B, *Pinus palustris*; C, *Picea sitchensis*; D, *Pinus strobus*; all × 17, to show the different proportions of earlywood and latewood. Note also that in A and B the transition from earlywood to latewood is abrupt whereas in C and D it is gradual.

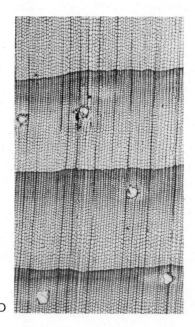

they form a pit-pair, in which only the thin pit membrane (formed by the middle lamella and the primary walls on each side of it) separates the two cells.

In most types of cell the form of the pit cavity, as it is seen in a section through the cell wall, appears as a more-or-less parallel-sided depression in the wall, so that the pit aperture (i.e. the opening of the pit cavity into the cell lumen) is of much the same dimensions as the pit membrane. Seen in surface view both commonly appear approximately circular or elliptical in shape (Fig. 20); slit-like simple pits may also occur, though in these it is usually the pit aperture rather than the pit membrane which is elongated. In tracheids, however, (and also in hardwood vessel elements, see Chapter 5), although simple pits are often present, the characteristic form of pit is the bordered pit. A bordered pit is one in which the secondary wall over-arches the pit-membrane, so as to enclose the pit cavity except for the relatively small

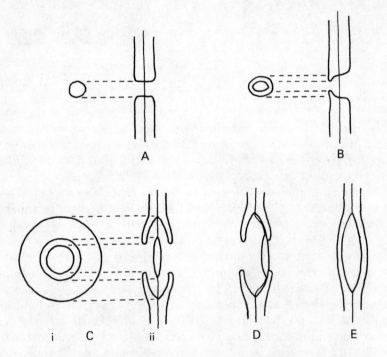

Fig. 20. Diagrams of pit structure. A, a simple pit, such as is formed between two parenchyma cells, in face view and in section; B, a half-bordered pit, such as may occur between ray parenchyma and axial tracheids; the border is on the tracheid side. Seen only in face view half-bordered pits may be indistinguishable from those which are bordered on both sides; C, a bordered pit between axial tracheids, in face view and section; D, the same, in section, in the aspirated condition; E, as it is often seen in sections; the plane of the section has gone through the border but not through the aperture or torus.

Fig. 21. *Picea abies*. T.S., Camera lucida drawing of the boundary between two growth rings. Bordered pits, mostly aspirated, can be seen in the radial walls of the large, earlywood tracheids; some may be seen in the tangential walls of the latewood tracheids. Simple pits, in face view, are to be seen in the ray parenchyma cell in the centre of the drawing. Scale bar = 50μm.

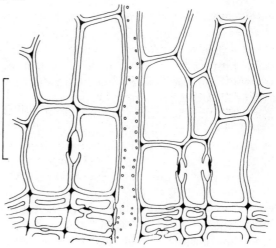

pit aperture. At maturity, in these types of cell, the protoplasts have of course disappeared, but the pit structures remain as permanent features of the cell wall. In tracheids they form the major pathway for water and solutes from one cell lumen to another.

The bordered pits of mature softwood tracheids are in general restricted to the radial walls, although in the last two or three members of a file of latewood tracheids, or in the first cells of the earlywood, some may be formed in the tangential walls (Fig. 21). Seen in face view, that is usually as they appear in radial longitudinal sections of the wood, the pits are circular or slightly elliptical in outline, and commonly some 10–20 μm in diameter. In transverse and tangential sections, in contrast, their structure is seen cut across, revealing the form of the pit membrane and the way in which the secondary wall extends over it. The relationships of the two views are displayed diagrammatically in Fig. 20C. In face view, Fig. 20C(i), the pit commonly appears as three concentric rings, representing respectively, from the outside inwards, the limits of the pit membrane, the edge of its thickened central region (termed the torus) and the pit aperture. In section, in favourable circumstances, these structures appear as in Fig. 20C(ii), though since wood sections may commonly be thicker than the diameter of the pit, the whole of the pit may lie within the thickness of the section; the identification of the pit apertures may then be a matter which calls for careful observation. They will only be seen in what is termed "optical section", that is to say by critical focussing, so that the chosen plane of focus is the "section" actually seen. Even so, especially if the section is unduly thick, or if its surface just grazes the pit aperture, so that this is not actually included in it, the pit-pair may appear as in Fig. 20E. The presence of a torus is characteristic of softwoods, though some species of *Thuja*, including *T. plicata* (Western red cedar) are usually described as lacking a torus. However, electron-microscopy indicates that there is something of this nature, distinguished from the remainder of the pit membrane by its density of structure rather than by its greater thickness, so that it is not visible in the light microscope; the bordered pits of *Araucaria* are similar in this respect (Jutte and Spit, 1963; Bauch *et al.*, 1972). The outer part of the pit membrane is termed the margo; it is minutely perforated with holes, which are mostly less than 1 μm in diameter. These perforations are thus near the limit of resolution of light microscopy (compare Chapter 6), though the larger ones are visible under favourable circumstances (Marts, 1955).

Bordered pits are very frequently to be seen in sections with the pit membrane displaced to one side of the middle lamella, so that the torus blocks the pit aperture on that side, as is represented in Figs. 20D and 21). This is not a difference of structure from that of Fig. 20C, but rather, one of condition; the pit is described as being aspirated. Aspiration may occur if, as a result of injury to the wood, air is admitted to the tracheid on one side of the pit-pair while on the other side the tracheid is still under the reduced pressure of the transpiration stream. Due to the small size of the perforations, and the relatively high surface tension of the xylem sap, the air/liquid interface does not pass through the perforations to equalize the pressures on the two sides, as perhaps one might at first sight expect. The pressure difference is thus not relieved, and in consequence the membrane becomes displaced (Gregory and Petty, 1973) and the torus blocks the pit. A bordered pit thus has a selective valve-like action; it will allow the passage of xylem sap from one tracheid to another while limiting the corresponding movement or expansion of an air bubble. Once a pit has become aspirated it tends to remain in this condition; the margo adheres closely to the inside of the pit border — hydrogen bonding (see p. 147) is thought to be involved here (Comstock & Côté, 1968; Thomas & Kringstad, 1971, 1972; Petty, 1972). In consequence, the margo, though indicated diagrammatically in Fig. 20D, may no longer be visibly distinct, by ordinary light microscopy, from the inner side of the pit border. Differences in pressure on the two sides of a pit membrane, sufficient to cause aspiration, commonly arise also in the drying of wood, so that in heartwood most of the pits are found to be aspirated (Harris, 1954; Puritch,

1971). The proportion varies in different softwood species, and is of technological interest and importance in that aspiration adversely affects the penetrability of timber to preservatives. The penetrability of heart-wood may be further reduced by the incrustation of pit membranes by phenolic and other substances, (Bauch & Berndt, 1973).

There is some variability in pit structure and in pit arrangement in softwoods which is worthy of note, especially as it has proved to be useful in the identification of some genera. In the true cedars (*Cedrus* spp.) the torus has a scalloped edge, so that it appears in face view somewhat like a miniature circular saw or toothed sprocket wheel, a feature sufficient to identify wood of this genus; (see Fig. 35*B*). In the hemlocks (*Tsuga* spp.) the torus may be irregular in shape in another way, often having transversely orientated more or less radial bands extending from its outer edge across the margo; (Fig. 35*C*). Although most softwoods show single axial rows of bordered pits in the radial walls of their tracheids, (the uniseriate arrangement) some have two or more rows, though where these occur they are usually limited to the wider tracheids of the earlywood. Pits may sometimes be in two rows (the biseriate condition) in redwood (*Sequoia sempervirens*) (Fig. 23) and swamp cypress (*Taxodium distichum*) or in three or more rows (multiseriate), also to be seen in swamp cypress, and characteristically in species of *Agathis* and *Araucaria*, genera which include kauri and parana pine respectively (Figs. 41 and 42). Where there is more than one row the pits are usually opposite, though in the last-named genera the alternate arrangement prevails. Moreover, these alternate pits are commonly so close together that they appear to be compressed, and their outlines are hexagonal instead of circular. Another feature sometimes seen in the bordered pitting of *Agathis* and *Araucaria*, though they are not alone in this respect, is that the pit apertures are more or less markedly elongated. The direction of elongation lies obliquely to the axis of the tracheid, reflecting the mean angle of orientation of cellulose molecules in its secondary wall (see Chapter 6). In a pit-pair seen in face view, as in a radial section, the microscope being focussed on the plane of the pit membrane, the two pit apertures may be seen, both somewhat out of focus, sloping in opposite directions, and so appearing to form a cross lying within the limits of the pit border (Fig. 42). Sometimes the pit apertures, though approximately circular, lie at the bottom of narrow, similarly oblique, grooves in the inner surface of the cell wall, overlying the pit cavity.

In addition to these different types of bordered pitting between contiguous axial tracheids, there is also, among softwoods generally, some diversity in the size, shape and number of pit-pairs between axial tracheids and ray cells. Some of these are also of value in the identification of timber; further reference to them is made below (see p. 66) in relation to ray structure.

The walls of axial tracheids exhibit certain other features of structure, besides pitting, some of which are also characteristic of certain genera. In general, in most species, the walls are smooth, but in yew and Douglas fir especially, spiral bands of thickening, (not to be confused with those of protoxylem) are laid down on the inner side of the secondary wall. These thickenings are very characteristic of yew, (see Fig. 39) in which all the tracheids show them; the wood of the related genera, *Torreya* and *Cephalotaxus*, is similar in this respect, though these do not show well-marked heartwood as does *Taxus*. In Douglas fir the spirals are best developed and most easily seen in the earlywood, and may be sparse in the latewood. Similar thickenings may occur very occasionally in spruce and larch, though in these genera they will be principally in the latewood. These spiral thickenings have sometimes been described as forming a tertiary cell wall layer, but there is no good reason for distinguishing them in this way. They are part of the S_3 layer of the secondary wall (Jutte and Levy, 1973).

Another type of localized thickening of the secondary wall occurs regularly in most species of *Callitris* (the cypress pines) and is rarely seen outside this genus. It takes the form of pairs of bars of thickening, not forming complete rings, on the radial walls of the tracheids, which partly overlie the bordered pits. It is known as callitroid or callitrisoid thickening (Fig. 22).

Fig. 22. *Callitris glauca*. Callitroid thickening, *A*, R.L.S., *B*, T.L.S. and *C*, T.S. (here the callitroid ridges are shown by the pecked lines). Camera lucida drawings; the scale bar represents 20μm.

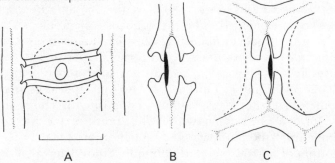

A   B   C

In examining tracheids for spiral thickening the student must guard against being misled by the regular spiral cracking or checking which is frequently to be seen, especially in thick-walled tracheids. Much of this is not present in the living tree, but develops during drying of the wood. It is then not infrequently associated with the pits, so that in radial sections the circular pit apertures may appear, quite falsely, to be drawn out into oblique slits. Another type of spiral sculpturing of the cell wall, which is not an artefact of drying but arises naturally in the course of tracheid differentiation, is one of the characteristics of compression wood, (see Chapter 9).

It is appropriate here to refer also to two other features of axial tracheid structure, both of which are widespread. One of them is of very frequent occurrence (except in *Agathis* and *Araucaria*); the other is rarely seen, but is of interest, if only for that reason, and our consequent lack of knowledge concerning its development. These are, respectively,

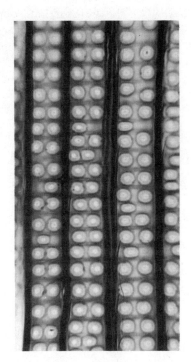

Fig. 23. *Sequoia sempervirens*. R.L.S. × 210. Biseriate opposite pitting in axial tracheids. Crassulae also occur above and below the pairs of pits.

the structures known as crassulae (formerly also as bars, or rims, of Sanio, now obsolete terms) and trabeculae.

The term crassulae is applied to the slightly curved bands commonly to be seen within the thickness of the radial walls of tracheids. They lie transversely above and below the bordered pits; where the pitting is biseriate and opposite, two laterally adjacent pit-pairs may lie within crassulae common to both of them (Fig. 23). Crassulae are localized thickenings of the middle lamella and primary wall, and probably indicate the boundaries of the primary pit-fields over which the pits of the secondary walls subsequently developed (Jane, 1970; Barnett, 1981a). Similarly localized thickenings of primary walls, adjacent to the edges of pit-fields, can sometimes be seen in other types of cells.

Trabeculae are radially orientated bars of cell wall material which are not part of the wall in the ordinary sense, but span the cell cavity from one tangential wall to the other. They occur rarely and sporadically in both coniferous and dicotyledonous wood. When they occur, they are not usually formed singly, i.e. within one cell, but a series of them develops, passing across the cavities of a variable number of tracheids in a radial file (Fig. 24). They are approximately circular in section,

Fig. 24. Trabeculae in *Callitris glauca*. R.L.S., × 200. In one instance trabeculae were observed to extend radially over more than 60 axial tracheids. Note also the callitroid thickening, mostly somewhat out of focus.

and some have been described as being hollow, thus appearing to have developed first as thin threads which have subsequently become coated with secondary wall material: others, however, are considered to be solid. Their origins, and function, if any, are not known. They have been regarded as arising in the cambial zone from folds in the radial walls of fusiform initials, or from localized adhesions between their tangential walls (Priestley, 1930). McElhanney *et al.* (1935) suggested that they are formed around a fungal hypha growing across a fusiform initial and perpetuated in its derivatives; this however can hardly explain their undeviating radial and also strictly transverse orientation. A recent study (Butterfield and Meylan, 1979), though based on hardwoods, includes a general discussion of the problems which trabeculae present.

The remaining axial elements of the wood (resin canals apart) comprise two types of cell, a different form of tracheid, and axially orientated parenchyma. Both of these are relatively few in number, and both arise in consequence of transverse divisions of a fusiform initial. Thus they are alike in form, both being approximately brick-shaped. They occur in short axial columns, referred to as strands; mixed strands, comprising both tracheids and parenchyma, may also occur.

Strand tracheids, as they are called, though parenchyma-like in shape, resemble other tracheids in developing bordered pits and in losing their living contents at maturity. Bordered pits occur in all their

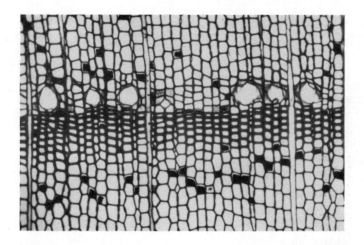

Fig. 25. *Sequoia* sp., T.S., × 65. The cells with dark contents are resin cells (i.e. axial parenchyma). Where the contents have been lost a pitted transverse wall can be seen in face view. There is a row of traumatic resin canals at the beginning of the growth increment.

walls; these pits are rather smaller than those of the principal axial tracheids, but are otherwise similar, being approximately circular in outline and possessing a torus. Strand tracheids are often associated with the parenchyma surrounding axial resin canals, and may also be formed in response to wounding. In Douglas fir and species of larch they sometimes occur also in the outer parts of the latewood.

The cells of axial or strand parenchyma, though similar in shape to strand tracheids, are commonly, but not invariably, conspicuous, in contrast to the empty appearance of the latter, by virtue of their dense resinous contents; they are then often referred to as resin cells (Fig. 25). Bordered pits are of course lacking, but simple pits, and also the presence of localized cell wall thickening, may give the walls a markedly beaded appearance: these are described as being nodular (Fig. 26).

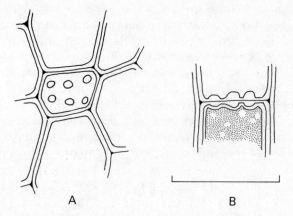

A   B

Fig. 26. Axial parenchyma in *Cryptomeria japonica*. *A*, T.S., showing the nodular end walls between two members of a parenchyma strand, seen here in face view. *B*, T.L.S., showing parts of two such cells and their nodular end walls in section. Camera lucida drawings; the scale bar represents 20μm. (Nodular end walls, which are sometimes useful in the identification of a wood, are best looked for in longitudinal sections).

Axial parenchyma is never abundant in softwoods to the extent that it is in some hardwoods. It is altogether lacking in yew, and other members of the Taxaceae, and also in *Agathis* and *Araucaria* (Araucariaceae). It is also absent from the pines and spruces (Pinaceae), but may occur occasionally but always sparsely in some of the other genera of this family; among them it is usually to be found in *Abies*, the true firs. It is usually present and relatively frequent in members of the Podocarpaceae (e.g. *Podocarpus* spp.), in the Taxodiaceae (e.g. *Taxodium* and *Sequoia*) and in the Cupressaceae (e.g. *Cupressus* and *Thuja*).

As seen in transverse sections the strands are often scattered in the growth increments, but they may occur in concentric bands, and are then said to be zonate in their distribution.

The rays of softwoods (leaving aside those containing resin canals) are each, with few exceptions, derived from a single axial column of ray initials in the cambium, and so are only one cell wide. They appear as single rows of cells in both transverse and tangential longitudinal sections, and hence are termed uniseriate (Fig. 15*C*). Biseriate rays (two cells wide) are, however, not infrequent in *Sequoia* and *Cupressus*, and may be seen in a few other timbers; often they are biseriate only in part (Fig. 40). In radial longitudinal sections rays appear as sheets of tissue in which the cells are arranged in a manner recalling that of the bricks in a wall; they lie in regular transverse courses, but considered in the axial direction their arrangement is irregular. Though ideally it might be thought possible to cut a radial section so as to show the whole of a ray, in practice the normal slight irregularities of growth have the effect that the rays are seldom straight for more than rather short distances, so that usually only a correspondingly short length of a ray is to be seen in any one section. This will be of course where the plane of the ray happens to lie within the thickness of the section (Figs. 14 and 15B). Rays of softwoods vary in their height from two cells (sometimes, but rarely, only one) to forty cells or more, a range of variation which is partly referable to characteristic differences between different kinds of tree, but which in an individual specimen may also be affected by its age and rate of growth (see Chapter 8).

In the cambial zone divisions in the ray initials are less frequent than in the fusiform initials (Wodzicki and Brown, 1973), so that ray cells are radially elongated, commonly reaching a length of some 3–7 times the radial width of adjacent axial tracheids. Their end walls (i.e. their nominally axial tangential walls) are frequently markedly oblique, both to the axial and tangential directions.

Ray cells are, in the main, parenchyma cells, and retain their living protoplasts for some years; they die in the transition from sapwood to heartwood. They usually show conspicuous simple pits, in both their axial and transverse walls (Figs. 34, 36 and 37). In some genera, however, at the upper and lower margins of each ray (and sometimes also in its middle) there are 1–3 rows of ray tracheids; radially elongated cells which develop bordered pits and when fully differentiated lose their protoplasts, remaining only as cell walls. Their bordered pits are smaller than those forming pit-pairs between axial tracheids (Fig. 27);

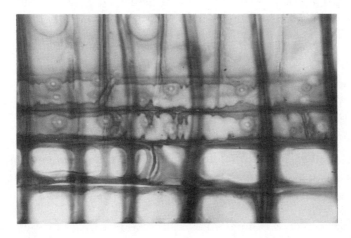

Fig. 27. *Pinus sylvestris.* R.L.S. × 450, showing the margin of a ray. There are two rows of ray tracheids with dentate walls and small bordered pits. The ray parenchyma cells have large window-like pits.

they may occur in any of the walls of the ray tracheids, thus connecting them with each other, with ray parenchyma above and below, (Figs. 34 and 36) and also with contiguous axial tracheids. Ray tracheids are regularly present in the rays of species of *Picea*, *Pinus*, *Larix*, *Pseudotsuga*, *Cedrus* and *Tsuga* and also in *Chamaecyparis nootkatensis* (yellow cedar). They also occur occasionally, in isolation, in other genera, including *Abies*, *Sequoia* and *Thuja*, where they are sometimes referred to as ghost tracheids.

Notwithstanding such differences as those of ray height, or the presence or absence of ray tracheids, to which reference has been made, there is a large measure of similarity in the rays of different softwoods. It has however been found, by critical observation and comparison, that there are a number of variations in what appear to be quite trivial details of structure of ray cells, but which are nevertheless characteristic, to a greater or lesser extent, of different kinds of softwoods, and are therefore valuable in contributing to their identification. These details include differences in cell wall thickness and sculpturing, and in the form and arrangement of the pit-pairs between ray parenchyma cells and contiguous axial tracheids. These features have been extensively studied by Phillips (1948), on whose work the following account is based.

Where ray tracheids are present, their walls may be smooth, and though varying in thickness, these variations will be of a gradual, undulatory nature. Alternatively, their walls may bear more or less conspicuous peg-like or tooth-like ingrowths, projecting into the cell lumen, when the walls are said to be dentate, or extending almost completely across it, when the cell is described as reticulate. Smooth ray tracheid walls are characteristic of the soft pines (for example the yellow pine, *Pinus strobus*) and Douglas fir, though in the latter spiral thickenings may be present in these cells, as they are in the axial tracheids. In the larches the walls may be smooth, or occasionally minutely dentate. Some small degree of dentation is sometimes, but not invariably, to be found in the spruces, while in some of the pines, including the Scots pine (*Pinus sylvestris*), the ray tracheids are markedly dentate. In the pitch pines (*P. palustris* for example) they are also dentate, or may be reticulate. In the ray parenchyma the horizontal walls may be thick or thin (a feature to be looked for in the earlywood), and may or may not be conspicuously pitted, best observed in the latewood. The end walls of these cells may also differ in their pitting (Figs. 34 and 36).

The pitting of the horizontal walls shows also a further point of interest. In *Picea* and *Cedrus*, for instance, where these walls are thick and well-pitted, careful observation reveals some pits which appear to be isolated, in the sense that they are not aligned with corresponding pits in the walls of adjacent cells to form pit-pairs in the usual way (Figs. 34 and 36). Such pits are termed blind pits; here they are in fact directed towards the intercellular spaces which extend along the radial edges of the parenchyma cells, between them and the axial tracheids (Laming, 1974; Butterfield and Meylan, 1980). Presumably these pits serve, in the sapwood, to facilitate gaseous diffusion between the protoplasts of the ray cells and the (air-filled) intercellular spaces.

There is another, rather different, feature of the horizontal walls of ray parenchyma which calls for brief reference; this is the presence of indentures. Indentures are depressions in these walls, somewhat resembling shallow pits, which are sited at the ends of the cells and within which the (tangential) vertical walls are set. They have been found sometimes to be of minor or confirmatory value in distinguishing certain softwoods, especially within the families Cupressaceae and Taxodiaceae. They are however also widely and somewhat variably distributed in other families; examples are shown in Fig. 36 (*Taxus*) and Fig. 37 (*Podocarpus*).

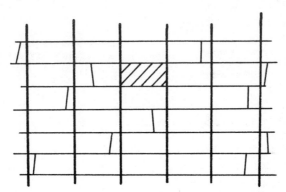

Fig. 28. Diagram illustrating the concept of a cross-field, an area of contact between an axial tracheid and a ray parenchyma cell, marked out by the axial walls of the tracheid and the horizontal walls of the parenchyma cell. One such cross-field has been shaded.

In the study of the pitting in the radial walls of ray parenchyma, between them and contiguous axial tracheids, the form and arrangement of the pits are, by convention, considered not in relation to their number or position in a whole parenchyma cell, nor in a whole tracheid, but by reference to what is termed a cross-field. A cross-field is a rectangular area of contact between a ray parenchyma cell and an axial tracheid; it is thus to be seen in a radial section, delimited by the upper and lower transverse walls of the ray cell and the tangential walls of the tracheid (Fig. 28). In this way each individual tracheid forms a cross-field with each tier of parenchyma cells in a ray, and any one parenchyma cell forms cross-fields with a few members of a radial file of tracheids. Cross-fields will clearly vary in their radial width according to their position in the growth ring; for this reason descriptions and comparisons of cross-field pitting must be made by reference to the earlywood.

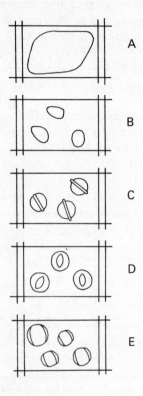

Fig. 29. Diagrams of the five types of cross-field pitting. *A*, large window-like (fenestriform); *B*, pinoid; *C*, piceoid; *D*, cupressoid and *E*, taxodioid.

In the diversity of cross-field pitting Phillips (*loc. cit.*) has recognized five fairly definite types. His descriptions of them refer to the appearance of the pit-pairs in face view, that is as they are seen in radial sections of the wood. The types (Fig. 29) are:

1. *Window-like* (sometimes called fenestriform) pitting: pits large, 1–3 in number, occupying the greater part of the cross-field. They may appear simple, or slightly bordered (Fig. 30). Such pitting is found in certain of the pines, including Scots pine, and also in *Dacrydium*, *Phyllocladus*, and matai (*Podocarpus spicatus*).

2. *Pinoid*: small pits, 1–6 in the cross-field, simple or slightly bordered, and often of irregular shape. They are found in many of the pines, including the pitch pines.

3. *Piceoid*: small bordered pits with narrow, obliquely orientated apertures, the ends of which often extend beyond the pit border. They are typical of spruces (*Picea*), larches (*Larix*) and Douglas fir (*Pseudotsuga*), and also occur in some other genera.

4. *Cupressoid*: 1–4 small bordered pits in the cross-field, with elliptical apertures, which are rather narrower than the crescent-shaped areas of the border on each side of them. The pit apertures do not extend beyond the limits of the border, but are included within it; they may vary markedly in their orientation within a specimen. This type of pitting is characteristic of *Cupressus* and most of the Cupressaceae. It also occurs elsewhere, in *Taxus* and *Araucaria* among other genera.

5. *Taxodioid*: 1–5 pits in the cross-field, bordered, but with broadly elliptical or nearly circular included apertures, which are wider than the narrow crescentic areas of the border on each side of them. They occur not only in the Taxodiaceae (which includes *Sequoia* and *Taxodium* among other genera), but are also found in *Abies*, *Cedrus*, *Thuja* and others. In some cases cupressoid pits may also be present.

Seen in sectional view, as they would appear, for instance, in transverse or tangential longitudinal sections of the wood, these pits present a corresponding variety of form. Among the pines the pits may sometimes be seen to be entirely simple, as the foregoing descriptions indicate. Alternatively, as may commonly occur, for example, in Scots pine and yellow pine, the pit-pairs (as strictly, they should be called) are bordered on the axial tracheid side and simple on the ray parenchyma side; such pits are said to be half-bordered (Figs. 20*B* and 30). Piceoid, cupressoid and taxodioid pits, though smaller and less easily seen in sections, are however similar in this respect, though it follows, from their apertures being more or less elongated, that the apparent relative widths of the aperture and the border must depend on the orientation of the pit in relation to the plane of section. In an extreme case, of a section of a taxodioid pit cut parallel to the axis of the pit aperture, the pit pair would appear to be simple on both sides, and not half-bordered.

These minutiae of structure apart, it is also of interest to examine how such pit-pairs as these, between axial tracheids and ray parenchyma, are arranged along a tracheid (as distinct from their arrangement in a cross-field). This aspect of their distribution emphasizes another feature of the interrelationships of rays and axial tracheids. It is most easily observed in woods such as Scots pine which have window-like pits between the tracheids and rays.

In order to locate these along a tracheid it is necessary to be able to examine individual tracheids, in their entirety, unencumbered by other cells. This requires that the wood should first be macerated, so as to break down the middle lamellae and enable the individual cells to be

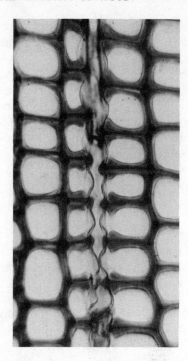

Fig. 30. *Pinus sylvestris*. T.S. × 450, showing the large window-like (fenestriform) pits between axial tracheids and ray cells. These are slightly bordered on the tracheid side.

separated. Wood does not macerate readily; since its middle lamellae consist of a polymeric carbohydrate framework which has subsequently been heavily impregnated with lignin, (see Chapter 6) its dissolution requires the hydrolysis of the carbohydrate and the oxidative breakdown of the lignin; for this reason macerating media for wood are usually both acid in reaction and strongly oxidising. The simplest satisfactory method of maceration is to treat small slivers of the wood in a mixture of equal volumes of 10% solutions of concentrated nitric acid and chromium trioxide, in the warm (40–50 °C); the process may take 2 to 3 days. Alternatively the wood fragments may be simmered gently for a few hours in a mixture of equal volumes of glacial acetic acid and hydrogen peroxide (20 vol.); this should be done in a flask fitted with a reflux condenser. Whichever process is used, its progress must be watched; if it is taken too far the wood will become totally disintegrated.

In wood so macerated and teased out gently on a microscope slide, individual cells may be observed in their various aspects and their shape in three dimensions may be the better appreciated. Axial tracheids may be measured for length, and the sometimes distorted shapes of their ends (a consequence of the intrusive growth in their early stages of differentiation) may be seen; in particular the distribution of their pitting can be examined. This is most readily done in tracheids of the earlywood; since those of the latewood are commonly wider tangentially than radially, they tend to lie on their tangential faces and their radial walls are less frequently seen in face view.

It may seem, at first sight of this view of macerated tracheids, that their bordered pits have disappeared. The borders of the pits may be only faintly visible, if at all, and their tori will no longer be evident. The reasons are that in a bordered pit of a macerated tracheid only

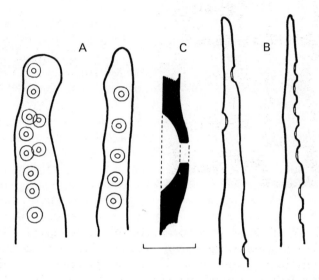

Fig. 31. Tracheid ends, from a macerate of Scots pine (*Pinus sylvestris*). *A*, radial walls, with bordered pits, in face view; *B*, tangential walls in face view and the bordered pits in optical section; the pit membranes have been destroyed in the macerating process. *C*, a diagram of such a pit in sectional view, further enlarged. (The scale bar for the drawings represent 50μm).

half the wall structure of the former pit-pair remains — the other half is, of course, in an erstwhile adjacent tracheid — and the pit membrane has been dissolved away in the maceration process. In surface view the pit thus appears as in Fig. 31*A*, and in section as in Fig. 31*B*.

The edge of the slight depression in the outer surface of the tracheid wall (the limit of the pit border), now lacking the sharp V-shaped margin of the total cavity of the complete pit-pair, is less optically refractive and so may be barely visible in face view. However, when this point is appreciated, the series of circular pit apertures, extending over considerable proportions of the lengths of all the tracheids, will be recognized for what they are.

Elsewhere in the radial walls patches of window-like pits will be clearly seen, marking the areas of contact with ray parenchyma, the cross-fields, and showing that, in contrast to the impression afforded by the examination of transverse sections, every axial tracheid makes contact with a ray and frequently with three or more. Thus the rays, in aggregate, form a much more intensively distributed component of the wood than is immediately evident; in softwoods generally they commonly comprise some 5–7% of the total wood volume. Their living cells serve for the radial transport of organic food substances, which are stored in them principally in the form of starch or fat. Starch is accumulated in ray cells in the late summer months, and may largely disappear from them in the spring when new growth begins. Evidence of enzymic activity in ray cells, associated with the spring-time mobilization of starch, is described by Braun (1970).

We now turn to the systems of resin canals (or resin ducts as they are also termed), which occur regularly in some softwoods and sporadically in others. They are normally present in four commercially important genera; *Larix*, *Picea*, *Pinus* and *Pseudotsuga*, though in *Picea* they may be less numerous than in the others, and so may be overlooked in the examination of a small specimen. They comprise axially orientated canals, which, as seen in transverse sections, are scattered throughout the wood, and transversely orientated radial canals, most readily observed in tangential sections; these are formed in specialized fusiform rays, rather different from the more usual type of uniseriate ray (Figs. 14 and 15). Axial and radial canals, though superficially apparently separate, do in fact interconnect and so form a unified network (Jane, 1956 and 1970; Bosshard and Hug, 1980).

In some other genera, notably in *Cedrus* and *Sequoia* and less frequently in *Abies* and *Tsuga*, resin canals are occasionally formed as a response to injury to the tree; they are thus said to be traumatic. Traumatic canals may also occur in those genera in which canals are normally present, but can usually be recognized as such. Thus traumatic axial canals tend to be formed in tangential rows, rather than being dispersed throughout the wood (Figs. 25 and 120A); they are also, less obviously, commonly shorter than normal canals, often being in the nature of cysts rather than canals. Traumatic radial canals are much rarer, but are also usually conspicuous to the practised eye, by virtue of their greater than normal diameter.

Axial canals are formed schizogenously in columns of strand parenchyma derived from fusiform initials. These cells divide longitudinally and parts of their middle lamellae break down, so that as the cells enlarge laterally a longitudinal space is formed among them. This becomes the canal, which as it expands to its full diameter thus has a parenchymatous sheath separating it from the surrounding axial tracheids. The innermost layer of the sheath, concerned in the secretion of resin, is termed the epithelium. Radial canals, which of course are formed at right angles to the cambial zone, rather than parallel to it, also arise schizogenously, but in fusiform groups of ray initials. In some genera, *Larix*, *Picea* and *Pseudotsuga* (but not apparently in *Pinus*) the lumen of the canal is identifiable within the cambial zone and can be traced right through it, so that it is radially continuous between the xylem and phloem (Wodzicki and Brown, 1973).

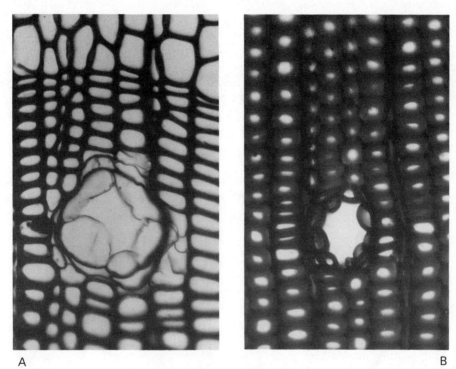

A   B

Fig. 32. Axial resin canals. *A*, *Pinus sylvestris*, T.S. × 270. The epithelial cells are thin walled. *B*, *Larix* sp. T.S. × 270. The epithelial cells are thick walled.

At maturity there are relatively minor structural differences among resin canals, some of which are useful pointers to identification of the wood in which they occur. Thus they differ in shape and in the nature of the epithelium; axial canals are more or less circular in section, and usually occur singly, though in Douglas fir they are not uncommonly formed in pairs. In *Pinus* the epithelium retains its initial thin-walled form, and so in mature wood is frequently found to be collapsed or to have become torn in the sectioning; thus it may not be seen intact. In *Larix*, *Picea* and *Pseudotsuga* however, the epithelium, though initially thin-walled in the young sapwood, soon becomes thickened, a change which probably marks the end of its secretory function, (Fig. 32). Radial canals, as they appear in tangential sections, also vary in shape; circular, elliptical and angular types can be recognised, with varied numbers of epithelial cells surrounding them. There are also, associated with these differences, others relating to the shapes of the rays in which the canals lie (Fig. 33). The ways in which these structural features, and the diversity they exhibit, may be made use of in the recognition of different kinds of softwood timbers are described in further detail below.

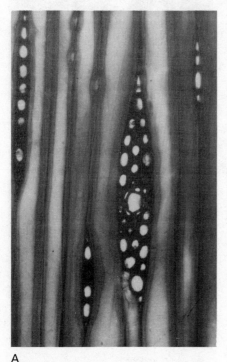 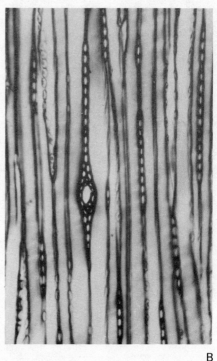

A   B

Fig. 33. Fusiform rays in A, *Pseudotsuga*, T.L.S. × 270, and B. *Larix* sp. T.L.S. × 130. The canal in *Pseudotsuga* is angular, while in *Larix* the canal is oval. In both, the epithelial cells are thick walled. The fusiform ray of *Larix* has markedly unequal 'tails'.

The reader may possibly feel that much of the foregoing outline of the diversity of structure of conifer wood is scarcely, if at all, anything more than a catalogue of rather trivial anatomical detail, of little real interest. Nevertheless, the general similarity among softwoods in larger matters, which springs from their shared fundamental features — the

almost wholly tracheidal nature of their axial elements and their inconspicuous rays — compel this kind of attention; it is necessary, if one is
interested at all in their recognition within narrower limits, to take note
of such minor differences of structure. To students of timber technology,
therefore, some understanding of these features, the differences which
may exist among them and the extent to which these differences may
be relied upon, is a necessary pre-requisite to their use in the recognition
of these timbers.

The general question then arises as to how far it may be expected to
be possible to distinguish different kinds. This will of course be, in large
measure, a matter of the experience and ability of the observer, and his
expertise as a microscopist, but there are also limits beyond which it
is not possible to go, at least at present, limits set by the essential
similarities of the woods themselves. Broadly speaking, however, the
timbers of the principal softwood trees of commercial importance can
be identified to the generic level, and a few are sufficiently distinctive
to be recognised as individual species, though how far this may be true
depends in some instances on what is included in a species: authorities
differ in these matters. In other cases, notably among the pines, groups
of species, rather than individual ones, may be recognized. The matter
is complicated by the natural variability of wood structure arising from
differences of site and rate of growth, so that while the timbers of certain
species might be distinguishable when grown in one area, they might
prove not to be so when grown in another.

In exemplification of the systematic use of structural differences
among softwoods in the recognition of their timbers, it is instructive to
consider the following genera, which include those timbers most likely
to be met with in Britain:

Pinus	Juniperus
Picea	Thuja
Larix	Taxus
Pseudotsuga	Sequoia
Cedrus	Taxodium
Tsuga	Araucaria
Chamaecyparis	Agathis
Abies	Podocarpus

Among the anatomical features referred to earlier perhaps the most
conspicuous is the presence of resin canals; if these are regularly present
in a sample of an unknown wood, it is narrowed down to one of the
four genera, *Pinus, Picea, Larix* or *Pseudotsuga*. In this context however,
it must not be forgotten that the resin canals in *Picea* may be relatively
sparse and so may not be seen in a small section. Moreover, some of
the other genera, especially *Abies, Cedrus, Sequoia* and *Tsuga*, as well as

the four already referred to, not infrequently develop resin canals in response to injury, and the characteristic arrangement of such traumatic canals in tangential rows (as seen in transverse sections) must be recognized for what it is. *Pinus*, *Picea*, *Larix* and *Pseudotsuga* also have ray tracheids, but since these occur also in other genera, their presence together with resin canals is only of limited confirmatory significance. Among these four, wood of the pines may be recognized by the thin-walled epithelial cells of its resin canals, usually seen in sections in a torn or fragmented state, and contrasting with the firmer, thicker-walled epithelia of the other three genera. Associated with this feature is the characteristic window-like or pinoid cross-field pitting, between ray parenchyma and axial tracheids, which is most easily recognized in radial sections. The uniseriate rays rarely exceed 12 cells in height; there is also a distinct heartwood.

The wood of *Pseudotsuga*, seen in longitudinal sections, is conspicuous is regularly possessing spiral thickenings in its axial tracheids, most easily seen in the earlywood, though this feature may also sometimes appear in species of *Picea* and *Larix*, notably in *Picea smithiana*, a commercially valuable Himalayan species. Elsewhere however its rare sporadic occurrence is usually in the latewood and is not likely to cause confusion. These three genera also have in common, besides the thick-walled epithelial cells already referred to, ray tracheids with smooth walls and cross-field pitting of the piceoid type (see Fig. 29) and differences in other features are contributory to their individual recognition. In *Pseudotsuga*, in transverse sections, the often paired axial resin canals and dense latewood, sharply distinct from the earlywood, are characteristic. In tangential sections the uniseriate rays are seen rarely to exceed eight cells in height, and the fusiform rays are also relatively low compared with those of *Larix* and *Picea*. They are dumpy in outline, tapering smoothly from the centrally placed resin canal to the markedly triangular profiles of the marginal ray tracheids (Fig. 33). The cavity of the canal is somewhat angular in shape, due to the small number of thick-walled epithelial cells, (usually less than six) which surround it. *Larix* also has a conspicuous, dense and sharply-defined latewood but its rays and resin canals are different. In tangential sections the uniseriate rays are seen to be commonly more than 20 cells in height, and in the fusiform rays the radial resin canal bulges rather abruptly from the "tails" of the rays above and below it. These "tails" are unequal in length, and according to Phillips (1948) the mean ratio of the longer to the shorter (defined in terms of the numbers of their cells) is usually between 2 : 1 and 3 : 1. The canals themselves are elliptical in section, with commonly 9–12 epithelial cells surrounding them. In *Picea*, in contrast with *Pseudotsuga* and *Larix*, the transition from earlywood to latewood is more gradual, and the latewood is less conspicuous; the timber as a whole is thus generally less dense. Also, though evident in the log, but not in microscopical preparations, *Picea* lacks the brown heartwood, sharply defined from a narrow pale sapwood, which is characteristic of *Larix*. Under the microscope these two timbers are much alike; their uniseriate rays are similar in height, and the radial canals of *Picea*, like those of *Larix*, are elliptical in section,

Fig. 34. Diagrams of radial longitudinal sections of various softwoods, showing parts of axial tracheids and part of a ray. *A*, Scots pine, *B*, a pitch pine; *C*, yellow pine; *D*, Douglas fir; *E*, a spruce; *F*, a larch. The subsidiary diagrams inserted in the top right-hand corner of the lower row show the type of cross-field pitting present. (From Jane, 1970).

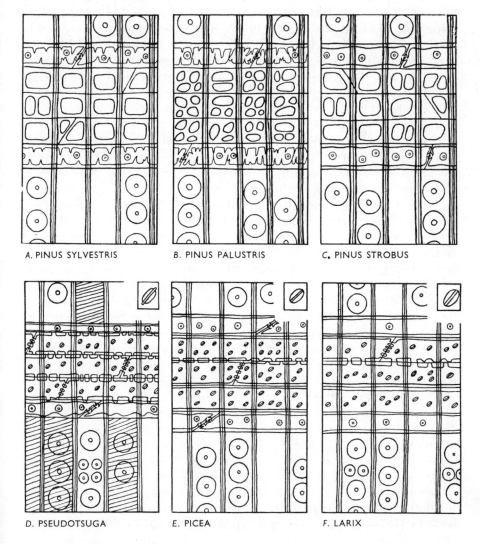

A. PINUS SYLVESTRIS   B. PINUS PALUSTRIS   C. PINUS STROBUS

D. PSEUDOTSUGA   E. PICEA   F. LARIX

though they tend to have rather fewer (commonly 7–9) epithelial cells surrounding them. The canals also tend to be more centrally placed in the fusiform rays than in *Larix*, the mean ratio of the number of cells in the "tails" of the rays usually lying between 1.5 : 1 and 2 : 1. *Picea* also lacks the occasional occurrence of biseriate pitting in the axial tracheids which is characteristic of *Larix*, but no one of these differences between the two genera is well-defined. Bartholin (1979) has proposed that certain minute differences between them, in the size of the bordered pits between their ray tracheids, and in the form of the pit borders, offer a diagnostically useful distinction.

Some other features of these four genera characterized by the presence of resin canals, which may be seen in radial sections, are shown diagrammatically in Fig. 34. The lower row of diagrams shows the similarity between *Larix* and *Picea*, and in *Pseudotsuga* the spiral thickenings of the axial tracheids, and the apparently very low marginal ray tracheids along the upper edge of the ray. This appearance is often to be seen in radial sections which are not quite median to the ray; it is a concomitant of the markedly triangular profile of the ray tracheid as it appears in a tangential section (Fig. 33).

The upper row of diagrams in Fig. 34 shows, in three species of *Pinus*, a diversity of structure within this genus that now calls for further consideration. *Pinus* is a genus of some 80–100 species, of which perhaps 30 are major sources of timber; *P. sylvestris*, the Scots pine, is the only one native to Britain, though many others are to be seen here in gardens and collections, and a few have been planted on a larger scale. Although their timbers cannot be reliably distinguished individually, they can be divided into seven recognizable groups, as Phillips (1948), in correlating and extending the work of many earlier investigators, has described. The timbers of the commercially important species fall into five of these groups,and in a somewhat simplified view of this classification which covers most of these species, three principal types can be recognised by their ray structure (Jane, 1956, 1970). These are shown diagrammatically in the upper part of Fig. 34, where they are represented by *Pinus sylvestris* (Scots pine), *P. palustris* (American pitch pine) and *P. strobus* (yellow pine).

P. sylvestris, and others like it, for example *P. resinosa* (Canadian red pine) and *P. nigra* (Austrian pine), are known as pines of the "red" or "red deal" type. Their ray tracheids are dentate and their cross-field pitting is window-like, usually with only one pit in each cross-field, as shown in the diagram. The *P. palustris* group, which also includes *P. elliottii*, *P. caribaea* and others, are the pitch pines. In these species the ray tracheids are strongly dentate or reticulate, and the ray parenchyma shows piniod pitting with 3–6 pits in a cross-field. Associated with this ray structure are strongly marked growth rings, arising from the abundant latewood, to which the transition from the earlywood is abrupt. These features account for the timbers of these species being heavier, stronger and harder than those of the red deal type. The name pitch pines derives from their abundant resin, another commercially valuable characteristic.

Both red and pitch pines are classed taxonomically as "hard" pines, though in the literal sense the timbers of the red deal type are inter-mediate in hardness between those of the pitch pines and those of the "soft" pines, which are represented in Fig. 34 by *P. strobus*. In this species and others of this group, for example *P. monticola* (Western white pine), window-like cross-field pitting (1–3 pits) in the ray parenchyma is associated with smooth-walled ray tracheids. These timbers also have in common rather poorly differentiated latewood and less-pronounced, though still distinct, growth rings than in the hard pines; in consequence they are relatively light, even-textured and easily worked. The wood of *P. strobus* is especially valued for these properties.

A point of special interest attaches to this sub-grouping of the pines. Though described here in terms of certain anatomical features of the timbers, it accords broadly with one based on differences in their leafy shoots. In all pines the twigs bear side shoots of limited growth, on which the needle-like foliage leaves are produced, and these short shoots (as they are termed) usually bear two or three or five foliage leaves. Most species show a high degree of constancy in this respect, with little random variation, so that they can be characterized as being 2–needle, 3–needle or 5–needle species. In this grouping, pines of the red deal type are 2–needle, the pitch pines are 3–needle and the soft pines are 5–needle. As in so many other biological classifications, however, there are exceptions to the general statement; for instance *P. banksiana* (jack pine), though a 2–needle species with wood which in its general charac-teristics is of the red deal type, has pinoid cross-field pitting like the pitch-pines, and the wood of *P. contorta*, another 2–needle species, is similar (Black, 1963). Some species of the pitch pine type also show variation in this shoot feature. It is relevant here to add that Howard and Manwiller (1969) have re-examined the anatomy of the trunk wood of the ten species of "southern pines" which make up the pine forests of the South Eastern United States. These are mostly, but not exclusively, 3–needle species, and form an economically most important group. These investigators were however unable to find any significant ana-tomical difference among the timbers of these trees which would serve to distinguish individual species.

Among the softwoods which lack regular resin canals two genera, *Cedrus* (the true cedars) and *Tsuga* (the hemlocks), together with one species of a third, *Chamaecyparis nootkatensis* (yellow cedar), normally possess ray tracheids; other *Chamaecyparis* spp. do not share this feature.

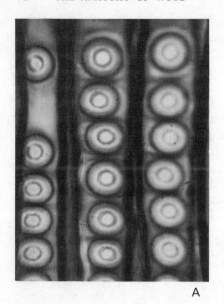 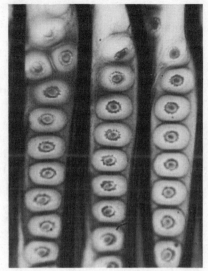

A   B

Cedrus has clearly marked growth rings and a brown heartwood with a pleasant pungent odour. It is distinguished also by the scalloped margin of the torus of its bordered pits; this is a unique microscopic feature, readily visible in radial sections (Fig. 35B). Axial parenchyma, if present at all, is never more than sparse, and has nodular end walls. The cross-field pitting is variable; piceoid, taxodioid and cupressoid types may be seen, even within a small microscopic preparation. The wood of *Tsuga* also has distinct growth rings, but differs from that of *Cedrus* in commonly having a rather sour smell, and also in the pit membranes of its axial tracheids. Seen in face view, as in radial sections, they usually show more or less transversely orientated bars extending across the margo from the torus to the pit border (Fig. 35C). The pits are also sometimes biseriate. Like that of *Cedrus*, axial parenchyma, if present, has nodular end walls. The rays however are lower; while they may be 40 cells in height and occasionally biseriate in *Cedrus*, in *Tsuga* they rarely exceed 16 cells: the cross-field pitting is cupressoid. In *Chamaecyparis nootkatensis* the wood differs from that of *Tsuga* in showing less prominent growth rings, with proportionately less latewood, and if axial parenchyma is present the end walls are not nodular. The rays are also lower, usually not exceeding 12 cells in height.

The wood of other species of *Chamaecyparis* — the principal commercial one is *C. lawsoniana* (Port Orford cedar) — resembles that of the related genera, *Juniperus* and *Thuja*, especially the latter. The chief differences in microscopical features are the abundant axial parenchyma

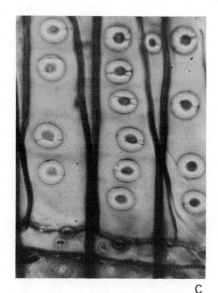

C

Fig. 35. Bordered pits in axial tracheids. *A, Pinus sylvestris*, R.L.S. × 460, with relatively smooth edges to the torus. *B, Cedrus* sp. R.L.S. × 460. The bordeed pits have scalloped tori. *C, Tsuga heterophylla*. R.L.S. × 460. The bordered pits have bands of thickening across the margo, usually present in *Tsuga* species. A ray tracheid runs along the margin of the ray.

and exclusively cupressoid cross-field pitting of *Chamaecyparis*, compared with the sparse parenchyma and generally taxodioid, but sometimes cupressoid, pitting of *Thuja*. In the log *Chamaecyparis lawsoniana* has a pale pinkish or yellowish-brown heartwood, hardly differentiated from the sapwood; it possesses a gingery smell and an unpleasant spicy taste. The principal *Thuja* species to be seen in Britain, both imported and home-grown, is *Thuja plicata*, (Western red cedar) which has a white sapwood and a well-differentiated pinkish or reddish-brown heartwood, with a somewhat cedar-like smell and a slightly bitter taste. Its rays, 1–12 cells in height, tend to be somewhat higher than those of Port Orford cedar, which are normally in the range of 1–6 cells. Another confirmatory difference is that in *Thuja plicata* the bordered pits at the ends of the axial tracheids in the earlywood tend to be paired (Fig. 37).

Among the junipers, the commercially important woods of *Juniperus procera* and *J. virginiana*, the pencil cedars, are distinctive by their familiar smell, that of a freshly sharpened pencil; the principal commercial use of these woods is in pencil manufacture. There is very little latewood in the growth ring, giving the wood an even texture, a factor in its good whittling properties. The heartwood, especially the rays, contains abundant dark resinous material, the cause of its reddish-brown colour. The rays are low, seldom exceeding six cells in height, and the cross-field pitting, though usually cupressoid, may sometimes be taxodioid, with 1–4 pits in a cross-field. A distinctive feature of *Juniperus* spp., to be seen in transverse sections, lies in the somewhat rounded form of

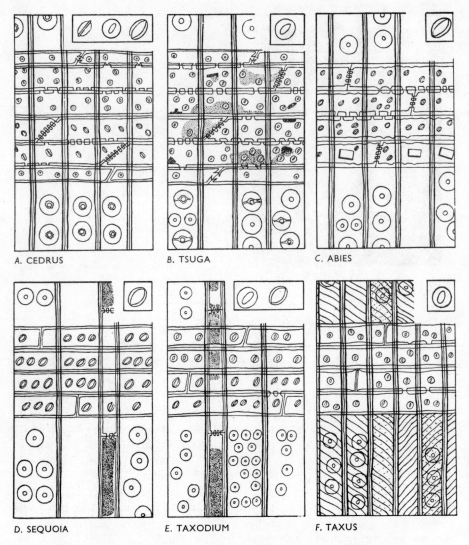

Fig. 36. Diagrams of radial longitudinal sections of various softwoods, showing parts of axial tracheids, axial parenchyma and part of a ray. *A*, a true cedar; *B*, a hemlock; *C*, silver fir; *D*, redwood; *E*, swamp cypress, *F*, yew. Resin is shown by stippling, and the presence of crystals in the ray cells of silver fir is indicated. The subsidiary diagrams inserted in the top right-hand corners show the cross-field pitting. (From Jane, 1970).

the axial tracheids, so that there are intercellular spaces between them at the cell corners (Fig. 38).

The pale coloured timbers of the firs (*Abies* spp.), lacking a pigmented heartwood, may commonly be shipped with those of *Picea* spp. (the

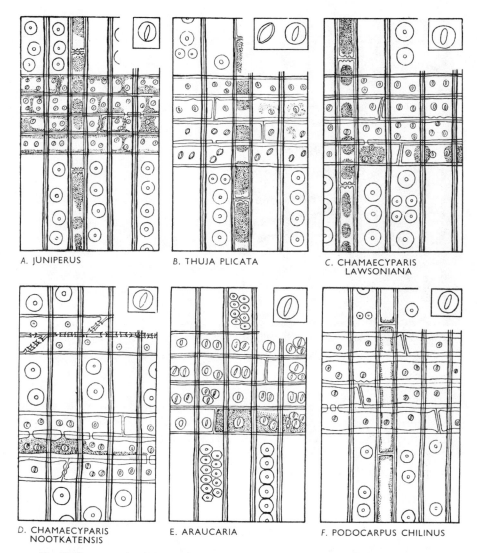

A. JUNIPERUS

B. THUJA PLICATA

C. CHAMAECYPARIS
   LAWSONIANA

D. CHAMAECYPARIS
   NOOTKATENSIS

E. ARAUCARIA

F. PODOCARPUS CHILINUS

Fig. 37 Diagrams of radial longitudinal sections of various softwoods showing parts of axial tracheids, axial parenchyma and part of a ray. A, pencil cedar; B, Western red cedar; C, Port Orford cedar; D, yellow cedar; E, Parana pine; F, manio. Resin is shown by stippling, and the subsidiary diagrams inserted in the top right-hand corner show the types of cross-field pitting. (From Jane, 1970).

spruces); these they resemble in general macroscopic terms, though they are somewhat coarser in texture. Normally, of course, they are to be distinguished microscopically from *Picea* by their lack of resin canals and ray tracheids, though traumatic canals may occur, and so too,

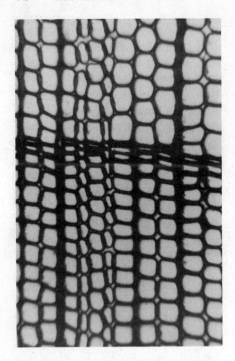

Fig. 38. *Juniperus* sp. T.S. × 200. The tracheids are rounded in cross-section so that intercellular spaces occur. There is comparatively little difference in wall thickness between earlywood and latewood tracheids.

occasionally, may ray tracheids. In the rays the end walls of the parenchyma are strongly pitted, like those of *Picea*, but the 2–3 pits of the cross-fields are taxodioid, not piceoid (Fig. 36). The ray parenchyma, especially of the upper and lower margins of the rays, also commonly contain large conspicuous crystals of calcium oxalate. As in *Cedrus*, the rays sometimes exceed 30 cells in height, and may be partly biseriate.

Taxus (the yews) are regarded by some authorities as comprising a group of about seven closely related species, but by others as the monotypic *T. baccata*; in the context of wood anatomy this is the realistic view. Native in Britain, and widely distributed in the Northern hemisphere, the yew is a minor source of timber, limited in its use by the small quantities and sizes available; it is however, valued for its decorative qualities. It has a narrow pale sapwood and a sharply distinguished orange- or purplish-brown heartwood; the short bole of the tree has often been formed by the lateral fusion of a number of vertical shoots, which eventually have become thickened by the activity of a single vascular cambium, so that it is often fluted and the growth rings are irregular in shape and variable in width. They are well-defined by a narrow, dense latewood, and the timber as a whole is among the

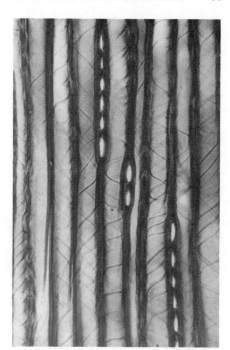

Fig. 39. *Taxus baccata*. T.L.S. × 200, showing the spiral thickening in the axial tracheids. The rays are mostly uniseriate, but may occasionlly be partly biseriate.

densest and hardest of the softwoods. It is distinguished microscopically by the absence of resin canals and the presence of spiral thickenings in all the tracheids (Figs. 36 and 39). The rays may be up to about 25 cells in height, and are occasionally partly biseriate. The cross-fields show 1–4 pits, of the cupressoid or taxodioid type.

Sequoia, represented by *S. sempervirens* (Californian redwood), is an important Californian tree, and is to be seen in Britain in small plantations and individually as ornamental specimens. It is conspicuous by virtue of its thick, red, fibrous bark. The wood shows a narrow, pale sapwood, from which the transition to the reddish- or purplish-brown heartwood is abrupt; in these respects it resembles Western red cedar. The zone of flattened, thick-walled tracheids of the latewood, though sharply defined from the much larger-celled, thin-walled earlywood, is relatively rather narrow; thus the wood as a whole is somewhat coarse in texture and is light in weight. Microscopically it shows abundant axial parenchyma (Fig. 25), conspicuous on account of its resinous contents; the end walls of these cells are variably, but not markedly nodular. The bordered pits of the axial tracheids are frequently rather small and biseriate, and the ray cell pitting is taxodioid, with usually 2–3 pits in the cross-field. The rays are variable in height, but generally

Fig. 40. *Sequoia* sp. T.L.S. × 90, showing, centre, a biseriate ray; resin is present in some of the adjacent axial cells.

rather low; they are frequently biseriate (Fig. 40). The large size of the ray cells is conspicuous, especially in their appearance in tangential sections.

Taxodium distichum (swamp cypress or bald cypress) is the only species of *Taxodium*, and is related to *Sequoia*. It is a valuable timber tree in the South-Eastern United States, and individual specimens are to be seen in Britain in parks and gardens, often adjacent to a lake; the tree is unusual in being especially tolerant of water-logged or marshy ground. The sapwood is a pale yellowish white, passing into a brown heartwood which may vary in colour through reddish shades to almost black, especially on the wetter sites; it has a characteristic sour smell, a greasy feel and a rather grubby appearance. In the axial tracheids the bordered pits are in 2, 3 or 4 rows, oppositely arranged; the latewood is sharply distinguished, variable in amount from growth ring to growth ring, and its tracheids show numerous small bordered pits in their tangential walls. As in *Sequoia*, there is abundant resinous axial parenchyma, the cells of which differ from those of *Sequoia* in their markedly nodular end walls. The ray parenchyma pitting is either taxodioid or cupressoid, up to 3–4 in a cross-field, commonly in a single transverse row. The rays are occasionally biseriate, but not frequently so, as in *Sequoia* (Fig. 36).

Araucaria and *Agathis* are two essentially Southern hemisphere genera,

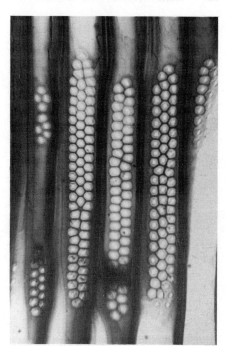

Fig. 41. *Agathis vitiensis*, R.L.S. × 200.
Multiseriate, alternate pitting in the
walls of the axial tracheids. A resin plug
can be seen at the lower end of the
central tracheid.

important as timber trees; *Araucaria* especially in South America and
Australia, and *Agathis* in South-East Asia, Australia and New Zealand.
Araucaria is also represented in Britain, by two ornamental species, *A.
araucana*, the monkey puzzle, and *A. excelsa* (formerly *A. heterophylla*), the
Norfolk Island pine, an indoor and greenhouse tree. The wood of *A.
angustifolia* (Parana pine) is imported into Britain, and may often be
seen in good quality internal joinery. It is pale in colour, with frequent
irregular pinkish streaks, and is rather uniform in texture, showing
barely distinguishable growth increments. *Agathis* includes three or four
species of which the wood is of commercial importance; that of the New
Zealand species *A. australis* (Kauri pine) is the most valuable. *Araucaria*
and *Agathis* are very similar in their timbers, which cannot be reliably
separated microscopically, but both are distinguished from all other
softwoods by the alternately arranged multiseriate pitting of their axial
tracheids, sometimes in *Agathis* in up to four rows, but more usually,
in both genera, in not more than two or three (Figs. 37 and 41). The
pits are closely ranked, and often of hexagonal shape; crassulae are
not formed. No torus is visible by light microscopy, though electron
microscopy indicates that the central part of the pit membrane is denser,
rather than thicker, than its peripheral region, and may thus constitute
an effective torus (Bauch *et al.*, 1972).

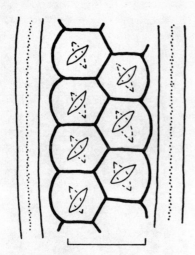

Fig. 42. *Araucaria* sp. R.L.S. Camera lucida drawing of part of an axial tracheid; the alternate pitting shows crossed pit apertures i.e. the slope of the pit aperture in the focal plane is approximately at right angles to the one in the adjacent tracheid. (The scale bar represents 20 μm).

Lastly in this outline survey of the diversity of softwood anatomy, is the genus *Podocarpus*. The trees of this genus are in the main Southern hemisphere species, in South America, South Africa and New Zealand; moreover *Podocarpus* is unusual among conifers in that a number of the species are tropical, in Central America and especially in East Africa. There are several that are valued for their timber, which, in the main, is used locally where it grows, though manio, derived principally from *P. salignus* (= *P. chilinus*) in Chile, is occasionally imported into Britain; the tree itself may also sometimes be seen here in gardens. The timbers of the East African species are collectively known as podo, and those of New Zealand include totara, derived from *P. totara* and *P. hallii*, and matai, from *P. spicatus*. Totara is more durable than the wood of the other species, and, unusually among softwoods, is resistant to the attacks of marine borers. *Podocarpus* wood lacks a single clear distinguishing character, but in general it is pale coloured, with barely differentiated latewood; the growth rings are indistinct, and the wood, unlike that of European softwoods, is even-textured. A few species develop a coloured heartwood; in totara, reddish-brown, and in matai, orange-brown. Axial parenchyma is usually present and abundant (Fig. 43), but may be sparse. Neither ray tracheids nor resin canals are present, and the ray parenchyma cells of most species have thin, unpitted walls, though in *P. salignus* these walls are relatively thick, comparable in this respect with those of the axial tracheids (Fig. 37). Cross-field pitting is usually small, cupressoid or taxodioid, though some species, including *P. spicatus*, have large window-like cross-field pits, resembling those of the *Pinus* spp. of the "red deal" type.

As the foregoing description of the timbers of these softwood genera exemplifies, they have, as a group, a uniformity of basic structure, which is overlaid by individual diversity in a number of different kinds of minor anatomical features, some of which seem to be of a very trivial nature. However, critical study of the features we have touched upon has established their value in characterizing the wood of the great majority of the genera, and to a very limited extent, that of certain of the species, of commercially important softwoods. Within these limits, therefore, specimens of unknown origin may be identified by systematic reference to the appropriate microscopic features of their anatomy (see Chapter 10).

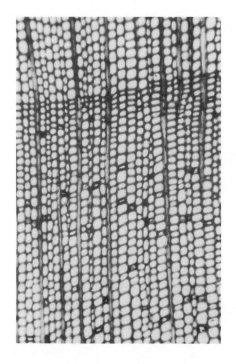

Fig. 43. *Podocarpus nubigenus*. T.S. × 95. The wood has an even texture. The scattered parenchyma cells are relatively thick walled.

5

The Anatomy of Secondary Xylem

II. Dicotyledons (Hardwoods)

As even a cursory glance at the figures in this chapter will show, hardwood timbers, in comparison with softwoods, are much more diverse in their anatomy; their cells are more varied, both individually and in their distribution in the wood as a whole. Whereas in softwoods the axial elements are almost wholly tracheidal in nature, with no more than a small proportion — if any at all — of parenchyma, in hardwoods the axial elements comprise, as a rule, not only tracheids and parenchyma, but also vessel elements (forming vessels), fibre-tracheids and fibres. These five cell types may be seen, in different timbers, in different proportions and patterns of arrangement. The rays of hardwoods, considered as a group, are also very diverse. They exhibit a considerable range of size in both height and width, and although, unlike those of certain softwoods, they do not contain ray tracheids, their parenchyma may take a number of recognizably different and characteristic forms (Metcalfe and Chalk, 1950, 1983). Thus among hardwoods, as among softwoods, features of both axial elements and rays are made use of in the recognition and identification of different kinds of wood. The details of such features, which have proved valuable in this respect, are however, very different in the two groups of timbers.

Though there are a few species of hardwoods (of little or no commercial importance) which do not have vessels, nevertheless the presence of vessels, more than any other single feature, is characteristic of hardwoods as a group. A vessel is a composite structure, formed from an approximately axial column of vessel elements (or vessel members), each of which is a derivative of a single fusiform initial. In its development into a vessel element the initial cell grows transversely to a varied extent (vessels may range in diameter from 20 μm or so up to about 400 μm), though with little change in length. It then lays down

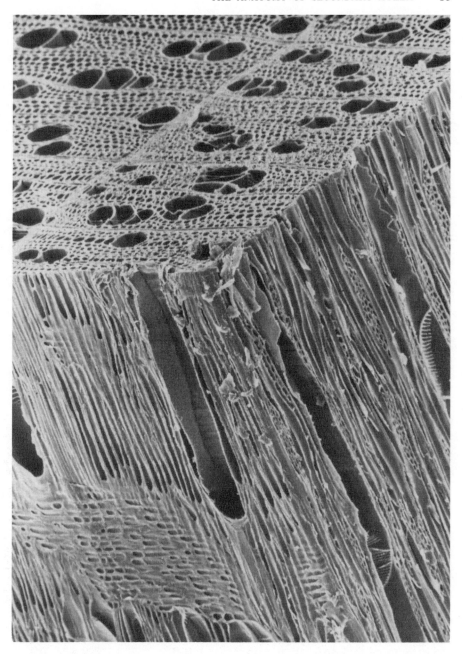

Fig. 44. Scanning electron micrograph of a small block of European birch (*Betula* sp.), showing transverse, radial and tangential surfaces (× ca. 70). Note the vessels, with scalariform perforation plates.

a conspicuously pitted secondary wall, which subsequently becomes lignified, but certain well-defined areas of its walls, at or near the ends of the cell, remain apparently unthickened by secondary deposition. In these unthickened areas some swelling may take place, giving an appearance of secondary thickening, but this swelling is a preliminary to the enzymic dissolution of the middle lamella and primary walls, and their eventual complete breakdown, so that the wall becomes perforated, and this behaviour, occurring in a column of cells, leads to the formation of an open tube. Within it the individual protoplasts of the vessel elements may briefly persist, until they too are dissolved and disappear, leaving the mature vessel, an inert pipe, now filled with the sap of the transpiration stream (Esau, 1965a; Murmanis, 1978; Butterfield and Meylan, 1980, 1982; Meylan and Butterfield, 1981).

The end walls of the vessel elements, which abut on to similar cells above and below them, and in which the vessel perforations are formed, are known as perforation plates. Like the wedge-shaped tapered ends of the fusiform initials from which the vessel elements arose, the perforation plates tend to lie radially but obliquely to the longitudinal direction. Perforation plates thus usually present very different appearances in radial and tangential longitudinal sections. However, in the formation of relatively wide vessels, such as those of the earlywood of oak, changes in the shapes of the vessel elements in the course of their increase in diameter usually result in the perforation plates becoming transversely orientated and the vessel elements becoming barrel-like in shape. However (as may be seen in macerations) vessel elements with more or less transversely orientated perforation plates may sometimes show short pointed "tails", extending longitudinally beyond their perforation plates; these "tails" may be regarded as relics of the tapered ends of the fusiform initials from which the elements arose. Another aspect of the shapes of vessel elements is to be seen most readily in transverse sections, which reveal a variety of cross-sectional shapes. These may be almost circular, as for instance in some maples (*Acer* spp.) and in kokko (*Albizzia lebbeck*), markedly oval, as in the chestnuts (*Castanea* spp.), or angular as in poplars and willows, (species of *Populus* and *Salix*), especially where the vessels are laterally contiguous.

The forms of perforation plate vary in ways which are sometimes usefully characteristic of certain timbers. The commonest form, with a single circular or elliptical hole, is described as having a simple perforation (Fig. 45). This may occupy only a small proportion of the perforation plate (which elsewhere may also bear bordered pits), or it may extend virtually to the whole of the interface between axially adjoining vessel elements, so that the perforation plate is then reduced to no more than a narrow, annular perforation rim around the inside of the longitudinal walls of the vessel (Fig. 115). Various forms of

multiple perforation also occur, with varied numbers of separate perforations. The commonest of these is the scalariform type, which
resembles a ladder, and is seen in longitudinal sections lying
obliquely — sometimes nearly longitudinally — across the vessel cavity.
The ladder-like form is best seen in radial longitudinal sections, in
which it appears in face view; in tangential sections the "rungs" of the
"ladder" are cut transversely to their length and are less conspicuous.
Scalariform perforations occur in many genera and families of woody
plants, in some in all the vessels, in others only sporadically. For
instance among European trees they are characteristic of alder (*Alnus*)
and birch (*Betula*) (Fig. 46), while in beech (*Fagus sylvatica*), where the
great majority of the perforations are simple, a few of the scalariform
type may usually be found scattered in the late wood. Scalariform
perforations may also differ, in different genera, in the number and
thickness of the bars across them. In alder and holly (*Ilex aquifolium*)
there are characteristically more than 20 bars, in birch and in the tulip
tree (*Liriodendron tulipifera*) rather fewer, while in boxwood (*Buxus* spp.)
the bars are thicker than in these genera, and up to about 8–10 in
number. In all these timbers the scalariform perforations occupy virtually the whole of the total area of the perforation plates, while in

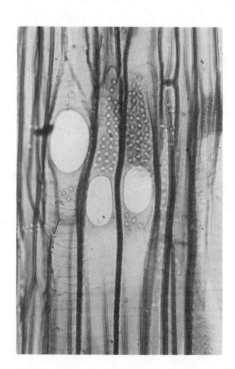

Fig. 45. Horse chestnut (*Aesculus
hippocastanum*). R.L.S., × 310. The
vessels have oblique perforation plates,
with simple perforations, seen here in
face view. The 'tails' of the vessel
elements extend beyond the perforation,
and show bordered pits in this region.
The characteristic spiral thickening of
the vessels, though somewhat out of
focus, can also be seen.

Magnolia the plates may often show scalariform perforations (with only a few bars) which occupy only part of the plate, but which are accompanied also by conspicuous scalariform bordered pitting in its unperforated part. The bars of scalariform perforations may occasionally branch; perforation plates in which this branching is regular or frequent are said to be reticulate, a form characteristic of some timbers.

Another type of multiple perforation, much less common than the scalariform pattern, takes the form of a number of roundish holes, and is described as ephedroid or foraminate. The term ephedroid derives from the presence of vessels with this type of perforation in *Ephedra*. This is a genus of small shrubs, the wood of which is of no commercial value; it is however of some botanical interest, because *Ephedra*, in common with the softwoods, is a gymnosperm, and is thus exceptional in that group in having vessels at all. Scattered ephedroid perforations may be seen occasionally in a number of genera, including some of the Rosaceae, for example, *Sorbus* and *Pyrus*. Various types of perforation plate are described and most strikingly illustrated, by means of scanning electron microscopy, by Butterfield and Meylan (1980). The same authors (1972) have also described, in detail, the formation of scalariform perforation plates in *Laurelia*.

Like the common "wall" between any two cells, that between two axially contiguous vessel elements is a compound structure. It consists of two perforation plates (one from each vessel element) cemented together by the middle lamella, and when actual perforation occurs this almost always takes the same form in both of them. Seen in microscope sections, therefore, the two fused perforation plates appear to be a single structure. However, when the wood is macerated, and the vessel elements fall apart, the dual nature of this structure becomes clear; the perforation plates of the two vessel elements separate at the middle lamella between them, and each element displays its own perforation plate. Occasionally, in woods in which more than one type of perforation plate occurs, the two fused perforation plates at a junction between two vessel elements may be of different types, as for instance, one being simple and the other scalariform (Butterfield and Meylan, 1980).

The axial walls of vessels are conspicuously pitted, and in common with the pits of softwood tracheids, their pits are bordered. They form pit-pairs not only with the pits of adjacent vessels, but also with those of the cells of the wood generally, whichever of those may happen to be contiguous to them. Different types of pit may be recognized, which are distributed over the vessel surfaces according to the nature of the contiguous cells and the areas of contact with them.

The pits between adjacent vessels (intervascular pits) are thus bordered on both sides. They are, however, very different from the intertracheid pits of the softwoods. They are generally much smaller than

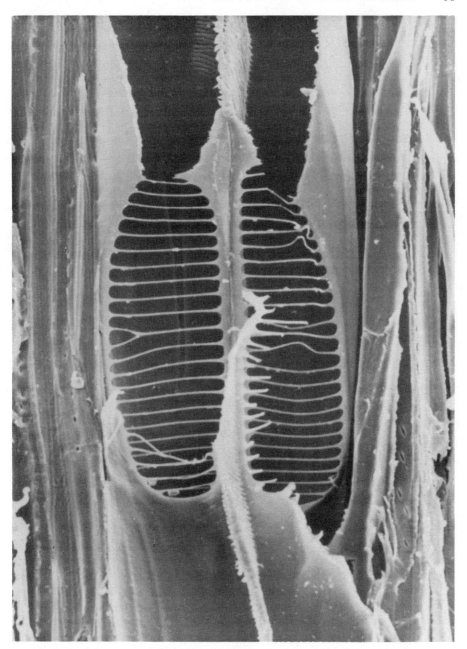

Fig. 46. European birch (*Betula* sp.);
scanning electron micrograph (×
ca. 300) of scalariform vessel
perforations, as seen on a radial surface.

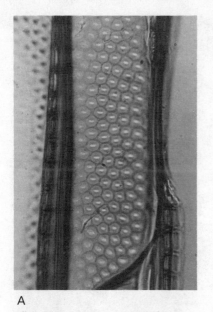

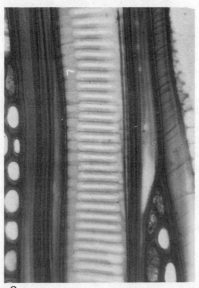

Fig. 47. Types of intervessel pitting, as seen in face-view in longitudinal sections, (× 320). *A*, poplar (*Populus* sp.), multi-seriate alternate; *B*, American whitewood (*Liriodendron tulipifera*), multiseriate opposite; *C*, magnolia (*Magnolia grandiflora*), scalariform. The vessels of this species also have spiral thickening, as may be seen in the vessel on the left of the figure.

the softwood pits, being commonly some 5–12 μm in diameter, and approximately circular in shape, though when the pits are very close together they may be more or less polygonal. The pit apertures are usually somewhat elongated, the elongation being in the transverse direction, or inclined at a small angle to it; there is no torus (Fig. 47).

In some timbers, these pits may be conspicuously minute, less than 3 μm in diameter, as for instance in birch and box, and in many members of the Meliaceae, including the African mahoganies (*Khaya* spp.). Intervascular pitting is usually alternate in arrangement (Fig. 47*A*), often somewhat irregularly so, though in some timbers, for example that of the tulip tree, the pits are opposite (Fig. 47*B*), and in alder both types of arrangement may be seen. In a few timbers the intervascular pits are markedly elongated, in the transverse direction, so that their regular arrangement gives the vessel wall a ladder-like appearance. This is scalariform pitting, and may be seen, for example, in *Magnolia* spp. (Fig. 47*C*), and in American red gum (*Liquidambar styraciflua*). It is, of course, quite a different matter from the scalariform pattern of certain perforation plates, though this is also to be seen in both these timbers.

Another variant of bordered pit structure is the presence of vestures, which are minute outgrowths of the secondary wall, often branched, on the insides of the pit cavities. Their dimensions are at the limit of resolution of light microscopy, so that as the pits are seen in face view in longitudinal sections, the vestures seem to be no more than masses of refractive granules occupying the pit apertures. They are, however, clearly resolved by electron microscopy and have been described in detail by Schmid and Machado (1964) and Schmid (1965). They are also illustrated, by scanning electron microscopy, by van Vliet (1978) and Butterfield and Meylan (1980). Vestured pits occur in most woody members of the Leguminosae, and may be seen, for instance, in laburnum (*Laburnum anagyroides*) and in afrormosia (*Pericopsis elata*), among many other timbers. They are also common among members of the Dipterocarpaceae (Fig. 48).

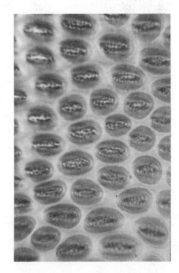

Fig. 48. Vestured pits in afrormosia (*Pericopsis elata*). Part of a vessel wall in face-view (× 1050).

Pit pairs between vessels and tracheids are bordered on both sides, like intervascular pits, though they usually differ from these in size or some other feature. Where vessels are in contact with parenchyma or fibres the pit-pairs are either half-bordered or wholly simple in structure. These pits are considered further below in relation to the other cellular components of the wood.

As well as the various forms of pitting, the walls of the vessels of many hardwoods, like those of the tracheids of certain softwoods, characteristically possess narrow, spiral (strictly helical) bands of thickening superimposed on their inner surfaces. Spiral thickening of this kind is, of course, not to be confused with that of protoxylem elements. It was formerly termed tertiary thickening, but is now regarded as a localized form of extra thickening of the secondary wall. It is to be seen, for instance, in the hackberries (*Celtis* spp.), the elms (*Ulmus* spp.), both members of the Ulmaceae, in sycamore and the maples (*Acer* spp.), the limes (*Tilia* spp.), the horse chestnuts (*Aesculus* spp.), laburnum and in some members of the Rosaceae. It is sometimes a useful aid to the identification of a timber (Figs. 45, 47*C* and 77).

Tracheids are not universally present in hardwoods, though two types occur. One of these, the vasicentric type, is so-called because it occurs characteristically in association with the vessels, as for instance in chestnuts and some oaks, including the British species, and in *Eucalyptus* spp. Vasicentric tracheids, in contrast with the tracheids of softwoods, are not greatly elongated; moreover, they have rounded ends and bordered pits in all their walls. They are often distorted in shape, being bent longitudinally and flattened transversely, a consequence of the lateral expansion of adjacent vessels and the inevitable radial pressures and tangential tensions which this expansion produces and imposes on nearby cells (Fig. 49).

The second type is the so-called vascular tracheid, such as occurs in the latewood of elm. Vascular tracheids resemble small vessel elements, in that they are formed in axial columns, but their more or less oblique end walls, though pitted, are not perforated. Thus in a sense, they appear as incompletely differentiated vessel elements, in which the perforations have failed to form; indeed it may sometimes happen that an axial column of vascular elements consists in part of vascular tracheids and in part of vessel elements.

In this context, it is appropriate to refer briefly to the wider, more general question, albeit one of greater interest perhaps to plant physiologists than to wood anatomists; the question of the length of wood vessels generally. For instance, do vessels extend indefinitely throughout the height of a tree? Or are there, at intervals along an axial column of vessel elements, end walls which have failed to perforate? If so, how far apart are they? These are not easy questions to answer, but what evidence there is suggests that while some vessels in ring-porous trees may extend for many metres (and possibly, indeed, throughout the height of a tree), in diffuse-porous trees the maximum vessel length is likely to be much less, about a metre or so. Within these maxima the majority of vessels in both types of wood are probably much shorter, 20 cm or less. Even at 20 cm, a vessel would, of course, comprise a

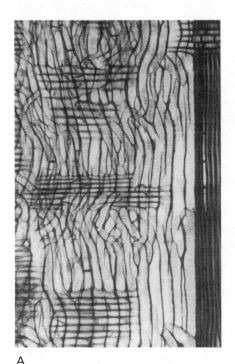
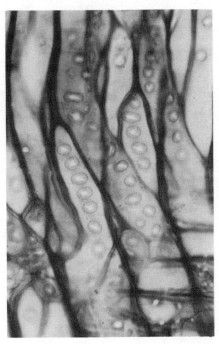

A   B

Fig. 49. Vasicentric tracheids in American chestnut (*Castanea dentata*). R.L.S., *A*, × 95; *B* × 450. Note the distorted forms of these tracheids, and in *B* their bordered pits.

few hundred vessel elements, so that the end of a vessel, marked by the occurrence of an imperforate end wall in a vessel element, is not very likely to be seen in a section. There seems to be no regularity, in the distribution along an axial column of vessel elements, of end walls which have failed to perforate (Greenidge, 1952; Scholander, 1958; Skene and Balodis, 1968; Zimmermann and Jeje, 1981; Zimmermann, 1983).

The vessels and tracheids of hardwoods are, in the main, water-conducting structures, which mechanically are rather weak; the mechanical strength of hardwoods resides principally in their fibres. These are long, narrowly fusiform or almost needle-like cells, angular in cross-section, and strongly adherent; typically they have fairly uniformly thickened cell walls which become heavily lignified. On completion of their cell wall development their protoplasts usually break down, but in some instances, the cells may remain alive for the duration of the sapwood, and during this period they may also store starch, as wood parenchyma does (Braun, 1961, 1970; Fahn and Arnon, 1963; Fahn and Leshem, 1963).

While vessel elements are of much the same length as the fusiform initials from which they were differentiated, fibres are often some 2–5 times the length of the fusiform initials, this increase in length in the course of their differentiation being achieved by intrusive growth of the cell tips. Evidence of this mode of growth is frequently to be seen in macerations of hardwoods, since, in intruding among other cells, the tips of fibres often become markedly distorted by the shapes of the contiguous cells between which they have intruded. Thus, adjacent to a ray, of which the cells have rounded, bulging radial walls, a fibre tip may develop a scalloped or almost serrated form, or, in meeting the edge of a ray, the tip of a fibre may fork and continue to grow, up or down both sides of it; examples of the shapes which fibre ends may adopt have been illustrated by Wardrop (1964a) and especially by Süss and Müller-Stoll (1969); see also Fig. 12. An account and discussion of the process of intrusive growth in the fibres of *Salix viminalis* has been given by Wenham and Cusick (1975). Fibres occur in wood in relatively large groups, and their well-developed capacity for intrusive growth has the consequence that they interdigitate markedly. This tends greatly to increase the intercellular cohesion within a group of fibres, and so to enhance the mechanical strength of the group as a whole. It also has the result that, in a transverse section cut at any level through a group of fibres, these show a range of diameters according to whether the individual fibres happen to have been cut across their widest middle parts, or near their pointed tips. This appearance is quite characteristic of fibrous tissue, and is an aid to its recognition in transverse sections.

The pits of hardwood fibres are small, but show some diversity in their structure. In some genera, as for example in *Platanus* and *Laurelia*, they are clearly bordered, though in others, *Alnus*, for instance, the borders are narrow and inconspicuous. The pit apertures are elongate and slit-like, in the form of flattened funnels in the thick cell walls, so that their appearance in sections depends on the plane of the section in relation to the orientation of the slits (Fig. 50). In longitudinal sections in which the fibre walls may be observed in face view, the pit apertures are usually to be seen orientated at small angles to the axis of the fibre, so that in a pit-pair they appear as a cross superimposed on the pit border. They may however be so nearly axially orientated that the cross effect is not produced. There is also some variation in the length of the pit apertures, so that the arms of the cross may or may not extend beyond the limits of the pit border. The presence in these fibres of bordered pits means of course that they are tracheids, in the strict sense of that term, but as they differ so markedly from other types of tracheid, they are distinguished from them by being termed fibre-tracheids.

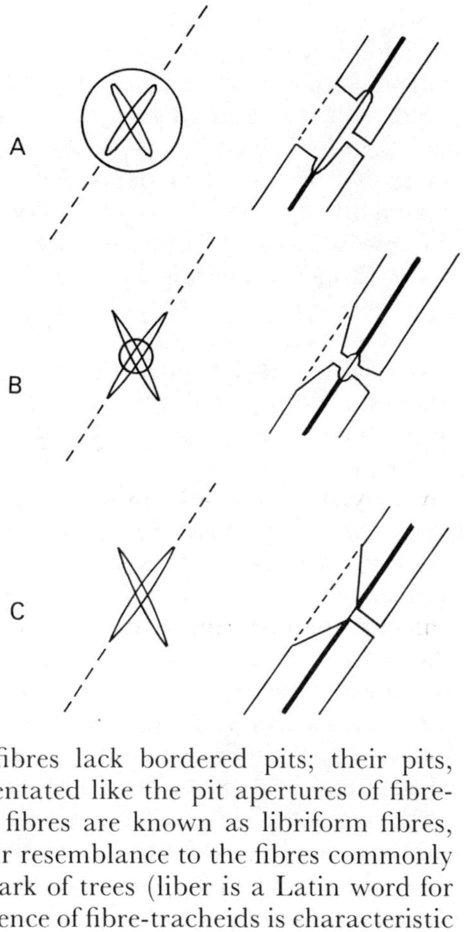

Fig. 50. Diagrams of common types of fibre pitting, in face-view and section. The plane of section drawn is indicated by the broken line in the face-view diagram. A, a bordered pit-pair between fibre tracheids; B, similar to A, but with the pit apertures extended beyond the pit border; C, a simple pit-pair, as between libriform fibres. Where the pit border in B is narrow it is easily overlooked, so that the distinction between B and C is not, in practice, a clear-cut one.

Usually, however, hardwood fibres lack bordered pits; their pits, though slit-like and obliquely orientated like the pit apertures of fibre-tracheids, are simple pits. These fibres are known as libriform fibres, the term libriform referring to their resemblance to the fibres commonly present in the phloem, or inner bark of trees (liber is a Latin word for the inner bark). Although the presence of fibre-tracheids is characteristic of the timbers of some genera, and may be an aid to their identification, the often inconspicuous pit borders are easily overlooked. In everyday usage both types of fibre are referred to simply as fibres, without the distinction between them being made; what, in practice, is more important, is the great range, among different kinds of wood, in the thickness of their fibre walls.

The mechanical strength of timber is related closely to its "weight" — more accurately of course, to its density or weight per unit volume — and this in turn depends largely on the proportion of fibre cells in its make-up and the thickness of their cell walls. Extreme values are exemplified by lignum vitae (*Guaiacum* spp.), an exceptionally hard timber, best known perhaps in everday circumstances in the "woods" used in the game of bowls, and balsa (*Ochroma pyramidalis*), well-known to model makers for its softness and ready whittling properties. Lignum vitae has a density of about 1200 Kg/m^3 (75lb/ft^3) when seasoned, so that it sinks in water; its fibre walls are so thick that the cell cavities are almost obliterated. Balsa, on the other hand, is likely to have a density of the order of 170 Kg/m^3 (= 11 lb/ft^3) at 12% moisture content (Farmer, 1972) and its fibre walls are exceptionally thin and delicate in appearance. Hardness is, of course, only one aspect of the mechanical strength of wood. Other properties, for example the outstanding toughness and bending qualities of European ash (*Fraxinus excelsior*), which is intermediate, in its hardness and density, between lignum vitae and balsa, cannot be specifically referred to features of its anatomical structure.

Fibres rarely show spiral thickening of the kind described in vessel elements (and in softwood tracheids), but this does occur, in both fibres and vessels, in holly (*Ilex aquifolium*).

Another variant of fibre structure is the septate fibre, which may be of either the fibre-tracheid or libriform type (Bailey, 1936). In the differentiation of this type of fibre the secondary wall is formed in the usual way, and following this the protoplast divides and a number of transverse walls (the septa) are laid down, so that the fibre becomes divided into a file of parenchyma cells. These cells, usually 4–8 in number, have a distinctive appearance in longitudinal sections, since the septa usually remain thin, in marked contrast with the thick axial walls of the fibre; moreover, they extend only across its lumen, having no connection to its primary wall or to the adjacent middle lamella. In this way a septate fibre comes to resemble, in some respects, a column of axial parenchyma cells (see below), but the special features of its cell walls are sufficient, on close inspection, for its correct identification (Parameswaran and Liese, 1969). The resemblance is however, enhanced in some instances by the capacity of septate fibres to remain living while in the sapwood, and to store starch or other metabolic products during this period. Septate fibres are of wide occurrence, more especially among tropical trees; they are well shown, for instance, in sapele (*Entandrophragma cylindricum*) and utile (*E. utile*), and in the American mahoganies (*Swietenia* spp.). In a survey of 6250 species, in 2280 genera, Spackman and Swamy (1949) found that 25% of genera include species in which septate fibres occur, and that, in broad terms, there is a tendency for them to be most abundant in species in which axial parenchyma is not well developed (Fig. 51).

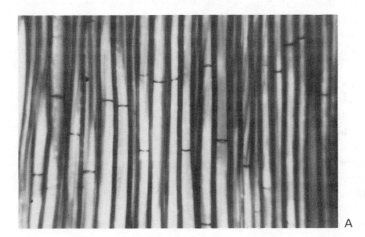

A

Fig. 51. Septate fibres in sapele (*Entandrophragma cylindricum*). R.L.S., *A*, × 200; *B*, × 610. The septa are thinner than the axial walls of the fibres, and are attached to their inner surfaces; they do not extend to the middle lamellae. In *B* part of a transverse 'wall' between two parenchyma cells is shown to the right of a fibre septum, emphasizing the difference between the two types of dividing 'wall' in their relationships to their axial walls.

B

Axial parenchyma is formed by transverse divisions of fusiform derivatives of the cambium, but these divisions, in contrast with those which occur in septate fibres, take place at a much earlier stage in the differentiation of the fusiform cells. Thus, as the daughter cells mature into parenchyma, their transverse walls thicken at the same time, and to similar degree, as their axial walls, and they develop simple pits; they do not remain conspicuously thin like those characteristic of septate fibres. A single fusiform derivative thus usually produces an axial column of a few parenchyma cells; in storied woods however, in which the fusiform cells are relatively short, these may each differentiate into a single fusiform parenchyma cell, or may divide once or twice only to form a column of two or four cells (Figs. 72 and 116B).

At maturity axial parenchyma cells are commonly in the range of 50–150 μm in length, and 20–30 μm wide. They are rectangular or polygonal in cross-section, and while those at the ends of the column tend to show the tapered form of the fusiform initial (Fig. 56B), the end walls generally are substantially transverse. Parenchyma cells formed in this way, from scattered individual fusiform initials in the cambial zone, would, of course, come to exist, in the mature wood, as similarly scattered, single axial columns or strands; these are often apparently isolated from each other, in a general background of fibres. They occur like this in many timbers, for example, in alder and plane, and as they are seen in transverse sections they are relatively inconspicuous and may be difficult to identify. In the sapwood attention may be drawn to them by their starch content, and in the heartwood by the occasional appearance within the thickness of the section of a pitted transverse wall. When the strands are short, as they are in alder, their appearance in tangential longitudinal sections may also be confusing, in giving them a superficial resemblance to uniseriate rays; careful study of the orientation of the individual cells should, however, dispose of this ambiguity. In the walnuts, the strands are longer, and often associated, two or three together; they are thus more readily recognized (Fig. 56).

Very frequently parenchyma cells in wood are found in larger aggregates, rather than in single strands, a result of the correlated activity of groups of fusiform initials. Some of these aggregates, as they appear in transverse sections, have characteristic forms which are of value in the identification of timbers; they are considered further below.

Axial parenchyma remains alive much longer than other axial cells of the wood, normally for the duration of the sapwood. It has an important storage function, usually containing starch grains or other metabolic products; oil, mucilage and other substances may be held in somewhat enlarged specialized cells. As the sapwood is converted into heartwood the starch is mobilized and disappears, presumably serving as a substrate in the synthesis of the numerous other organic substances which are deposited in the heartwood. In some timbers crystals of various shapes are formed in axial parenchyma; they are usually of calcium salts, especially calcium oxalate. Silica may also occur, either as fine granules or as amorphous deposits.

Cells containing conspicuous crystals are said to be crystalliferous. In the wood of many trees they do not differ, except in their contents, from other axial parenchyma; examples of this type may be seen in ramin (*Gonystylus macrophyllum*), and afara (*Terminalia superba*). In many other timbers, however, crystalliferous cells of a more specialized type are formed. The protoplasts of certain axial parenchyma cells divide transversely and additional transverse walls are laid down, so giving rise to columns of shorter cuboidal cells; the additional transverse walls often remain thin (like those of septate fibres) and so can be recognized even in the mature wood. Alternatively, a fusiform derivative of the

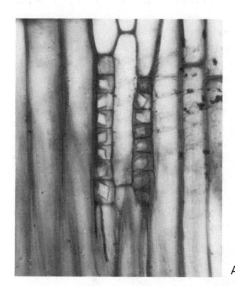

Fig. 52. Crystals in wood cells. *A*, in a chambered crystalliferous cell in *Albizzia falcata*; R.L.S., × 300. *B*, in the marginal cells of a ray in *Mansonia altissima*; R.L.S., × 95.

A

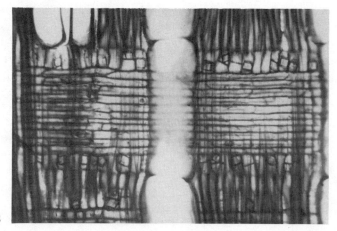

B

cambium may divide, from the beginning, into a similar column of small, almost cuboidal or barrel-shaped cells, which again can be recognized as having arisen from the sub-division of a single initial cell. Whichever way the columns of smaller cells may have been formed, each cell usually develops a single rhomboidal crystal, and the whole column, having been derived from a common mother-cell, is termed a chambered crystalliferous cell. Examples may be seen in the albizzias (Fig. 52A), in afrormosia (*Pericopsis elata*), swamp sepetir (*Pseudosindora palustris*), African walnut (*Lovoa trichilioides*) and other timbers.

There is a further aspect of the diversity of axial parenchyma in wood, which relates to its part in the formation of intercellular ducts or canals. Canals of this type are not of wide occurrence in hardwoods, but are characteristic of the timbers of certain families, notably those of the Dipterocarpaceae of India and South East Asia. The canals of these timbers are all broadly similar in structure to the axial resin ducts of softwoods, but they show differences in their arrangement in the wood which are of some diagnostic value. As they are seen in transverse sections, they may be scattered singly in the wood, as in mersawa or krabak (*Anisoptera* spp.), or, as in a number of other genera, they may be arranged in tangential lines (Fig. 53). These are relatively short in *Dipterocarpus* spp. (from which the timbers eng, keruing and others are obtained) or conspicuously longer in *Dryobalanops* spp. (which yield kapur) and in the merantis (*Shorea* spp). The canals are commonly filled with gum or a pale yellowish or white deposit of dried resins.

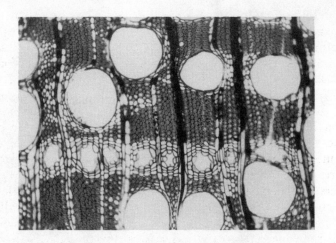

Fig. 53. *Dryobalanops aromatica*. T.S. × 65, showing a tangential row of axial ducts, which would normally contain gum or resinous material. The ducts do not have a wall of their own, as vessels do, but are cavities in the wood bordered by parenchyma cells.

Another quite different type of intercellular cavity, found characteristically in timbers of the family Apocynaceae, derives from the presence of systems of latex tubes in the wood. These are surrounded by unlignified thin-walled parenchyma, and the parenchyma and embedded latex tubes are known as latex traces. When the green timber is freshly sawn the latex exudes, but as the wood is dried the parenchyma shrivels, leaving cavities which appear on longitudinal surfaces as lenticular holes a few millimetres wide and 2–3 cm long. These occur, for instance, in the alstonias of tropical Africa (*Alstonia* spp.) and in jelutong (*Dyera* spp.) of South East Asia. Smaller latex tubes are also to be seen in the rays (Fig. 70).

The four principal components of the axial structure of wood; vessels, tracheids, fibres (in the broad sense of that term) and parenchyma, which are derived from identical fusiform initials in their various ways, are intermingled in the mature wood. Here they display considerable variation, not only in their individual sizes and shapes, but also in the proportions in which they are present, and in their arrangement. Although there is what seems to be a markedly random element in these matters, nevertheless certain types of pattern can be recognized, which contribute to the figure of wood (see Chapter 7), or facilitate its identification. While transverse sections, or endgrain surfaces, are in many instances the most revealing and most useful in the latter respect, figure is most evident on longitudinal surfaces and its full understanding commonly calls for reference to all three planes of section. We now turn, therefore, to some consideration of the nature, recognition and terminology of these patterns which are most conspicuous in relation to the distribution of vessels and parenchyma. The rays also contribute another group of structural patterns, but the anatomy of rays, in its finer points, is complex, and is most conveniently considered separately.

In most hardwood timbers, both temperate and tropical, the vessels, as seen in transverse sections, are scattered fairly uniformly throughout the total structure, and even where there are discernible growth increments there is no great gradient of vessel diameter or spacing across the season's growth. Such timbers are described as diffuse-porous; among British trees, beech, birch, lime and many more are of this nature (Figs. 76 and 81).

In others, however, there is in the early wood a more or less continuous zone of vessels which are of conspicuously greater diameter than those produced later in the growing season, and moreover the transition from one type to the other is abrupt and clear-cut. This is the ring-porous condition, in which the earlywood zone, one to several vessels wide radially, is usually visible to the unaided eye as a pore-ring. Ring-porous trees are always deciduous, though it will be evident from the previous paragraph that the converse is not true. However, the deciduous oaks (including the British species) are all ring-porous, while the evergreen oaks (including *Quercus ilex*, which is often planted here) are not. Among our other native trees, ash, elm and sweet chestnut are all ring-porous (Fig. 74).

A third category of vessel distribution is also recognized, in which the earlywood vessels are unevenly spaced, so that the pore-ring is interrupted; this arrangement is described as semi-ring-porous. The walnuts (*Juglans* spp.) and the hickories (*Carya* spp.) are semi-ring-porous; so also usually is teak (*Tectona grandis*) (Fig. 60*A*) but teak is more variable and sometimes has a more or less complete pore-ring. Teak is a deciduous tree, and the variability of its pore-ring is thought to be related to its conditions of growth and the period of the year for which it retains its leaves.

Within these generalized patterns of vessel arrangement, other variations, which prove useful in distinguishing certain timbers, may be recognized in transverse sections. Vessels may be solitary, as for instance in box (*Buxus* spp.) (Fig. 83*C*) and apple (*Malus sylvestris*), where they are small, and in obeche (*Triplochiton scleroxylon*), where they are of much larger diameter. A fair proportion may sometimes characteristically appear in pairs, as in the maples (*Acer* spp.) (Fig. 81*B*), and radial chains of 2–6 together, with much flattened faces of contact, are also commonly to be seen as in the alders (Fig. 79*B*) and in hornbeam (*Carpinus betulus*), among genera represented in Britain, and in the ebonies (*Diospyros* spp.) among tropical ones; in basralocus (*Dicorynia paraensis*) these vessel chains are exceptionally long, extending to 25 or more vessels. In some woods radially orientated vessel clusters, rather than chains, are frequent, as in the limes (*Tilia* spp.) and in the latewood of robinia (Fig. 116), and in others again the vessel arrangement may be predominantly in tangentially orientated bands or clusters, exemplified in Australian silky oak (*Cardwellia sublimis*) and in the latewood of elms (Fig. 74*B*). Obliquely orientated lines or clusters of vessels, lying at various angles between the radial and tangential directions are also characteristic of some timbers, and are well shown in the chestnuts (*Castanea* spp.), and in some *Eucalyptus* spp. (Fig. 74*C*). The vessels are often actually solitary, being slightly separated by other types of element, but the oblique orientation of their grouping is none the less clear.

The distribution of axial parenchyma in wood, like that of vessels, shows marked diversity. When much is present it can easily be seen on end-grain surfaces with a hand lens, and is useful in the identification of certain timbers. The various patterns of its arrangement have therefore been classified and defined so that they may be referred to in concise terms. The following classification is essentially that of Jane (1956, 1970) (Fig.54). It is satisfactory for most purposes, and

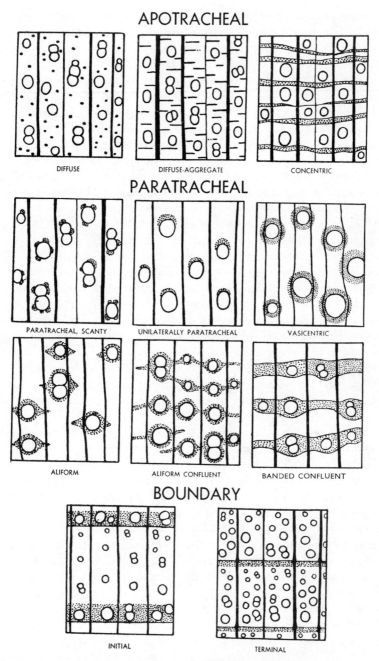

Fig. 54. Diagrams illustrating the principal types of distribution of axial parenchyma in hardwoods, as seen in transverse sections. The parenchyma is shown stippled, except in the first diagram where it is represented by isolated dots, and in the second, where it is shown as horizontal lines. (From Jane, 1970).

adequately encompasses the range of types of distribution which occur; some timbers may show more than one of these. The scheme is based entirely on the appearance of the parenchyma as it is seen on end-grain surfaces or in transverse sections, and should be read with this in mind. For instance, the apparently scattered cells of diffuse parenchyma, though described as isolated, are not so in reality; each is a member of an axial file of cells, as may be seen in longitudinal sections.

A. *Apotracheal parenchyma.* Axial parenchyma which is not pre-dominantly associated with vessels or vascular tracheids.

1. *Diffuse.* Isolated parenchyma cells scattered among the fibres, as in alder and the chestnuts (*Castanea* spp.). Diffuse axial paren-chyma is not visible with a hand-lens; even under the microscope it is usually not conspicuous in transverse sections, though its transverse walls, seen in face value, may draw attention to its presence. It is distinct enough in longitudinal sections (Fig. 55).

2. *Diffuse-aggregate*, also known as *diffuse-in-aggregates*. Cells as in (1), but mostly associated a few together, in short tangential rows, as in walnut and lime (Fig. 56*A*).

3. *Banded.* Bands of parenchyma, one to several cells wide in the radial direction, concentric within the growth increment (i.e. dis-

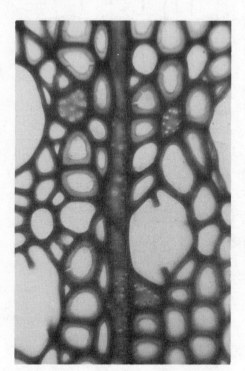

Fig. 55. American chestnut (*Castanea dentata*). T.S. × 475, showing diffuse parenchyma. In three places in the field of view pitted horizontal walls of axial parenchyma strands occur within the thickness of the section, and thus appear in face-view.

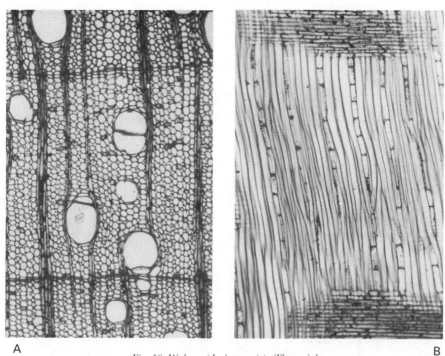

A

B

Fig. 56. Walnut (*Juglans regia*). The axial parenchyma is in short tangential lines, i.e. diffuse-in-aggregates. *A*, T.S., *B*, R.L.S. Both × 95.

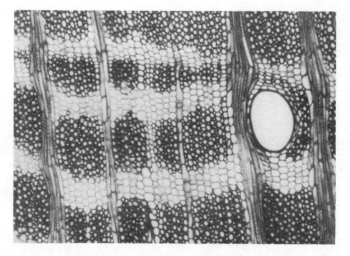

Fig. 57. *Sterculia oblonga*. T.S., × 70. The axial parenchyma is in concentric bands, which are 5–6 cells wide in the radial direction.

tinct from boundary parenchyma) and usually easily seen with a hand-lens. Banded parenchyma occurs in many timbers. Bands one cell wide are to be seen in holm oak (*Quercus ilex*) and often in other oaks; in the hickories (*Carya* spp.) the bands are 1–3 cells wide; in the alstonias (*Alstonia* spp.) 2 cells wide, and in the sterculias (*Sterculia* spp.) and ekki (*Lophira alata*) some 5–7 cells in width. The spacing of the bands may also differ in different timbers in characteristic ways (Figs. 57 and 58).

A

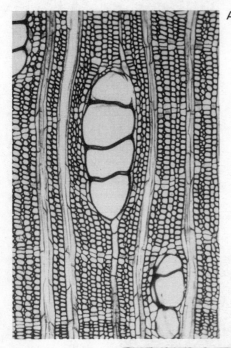

Fig. 58. *Alstonia boonei*. Concentric banded axial parenchyma, the bands here being 2 cells wide, and comparatively inconspicuous in transverse sections. *A*, T.S. and *B*. R.L.S., both × 60.

A also shows a radial latex canal, cut longitudinally, in the ray to the left of the chain of four vessels. (Compare Fig. 70*A*).

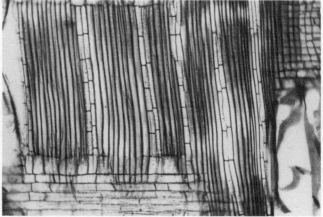

B

B.   Paratracheal parenchyma.   Axial parenchyma predominantly associated with vessels or vascular tracheids.

  1. *Scanty paratrachael.*   Parenchyma adjacent to vessels, isolated, or forming partial sheaths around them; it may often be incon-

A

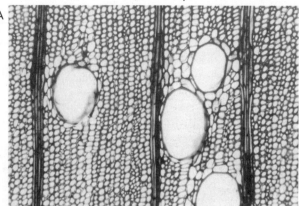

B

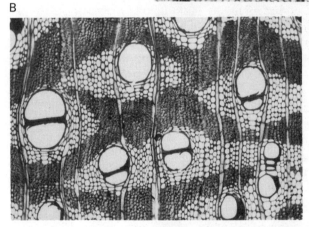

Fig. 59. Some forms of
paratracheal parenchyma.
A ,Lovoa trichilioides,
scanty paratracheal;
T.S., × 95
B. Mora excelsa,
aliform confluent;
*C, Haematoxylon
campechianum,*
banded confluent.
Both T.S., × 60.

C

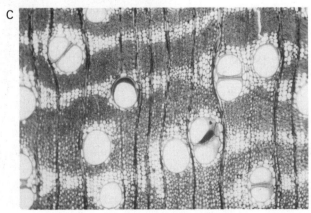

spicuous. It occurs, for example, in elms (*Ulmus* spp.) in some *Eucalyptus* spp. and in African walnut (*Lovoa trichilioides*) (Fig. 59*A*).

2. *Unilateral paratracheal*. Aggregates of axial parenchyma occurring to one side of the vessels (almost always the outer side) so that the vessels, as seen in transverse sections, appear to have "caps" of parenchyma, as in idigbo (*Terminalia ivorensis*).

3. *Vasicentric*. Parenchyma forming a circular or oval "halo" around the vessels as in the latewood of ash (*Fraxinus* spp.) (Fig. 74*D*), in ogea (*Daniellia* spp.) and the African mahoganies (*Khaya* spp.). Vascentric parenchyma is usually visible with a hand-lens, though when it is sparse it may be difficult to distinguish from scanty paratracheal; the parenchyma of *Lovoa* has been described under both headings.

4. *Aliform*. Aggregates of parenchyma surrounding the vessels, as in the vasicentric pattern, but extending tangentially into lozenge-shaped or winged profiles, for example in satiné (*Brosimum paraense*) and ramin (*Gonystylus macrophyllum*).

5. *Confluent*. Groups of parenchyma, linking two or more vessels;
   (a)   *Aliform confluent*. The "wings" of aliform parenchyma are more extended tangentially, so that they join up with those surrounding nearby vessels, for example in mora (*Mora excelsa*), iroko (*Chlorophora excelsa*) and Indian rosewood (*Dalbergia latifolia*) (Fig. 59*B*).
   (b)   *Banded confluent*. Bands of parenchyma, rather than "wings", which link vessels in the tangential direction, for example in basralocus (*Dicorynia paraensis*) and logwood (*Haematoxylon campechianum*) (Fig 59*C*).

C. *Boundary*. Axial parenchyma formed at the beginning or end of the year's growth. There are thus two forms, though it is often difficult to distinguish them.

1. *Initial parenchyma*. A zone of parenchyma formed at the beginning of the year's growth and thus occupying the innermost part of the growth increment. This is apparently rather rare, but is well shown in teak (*Tectona grandis*), where the semi-ring-porous arrangement of the vessels enables the parenchyma to be more readily seen among them (Fig. 60*A*).

2. *Terminal parenchyma*. A zone of parenchyma, usually only a few cells wide in the radial direction, as occurs, for example, in the magnolias (*Magnolia* spp.) and American whitewood (*Liriodendron tulipifera*). A zone of this kind can usually be seen on an end-grain surface with a hand-lens, though its true nature is likely then still to be in doubt. A terminal zone of radially flattened parenchyma may look very similar to fibres, even under the microscope, unless radial longitudinal sections, as well as transverse sections, are examined (Fig. 60*B* and *C*).

A

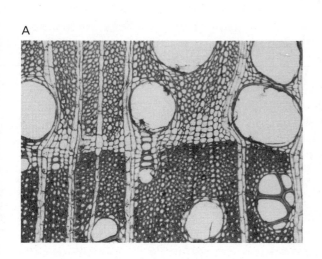

C

B

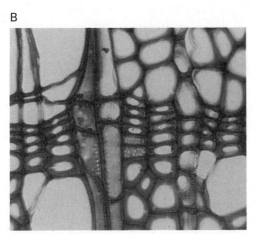

Fig. 60. Boundary parenchyma. *A*, teak (*Tectona grandis*). T.S., × 60; a growth-ring boundary, showing initial parenchyma, i.e. formed at the beginning of the season's growth; note also the interrupted pore ring. *B* and *C*, American whitewood (*Liriodendron tulipifera*); here the parenchyma is terminal, i.e. formed at the end of the season's growth. *B*, T.S., × 120; two parenchyma cells to the right of the ray have been cut so that a horizontal wall with simple pits is visible. *C*, the parenchyma in R.L.S., × 260; the outlines of the cells are in sharp focus, so that their pitted radial walls, within the thickness of the section, are less clearly shown.

The rays of hardwoods consist entirely of parenchyma, which, like axial parenchyma, remains alive while it is in the sapwood, and during this period commonly stores starch; in many instances oils and other metabolic products may also be present, or certain cells may become crystalliferous (Figs. 68 and 52*B*). Though lacking ray tracheids, hardwood rays show a considerable diversity of structure, both in their dimensions and in the form of their constituent cells. Not only may their rays be uniseriate or biseriate, as in softwoods, but multiseriate rays are also commonplace. Moreover, the multiseriate rays of different species may differ considerably and characteristically in their width. For instance in lime and sycamore the rays rarely exceed 8 cells in width, while in beech they commonly extend to 30 cells or so. In actual dimensions the width of hardwood rays may range from about 10 μm to 500 μm or so, and, similarly, while the uniseriate rays may be only a few cells high (50 μm), the multiseriate rays of some species may extend in height to a few centimetres (Fig. 101C). Most rays, however, do not exceed about a millimetre in height. Since wide rays taper to narrow upper and lower margins, their full height and width can be seen only in tangential longitudinal sections; their apparent dimensions, as they appear in transverse and radial sections, are likely to be mis-leading.

In many hardwoods, as for instance in the willows (*Salix* spp.), the horsechestnuts (*Aesculus* spp.), afara (*Terminalia superba*) and ramin (*Gonystylus macrophyllum*), the rays are exclusively uniseriate, and are barely visible (if at all) with a hand-lens. More usually, however, uniseriate and multiseriate rays occur together; in this respect the oaks offer an extreme example. Among their conspicuous and relatively infrequent broad rays, approaching 0.5mm in width and a few centi-metres in height, there are large numbers of very fine uniseriate rays which are less than 0.5mm high.

Where multiseriate rays cross the boundaries of the growth increments their cells (though not increased in number) may be locally enlarged in the tangential direction, so that the rays, as they appear in transverse sections, appear swollen in these regions. They are then described as noded, and the presence of noded rays may be a useful pointer to the identification of an unknown specimen. They are charac-teristic of the wood of magnolias and limes, among other trees (Figs. 60B and 76D).

In some timbers, in addition to their generally distributed and rela-tively low uniseriate and biseriate rays, there appears to be a much smaller number of wide rays, which may, moreover, extend to several centimetres in height. These prove, on close examination of tangential longitudinal sections, to be made up of extensive more-or-less fusiform groups of very numerous and closely aligned finer rays, those within each group being only narrowly separated from each other by axial fibres. Such groups of rays are termed aggregate rays; they are charac-teristic of alder (where their constituent rays are uniseriate) (Fig. 80) and hornbeam (*Carpinus betulus*), in which the individual fine rays range from uniseriate to narrowly multiseriate (Fig. 61).

Rays are also sometimes distinguished by the extent of their diversion from the straight radial direction, as they appear in transverse sections. Rays which take a somewhat sinuous course, having been markedly deflected by the developmental expansion of vessels adjacent to them,

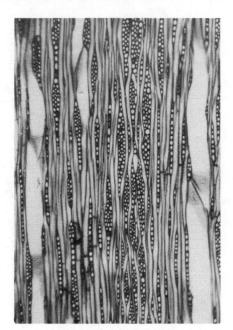

Fig. 61. Hornbeam (*Carpinus betulus*).
T.L.S., × 65, showing part of an
aggregate ray.

are said to be weak rays; in timbers in which they are not so deflected
they are termed strong rays.

The various types of ray tissue and ray structure, considered at the
cellular level, have been classified by Kribs (1968); see also Jane
(1970). Kribs' classification provides a concise system of describing the
rays of hardwoods (it is not applicable to softwoods) and has been
generally used in relation to the description and identification of timbers
(Brazier and Franklin, 1961; Barefoot and Hankins, 1982). The student
thus needs some understanding of it; it is depicted in outline in Fig.
62.

The commonest type of ray cell is one which is elongated radially,
so that its long axis lies in the transverse plane of section of the wood;
such cells are thus said to be procumbent. In tangential sections,
therefore, they are cut across at right-angles to their length and appear
more or less square or polygonal in this view; those of uniseriate rays
often appear barrel-shaped.

In the majority of hardwoods the ray cells are all procumbent, and
those of a given species are much alike. Ray tissue consisting wholly of
procumbent cells is termed homogeneous, irrespective of whether the
rays are exclusively uniseriate, as for example in poplars, horse-chest-
nuts and ramin, or whether some are uniseriate and some multiseriate,
as in elms (*Ulmus* spp.), oaks (*Quercus* spp.) and maples (*Acer* spp.).

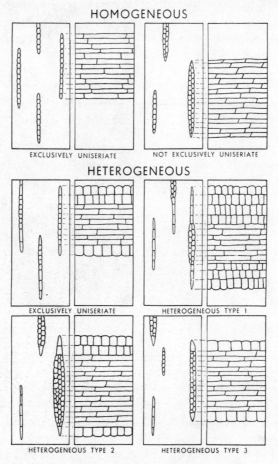

Fig. 62. Diagrams illustrating Kribs'
classification of the different types of ray
tissue in hardwoods, as they are seen in
tangential and radial longitudinal
sections. (From Jane, 1970).

However the rays of many timbers contain cells which are not procumbent, but which, as seen in radial longitudinal sections, appear
approximately square or somewhat elongated in the axial direction;
these cells are known as square or upright cells respectively. Some
uniseriate rays may consist entirely of square or upright cells, but cells
of these types are most frequently to be seen, in one to several tiers,
along the upper and lower margins of rays which otherwise consist of
procumbent cells, and which may be either uniseriate or multiseriate.
Ray margins of this kind are always uniseriate, and where they are
well-developed they form the so-called "tails" of the rays (from their

appearance in tangential sections); their cells are often referred to as tail cells or marginal cells. Ray tissue which contains square or upright cells is termed heterogeneous, again irrespective of whether the rays are uniseriate or multiseriate or of both types together.

In timbers in which the rays are wholly uniseriate and are also heterogeneous, the heterogeneity usually takes the form of the presence of 1–2 rows of square or upright cells along the margins of the rays. This combination of exclusively uniseriate rays with heterogeneous ray tissue is an uncomplicated one, and is sufficiently described in these terms; it may be seen, for instance, in willows (*Salix* spp.).

Among timbers possessing both uniseriate and multiseriate rays, however, the heterogeneous condition is more frequent and more diverse; procumbent, upright and square cells may be found in different

A

Fig. 63. *Wrightia tomentosa. A*, T.L.S., *B*, R.L.S., both × 65. The ray tissue is heterogeneous, type I.

B

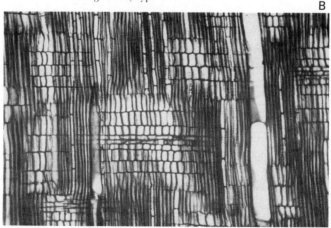

proportions and configurations. These were classified by Kribs under three headings, which he termed heterogeneous types I, II and III. These "shorthand" terms are to be read as conveying the following definitions:–

Heterogeneous Type I .Ray tissue consisting of uniseriate rays composed entirely of upright or upright and square cells, together with multiseriate rays with uniseriate upper and lower margins which (as seen in tangential sections) are as long as, or longer than, their multiseriate parts. The uniseriate margins thus form conspicuous tails to the rays, consisting of cells similar to those of the uniseriate rays, as for example in opepe (*Nauclea diderrichii*) and *Wrightia tomentosa* (Fig. 63).

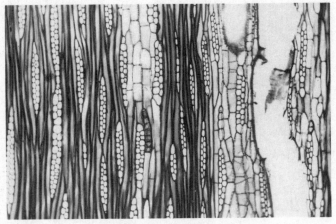

A

Fig. 64. Black bean (*Castanospermum australe*). *A*, T.L.S., *B*, R.L.S., both × 65. The ray tissue is heterogeneous, type II.

B

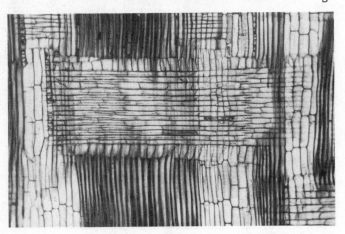

Heterogeneous Type II   .Ray tissue consisting of uniseriate rays com-posed entirely of upright or upright and square cells, together with multiseriate rays with uniseriate tails which are shorter than their multiseriate parts. The tails consist of upright or square cells, or there may be only single marginal rows of such cells. Rays of this type are characteristic of European boxwood (*Buxus sempervirens*), American red gum (*Liquidambar styraciflua*), African celtis (*Celtis* spp.) keruing (*Dipterocarpus* spp.), black bean (*Castanospermum australe*) and many other timbers (Fig. 64).

Heterogeneous Type III   .Ray tissue consisting of uniseriate rays usually of two sorts, some composed entirely of procumbent cells and others of square cells, or of mixed procumbent and square cells, together with multiseriate rays with square marginal cells which are usually in single rows only. If tails are present they are composed wholly of square cells. Heterogeneous Type III ray tissue is characteristic of the beeches, including the European beech (*Fagus sylvatica*), West African bombax (*Bombax* spp.), sapele (*Entandrophragma cylindricum*), Queensland walnut (*Endiandra palmerstonii*) and other timbers (Fig. 65). In many timbers heterogeneous ray tissue of either Type II or Type III may be found, as for instance in the American mahoganies (*Swietenia spp.*) so that these categories are not mutually exclusive in their occurrence even within the same species. Identification of these

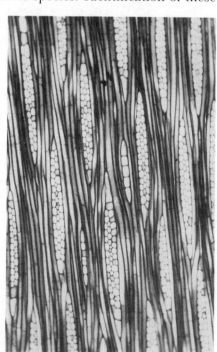

Fig. 65. American mahogany (*Swietenia* sp.). T.L.S., × 65. The ray tissue is heterogeneous, type III.

rays tissue types calls for the inspection of a sufficient sample of both uniseriate and multiseriate rays (where both are present) and may sometimes prove to be a laborious matter, especially for instance where uniseriate rays are relatively sparse.

Although the multiseriate parts of the rays referred to in this classification usually consist entirely of procumbent cells, in some timbers they also contain one or both of two other cell types, known as tile cells and sheath cells. When these are present they confer additional elements of heterogeneity (in the general sense of that word) on the ray tissue. This is, however, a matter quite separate from the Kribs system of ray classification.

Tile cells (Chattaway, 1933) are so-called on account of their characteristic shape. They occur in radial files in the rays, and after having been cut off from the ray initials of the cambial zone they undergo little or no radial elongation, so that in transverse and radial longitudinal sections they are seen to be much shorter radially than the procumbent cells; in tangential longitudinal sections they appear squarish or polygonal. They tend to lose their contents earlier than do the adjacent procumbent cells, and may be additionally conspicuous on this account. In some timbers, for example *Durio*, the tile cells are about the same

A
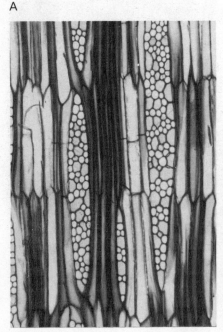

Fig. 66. Obeche (*Triplochiton scleroxylon*). *A*, T.L.S., *B*, R.L.S., both × 95, showing tile cells of the *Pterospermum* type in the rays. In *A* the tile cells are the distinctly larger cells of the ray tissue; in *B* they can be seen to be flattened radially and about twice the height of the procumbent cells. In *A* the storied arrangement of the fibres is also shown.

B
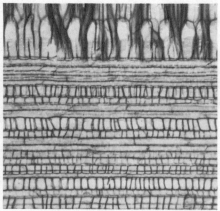

height as the procumbent cells of the ray, while in others, for example *Pterospermum*, they are much higher, twice as high or more. These two types of tile cells are thus known respectively as the *Durio* and *Pterospermum* types. Tile cells are well shown in obeche (*Triplochiton scleroxylon*), where they are of the *Pterospermum* type (Fig. 66).

Sheath cells are upright cells which form a more-or-less complete layer, one cell thick, over the surfaces of multiseriate rays, not merely along their upper and lower margins. They are thus most clearly visible in tangential sections, appearing, as their name implies, to form a complete or partial sheath enclosing the ray. They occur, for instance, in the sterculias of West Africa (*Sterculia* spp.) (Fig. 67).

A number of other variants of ray structure call for brief reference. Where oil or mucilage are held in rays they are often contained in markedly distended thin-walled cells, known as oil cells or mucilage cells respectively. Oil cells are characteristic of some families, for example the Lauraceae, which includes sassafras (*Sassafras officinale*) (Fig. 68); the oil is extracted for medicinal and other purposes. As we have already noted, ray cells of many timbers may also be crystalliferous, as in ramin (*Gonystylus macrophyllum*), African mahogany (*Khaya* spp.) and *Mansonia altissima* among others. In timbers in which the ray tissue is heterogeneous (as in the last two species), the crystals are more likely to be present in the marginal upright or square cells of the rays than in

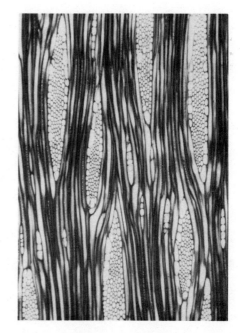

Fig. 67. *Sterculia oblonga*. T.L.S., × 65, showing multiseriate rays with sheath cells. These are the larger cells which form a more-or-less complete layer on the sides of the rays.

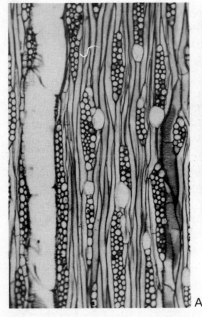

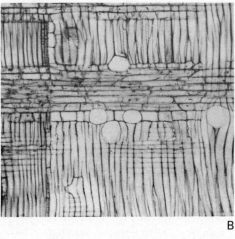

B

Fig. 68. *Sassafras officinale*. *A*, T.L.S., *B*, R.L.S., both × 65, showing oil cells. These are enlarged marginal ray parenchyma.

A

the procumbent cells (Fig. 52*B*). Radially orientated intercellular canals or gum ducts (structurally similar to the radial resin canals of some softwoods) also occur in the rays of some hardwoods, notably among

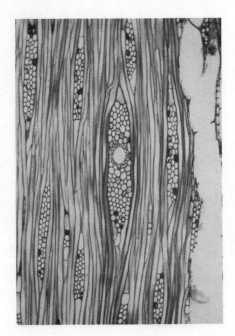

Fig. 69. *Antrocaryon* sp. T.L.S., × 65, showing a radial gum duct in a ray. Note the presence of an epithelium lining the duct.

members of the Burseraceae and Anacardiaceae, families of tropical trees and shrubs. They are to be found, for instance, in Malayan canarium or kedondong, derived from a number of species of *Canarium*, and in *Antrocaryon* sp. (Fig. 69). Radial ducts often connect with elaborate duct systems in the cortex; they are not usually present in the wood together with axial ducts, though both are to be seen in the wood of the yellow merantis (*Shorea* spp.). Among members of the Apocynaceae radial duct-like cavities may arise in the rays from the presence of latex tubes, which appear in tangential sections as elliptical intercellular spaces (Fig. 70A). Latex tubes are also characteristic of members of the Moraceae, and may sometimes be seen in the rays of iroko (*Chlorophora excelsa*) which belongs to this family (Fig. 70B).

The pits between ray cells are, of course, simple pits, which in general are small, lacking in distinctive features and variable in number. The pits between ray cells and vessels, however, call for further comment. These may be half-bordered, or apparently wholly simple, and show some diversity of size and shape. Most commonly they are small (less, often much less, than 10 μm in diameter), and very numerous, as may be seen, for example, in the birches (*Betula* spp.) and ashes (*Fraxinus*

Fig. 70. Latex tubes in rays. *A, Alstonia boonei*, T.L.S., × 65; *B*, iroko, (*Chlorophora excelsa*), T.L.S. × 95. *Alstonia* also shows heterogeneous type II ray tissue.

A

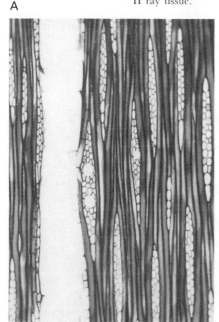

B

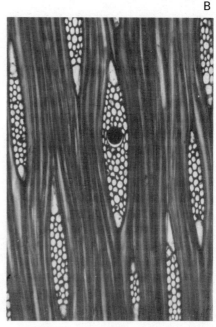

spp.) among temperate genera, and in ramin (*Gonystylus macrophyllum*), obeche (*Triplochiton scleroxylon*), the mahoganies and other members generally of the Meliaceae among tropical genera. In some other timbers the ray-to-vessel pits are larger (more than 10 μm in diameter), and round or rounded-polygonal in shape. This type is well shown in the willows (*Salix* spp.) and *Eucalyptus* spp. In other timbers again, the large ray-to-vessel pits are extended transversely into gash-like shapes, as for example in the beeches (*Fagus* spp.), the magnolias (*Magnolia* spp.) and Chilean laurel (*Laurelia aromatica*) (Fig. 71).

In many timbers the pits between ray cells and vessels (and also those between axial parenchyma and vessels) may be sites of the growth of tyloses into the vessels in the course of the changes in the wood which mark the transition from sapwood to heartwood (see Chapter 8).

Contiguity of ray cells and vessels does not necessarily imply that pits are formed in the walls between them. In some timbers this pitting is restricted to certain cells of the rays, which (rather unfortunately perhaps) have been termed contact cells, in distinction from other ray cells lacking these pits, known as isolation cells (Braun, 1970). The difference is well shown in the willows, in which the large, rounded ray-to-vessel pits are restricted to the marginal cells of the (heterogeneous uniseriate) rays (Fig. 78*K*); the procumbent cells are thus never contact cells. A comparable situation exists in *Laurelia* spp., in which the rays are heterogeneous type II and the scalariform gash-like pitting, referred to above, is restricted to the square or upright cells (Fig. 71). However,

Fig. 71. *Laurelia serrata*. R.L.S., × 130.
The ray tissue is heterogeneous type II,
and the large gash-like ray-to-vessel pits
are restricted to the marginal ray cells.

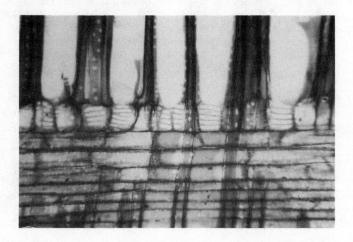

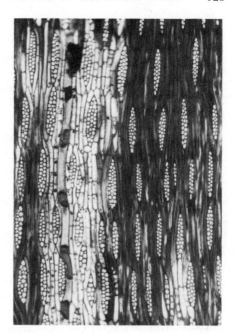

Fig. 72. Afrormosia (*Pericopsis elata*). T.L.S., × 65, showing storied rays. The axial parenchyma, just to the left of centre in the figure, is also storied.

the distinction between contact and isolation cells can still be recognized in some other timbers, even though their rays are homogeneous. This may be seen in poplars (*Populus* spp.), European ash (*Fraxinus excelsior*) and sycamore (*Acer pseudoplatanus*), where the ray-to-vessel pitting is restricted to certain of the horizontal tiers of the ray cells (Braun, 1970).

There is a more generalized structural pattern which is characterisic of many hardwoods and is most evident in tangential longitudinal sections and surfaces. We refer here to the storied arrangement of their elements (or some of them), often to be seen, for example, among members of the Leguminosae and Meliaceae. It arises, of course, from the formation of the wood by a storied cambium (Chapter 3), but the degree to which the storied structure may be evident in the mature wood is variable. This is because, as the various types of cambial derivatives grow, divide and differentiate in their various ways, their initial regularity of arrangement may become correspondingly differently disturbed. Vessel elements and parenchyma are commonly storied, though as regards the latter it is of course the axial strands of parenchyma which correspond to the tiers of cambial initials. In trees with storied cambia these strands commonly consist of 2–4 parenchyma cells (Figs. 72 and 116*B*). Fibres as well as parenchyma may also be storied, as is to be seen in obeche (*Triplochiton scleroxylon*) (Fig. 66*A*), though in timbers in which the fibres undergo a marked and variable degree of intrusive tip growth, their basically storied origin may be correspondingly variably obscured, even though adjacent parenchyma retains its storied arrangement. This is well shown, for instance, in robinia (*Robinia pseudoacacia*). Rays, similarly, may be storied or not. Small rays are more likely to be storied than larger ones, as for example the (uniseriate) rays of cocus wood (*Brya ebenus*) and lignum vitae (*Guaiacum* spp.), and the relatively low (bi- or multi-seriate) rays of mansonia and afrormosia (*Pericopsis elata*) are storied (Fig. 72). In the American mahoganies (*Swietenia* spp.) and sapele (*Entandrophragma cylindricum*) the rays may or may not be storied, whereas in obeche, while some regions of storied arrangement may be evident among the smaller rays, the larger ones, extending in height over two, three or four stories of the other elements, are less regularly arranged.

Although different patterns of wood structure, such as are described in the foregoing pages, may be identified in sections cut in different planes, there are nevertheless certain aspects of cellular inter-relationships in wood which are barely, if at all, recognizable by the ordinary methods of microscopic examination of sections and macerations. For instance, we have referred to the occurrence of apparently isolated strands of axial parenchyma (such as are seen in alder), and this is how they appear to be. Yet they can hardly be really isolated among surrounding dead cells, or how could they accumulate starch? Again, it is customary to describe the arrangement of vessels in wood, in terms of their appearance in transverse sections, as being solitary or as occurring in various types of multiple groups. This then raises the interesting question as to whether apparently solitary vessels really are solitary; do they indeed form isolated channels of water transport over long distances in the tree? Or do they associate with other vessels in some transitory fashion? Similarly, does a multiple group of vessels have an aggregate unity? Or do exchanges take place between the vessels of one group and those of neighbouring groups? If so, of course, this would mean that the groups we see in any one transverse section represent strands of a network, not real structural entities.

Answers to questions of this kind, affording additional insights into wood structure, derive from the close study of long series of transverse sections, and the reconstruction, from the changing patterns that they present, of the intercellular relationships, in three dimensions, of the tissue elements under examination. This is a laborious procedure, and has therefore, in general terms, been applied only to very small volumes of wood, of the order of size of a few cubic millimetres; the technique developed by Zimmermann and Tomlinson (1967), using repetitive photography of the wood surface from which the sections are being cut, rather than of the sections themselves, facilitates the exploration of larger volumes.

Studies even of very small volumes of wood are nevertheless revealing.

In *Populus* wood the vessels are to be seen in transverse sections as occurring singly or in short radial groups of two or three together. Braun (1959) showed, however, in a three-dimensional reconstruction, which is reproduced also by Esau (1965a), that even within a volume of wood of less that 1 mm³, this association of the vessels in twos and threes is of very limited extent axially; the groups divide and their members associate with others, and many of the vessels which, in an isolated transverse section, appear to be solitary, are solitary only in the course of their somewhat oblique passage from membership of one group to membership of another. Thus, as Braun emphasized, the vessels form a network, or plexus, in the wood; see also Braun (1970).

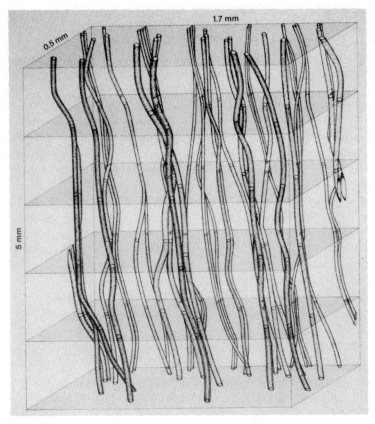

Fig. 73. European ash (*Fraxinus excelsior*). A diagram of the courses of the latewood vessels in a small volume of the wood of the third growth increment; the back of the block shown here was the growth increment boundary. Note that different scales of drawing have been used in the axial and transverse directions. Successive 1 mm levels are shown by shading, and the positions of the vessels at each of these levels are indicated. (From Burggraaf, 1972); see text.

The observations of Skene (1969) on *Eucalyptus maculata*, of Zimmermann and Tomlinson (1967) and Burggraaf (1972) on *Fraxinus excelsior* (Fig. 73) and of Zimmermann and Brown (1971) on *Cedrela fissilis* reveal the existence of similar networks in the wood of these trees, so that vessel networks of this kind seem likely to be general features of wood structure. As Burggraaf has pointed out, the existence of such networks, in which vessels "wander" from one network strand to another, often in the radial direction, raises certain problems. It complicates our comprehension of what it may be, in the inner cambial zone, which determines the types of mature axial elements that fusiform derivatives, considered individually, are to become.

Intercellular relationships among other types of wood elements can also, of course, be investigated by similar methods. Thus in *Eucalyptus maculata*, in which the axial parenchyma is diffuse or diffuse-in-aggregates, Skene (1969) found that 121 parenchyma strands, which were closely studied, made contact with 135 rays, and only four were without an observed contact with another strand or a ray. The rays and axial parenchyma thus together form another integrated network, which, in the sapwood, is a living network. Since the rays extend also into the phloem, the recognition of their close connection with axial parenchyma makes the accumulation and mobilization of starch in these cells the more comprehensible. Skene also found vessels to be in contact with rays virtually throughout their length, and Kučera (1975), working with beech, has also emphasized the frequency of contacts of this kind. Evidence bearing on the physiology of ray-to-vessel contacts, in relation to starch mobilization in ray cells, has been described and discussed by Braun (1970) and Sauter *et al.* (1973).

It is instructive, in the light of the outline survey of the nature of the diversity of hardwood structure in the earlier part of this chapter, to examine a group of timbers which exemplify various combinations of the anatomical features to which reference has been made. The timbers of the genera listed below, which all include familiar common British trees, as indicated, suffice to illustrate the use of most of these features in their recognition.

Acer	sycamore	*Ilex*	holly
Aesculus	horse chestnut	*Populus*	poplar
Alnus	alder	*Quercus*	oak
Betula	birch	*Salix*	willow
Castanea	chestnut	*Tilia*	lime
Fagus	beech	*Ulmus*	elm
Fraxinus	ash		

These genera are also widely represented in Europe, often by the same species as those which occur in Britain, and in North America and elsewhere in the North Temperate zone, largely by other species. In general these have timbers with basic anatomical features very much in common with those of the British and European representatives, and the differences from them are in most instances relatively small.

We are concerned here, however, with the generic characters of the wood of these trees, and not with the extent, if any, to which the various species of a genus differ among themselves, and by which they may be distinguished — if indeed that is possible at all. In most of the genera in our list, therefore, the wood described and illustrated here may be regarded as representative of that of the genus as a whole. The conspicuous exception among them is afforded by the oaks, *Quercus* spp. This genus includes upwards of 300 species, which for present purposes may be regarded as falling into three main groups, the so-called red oaks and white oaks, and the evergreen oaks. The red oaks and white oaks are deciduous trees, with broadly similar ring-porous timbers, those of the two groups differing in their capacity to form tyloses (see p. 212) and certain other features, while the wood of the evergreen oaks is rather different, in being, *inter alia*, diffuse porous. European oak is classed as one of the white oaks, so that although its timber is representative of an important proportion of the species of the genus *Quercus*, it cannot be regarded as typical of them all.

Among this list of 13 genera, 4 are markedly ring-porous; these are *Castanea*, *Fraxinus*, *Quercus* and *Ulmus*, and this feature of their wood anatomy is evident to the unaided eye in the pore-rings shown on their end-grain surfaces (Figs. 74 and 75). On longitudinal surfaces the pore-rings are represented by lines of scratch-like marks, which, as can be seen with the aid of a hand-lens, are individual earlywood vessels. On radial surfaces they form parallel bands, the spacing of which is indicative of the width of the growth increments; on tangential surfaces these bands lie in series of U's or V's.

The wood of oak stands out from those of the other three genera by virtue of its large rays, up to 400 μm in width and 4 cms or so in height. These are thus readily visible to the unaided eye; they appear as dark vertical flecks on tangential surfaces, and as variable, more or less irregularly shaped, lighter areas on radial or near radial surfaces; this is, of course, the so-called "silver grain" or "flower" of oak, familiar in the traditional use of oakwood in furniture and panelling (see Chapter 7). Among them there are also very large number of finer rays, uniseriate and only a fraction of a millimetre in height, which are barely visible by hand-lens. The vessels of the pore ring are rounded and approximately circular in cross section, and commonly some 300–400 μm in diameter. There is an abrupt transition to those of the latewood, which, in sharp contrast, are commonly 50–100 μm across. Seen in transverse sections they occur in radial or near radial lines, embedded in rather irregular

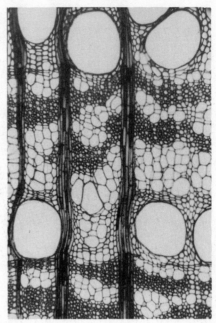

A   B

C   D

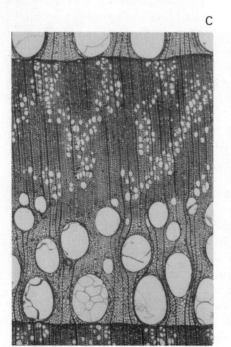
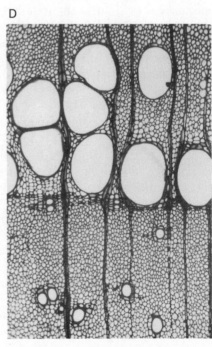

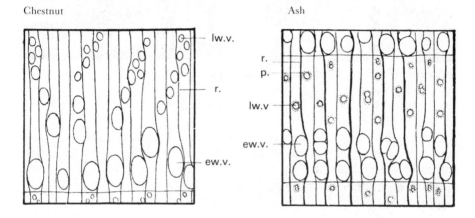

Oak

Elm

lw.v.
s.r.

ew.v.
l.r.

r.

r.

lw.v.

ew.v.

Chestnut

Ash

lw.v.

r.

ew.v.

r.
p.

lw.v

ew.v.

Fig. 74. Transverse sections of ring-porous timbers: A, European oak (*Quercus* sp.), × 30; B, English elm (*Ulmus procera*), × 60; C, American chestnut (*Castanea dentata*), × 24; D, American ash (*Fraxinus nigra*), × 60. For oak, elm and chestnut the whole width of the growth increment is shown, to display the different patterns of distribution of the latewood vessels. In the case of ash, a magnification which was sufficient to show the characteristic latewood parenchyma clearly, did not allow the whole growth increment to be represented, so the growth ring boundary has been placed across the middle of the field of view.

Fig. 75. Simplified (caricature) drawings of transverse sections of the wood of oak, elm, chestnut and ash, to emphasize their characteristic features and the differences between them. *ew.v.*, earlywood vessel; *lw.v.*, latewood vessel; *l.r.*, large ray; *p*, parenchyma; *r*, ray; *s.r.*, small ray. (Compare these drawings with the photomicrographs on the facing page). (From Jane, 1970).

radially disposed wedge-shaped masses of tracheids and parenchyma, which alternate tangentially with similar bands of fibrous tissue. Seen in the log the pale sapwood is distinct from a rich brown heartwood, somewhat variable in colour.

Elm wood also has rays of two sizes, the larger of which, though more numerous than the large rays of oak, are much smaller than those. Many are just visible to the unaided eye, as fine lines on transverse surfaces, and as transverse bands, up to about 0.5 mm in height, on radial surfaces; on tangential surfaces their general effect is to produce a coarse stippling. These features are clearly seen by hand lens. There are a few finer rays among them, uniseriate or biseriate, but which are visible only by microscopy.

In elm, as in oak, the wide vessels of the pore ring give way abruptly to the much narrower ones of the latewood, but in contrast to oak, these, together with vascular tracheids, form somewhat undulating tangential bands of conducting elements. These alternate with similar tangential bands of fibres (Fig. 74B), so that the latewood gives rise, on plane-sawn surfaces, to zig-zag bands of latewood vessel lines among the less numerous but wider bands of vessel lines due to the pore rings (Fig. 100). The sapwood is pale in colour, passing into a reddish-brown heartwood which is variable in shade.

Chestnut and ash differ conspicuously from the other two ring-porous members of our list, in that their rays are all fine and not visible to the naked eye. In *Castanea* they are entirely uniseriate; in *Fraxinus* they may be 1–3 cells wide. In chestnut the earlywood vessels, though about the same size as in oak, are markedly oval in cross-section, but they grade off smoothly in size to those of the latewood, in which, as seen in transverse sections, they are disposed in oblique lines or flame-like groups (Fig. 74C). In the solid, chestnut much resembles oak without its wide rays; also, like oak, it is rich in tannins, giving a colour reaction with ferric chloride solution, and tending, under moist conditions, to stain when in contact with steel fastenings.

In ash the sharply defined pore-ring of somewhat oval earlywood vessels, some 200–300 μm in diameter, passes abruptly into the latewood, which consists almost wholly of fibres. Latewood vessels are much smaller and rather sparse, scattered among the fibres, either singly or in pairs, each surrounded by a conspicuous "halo" of vasicentric parenchyma; the parenchyma groups tend to become confluent towards the end of the growth increment (Fig. 74D). In the solid wood the vessel lines are conspicuous on longitudinal surfaces, but there is no coloured heartwood.

Of the nine diffuse-porous woods in the list on p. 128, poplar, willow horse chestnut and lime form a group of similar appearance in the solid; soft and even-textured, and white or near white in colour. Willow is the only one of the four to produce a distinct heartwood, brown in colour, as a regular feature; some poplars may do so occasionally, but in horse chestnut and lime the heartwood is not visibly different from the sapwood.

Under the microscope lime wood may be distinguished from that of the other three genera in having both multiseriate and uniseriate rays; in the others the rays are exclusively uniseriate (Fig. 76). The multiseriate rays of lime are up to about six cells wide and are seen in transverse sections to be noded at the growth ring boundaries, and in longitudinal sections appear up to about 0.5 mm in height. The vessels, as seen in transverse section, are individually angular in form, and grouped in short radial chains, or in clusters, and in longitudinal sections they show simple perforations and abundant spiral thickenings (Fig. 77). The apotracheal, diffuse-in-aggregates parenchyma appears in transverse sections as forming short, rather irregular bands, one cell wide, more or less tangentially orientated (Fig. 76D).

The vessels of poplar, willow and horse chestnut, like those of lime, are somewhat angular in transverse section, with simple perforations. They occur singly, or grouped in short radial or sometimes oblique chains; in horse chestnut, as in lime, they have spiral thickenings, which, however, are not present in poplar and willow. These two genera (both members of the Salicaceae) also differ from the other two in producing tyloses (see Chapter 8) in their heartwood. Their timbers are very similar anatomically, (Figs. 76 and 78) and in microscopical preparations can be reliably distinguished only by detailed examination of the rays, as these are seen in radial longitudinal sections. In poplars the rays consist entirely of procumbent cells, and in those of their cells which have ray-to-vessel pitting, this is in the form of two or three horizontal rows of conspicuous rounded pits. In the willows, however, the ray tissue is heterogeneous; while the rays consist mainly of procumbent cells, there are one or two rows of upright or square cells along their margins, and the ray-to-vessel pitting is restricted to these marginal cells. Moreover, the pits, though similar to those of poplars, are in five to eight rows in the ray cells (Fig. 78K). Horse chestnut, like poplar, has homogeneous ray tissue, but the ray-to-vessel pits are smaller and are in five to nine rows in the ray cells. It may be noted in passing that there is no evident anatomical reason why the wood of *Salix alba* var. *coerulea* (the cricket-bat willow), among these rather similar timbers, or even among the many other species of willow, should be the best for the manufacture of cricket bats.

Alder and birch are conveniently considered together as a (related) pair of even-textured, light-coloured woods; though alder sapwood freshly cut from the tree may show a marked orange colour, this fades on exposure to the air to a pale reddish brown. Birch wood is white to

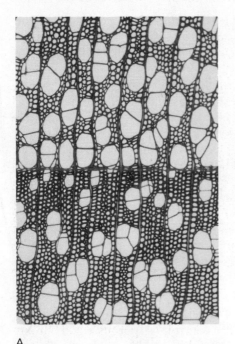

A

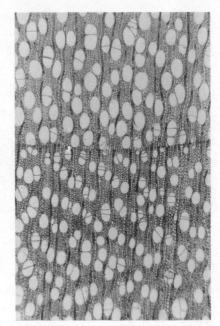

B

Fig. 76. Transverse sections of some diffuse-porous woods. *A*, poplar (*Populus* sp.), × 60; *B*, willow (*Salix nigra*), × 30; *C*, horse chestnut (*Aesculus hippocastanum*), × 60; *D*, lime, (*Tilia cordata*), × 60.

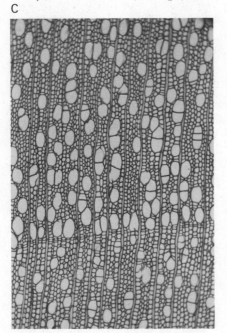

C

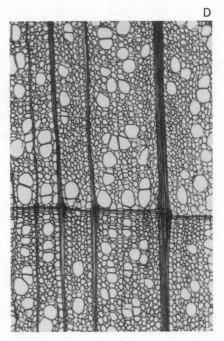

D

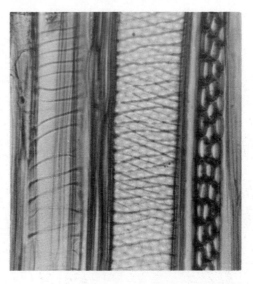

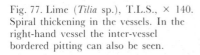

Fig. 77. Lime (*Tilia* sp.), T.L.S., × 140. Spiral thickening in the vessels. In the right-hand vessel the inter-vessel bordered pitting can also be seen.

a very pale brown, and both timbers lack a visually distinct heartwood. They are distinguished from the other soft diffuse-porous woods in our list by their vessels, in which the perforation plates are always scalariform. These lie at acute angles to the longitudinal direction, and are oriented more or less in the radial plane (Figs. 46 and 80*C*), so that they are best seen in radial longitudinal sections. They have numerous bars, characteristically more than 20 in alder, and rather fewer in birch. The vessels of alder are somewhat angular in transverse section; they may occur singly, but are more usually in radial chains or clusters of up to six or eight together, whereas in birch the vessels are usually single, and oval in section, or slightly angular and in short radial chains of two or three (Figs. 79*A* and *B*). The rays of the two woods are also distinctive; in birch, one to five seriate, noded slightly at the growth increment boundaries, but generally inconspicuous, while in alder they are exclusively uniseriate. Here, however, a proportion of them are grouped into very high aggregate rays (Figs. 80*A* and *B*), which are also wide enough to show up on tangential surfaces. The growth rings are marked in birch by narrow bands of thick-walled, flattened boundary parenchyma; these are visible on wood surfaces, because, on account of their denser structure than the rest of the wood, they take a shine when the surface is planed or polished. In alder, in contrast, the growth increments terminate in narrow bands of flattened fibre-tracheids, which, as seen in transverse sections characteristically dip inwards, towards the cenre of the trunk, between the aggregate rays.

Beech and sycamore, though not closely related, share a general similarity of anatomy. Neither forms an obvious heartwood, and both

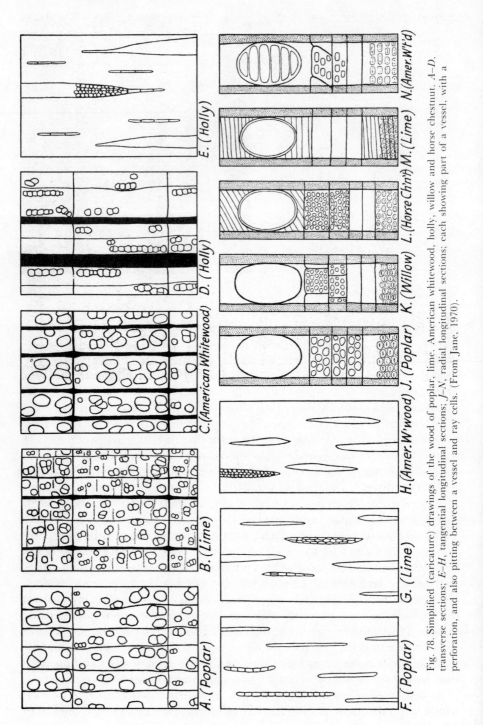

Fig. 78. Simplified (caricature) drawings of the wood of poplar, lime, American whitewood, holly, willow and horse chestnut. A–D, transverse sections; E–H, tangential longitudinal sections; J–N, radial longitudinal sections; each showing part of a vessel, with a perforation, and also pitting between a vessel and ray cells. (From Jane, 1970).

A. (Poplar) B. (Lime) C. (American Whitewood) D. (Holly) E. (Holly)

F. (Poplar) G. (Lime) H. (Amer.W'wood) J. (Poplar) K. (Willow) L. (HorseChn't) M. (Lime) N.(Amer.W't'd)

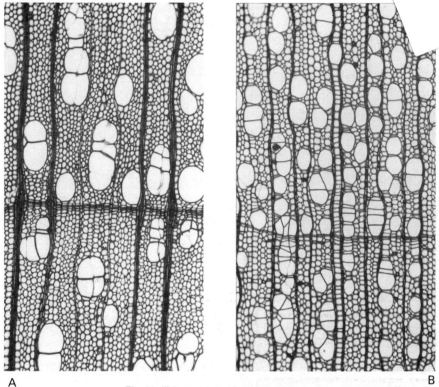

A   B

Fig. 79. T.S. *A*, birch (*Betula pendula*) and
B, alder (*Alnus glutinosa*); both × 70.

show clearly marked growth increments; in both also there are rays of
two different ranges of size, the large rays giving rise to a readily visible
and characteristic figure. In beech the large rays are commonly up to
three or four millimetres high and up to 25 cells in width, and noded
at the growth ring boundaries (Fig. 81*A* and *B*); they are thus clearly
visible to the naked eye as irregular transverse bands on radial surfaces
and as longitudinal flecks on tangential surfaces. Among these large
rays are numerous smaller ones, commonly one to four cells wide, and
visible only with a lens. The wood thus shows a ray figure which is
basically similar to that of oak, though on a much smaller scale, and
the distinction between large and small rays is not so well defined as
in oak. In sycamore the large rays, though smaller than in beech, are
still visible on radial surfaces; they range up to about 1 mm in height
and 7–8 cells wide, and like those of beech are noded at the growth
ring boundaries; the smaller rays are uniseriate. Under the microscope
they can be seen to be homogeneous, in contrast with those of beech,
which in Kribs' nomenclature are heterogeneous type III. Although the

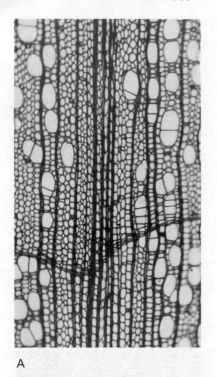

A

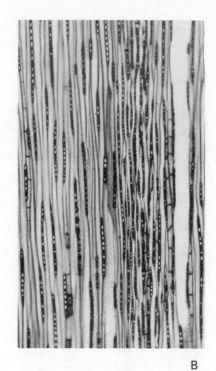

B

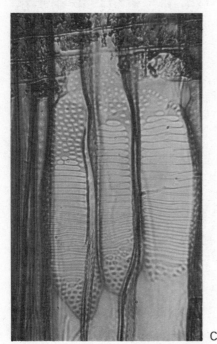

C

Fig. 80. Alder (*Alnus glutinosa*). *A*, T.S.
and *B*, T.L.S., both × 70, showing an
aggregate ray. Note also the diffuse
axial parenchyma. *C*, R.L.S., × 130;
showing scalariform perforation plates in
three contiguous vessels.

rays of sycamore may thus not be much larger than those of birch, they differ from the latter in their appearance in tangential sections; the ray cells appear rounded in shape, while those of birch are laterally flattened (Fig. 82E and F). In transverse section beech shows vessels in irregular groups, most frequent in the earlywood and diminishing in number and diameter from earlywood to latewood. Spiral thickenings are not present and vessel perforations are predominantly simple; scattered scalariform ones are however not difficult to find. In sycamore, in contrast, the vessels are mostly solitary, or in groups of two or three together, and are of much the same diameter throughout a growth increment. The vessel perforations are always simple and spiral thickenings are regularly present. The growth rings in beech have a somewhat irregular contour, usually dipping inwards towards the centre of the trunk, either at their intersections with the large rays, or else in between them; they differ markedly in this respect from the smoothly-contoured growth rings of sycamore. Parenchyma in beech is inconspicuous, diffuse or diffuse-in-

Fig. 81. T.S. A, beech (*Fagus sylvatica*) and B, sycamore (*Acer pseudoplatanus*); both × 70.

A

B

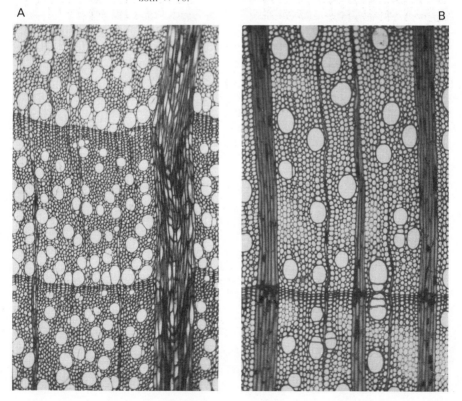

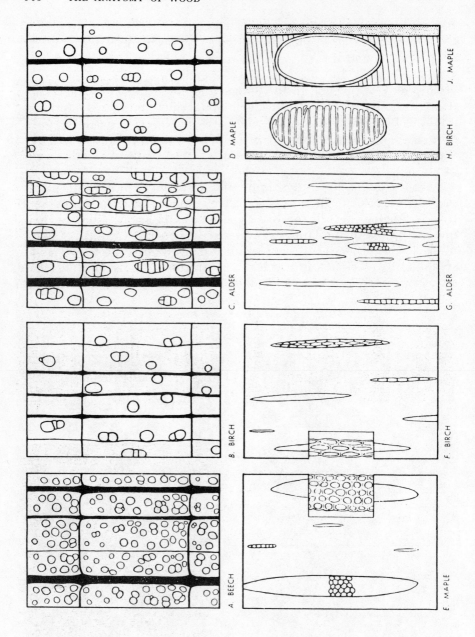

Fig. 82. Simplified (caricature) drawings of the wood of beech, birch, alder and maple (includes sycamore). A–D, transverse sections; E–G, tangential longitudinal sections. In E and F parts of the rays are drawn on a larger scale to show the characteristic shapes of the cells. H and J each show part of a vessel, with a perforation, as seen in radial longitudinal section. (From Jane, 1970).

aggregates, whereas in sycamore the thick-walled boundary parenchyma, though rather sparse, contributes to the distinctness of the
growth ring boundaries.

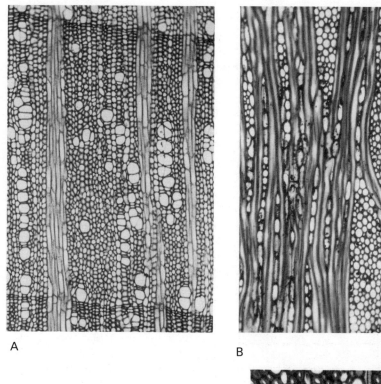

A

B

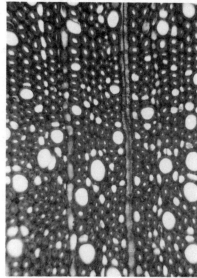

Fig. 83. Two fine-textured woods; *A*
and *B*, holly (*Ilex aquifolium*) and *C*, box
(*Buxus* sp.). *A*, T.S. × 70; *B*, T.L.S. ×
95. Note the tails of the multiseriate
rays. The ray tissue is heterogeneous
type II.
C, T.S. × 200. Here the vessels are
mostly solitary.

C

Holly, the remaining timber on our list, is rather different in its general character from the others, though it has many similar anatomical features, albeit on a smaller scale of construction (Fig. 83A). The wood is white or pale cream in colour, sometimes greenish or greyish, and denser and harder than the others we have been considering; there is no distinct heartwood. It has a very close, fine texture; even the vessels are barely visible with a lens. The rays are of two sizes, the larger ones ranging up to about ten cells wide and 1–1.5 mm in height, sufficient to produce an inconspicuous ray figure on surfaces of the wood, and among them there are numerous lower uniseriate rays. The larger rays consist principally of procumbent cells, but their margins are extended into uniseriate "tails" made up of squarish or upright cells; the "tails" are often of unequal length, and commonly only one, at either the upper or lower margin of the ray, may be present. The uniseriate rays consist entirely of square or upright cells. Thus in Kribs' terminology the rays are heterogeneous type II (Fig. 83B). The vessels form a discontinuous and ill-defined pore-ring on the earlywood, and smaller vessels occur in the middle and latewood in the long, interrupted radial files. They have scalariform perforations with many bars, often 20 or more, and spiral thickening; the two together often presenting a confusing picture to the observer. Spiral thickening is also present in the fibres. The parenchyma is apotracheal, diffuse and diffuse-in-aggregates.

In this chapter and the preceding one we have described some of the diversity of anatomical detail which, within the fundamental common basis of the structure of wood, has been found to be useful in distinguishing one timber from another. The student who has worked through these chapters and achieved some understanding of them, not only in the abstract, but also in locating and recognizing the relevant features in microscopical preparations, will be well on the way to being able to embark on the use of the many keys which exist for timber identification (Chapter 10).

6

The Ultrastructure of Wood; its Importance in Understanding Wood Properties

Consideration of the ultimate structure of wood involves firstly, the nature of the molecules of which the wood substance is made up, that is to say, its chemistry, and secondly, the way in which the different kinds of molecule are arranged and inter-related in wood cell walls. In these matters we are thus concerned with structural features of the cell wall which are very much smaller than those visible by ordinary light microscopy, features for which the unit of measurement is the nanometre (nm) or 10^{-9} metre; (the Angstrom Unit (AU), previously widely used in ultrastructural studies, but now obsolescent, is 1/10th of one nm, or 10^{-10}m). One nm is thus 1/1000th part of one micron (μm), the familar unit of light microscopy, and it may usefully be recalled here that the smallest structural detail revealed by light microscopy (its limit of resolution), under the best conditions, is about 0.25 μm, or 250 nm. In less critical "everyday" usage it is likely to be two or three times greater than this, and the student whose first-hand acquaintance with wood anatomy does not extend beyond that afforded by ordinary light microscopy may thus feel that this submicroscopic structure is beyond his concern. While in matters of detail this may well be so, nevertheless an outline acquaintance with its principal features is most valuable. It furnishes a background of understanding of certain aspects of the anatomy of wood as they appear in ordinary microscopy, and also an explanation of some of the physical properties of wood which are of importance both technologically and botanically.

The chemistry of wood is very complex and difficult of study, and in spite of its having been much investigated, largely in relation to the manufacture of wood-pulp, paper, rayon and other cellulose derivatives, it is still incompletely understood. One general difficulty is that some of the various chemical substances present in wood cell walls are, in

143

their natural state, very intimately interconnected, so that chemical procedures aimed at separating them tend also to degrade them into smaller fragments; thus their true nature may be lost sight of. Nevertheless there is a readily comprehensible general picture which is adequate for our purpose and which we need not pursue in great detail (Timell, 1965, 1967).

To a first approximation, wood may be described as consisting of holocellulose, lignin and extraneous materials. The last of these refers to substances which are present in wood but are not part of its essential anatomy; some of them can be dissolved from wood in neutral solvents such as acetone or ether, and are then referred to as extractives. Extraneous materials include mineral deposits (e.g. silica, and calcium salts, mainly carbonate, phosphate and oxalate) and a great variety of organic substances; oleo-resins, oils, fats, gums, flavonols, anthocyanins, tannins, glycosides, polyphenols, sugars, starch and others. The quantities present may amount to 1%, or less, of the dry weight of the sapwood, ranging, in the heartwood of some timbers, up to 20% or so of its dry weight. Though generally of no structural significance, they commonly have some other bearing, often an important one, on the properties of the timber, especially the heartwood, and its commercial use and value (Hillis, 1962, 1968b, 1971).

Of the remaining dry substance, normally some 65–80% is holocellulose and some 20–35% is lignin; the lignin content of softwoods tends to be somewhat higher than in hardwoods. Moreover in different species, or even in different specimens of the same species, the proportions can vary widely. We must not however lose sight of the fact that, in addition, wood contains water, and although in the growing tree most of it is free to move in the cell cavities, a considerable fraction is held in the submicroscopic spaces of the cell walls, where some remains, even in air-dry or fully seasoned timber. From the ways in which the properties of timber are influenced by its water content, it may be inferred that this fraction must be intimately associated with the cell wall solids, and is thus in a very real sense part of the cell wall structure. We shall return to this topic later.

Holocellulose is not a pure substance, but includes a number of compounds; cellulose in the strict sense, together with other somewhat similar carbohydrates and related substances, which are collectively referred to as hemicelluloses. These include also a small proportion of pectic compounds. They are all large molecules, polymers of sugars and uronic acids; the molecular structure of their principal monomers is shown in Fig. 84. Among them, cellulose itself, though not necessarily the most abundant of them, has a special role in cell wall structure, for reasons which are explained below, and is thus conveniently considered first.

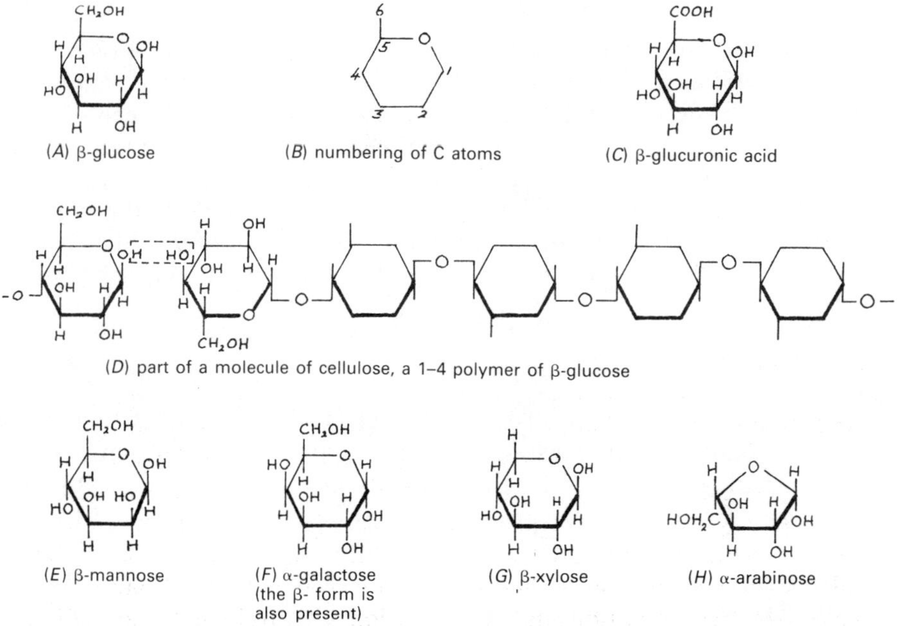

(A) β-glucose   (B) numbering of C atoms   (C) β-glucuronic acid

(D) part of a molecule of cellulose, a 1–4 polymer of β-glucose

(E) β-mannose   (F) α-galactose (the β- form is also present)   (G) β-xylose   (H) α-arabinose

Fig. 84. The chemical constitution of cellulose and some of the monomers present in hemicelluloses (see text). The molecules are represented conventionally; the atoms of the ring structures in flat planes, with the atoms and radicals attached to them lying above or below the planes of the rings. The distance between successive oxygen atoms linking the glucose units in the cellulose molecule is about 0.5 nm.

Chemically, cellulose is a straight-chain polymer of the hexose, or 6–carbon sugar, β–glucose, the link beteen adjacent sugar units being between carbon atoms numbers 1 and 4; it is thus described as a β 1-4 glucan; see Fig. 84 A and D. The number of glucose units (monomers) in the cellulose molecule (i.e. what is commonly called its degree of polymerisation, abbreviated to DP) is variable. In wood it is about 8000 to 10000, so that since a glucose molecule is about 0.5 nm across, the length of a cellulose molecule is 4-5 μm, and its molecular weight is of the order of 1.5×10^6. About 40-45% of wood substance is cellulose.

Though not strictly relevant here, it is not without interest that α–glucose, which differs from β–glucose only insofar that the positions of the H and OH on carbon atom No. 1 (Fig. 84B) are interchanged, is the monomeric unit of which the starch molecule is constructed. This apparently rather trivial difference between the two forms of glucose is sufficient to result in their giving rise to two very different polymers, which have widely different physiological functions in plants, and are metabolized by quite different enzyme systems.

In contrast to cellulose, the hemicelluloses show considerable diversity, as Preston (1979) has recently emphasized. The hemicelluloses of wood may be described in outline as follows. They are smaller molecules than cellulose, with DP values in the region of 150–200, and are built up of sugar units which, besides glucose, include the hexoses mannose and galactose, Fig. 84E and F; some of them also include the pentose (5–carbon) sugars, xylose and arabinose, Fig. 84G and H. Furthermore the hexoses may contain methoxyl (CH_3–O–) or acetoxyl

$$(CH_3–C–O–)$$
$$\|$$
$$O$$

groups, replacing certain of the hydroxyl (HO–) groups of their ring structure, and in other instances these sugars may be present as the corresponding uronic acids; these are formed from the sugar by the oxidation of the –CH_2OH group (C atom No. 6) to a carboxyl group, –COOH; Fig. 84A and C. Galacturonic acid is related to galactose (Fig. 84F) in the same way as glucuronic acid is to glucose. In softwoods the predominant hemicelluloses are a range of what are termed galacto-gluco-mannans; these are 1–4 polymers of glucose and mannose, in which mannose units (some acetylated) predominate, while the galactose units are borne laterally on this main chain. In hardwoods the most frequent is a methyl-glucurono-xylan, a 1–4 polymer of xylose units (some of which are acetylated), bearing methylated glucuronic acid units laterally. A number of other types of hemicelluose are also known, both in softwoods and hardwoods. In aggregate, in wood, the hemicelluloses make up some 25–40% of its dry weight (Timell, 1967).

The pectic compounds of softwoods and hardwoods are 1–4 polymers of uronic acids, principally galacturonic acid, though a proportion of their carboxyl groups are esterified with methanol. Though important in the young primary wall, pectic compounds comprise only 1% or less of mature wood.

Although the non-cellulosic carbohydrates of wood thus differ from cellulose in being much shorter, branched molecules, assembled from a variety of monomers, the chemical bonds between adjacent sugar units are of the same general kind, in the sense that their formation may be visualized as involving the removal of the atoms of a molecule of water at each sugar–sugar junction, as is indicated in Fig. 84D for cellulose. The biochemical processes leading to the formation of these bonds are a great deal more complex than this description of them implies, but these problems need not concern us here. The polymers are, however, fairly readily hydrolyzable, either enzymically or by appropriate acid treatment. Hydrolysis involves the re-introduction of the atoms of a water molecule at each junction, so that the molecular chains are broken down into their constituent monomeric units.

The chemical bonds indicated in the diagrams of cell wall carbohydrates in Fig. 84 are covalent bonds, the usual type in organic compounds. There are, however, in addition to these, other, perhaps less familiar, bonds, involved in biological structures, which are termed hydrogen bonds. These are of great importance biologically; they are referred to here primarily because they play an essential part in the inter-molecular relationships of the various polymers present in plant cell walls, including those of wood. More widely, and more fundamentally, however, they are also concerned in the structure of proteins, and thus in the structure and functioning of the living substance of all cells.

A hydrogen bond is one which, if molecular configurations allow, may be formed between the H atom of an –OH or –NH group in a molecule, and an O atom or an N atom in the same or another molecule; for example –OH------O– or –NH------O–. Among carbohydrates, which of course do not contain nitrogen as proteins do, it takes the first of these two forms.

A hydrogen bond is a "longer-range" bond, about twice the length of covalent bond. It is also much weaker, its bond energy (that is, the energy required to break it) being about one-tenth (or less) of that of a corresponding covalent bond. However, where long-chain carbohydrate polymers, bearing numerous –OH groups, are in suitably close lateral association, it is possible for large numbers of hydrogen bonds to be formed between them. Thus the number of these bonds may compensate for their individual lower bond energies; collectively they are a very powerful force in the establishment and maintenance of the coherence of plant cell walls of all kinds.

Water molecules, $\begin{smallmatrix} H \\ H \end{smallmatrix}\!\!\diagdown\!\!O$, also form hydrogen bonds, both among themselves and also with carbohydrate molecules. These bonds have an important bearing on the solubility and swelling properties of carbohydrates in water, and are thus concerned in the influence of the water content of wood on its physical properties and behaviour (see p. 172).

Lignin lies entirely outside the range of polymeric carbohydrates to which reference has been made. In spite of much investigation it has proved extremely difficult to study, and its chemistry is not fully known; but see, for instance, Kratzl (1965) and Adler (1977). Moreover, there is not merely one lignin; the lignins of hardwoods and softwoods are different, and so may be also those of plant tissues other than wood. The lignins are polymers too, but three-dimensional ones rather than linear chains. They are not hydrolyzable into constituent units as the long-chain carbohydrates are, but other forms of chemical breakdown have been found to give rise to a range of products which, though differing in molecular detail, have in common a structural carbon skeleton of the form shown in Fig. 85.

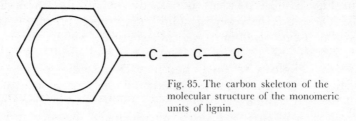

Fig. 85. The carbon skeleton of the molecular structure of the monomeric units of lignin.

Molecules of this basic structure — a six-membered ring with a side chain of three carbon atoms — are the monomers of which lignin is built up; they are thus very different indeed from those of the holocellulose compounds. The molecular weight of lignin, after its extraction from wood, is estimated to be about 11000, which means that its molecule might consist of about 60 of these monomeric units; however, it might well be larger than this in the form in which it exists in the intact cell wall. The existence in cell walls of ligno-cellulose, a postulated compound of lignin and cellulose, has been debated for a long period. It seems probable now that lignin does form compounds of this nature, but with components of the hemicellulosic matrix of the wall, not with cellulose in the strict sense (Eriksson *et al.*, 1980; Wardrop, 1981).

The special place of cellulose among other cell wall substances lies in the manner in which its molecules are associated in the cell wall to form larger structural units with distinctive physical properties. In the majority of plants, cellulose molecules are closely linked laterally, in aggregates of a few hundreds, which are termed microfibrils. As revealed in the electron microscope, these are of indefinite length, unbranched and of somewhat ribbon-like form; they are about 10 nm wide and 5 nm thick, and are thus far below the limit of resolution of light microscopy (Fig. 90). In general, within a microfibril, the lateral linkages between cellulose molecules are uniformly ordered (uncounted hydrogen bonds are involved in them), so that the greater part of the interior of the microfibril consists of a regular three-dimensional array of glucose units; that is, it is crystalline. Its crystallinity is however interrupted along its length by numerous localized regions in which the molecules are less regularly packed, the crystalline regions between them being some 50–60 nm in length. Such microscopically invisible crystals are known as crystallites or micelles. The term micelle, which was originally applied to them, is however now used in some contexts in a somewhat different sense, without an implication of crystallinity, an ambiguity which is to be avoided.

Since wood cell walls, in common with other types of secondary wall, contain closely packed and approximately parallel arrays of microfibrils, the similarly parallel crystallites within the microfibrils act, in the aggregate, to confer on the wall as a whole some of the attributes of an overall crystalline structure. Thus cell walls have been studied by crystallographic methods, including X-ray diffraction analysis; the X-ray diffraction diagram of cellulose is known, and a corresponding crystal structure has been formulated. Similarly, arising from its crystallinity, cellulose (and cell walls generally) are optically birefringent and lend themselves to study by polarization microscopy, another classical crystallographic tool. It is an interesting aspect of the history of our knowledge of cell wall structure that long before the development of electron microscopy made microfibrils visible (the first electron micrographs of microfibrils were published in 1948) the existence, nature and arrangement of crystallites in cell walls had been inferred, with a considerable degree of accuracy, from the indirect evidence deriving from these older methods.

Softwood tracheids have been intensively studied by these and other techniques, and thus serve well to exemplify a type of cell wall microstructure which is found, though not invariably, in the fibres of hardwoods (Wardrop and Dadswell, 1957; Meylan and Butterfield, 1978). The walls of vessel elements have been much less widely studied in this respect than fibre walls. In some instances they seem to be basically similar to the latter, but their structure is greatly complicated by their characteristically large numbers of bordered pits, around and among which the microfibrils follow sinuous courses. General accounts of the ultrastructure of wood cell walls, with reference to the extensive literature bearing upon it, have been given, *inter alia*, by Roelofsen (1959), Wardrop (1964a), Harada (1965a and b) and Preston (1974).

The assembled evidence from polarization microscopy, X-ray diffraction, electron-microscopy and other methods of study shows that the walls of fully-grown softwood tracheids have a complex microfibrillar framework. This may be represented diagrammatically in a somewhat simplified form, as in Fig. 86, which, it may be noted, shows a structure not greatly different from that proposed by Bailey and Kerr in 1934–5; see also Bailey (1954). In this figure a short length of an isolated tracheid has been visualized, in which each of certain principal layers of its wall has in turn been drawn out axially from within those external to it, rather in the manner in which a telescope is extended for use. No pits are shown in this diagram, since these involve local perturbations of wall structure which are better considered separately (see p. 159).

Beginning with the outside of the cell, the figure shows first the middle lamella, the intercellular material which cements it to its neighbours; this is not part of the cell wall proper, and it contains no cellulose. In young, still growing, tracheids it is largely pectic in nature, but as they mature it becomes heavily lignified.

Within the middle lamella may be seen the primary wall (P) which

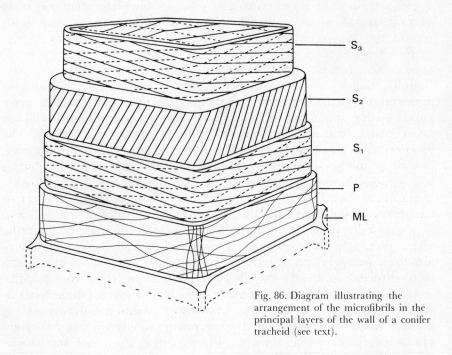

Fig. 86. Diagram illustrating the arrangement of the microfibrils in the principal layers of the wall of a conifer tracheid (see text).

at an earlier stage was the only wall of the young tracheid during its period of expansion, after being cut off from a fusiform initial in the cambial zone. Then follows the secondary wall which was laid down as the cell approached maturity, and within which three distinct layers or zones can be recognized. These differ in their microfibrillar organization (and in other features also); they are referred to as S_1, S_2 and S_3, in the order of their formation, i.e. from the outside inwards. These layers are not usually distinguishable in mature tracheids by ordinary light microscopy, though associated differences in their lignin content may sometimes distinguish them by differences in their staining reactions.

In the primary wall, most readily studied, of course, at an earlier stage of tracheid differentiation, before the secondary wall has been laid down, the microfibrils are in the main rather sparse, and arranged more or less transversely, or in flat helices, though with a good deal of "scatter" about their mean direction. In addition there are other groups of them, lying axially, at the corners of the cell. In the young growing tracheid the sparse microfibrils, embedded in a matrix of hemicelluloses and pectic compounds, form a plastic, extensible wall, the structure of which is characteristic of plant cells generally at this, the expansion phase, of their development.

In the mature tracheid the primary wall, being relatively very thin in comparison with the secondary wall, tends to be lost sight of at light-microscopy magnifications, though it is revealed by electron microscopy.

In the secondary wall the organization of the microfibrillar framework is quite different. There is not only a higher proportion of cellulose, but the microfibrils are laid down in substantially parallel arrays. Its outer part, the S_1, shows more closely packed and less diffusely aligned microfibrils than in the primary wall, arranged in what may be described as right- and left-handed helices around the cell. However, in view of the possible ambiguity of the terms right- or left-handed, it has become the practice to define the direction of a helix by reference to the direction of its apparent slope on the side of the cell nearer to the observer, and to identify this slope by reference to the letters S and Z, the middle parts of which slope in opposite directions. Thus the screw thread of an engineer's normal right-handed bolt, and more familiarly perhaps, the helical shaft of a corkscrew, are Z-helices; a left-handed thread is correspondingly an S-helix. In the S_1 the microfibrillar helices lie at a mean angle of some 50 °–75 ° to the cell axis; both S- and Z- helices are present, but one of the two directions, usually, if not invariably, the S-orientated, is preponderatingly the more strongly developed. The next layer within, the S_2, differs again, its microfibrils being more steeply orientated and more closely packed. They lie in Z-helices, and their mean angle to the cell axis is commonly in the range 10 °–30 °. Finally, in the S_3, the youngest part of the secondary wall, there is a reversion to flatter S-helices, at a mean angle of some 60 °–80 ° to the cell axis. In *Pinus radiata* Wardrop (1964a) reported evidence of the presence here also of more faintly developed Z–helices, as are found in the S_1 layer, but again, the S-helices were predominant. Thus in broad terms, the secondary wall as a whole shows an alternation of microfibril angle and direction, S, Z, S, in its three layers. In the earlywood tracheids of a growth ring the three layers of the cell wall are of much the same thickness; the greater cell wall thickness characteristic of latewood tracheids arises almost entirely from an increased thickness in the S_2 (Fig. 88). An added complication in the formation of the secondary wall is that although at any one point in the tracheid or fibre the S_1, S_2 and S_3 are laid down in that order, the timing of this sequence is not necessarily simultaneous throughout the cell. Secondary wall formation commonly begins in its middle parts, even perhaps while the ends are still undergoing intrusive extension growth, and spreads towards them. Thus the middle part of the cell might reach the S_3 stage of wall formation, while near the tips the S_2, or even S_1, might still be in the course of deposition (Wardrop and Harada, 1965).

There are two important features of this microfibrillar framework, which, for the sake of clarity, have been omitted from Fig. 86. The first of these is that the three principal layers of the secondary wall are themselves built up of many much finer layers or lamellae, the thickness of which is about 0.1 μm or less. Though this is below the limit of resolution of the light microscope, the lamellae can be revealed by the application of suitable swelling techniques, as Bailey and Kerr (1935) showed; the existence of these lamellae has since been confirmed by numerous investigators using electron microscopy (Preston, 1974). Similar fine lamellations are characteristic of thick cell walls generally. Secondly, there may be, in the microfibrillar orientation of some of these finer lamellae, transitional regions between the S_1 and S_2, and between the S_2 and S_3, so that these three principal layers of the secondary wall are not always quite so sharply defined and distinct from one another as the diagram indicates (Harada, 1965a; Dunning, 1968).

As the wide-ranging studies of Meylan and Butterfield (1978) have shown, the tracheids of softwoods are remarkably similar in this pattern of microfibrillar structure; there are however some distinct variants. The S_3 is regularly lacking in some woods, as in most, if not all, species of *Picea*. Its absence is also a regular feature of the compression wood of conifers, the type of wood produced on the underside of branches and leaning trunks (see Chapter 9). Another variation is the additional presence, as for example in *Pseudotsuga* and *Taxus*, of spiral thickenings on the inner side of the cell wall. These are localized thickenings of the S_3, with a similar microfibrillar orientation.

An important part of the evidence on which Fig. 86 is based is illustrated in Fig. 87. This is a polarization photomicrograph of a transverse section of the wood of *Pinus strobus*. The optical reasoning lying behind the interpretation of photographs of this kind is complex, and would be out of place here. A greatly simplified and hence very incomplete explanation is given by Jane (1970); otherwise the student who wishes to pursue the matter must learn something of crystal optics (textbooks of mineralogy are helpful here) and dip into a more rigorous treatment of cell wall optics, such as that given by Preston (1952).

However a greatly simplified partial explanation, sufficient it is hoped to convey some general understanding of the matter, is attempted in the following paragraphs. In a polarizing microscope two discs of the synthetic material "polaroid" are fitted in the optical system of the instrument, one in the microscope tube and one in the substage. Thus the specimen, mounted on the stage in the usual way, is viewed as it appears lying between the two polaroids. The microscope is also fitted with a rotatable stage, and in addition there are cross-wires mounted in the eyepiece.

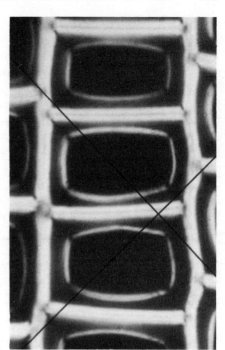

Fig. 87. *Pinus strobus*. T.S. latewood (polarizing microscope, × 1200). Three layers in the cell walls are visible; P + S_1, S_2 and S_3, (see text). The middle lamella appears dark because it contains no cellulose, and is not birefringent.

Polaroid is obtainable commercially and may perhaps be familiar to the reader from its use in sun-glasses, or in certain photographic filters and in the special spectacles used for the viewing of stereoscopic cinema films. It has the property of so modifying a ray of light passed through it that the ray emerges in the plane-polarized condition; that is to say, in simple terms, that the wave-motions of the light are to be visualized as "vibrating" only in one plane, the polarization plane of the polaroid, rather than in all planes radial to the axis of the ray which is the usual condition.

If a ray of light (non-polarized) is directed towards two sheets of polaroid, one behind the other, which are so orientated that their planes of polarization are at right-angles to one another, the ray is cut off completely, because the plane-polarized ray produced by the first polaroid cannot in this circumstance pass through the second polaroid. The polaroids are then said to be "crossed". The polaroids of the polarizing microscope are for most purposes arranged in the crossed condition, so that, therefore, the field of view of the instrument appears dark. Moreover the cross-wires in the eyepiece of the microscope are set so that they are parallel to the polarization planes of the two polaroids.

The light-transmitting properties of two polaroids, in the crossed and non-crossed positions, can easily be demonstrated by experimentation with two hand specimens of the material, so that although a full explanation of these phenomena is complex, their effects may become familiar in practice. They relate also to the use of polaroid in sunglasses, which arises from the fact that sunlight, as reflected, for instance, from a water surface, becomes partially plane-polarized in its reflection. Thus polaroid sunglasses, appropriately orientated so that their polarization plane is at right-angles to that of the reflected light, will reduce the transmission of the latter and so greatly diminish the glare it produces.

Most crystals, as they are seen in a polarizing microscope between crossed polaroids, appear illuminated against the dark field, by virtue of what is termed their birefringence, a directionally non-uniform optical property. If however, the microscope stage is rotated, a visible crystal becomes darkened and seems to disappear at certain positions of its rotation; in these positions it is said to become extinguished. At the extinction positions a certain direction within the crystal, termed its optic axis, lies parallel to one or other of the polarization planes of the microscope, and hence also to a cross-wire visible in the eyepiece. Thus the orientation of the optic axis of a crystal, referred to its position of rotation in the plane of the stage of the microscope, can be determined from its extinction position.

Although cellulose crystallites and microfibrils are of course far too small to be seen individually in the polarizing microscope, an approximately parallel array of them, such as exists within each of the three principal zones of the fibre wall, possesses optical properties similar to those of a single crystal; moreover, the optic axis of the array of microfibrils lies parallel to the mean direction of the microfibrils within each zone. Thus these aggregates of microfibrils appear illuminated, and show extinction positions, in much the same way as single crystals would. A sheet of cellophane, which has a similar sub-microscopic partially crystalline structure, will show extinction positions when observed between crossed polaroids.

In Fig. 87 the specimen is so orientated, in relation to the polarization planes of the microscope, that the principal faces of the cell wall apppear illuminated, but it will be noticed that at four positions around the cell the wall appears to show discontinuities. In these regions it is extinguished; it also lies parallel to a cross-wire, showing that the microfibrils are, on average, parallel to the cell wall surfaces.

In their illuminated parts the walls show internal differences of brightness, the outer and inner layers appearing distinctly brighter than the middle part between them. The bright outer region represents the $P + S_1$ layers of the wall (these are not separately recognizable) and the middle and inner layers are the S_2 and S_3 respectively. The question thus arises as to how these differences of illumination, shown in Fig. 87, are indicative of the steeper helical arrangement characteristic of the microfibrils of the S_2 layer (as shown in Fig. 86) compared with those of the S_1 and S_3 layers.

The answer to this question calls for a further excursion into the phenomena of crystal optics than we have made previously. So far, in considering extinction phenomena, we have tacitly assumed that the microfibrils (and hence their optic axes) are lying flat and parallel to the stage of the microscope, so that as they are rotated they are thus viewed along a direction at right-angles to their length. This, however, is not necesarily so; the microfibrils might, as far as we know, lie at any angle to the microscope stage, and thus might be being viewed along a direction at any angle to their optic axes. Moreover it is a feature of their crystal optics that their birefringence and the concomitant phenomena of illumination between crossed polaroids, and extinction at certain positions, such as we have described, are seen at their optimum when the microfibrils are viewed at right-angles to their optic axes, but disappear completely when they are viewed in a direction parallel to it, that is as they would be seen if they were erected at right-angles to the microscope stage. For intermediate directions of observation, the apparent birefringence and hence the illumination of a microfibrillar aggregate decreases progressively between the maximum and zero, so that the weaker illumination of the S_2 layer, seen in Fig. 87, compared with that of the S_1 and S_3 layers, is suggestive of the hypothesis that in the S_2 layer the microfibrils are arranged in a steeper helix than those of the other two layers.

This difference of illumination, between the S_2 on the one hand and the S_1 and S_3 on the other, here described in the simplest terms, can be rigorously quantified. As Wardrop and Preston (1947, 1951) showed, in sections cut obliquely at different angles to the transverse plane, the levels of illumination in the different layers of the wall change relatively to one another, and the change can be used as a basis for a more detailed analysis of the wall structure. Among a range of sections, of uniform thickness, which have been cut at different known angles of obliquity to the transverse, those in which a given wall layer shows its maximum birefringence are those which happen to have been cut parallel to the mean direction of orientation of the microfibrils in that layer; this angle of orientation is thus revealed. The application of this technique to a specimen of the wood of *Picea* showed that the mean microfibril orientation in the S_1 lay at an angle of about 38 ° from the transverse plane, and in the S_2 at about 72 ° from it (in *Picea*, as we have noted, the S_3 layer is not present).

In contrast with the complexities of structure (and hence of polarization optics) shown by tracheid walls as these are seen in transverse sections, their appearance in face view presents a much simpler picture. To see this correctly however it is necessary to be able to examine the

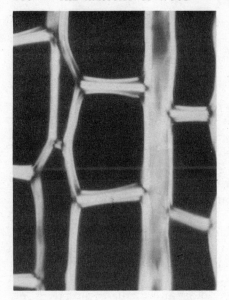 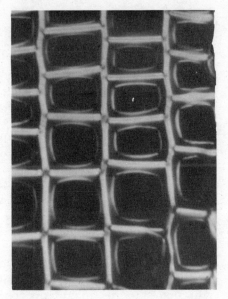

A   B

walls singly, which involves separating the tracheids and also cutting them in half longitudinally. This may be achieved by Preston's (1934) method, or alternatively by cutting a number of longitudinal sections, of thickness around 15 μm or less, and then macerating them (see Chapter 4). The macerate will be found to contain a significant proportion of tracheids which have been cut in two longitudinally, and which when spread on a slide thus show single walls in face view. Such single walls, seen in this aspect, appear to have a simple unified crystalline structure. They show a major extinction direction, which represents an over-all weighted mean of the microfibril orientation in the various layers of the wall, which are, of course, in this view, seen in superposition. This mean orientation, commonly in the range 50–70 ° to the transverse plane, depends principally on the microfibril orientation in the S_2 alone; it rarely differs from this by more than ±2 ° (Preston, 1974). The S_2 layer is the dominant influence in this respect, because its microfibrils are more nearly parallel than those of the S_1 and the S_3, and, especially in the latewood, it comprises a major component of the wall. The microfibril orientation in the S_2 may also be indicated by the presence of striations or cracks in the wall, or by decay due to certain wood-rotting micro-fungi (soft rots), such as *Chaetomium globosum*. The hyphae of this fungus, growing within the thickness of the S_2 layer, follow the alignment of the microfibrils and produce helically orientated cavities in this layer with characteristically

Fig. 88. *Pinus strobus.* T.S. *A*, earlywood and *B*, latewood (polarizing microscope, × 570). The difference in the cell wall thickness is due principally to the difference in the thickness of the S_2 layers.

Fig. 89. *Pinus sylvestris.* R.L.S. of partly rotted wood (polarizing microscope, × 570). The specimen had been attacked by the soft-rot fungus *Chaetomium globosum*, the hyphae of which grow within the thickness of the tracheid walls, following the 'run' of the microfibrils in the S_2 layer. Here they form cavities with conically tapering ends, which are readily visible by polarizing microscope in the otherwise intact cell wall, as a result of the dissolution of the cellulose by the fungus.

sharply tapered ends (Bailey and Vestal, 1937; Levy, 1965). These cavities are readily visible in the polarizing microscope (Fig. 89).

There is however a considerable range of variation in this angle of mean microfibril orientation, even within a single tree. This variation was first explored in a number of softwoods by Preston (1934); see also Preston (1952, 1974). He showed that there is a statistical relationship between microfibril angle and tracheid length, and that this relationship could be expressed in the form

$$L = A + B \cdot \cot \Theta$$

where L is the mean tracheid length, Θ is the mean microfibril angle measured from the axial direction, and A and B are constants. This equation means, in simple terms, that long tracheids tend on the whole to have more nearly axial microfibrillar helices in their walls than short ones; it does not mean that of two individual tracheids the longer will necessarily have steeper microfibrillar helices than the shorter.

This type of relationship has been found in other softwoods wherever it has been looked for, and also in bamboo fibres. Its fundamental basis is not understood, if only perhaps because the determining factors in microfibril orientation generally are not known. It is however an important relationship, of technological as well as botanical interest, since the strength and shrinkage properties of softwood have been found to be greatly influenced by its mean microfibril angle (Cowdrey and Preston, 1965, 1966; Cave, 1968; Meylan and Probine, 1969). That this in turn proves to be related to the mean tracheid length in the wood, which has long been known to vary according to the position in the tree from which it had been cut (Chapter 8) is thus very relevant to an understanding of the properties of juvenile wood (Chapter 8) and compression wood (Chapter 9).

Although it has been convenient here to refer, as we have done, to the microfibril angle in these cell walls, it is appropriate to recall that much of this kind of work was done before the advent of electron microscopy. This revealed the existence of microfibrils as the embodiment of the crystallites of the earlier workers and substantially confirmed the general picture of their arrangement in the tracheid wall, which had been very largely derived from polarization microscopy. But even now, the complexities of electronmicroscopic technique, and the limited fields of view which it affords, make it quite unsuitable for wide-ranging studies of the kind referred to in the previous paragraph, which have particular relevance to the properties of timber; the polarizing microscope is still an important tool in this field of study. Electronmicroscopy has however shown that the microfibrils of wood are

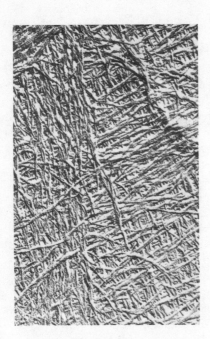

Fig. 90. An electron-micrograph of a cell wall preparation from a parenchyma cell, showing microfibrils. (× ca. 20 000).

similar to those of other cells of green plants, though they are less readily exposed to view since they are embedded in the lignified matrix of the cell wall; those shown here (Fig. 90) are from a non-woody cell. (See also Fig. 129 in Chapter 9.)

Where bordered pits occur in a tracheid wall the generalized structure of its microfibrillar framework is locally modified. The development of a bordered pit in a young differentiating tracheid first becomes evident, before the tracheid has acquired an obvious secondary wall, by the deposition of what is termed the initial pit border. Whether this is to be regarded as part of the S_1 layer, or as a separate structure, seems to be an open question (Harada and Côté, 1967; Preston, 1974); in it, however, the microfibrils are laid down in circular orientation around the pit aperture, this arrangement thus being entirely different from that of the S_1 generally. In the S_2 also, where it overlies the pit border, the microfibrils depart from their usual courses and sweep around the pit aperture in substantially circular pathways (Fig. 91). Thus the microfibrillar structure of the pit border, as it is seen in face view, is in large measure radially symmetrical, and in consequence it appears in the polarizing microscope as a bright circle, in the otherwise extinguished cell wall, with a dark Maltese cross in it (Fig. 92); the dark central spot which also appears in the figure is of course the pit aperture. The cross is indicative of the radial symmetry of the border; where the

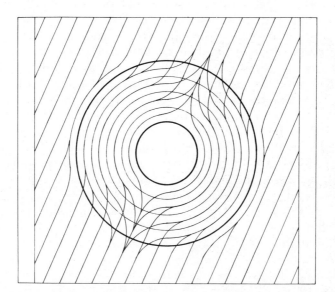

Fig. 91. Diagram illustrating the arrangement of the microfibrils in the S_2 layer of the tracheid wall in the region of a pit border (simplified). The circles represent the microfibrils of the initial pit border, and the oblique lines, sweeping round the pit aperture, represent those of the S_2 layer.

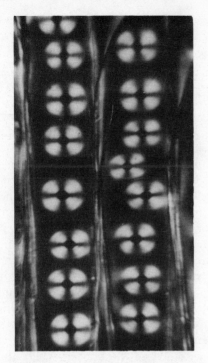

Fig. 92. *Pinus strobus*, R.L.S. (polarizing microscope, × 420). The bordered pits, seen in face view, appear as illuminated circles, each with a dark cross. This appearance indicates the essentially radially symmetrical structure of the pit border. The dark central disc is the pit aperture.

circularly arranged microfibrils happen to lie parallel to the polarization planes of the microscope they are extinguished in these regions, but elsewhere they appear illuminated. This type of polarization image is characteristically produced by radially symmetrical arrays of crystals, (as for instance also in starch grains); Preston (1952 and 1974) has discussed its interpretation in relation to bordered pit structure in greater detail. The circular arrangement of the microfibrils on the inner side of the pit border can be seen in Fig. 93.

The pit membrane is derived in the first instance from the middle lamella and primary walls of the adjacent tracheids, and thus comprises both microfibrillar and matrix components. In most softwoods, as the tracheids mature, further deposition of both types of wall substance takes place in the central part of the membrane, which thus becomes thickened to form the torus; here the pattern of additional microfibrillar deposition is random or more or less circular, taking different forms in different timbers. In the margo, in contrast, though additional microfibrils are laid down, the matrix substances are progressively dissolved (Barnett, 1981a), so leaving the torus suspended by a rather sparse, open fibrillar network, in which mainly radially arranged strands of aggregates of microfibrils predominate. The pit membranes thus afford open pathways for water movement from tracheid to tracheid, as indeed

Bailey (1913) demonstrated experimentally. He, and other later workers (Liese, 1965b) have shown that solid particles, up to about 0.2 μm in diameter, in suspension in water, can pass through the membranes of softwood pits. The openings in the pit membranes are especially characteristic of the sapwood; as this ages and develops into heartwood they tend to become closed off, to different degrees in different timbers, by the aspiration of the pits (see Chapter 4) or by the deposition of lignin-like extraneous substances in the pit cavities or on the pit membranes themselves.

Fig. 86, and the evidence relating to it, refer only to the arrangement

Fig. 93. *Cedrus libani*. Electron micrograph of a replica of the interior of a bordered pit, after removal of the warty layer (× ca. 5000). The torus is suspended by radially arranged bundles of microfibrils in the margo. Note the circular orientation of the microfibrils of the inner side of the pit border.

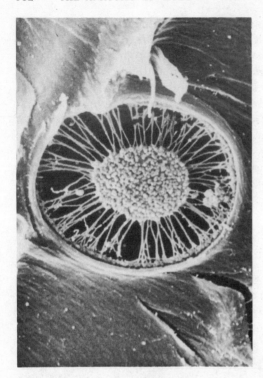

Fig. 94. *Pinus* sp. Scanning electron micrograph of the pit membrane of a bordered pit (× ca. 3000). There is a deposit of extraneous substances on the torus.

of the crystalline microfibrillar fraction of the tracheid wall; they tell us nothing about the molecular arrangement of the hemicelluloses and lignin, which form the major part of the matrix substances of the mature wall and middle lamella. While this is not known in detail, there is good reason to believe, for a variety of reasons, that the elongated essentially linear molecules of hemicelluloses which surround and link the microfibrils, will tend to be aligned more or less parallel to them, though not in a regularly crystalline spacing (Preston, 1974). Presumably the side chains of these molecules, which have been identified in holocellulose analyses, are involved in the molecular interconnections whch exist in the intact wall. In this context it is interesting to note that the microfibrillar fraction of the wall, when isolated, is found to include a proportion of xylan molecules, which are firmly attached to the surfaces of the microfibrils. This xylan may be visualized similarly as a link in the sytem of interconnections between the cellulose microfibrils and the hemicellulosic matrix generally.

As a concomitant of their looser and non-crystalline structure the middle lamella and the cell wall matrix are minutely porous on a submicroscopic scale. Initially the pores are occupied by water, but as the tissue approaches maturity lignin is deposited in some of them, forming a three-dimensional polymer among the microfibrils; it causes some swelling of the matrix and middle lamella. Lignification is thus a later and separate process from those of the formation of the holocellulosic structure of the wall. Lignification begins in the cell corners, remote from the protoplast, and spreads outwards into the middle lamella and inwards into the primary and secondary walls (Wardrop, 1981). As familiar staining reactions commonly show, the final concentration of lignin reaches a higher level in the middle lamella and primary wall than in the secondary wall. Nevertheless, the latter, on account of its much greater volume, contains most of the total lignin present (Fergus and Goring, 1970; Fergus, Procter, Scott and Goring, 1969). Although the molecular inter-relationships of lignin and holocellulose are incompletely known, these components of the wall form two very strongly attached and mutually inter-penetrating systems. Either may be extracted chemically without the tracheid as a whole losing its coherence of form.

Finally, as the protoplast dies, there may be deposited a thin additional structure, which forms a lining to the cell lumen, termed the warty layer (Liese, 1965a). This appears as a thin granular deposit, clearly revealed by electron microscopy, and in many instances coarse enough in texture to be detectable by light microscopy. It consists of scattered, more or less spherical granules, ranging in diameter from about 10 to 500 nm, overlaid by, and enclosed in, the remains of the plasma membranes, which adhere to the inner surface of the tracheid wall. The granules appear to be localized lignin-like deposits on the wall, together with remains of the protoplast, and the size and spacing of the "warts" to which they give rise are, up to a point, characteristic of individual species. When present, the warty layer completely lines the cell lumen, including the pit cavities, but although widely distributed, both in softwoods and hardwoods, it is not universal; to give just one example, some species of *Pinus* regularly have it, while others do not (Frey-Wyssling, 1976). It probably has little if any bearing on the physiological and structural functions of the wood.

A mechanical rather than a structural attribute of wood fibre cells, and one of some importance technologically, is that they tend to shrink longitudinally as they complete their maturation. This shrinkage is considered to be a consequence of the swelling of the cell wall matrix caused by the deposition of lignin in it; the loss of turgor following the death of the protoplast may also be a contributory factor. Since the maturing cells are bonded by their middle lamellae to earlier-formed wood, their longitudinal contraction tends to put them under tension, and correspondingly subjects the adjacent older wood to compression. As secondary thickening proceeds these effects are cumulative, and longitudinal stresses may built up to high levels within the wood. Since they originate in the natural processes of growth they are referred to as growth stresses (Jacobs, 1945; Boyd, 1950a and b; Dinwoodie, 1966a; Wilson and Archer, 1977; Chafe, 1979; Wilson, 1981), and are not to be confused with the very different internal stresses which develop in the drying or seasoning of timber (see p. 172).

Quantitative estimates of longitudinal growth stresses are based, in principle, on measurement of the distances between markers inserted in a freshly felled trunk before it is cut up, and the increase or decrease in these distances as the strains are relieved by nearby cutting; techniques have been described by Boyd (1950a) and Nicholson (1971). The stresses which must be applied artificially in order to produce comparable dimensional changes in adjacent samples of the timber can then be measured in laboratory test machinery to give the values which it is required to know. In some hardwoods the stresses are found to be of the order of 1000–2000 lb/in^2 (70/140 Kg/cm^2); in softwoods they are much lower, about 1/10th of these figures. For some purely comparative purposes it may be sufficient to adopt a simpler procedure and to record the dimensional changes themselves, expressed as percentages of the original dimensions; this is done, for instance, in the diagrams reproduced by Wilson and Archer (1977). In general terms, as these diagrams show, growth stresses result in the middle part of the trunk, especially the juvenile or core wood, being under longitudinal compression and the outer part in longitudinal tension; there may also be, in addition, lesser radial and tangential stresses, acting transversely. Various kinds of mechanical failure of the timber may occur in consequence (see Chapter 8).

Some understanding of the chemical and physical structure of the conifer tracheid wall, incomplete though it is, naturally leads to questions of how it is built up. The answers to these questions are at present largely hypothetical, but nevertheless a brief reference here to some general aspects seems appropriate. The basic feature of cell wall ultrastructure outlined in the foregoing pages, that is to say one comprising largely crystalline microfibrils embedded in an amorphous matrix, is universal in plant cells, though the chemical nature of both the microfibrils and the matrix may differ in different types of cell. In seed plants, where the microfibrils are always cellulose, the matrix may vary, as for instance is evident in the differences between the cell walls of collenchyma and sclerenchyma; in other groups of plants, as in some algae and fungi, the microfibrils also may consist of different crystalline polymers. The pattern which this basic structure takes in conifer tracheids and other wood cells, that is one in which lamellar arrays of closely aligned microfibrils are arranged in systematic helical fashion at different angles to the cell axis, is also a widespread one; it occurs, for instance, in various forms in other cells of higher plants. Furthermore, it is also most beautifully exemplified in certain algae, where it has been intensively studied, and it is also known in some fungal cells. Thus, putting aside the matter of specific biochemical pathways of the syntheses of individual cell wall substances, the wider problems of the manner in which such cell walls are built up are universal problems of plant growth, common alike to wood cells and to other kinds. Growing wood cells are of course difficult of access compared with many other types, for example the cells of various algae, which, as single cells or filaments, may be grown in culture. Thus it has come about that what may be inferred or hypothesized about the growth processes of wood cell walls leans heavily on evidence based on studies of the growth of other types of cell more amenable to investigation. The universality of the problems presented by the growth processes, and the broad similarities of the mature structures which these processes produce, justify this situation.

There are numerous accounts of the ultrastructure of cambial cells; see, for instance, Cronshaw (1965), Wardrop (1965a) and Robards (1968), concerned with hardwood cambia, and Cronshaw and Wardrop (1964), Murmanis and Sachs (1969) and Barnett (1977) with softwoods. It is clear that the young xylem mother cells of the inner part of the cambial zone exhibit much the same content of cytoplasmic organelles as many other plant cells. Thus, it seems most likely that in wood cells, as in other cell types for which the evidence is better, that the secretory structures of the cytoplasm, known as Golgi bodies (after their discoverer) or dictyosomes, are concerned in the formation of the cell wall matrix. They are about 0.5 to 1 μm in diameter and appear, almost universally, in electron micrographs of physiologically active cells, as stacks of disc-like hollow structures with tubular or swollen vesicular extensions to their margins; concise accounts of them have been given by Clowes and Juniper (1968) and Robards (1970). In growing plant cells vesicles about 0.1 μm in diameter, containing precursors of cell wall matrix substances, are budded off from the margins of Golgi bodies, and move towards the cell wall. These vesicles fuse with the plasmalemma and in doing so discharge their contents into the growing wall (Northcote and Pickett-Heaps, 1966).

Another type of cytoplasmic organelle, the microtubule, seems also to be involved in cell wall growth. Microtubules are proteinaceous tubular structures, of variable length, but of fairly uniform diameter, about 20–25 nm. Like dictyosomes they are common to both plant and animal cells, in both of which they have varied functions. For instance, they form the fibres of the mitotic spindle at nuclear division, and they are also constant components of the internal structure of flagella. In plant cells, in addition, they are commonly to be found in the cytoplasm near growing cell walls, adjacent or attached to the plasmalemma, and usually, but not invariably, orientated parallel to the microfibrils of the recently deposited wall (Robards, 1968; Robards and Kidwai, 1972; Pickett-Heaps, 1974; Preston, 1974). It is doubtful however that they are concerned specifically in microfibril orientation; an indirect role for them relating to the transport of precursors of cell wall substances to sites of synthesis, has been proposed. There is also evidence implying their involvement in the process of lignification of the cell wall (Nelmes *et al.*, 1973).

The production of the microfibrillar framework of the wall presents more complex problems in addition to those relating to the matrix, since here there are further structural features to be considered. Not only is there the matter of the synthesis of cellulose at the molecular level, but also those of the formation of the microfibrils as such, and the means whereby these are orientated in the cell wall in the rather precise patterns in which they are found. Leaving aside, once more, the purely biochemical aspects of cellulose synthesis, it might be supposed, by analogy with the behaviour *in vitro* of other crystal-forming substances, that molecular cellulose could be synthesized in the cytoplasm and extruded through the plasmalemma, the individual molecular chains then crystallizing into microfibrils in the cell wall by lateral association. However, if one considers the length of cell wall cellulose molecules — of the order of 5 μm — and the number of them involved in a single microfibril — of the order of a few hundreds — one cannot help feeling intuitively that this is an unlikely procedure. Moreover, there is crystallographic evidence to the contrary; if natural cellulose is dispersed in solution *in vitro* and then induced to re-crystallize, it takes up a slightly, but identifiably different, crystal structure from that of its original state. In addition, it forms anastomosing strands, of variable thickness, not the markedly uniform microfibrils characteristic of cell walls. For these and other reasons, therefore, there is a good basis for the belief that microfibril synthesis and cellulose synthesis are substantially simultaneous processes; that is to say that the microfibrils are synthesized as such by the repeated addition of glucose units to their constituent cellulose molecules (Roelofsen, 1958; Brown *et al.*, 1976). Furthermore, since microfibrils are not to be seen electronmicroscopically in the cytoplasm, they must arise at or very near to the plasmalemma surface. This conclusion then lends weight to the concept (for which there are other good reasons which we need not pursue) that their ordered arrangement in the cell wall must have its basis in their ordered origin in the plasmalemma, and, on the assumption that a microfibril must be generated by some kind of enzymic complex, such a complex, if large enough to encompass it, should be visible electronmicroscopically in or on the plasmalemma.

In the early 1950's Preston and his co-workers recognized indications in their electronmicrographs of systems of protoplasmic granules adhering to various cell wall preparations (including some of conifer cambium), which seemed to be related to microfibrillar orientation. Subsequently Frei and Preston (1961) showed that this kind of relationship was particularly clearly evident in the green alga *Chaetomorpha*, where similar granules were shown to lie in rows parallel to the two directions of orientation of microfibrils in the cell wall, and appeared to be closely associated with them. In 1963 Preston (1964) developed the concept of this association in formal terms in an "ordered granule hypothesis", which related microfibril synthesis and order to the activity of regularly arranged plasmalemma granules considered as microfibril synthesising systems.

The study of plasmalemma granules was greatly stimulated about this time by the development of the "freeze-etching" technique of electronmicroscopy. The principle of this technique, in barest outline, is to freeze the specimen in liquid nitrogen and then to cut "sections" of it in the frozen state with a similarly cooled knife. In these circumstances the specimen does not cut smoothly in the normal way, but tends to fracture, and the fractures may follow the surfaces of membranes within it. Membrane surfaces are thus exposed, and their structural contours can be revealed a little further by allowing a controlled and very thin layer of ice to sublime off their still frozen surfaces. A plastic replica can then be made of a surface so prepared, and after further appropriate treatment it can be electronmicrographed. Robards (1970) gives a concise explanatory account.

This technique enabled the demonstration of plasmalemma granules in other types of cell, granules which in some instances showed clear evidence of ordered arrangement relatable to microfibrillar patterns. The whole concept, and additional evidence bearing upon it, was discussed again by Preston (1974) in greater depth, and since that time evidence of the existence of ordered granules has continued to accrue; see for instance the work of Giddings *et al.* (1980) and Mueller and Brown (1980), and that of other workers cited by them. Granule complexes, in the form of hexagonal "rosettes", have been found in the plasmalemmas of several types of cell, and as the evidence suggests, have been postulated to be the sites of microfibril synthesis. Although this work refers to cells other than those of wood, similar "rosettes" have recently been reported in developing vessels of primary xylem (Herth, 1985). In the plasmamembranes of developing fibres of secondary wood, presumably complicated sequential changes in the arrangement of granule complexes are to be visualized, as the various layers of the wall are deposited.

Moreover since the middle and ends of a wood fibre may, at the same time, be at different stages in the deposition of the secondary wall

(Wardrop and Harada, 1965), different layers of the wall, with different microfibrillar orientations, may be being laid down simultaneously in these different regions of the cell.

Ideas alternative to some of those explicit in Preston's ordered granule hypothesis have also emerged in recent years, proposing a different interpretation of the role and action of plasmalemma granules. An essential feature of Preston's hypothesis is that the granules are stationary, and that the ends of microfibrils grow by the action of successive granules in the pattern with which they come in contact. In an alternative view, however, the granules are considered to be mobile, moving in a systematic fashion in the plasmalemma (presumably along predetermined tracks), each one leaving its newly synthesized microfibril behind it on the surface of the plasmalemma as it goes (Brown and Montezinos, 1976; Mueller and Brown, 1982). The formation of the microfibrillar framework of the cell wall by a mechanism operating in this way might thus be compared, in a very general sense, to the building of a spider's web by the highly ordered and systematic movements of the spider as it produces the strands of web substance from its spinnerets, and leaves them behind it, appropriately positioned. In a cell wall there would of course have to be a large number of synthetic granules behaving like the spider. Such a mechanism seems highly speculative and difficult to harmonize with certain aspects of cell wall structure and growth. Though the existence of ordered plasmalemma granules is clearly established, their role if any, in microfibrillar synthesis, and whether they are stationary or mobile, is still unclear.

These recondite matters apart, we see in the mature conifer tracheid (and similarly in other types of wood cells) a structure in which variously orientated microfibrils of cellulose, made up of very long molecules, and known to be of high tensile strength, are embedded in, and strongly linked by hydrogen bonds to, a matrix in which lignin, (a dense hard material) is a major component. The long-standing analogy, often repeated, which has been drawn between this two-phase structure and that of reinforced concrete, visualized on a sub-microscopic scale, is a striking and attractive one, and has a certain illustrative validity. The microfibrils represent, of course, the steel rods of the reinforced concrete, on which its tensile strength very largely depends, while the matrix of the cell wall, and especially the lignin, corresponds to the cement and aggregate mixture, the concrete itself; this is resistant to compression forces and supports the reinforcing bars in compressive situations. A structure of this nature seems appropriate to the varied mechanical demands imposed on wood cells; these include, for instance, the forces of compression, tension and shear, arising from the weight and wind resistance of the trunk, branches and foliage of the tree, together with the growth stresses generated within the wood itself. Of a somewhat different kind there are also stresses arising from the negative pressures, amounting to many atmospheres, which may develop in the elements of the wood of tall trees in relation to the maintenance of the transpiration stream, the upward flow of water from the roots to the leaves of the tree.

The "strength" of a timber, in the general sense, is approximately proportional to the amount of wood substance it contains. Heavy (i.e. dense) timbers thus tend on the whole to be stronger than light-weight timbers, though density enhanced by high extractive content is, not unexpectedly, largely ineffective in this respect. "Strength" of wood is, however, a complex matter; there is a variation in hardness, in strength under tension and compression, in resistance to impact and to splitting, and so on, so that the assessment of these properties, in relation to the uses to which the wood is to be put, is equally complex (Lavers, 1969; Dinwoodie, 1975, 1981; Desch, 1981). These are technological matters, but it is appropriate here to refer briefly to certain aspects of the strength of wood which can be seen, in a general way, as concomitants of its microscopic and sub-microscopic structure. Thus the tensile strength of wood, measured longitudinally, is some forty times that measured transversely; this is clearly a consequence of the longitudinally elongated, interdigitating form of the tracheids or fibres, in the walls of which the mean microfibrillar orientation also approximates to the longitudinal (but compare also juvenile wood, Chapter 8, and compression wood Chapter 9). If conifer wood breaks under longitudinal tensile stress, it does so following initial failures in the S_1 layer of the walls of the tracheids; the S_2 layer, being thicker and with more steeply orientated microfibrils, is much stronger in longitudinal tension, and pulls out of the S_1 (as one tube of a telescope might be pulled out of the others), before it fails completely itself (Mark, 1967).

Under longitudinal compression, failure takes a different form, and has an added interest in that early stages are not infrequently to be seen in longitudinal sections. As the load is slowly raised the wood eventually crumples (its compression strength along the grain is less than half its tensile strength), but before crumpling becomes outwardly evident, numerous microscopic regions of failure, termed slip-planes and compression failures, develop in the cell walls. These may be caused by loads as low as about 25% of those sufficient to cause ultimate failure of the wood; they may even be induced by the sectioning process itself (Dinwoodie, 1966b).

These minute failures can be seen in longitudinal sections as fine lines lying obliquely across the thickness of the double walls of adjacent fibres, commonly at an angle of 30–40° to the transverse plane. They may occur singly, or in V- or X-shaped configurations; though they are not very obvious under ordinary illumination they show up well

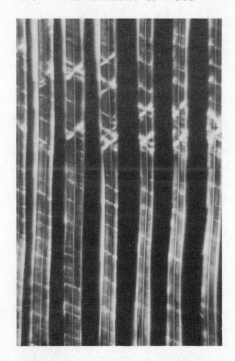

Fig. 95. *Abies balsamea*. R.L.S. (polarizing microscope, × 290). Slip-planes and minute compression failures in the double walls of adjacent tracheids are clearly revealed as oblique bright lines across the thickness of the walls. (compare Fig. 96 and see text).

under polarization microscopy (Fig. 95).

What has happened in these regions of incipient cell wall breakdown is shown diagrammatically in Fig. 96. The two halves of the double wall may fail in a unified way, as in *A* and *B* of that figure, or separately, in mirror-image fashion as in *C*, in this case more conspicuously disrupting the middle lamella. Although it may seem that in these regions

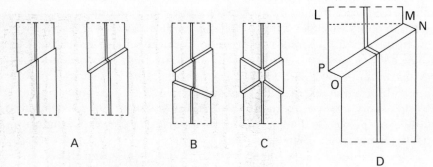

Fig. 96. Diagrams of *A*, slip-planes, *B* and *C*, minute compression failures in fibre walls (compare Fig. 95); *D*, a slip-plane on a larger scale; for explanation see text.

a portion of the wall has slipped laterally relative to the remainder (hence the term slip-plane), the discontinuity is not a matter of a slip in any literal sense, but is due to a minute sharp kink in the wall. This has involved a localized re-orientation of the microfibrils in the region of the kink, which is why this is so conspicuous under polarization microscopy (Dinwoodie, 1968; Keith and Côté, 1968).

In Fig. 96*D*, which represents a slip-plane on a large scale, it is clear that the distance PM along it is greater than the distance LM, the normal thickness of the wall. Within the region of the kink (PMNO) therefore, the volume of the wall has been increased, indicating that its normal structure must have been torn apart here to some degree (Frey-Wyssling, 1976), and it seems likely that this disruption will have involved the bonds between the microfibrils and the matrix of the wall. In consequence the microfibrils, less well supported by the matrix, have also given way and buckled under the load. Compression failures of this kind, though only of microscopic dimensions, are thus regions of permanent damage to the wall, and hence are regions also of potential weakness in it.

Under increasing loads these microscopic failures become more numerous, and may collectively give rise to a larger fold, involving many cell walls at about the same level, and extending through a long distance in the wood, producing what has been termed a compression crease (Fig. 97). As creases like this become deeper and more extensive, they eventually lead to outwardly visible failure of the wood, as may be seen in the course of laboratory compression testing (Keith, 1971;

Fig. 97. *Abies balsamea.* R.L.S. (× 95). Part of a compression crease. Obvious buckling of the tracheid walls extends over long distances in the wood.

Kučera and Bariska, 1982). Minute compression failures may also be induced inadvertently in articles made of wood, such as scaffold boards and ladders, by slight overloading, and Dinwoodie (1978) has drawn attention to the dangers which may arise in this way. Compression failures may occur, without outwardly visible sign, but the structure may have been permanently weakened and may be predisposed to premature complete failure when subsequently put under load.

Under natural conditions in the growing tree a similar sequence of developing cell wall failures may lead to the production of brittleheart, a not uncommon defect of the juvenile wood of some tropical trees (see Chapter 8 and Fig. 113). This is caused by growth stresses in the trunk which impose severe compressive loads on the core wood.

Attractive though the structural analogy between wood cell walls and reinforced concrete undoubtedly is, it must not be pushed too far. It leaves out of account the modifying effect of water, which is always present in wood, and which influences its mechanical properties and especially its dimensions. This water may be considered as consisting of two components, one of which comprises the water in the cell cavities, water which is mobile and accessible to the physiological needs of the tree, and the other the water which occupies the innumerable sub-microscopic pores (spaces up to a few nm in diameter) in the cell wall matrix. It is this second component — sometimes referred to as "bound" water — which is especially important in relation to the properties of wood as a structural material. Its importance stems from its involvement in the intermolecular hydrogen bonding between the microfibrils and the matrix, and among the matrix substances themselves.

When a tree is felled, and begins to dry out, or even in the natural drying of the heartwood of a standing tree, the more loosely held water in the cell cavities tends to be lost first, but the "imbibed" or "bound" cell wall water remains until a more advanced point in the drying process; it is in fact never lost in its entirety. A stage may thus be envisaged at which the cell cavities might be empty of water, while the submicroscopic spaces in the cell walls might still be full; this is the so-called fibre saturation point, often abbreviated as f.s.p. It corresponds to a water content of the timber as a whole which varies, but is commonly in the range of 25 to 35% of its oven-dry weight. There are various methods (Stamm, 1971) of estimating the fibre saturation point,which is in fact a somewhat theoretical parameter, insofar that the two phases of the drying process are not so entirely distinct as the foregoing may suggest; they overlap to some extent. Nevertheless the f.s.p. is a useful concept in that it relates to the stage in the drying process at which continuing loss of water involves its significant loss from the cell walls. At this stage therefore, shrinkage of the matrix begins, which leads to the onset of shrinkage of the whole wood substance. In consequence, since the crystalline structure of the microfibrils remains unchanged, shrinkage has the effect that internal drying stresses begin to develop between the matrix and the microfibrils. Stresses also develop as between adjacent cells, since a thick cell wall will tend to shrink by a greater amount than a thin one. Eventually these stresses reach levels sufficient to bring about distortion or partial breakdown of the structure, and warping and checking begin.

How far the drying of wood may proceed below its fibre saturation point is dependent on the water-vapour-pressure of its surroundings. This is because in this condition, that is to say, after the loss of the "free" water in its cell cavities, wood is hygroscopic; while it may continue to lose water vapour to a dry atmosphere, equally it may gain it from a moist one, with accompanying changes, downwards or upwards respectively, in its dimensions. This is the so-called "movement" of wood, which is not wholly preventable.

This property of wood in relation to its environment complicates its utilization, and makes some control of its moisture content necessary — the process of seasoning. Ideally the general principle of this process is to reduce the natural moisture content, in a controlled way and at a controlled rate, to a level such that the wood will be as nearly as possible in vapour-pressure equilibrium with the surroundings in which it is going to be used. This might, for example, be to about 18–20% moisture content for external woodwork, or to about 8–10% for furniture exposed to central heating; the figures might be different for different kinds of wood. In this way movement of the wood in service may be kept to a minimum. The seasoning process will ideally also be contrived to ensure that the wood dries evenly, throughout its bulk, so that the surfaces do not become unduly dry while the interior is still moist. Thus the disruptive effects of the shrinkage which unavoidably accompanies seasoning, and which leads to a variety of different forms of structural defect in seasoned timber, may be minimized. How far, and by what means, these aims may be achieved, is a considerable technological study, and is outside the scope of this book. It is discussed in detail by Kollmann and Côté (1968); concise accounts are given by Findlay (1975) and Desch (1981).

The disruptive effects of shrinkage are magnified by its directionally non-uniform nature. Thus "dry" timber, such as for example might be in equilibrium with a domestic indoor atmosphere, is likely to have shrunken from the green state by about 0.1 to 0.2% in the longitudinal direction, while its transverse shrinkage will have been some 20–50 times greater than this. This great disparity, familiar to the woodworker, has long been recognized, in a general way, as a consequence of the mean orientation of the crystallites in fibre and tracheid walls being approximately longitudinal; there is good experimental evidence and theoretical justification for this relationship. Moreover, in wood in which the mean orientation is less steep, as in juvenile wood and compression wood (Chapters 8 and 9 respectively), the extent and relative proportions of longitudinal and transverse shrinkage may be very different (Harris and Meylan, 1965; Meylan, 1968).

Transverse shrinkage, besides contrasting so markedly with longitudinal shrinkage, has a further directional character, in that shrinkage radially (commonly about 2–5%), is usually about half that which occurs tangentially. This difference accounts for certain changes of shape in converted timber which occur in the course of drying. For example, a plain-sawn board tends to become cupped in the direction away from the centre of the log, because its surface on that side is more nearly tangential than on the side facing the centre, and so shrinks the more. Similarly, a square-section batten may tend to become rhombic, especially if one of its diagonals happens to be tangential and the other radial (Fig. 98).

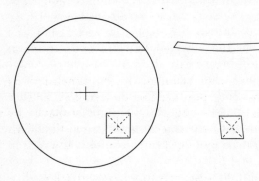

Fig. 98. Diagrams illustrating some effects of shrinkage on a plank and a batten cut from an unseasoned log. Because tangential shrinkage is greater than radial shrinkage, a plank tends to become cupped in the direction away from the centre of the log, and the square-section batten tends to become rhomboidal in section.

The difference between tangential and radial shrinkage may spring from a variety of causes. In the wood of beech and oak the lesser radial shrinkage is attributable to a restraining effect of the rays (McIntosh, 1955a and b and 1957; Schniewind, 1959). In these woods the rays form a comparatively large proportion (some 17–22%) of the total volume and ray tissue might well be expected to have some influence of this kind; this follows because the ray cells are radially elongated and the microfibrillar orientation in the S_2 layer of their walls (at least in beech) also approximates to the radial direction (Harada, 1965b). However, an explanation of this nature can hardly be universally applicable, because, for instance, pine resembles oak in its shrinkage properties, yet in pine, as in softwoods generally, the rays form a far smaller proportion, about 5–7%, of the total wood volume (Cave, 1969). Thus it would appear that in softwoods there must be some other reason, besides the effects of the rays, for the inequality of radial and tangential shrinkage (Boutelje, 1962; Barber and Meylan, 1964). Boutelje considered the growth increment structure, with its alternation of thin-walled earlywood and thick-walled latewood, to be significant in this respect, and Ylinen and Jumppanen (1967) developed this view in a theoretical treatment, citing experimental evidence in support of it. In essence, a thin cell wall tends to shrink a lesser amount than a thick one, so that along a radius, where zones of thin- and thick-walled cells alternate, the shrinkage will tend to be less than in zones where thick-walled cells lie in uninterrupted bands; that is, in the tangential direction in the latewood. This greater tangential shrinkage of the latewood has the effect of constraining the intervening bands of earlywood into similarly greater shrinkage, so that the wood as a whole behaves in this way. Reasons for the inequality of shrinkage have also been sought in differences between the radial and tangential walls of individual tracheids; differences in such features as their thickness, pitting, microfibrillar organization and degree of lignification have been regarded by other investigators as relevant (Frey-Wyssling, 1976). Evidently the balance of importance of the factors concerned in the inequality of radial and tangential shrinkage is different in different kinds of wood.

The effects of reduced cell wall water content on the dimensions of wood — effects which, if they could be produced by mechanical pressure alone, would call for enormous forces — emphasize the part played by water in the structure of wood and in its mechanical properties. This is further illustrated by the influence of the water content of wood on its resistance to bending.

If a piece of timber, for example a beam supported at each end, is suitably loaded for a short period, it becomes deflected, and when the load is removed it recovers. This is an elastic behaviour which is quantified in formal terms by reference to an appropriate modulus of elasticity, a parameter which may be thought of simply as a measure of the stiffness of the beam; the characteristic resistance of the timber to being bent. If however the load is left on for a long time the behaviour of the beam may become more complicated; when the load is removed part of the deflection will be recovered, but for the remainder the beam may be found to have acquired a permanent "set" — often shown, for instance, by heavily laden book-shelves. Thus the beam, though behaving partly in an elastic fashion, has also, in effect, flowed, to some extent, into a new shape, as if it were an extremely viscous liquid. Such complex behaviour of wood is thus commonly referred to in terms of its visco-elastic properties.

This kind of slow permanent change of shape or dimensions under load (which, incidentally, is also well shown by some plastics) is termed creep. In seasoned wood creep is relatively slight, but it will occur much more freely under moist conditions when the cell wall matrix is swollen; it involves some breakage and re-arrangement of hydrogen bonding in the inter-molecular structure of the wood, which takes place most readily in these circumstances. Creep is also facilitated at high temperatures, so that, for instance, wood to be used in the manufacture of bentwood furniture and articles such as hockey sticks, is heated to 100 °C in moist steam before being bent. After bending the pieces are held in the desired shape while they are partially dried at a lower temperature until they become set. Since bending in this way is achieved largely by compression of the wood on the inner side of the bend rather than by stretching it on the outer side, bending causes very numerous slip-planes in the cell walls. If it is properly done, however, no outwardly detectable structural failure is evident. Timbers vary greatly in their suitability for steam bending; for example, ash and beech are particularly suitable, but spruce and mahogany are very much less so (Stevens and Turner, 1970).

In the drying of moist timber its flexibility and plasticity are reduced and its stiffness and strength in general terms are improved; for instance, the compression strength of Scots pine seasoned to 12% moisture content is about $2\frac{1}{2}$ times its value in the green timber (Lavers, 1969). It may perhaps be visualized that as the matrix loses water and shrinks, some hydrogen bonds within it, which previously involved cell wall water, become internally satisfied; that is to say that they have been broken and formed anew between adjacent molecules of the wood substance (Preston, 1974), so adding to its inter-molecular coherence and hence to its strength and mechanical stiffness. Nevertheless, even in "dry" timber some water is still present, and moreover it cannot be entirely removed without some resultant breakdown of the wood structure.

In summary, it is evident that wood, considered at the sub-microscopic level, is a complex and highly ordered unity of a variety of substances, the individual attributes and interactions of which are the basis of its unique combination of mechanical properties. In this chapter, in ranging over this field of study in an inevitably summary fashion, we have done little more than to touch upon a variety of specialist topics, the sum of the knowledge of any one of which can be sought only in an extensive literature. Nevertheless, some acquaintance, in outline, with the ultra-structure of wood, no less than a knowledge of its more familiar microscopic features, contributes to an understanding of its remarkable properties.

7

Wood Surfaces and their Underlying Structure

In Chapter 2 we describe in broad, general terms the different outward appearances of transverse, radial longitudinal and tangential longitudinal surfaces of wood in relation to the underlying structural reasons for these differences. The features which are referred to there are fundamental ones, common to all timbers, though as Chapters 4 and 5 exemplify, the extent and manner of the expression of these features varies greatly among different kinds of trees, as for instance in the distinctiveness of the earlywood and latewood, and in the size and hence visibility of the rays. In this chapter we return in greater detail to this matter of the surface features of wood; some of which are very general and others more specific, but all of which have their origins in the mode of growth of the wood and its three-dimensional structure considered at the microscopic level.

The appearance of wood (and to some extent its other properties) may be referred to three groups of characteristics; its grain, its texture and its figure. Although these characteristics are inter-related, it is convenient to categorise them in this way.

Grain is a term often used loosely in various ways, but properly used, in its technical sense, it refers to the direction of the axial elements of the wood in relation to the long axis of the log, or, when applied to converted timber, of an individual plank. If the axial elements are aligned parallel to the length of the piece, this is said to be straight-grained, and thus any marked irregularity in the course of the axial elements affects the grain. Commonplace examples may be seen in the presence of knots, and localized diversion of nearby axial elements around them.

Also very frequent is the condition known as spiral grain, in which the axial elements are not aligned parallel to the axis of the trunk of the tree, but are laid down along helical paths, inclined tangentially at an angle to the truly axial direction. This angle is usually only a few degrees, but is very variable and may sometimes be much more. Spiral grain has been reported in over 200 spp., and in some it is so common as to be almost the normal condition (Noskowiak, 1963; Kozlowski, 1971; Harris, 1981). It may be seen occasionally in posts of Scots pine supporting telephone wires or minor power lines, the surface checking of the wood being clearly oblique to the axial direction. It is also not infrequent, for example, in sweet chestnut and hawthorn, where the influence of its presence may extend also to the fissuring of the bark. The condition of the bark is however not a wholly reliable indicator of the presence or absence of spiral grain.

Such external evidence of the presence of spiral grain may tend, perhaps, to be interpreted as indicative of a spirality of structure extending unchanged throughout the wood. In fact, however, a reversal of the direction of the spiral commonly occurs. In a number of softwood species the older corewood of the tree commonly shows an increasing left-hand, or S-spiral[1], which reaches a maximum after some 10–20 years. The grain of the later-formed wood then tends to reverse the direction of the spiral, changing progressively through the straight-grained condition to a right-hand, or Z-spiral[1], which is thus what is seen at the surface of the wood of older trees (Noskowiak, 1963; Bannan, 1966). In broad-leaved trees the predominant pattern seems to be in the opposite direction, from an initial Z-spiral to a later S-spiral, but considerable variability has been reported.

Conversion of a log with spiral grain produces planks similarly affected, their axial elements lying obliquely to the cut surfaces. Such planks are often described as being 'short in the grain', or the grain is said to 'run out at the side'. A similar effect may be produced if a straight-grained log is badly converted, so that the planks are cut somewhat obliquely. Although irregularities of grain may contribute to attractive forms of figure (see below), in structural timbers they are potential defects; the presence of markedly spiral grain, or of large numbers of knots, may result in mechanical weakness to an unacceptable degree.

The texture of wood is determined by its cellular construction. Texture refers essentially to the uniformity or otherwise of the cells of the wood, in their size and the thickness of their walls. Thus diffuse-porous woods, with vessels of moderate size, such as beech and lime (Figs. 76D and 81A), are even-textured; if, further, all the elements are small, as in boxwood and holly (Fig. 83), the wood is said to be fine-textured. On the other hand, woods like oak and chestnut, with their very open earlywood and dense latewood, have a coarse or uneven texture (Figs. 74A and C). Slow-grown oak, with a minimum of latewood, is thus

---

[1] See p. 151 for an explanation of this use of S– and Z–.

more even-textured than fast-grown timber; it is also less dense and is often preferred by cabinet makers for both these reasons, on account of its easier working.

Softwoods, though less diverse than hardwoods in their cellular make-up, nevertheless show comparable differences of texture. Thus in the pencil cedars (*Juniperus procera* and *J. virginiana*) there is little difference between earlywood and latewood, and all the tracheids are relatively thin-walled. The wood thus has a fine, even texture and cuts easily in all directions; hence its use for the casings of lead pencils. On the other hand, in Douglas fir there is an abrupt change from earlywood to latewood; the earlywood tracheids are relatively large and thin-walled, in marked contrast to those of the latewood, which are narrower and much thicker-walled. In consequence the alternation of zones of ear-lywood and latewood gives the timber a coarse and uneven texture, a feature which is shared in varying degrees by many other softwood species, for example by larch and the pitch pines (Fig. 19). Differences of texture affect not only the working properties of the wood, but also its resistance to wear. While a hard, close-textured wood will retain a smooth surface as it wears, coarse-textured woods tend to wear unevenly.

The surface of a piece of wood, when cleaned and smoothed, is rarely uniform in appearance; almost without exception it shows local variations of colour or structure which are evident to the unaided eye. Such variations, however caused, whether they are decorative or not, are known as figure. Though the term figure, in common usage, conveys a sense of decorative quality, technically the meaning is wider and has no aesthetic implications.

Figure may arise from a variety of causes, of which the simplest is perhaps irregular pigmentation, usually of the heartwood. One of the best examples of this is shown by European walnut, *Juglans regia*. The sapwood is a uniform oatmeal colour, but the heartwood has a greyish-brown backgound with darker, even black, streaks in it (Fig. 99*A*). The amount of such figuring varies; while French-grown walnut tends to be rather plain and uniform, Italian walnut is better, with the best coming from the Ancona region. Nowadays, however, the name Ancona tends to be applied to any well-figured walnut. Although *J. regia* may thus be nicely figured, American (black) walnut (*J. nigra*) is usually almost uniformly very dark in colour.

Among other hardwoods which may be figured by irregular pig-mentation are afara or limba (*Terminalia superba*), some of the ebonies (*Diospyros* spp.) and *Lovoa trichilioides*. The last of these often shows some irregular streaky colouring, a feature which probably prompted its trade name, African walnut. It is, however, not a walnut, but a member of the family Meliaceae, which includes the mahoganies. Among softwoods,

A

B

Fig. 99. Pigmentation as a cause of figure. *A*, walnut (*Juglans regia*); a veneer showing the characteristic somewhat irregular pigmentation. The vessels appear as short grooves. *B*, zebrano (*Microberlinia* sp.). Here pigmented and non-pigmented zones alternate fairly regularly. (The scales are in cm).

coloured figure may be seen in Parana pine (*Araucaria angustifolia*); this rather uniform, even-textured wood usually shows somewhat irregular reddish or pinkish streaks or bands.

Valuable though figure due to irregular pigmentation may be, figure most commonly has a structural basis, in which grain and texture are also involved. In consequence, while figure arising simply from pigmentation will be visible to some extent on a plank however the log may have been converted, figure deriving from a structural cause may be seen only if the log is converted in a manner appropriate to the cause; the position and orientation of the cut surface in which the figure is to be displayed may need to be carefully chosen for it to be shown to the best advantage.

The structural causes of figure are diverse. The commonest is the contrast between earlywood and latewood, which influences the distinctness of the growth rings, and hence their differing appearances on radial and tangential surfaces (see Chapter 2). In ring-porous timbers such as oak and chestnut the growth rings are well shown, but in diffuse-porous woods like birch and alder, in which the growth ring boundaries are marked only by a few rows of much-flattened cells, the figure is minimal. On radial surfaces the growth rings are barely visible, but may show up on worked timber as parallel fine shining lines, since the terminal bands of flattened cells (thick-walled and with narrow lumens) are closer-textured than the remainder of the wood and take a higher polish. This is more distinctly so in birch than in alder. When the timber is rotary cut, as in the manufacture of plywood, so that it displays a continuous tangential surface, the latewood shows up as faintly defined irregular smoother zones, somewhat reminiscent of a water-mark in paper.

A more complex contrast between earlywood and latewood is well shown by elm. Elm has a pore-ring in the earlywood, but in addition there are numerous smaller vessels and vascular tracheids in the late-wood, embedded in fibrous tissue, and these elements, as seen in transverse sections, are arranged in undulating tangential bands. Thus plain-sawn boards show not only the familiar U– or V–shaped markings of the pore-rings, but also, between these, finer and fainter but comparable somewhat irregular markings caused by the bands of latewood vessels and other elements associated with them. In polished elm these markings are considered to be reminiscent of the feathering of a partridge, and the effect they produce is known as partridge-breast figure. It may be well seen on the seats of Windsor chairs, or on elm-seated laboratory stools which have become highly polished by much use (Fig. 100).

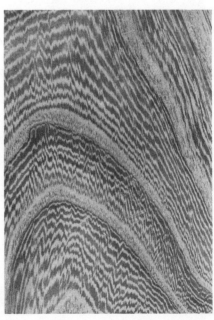

Fig. 100. Elm (*Ulmus* sp.). A slightly oblique tangential surface showing partridge-breast figure. This is caused by the undulating tangential bands of latewood vessels alternating with bands of fibres. (About 2/3 natural size).

In softwoods, contrast between earlywood and latewood is almost the sole cause of figure, which is characteristic therefore of species in which the wood is sharply differentiated in this respect. Mostly, of course, such figure shows no more than the usual arrays of parallel lines (on radial surfaces) or U's and V's (on tangential surfaces). Marked irregularities, bulges or indentations, in the growth rings are, however, not uncommonly present, rounded in their contour, and accompanied by local distortions in the grain. Tangential (plain-sawn) surfaces then show conspicuous variations of figure, which include irregular bands and systems of concentric zones of earlywood and latewood. Patterns of this kind, as may sometimes be seen, for instance, in pitch pine, are known as blister figure. In Douglas fir, which is much used for plywood, figure of this nature, displayed on the continuous tangential surfaces exposed by rotary cutting, may be very striking. The irregular growth rings, when rotary cut, sometimes give rise to repetitive patterns across the surfaces of large boards, patterns which change slightly at each repetition as a consequence of the knife having cut progressively deeper into the log at each rotation. Blister figure also occurs in hardwoods (see p. 188).

As Chapter 2 also indicates, the rays may be a cause of figure, which, in the classic case of oak, is very conspicuous. The large multiseriate rays, often 4-5 cms in height, show up clearly on radial (quarter-sawn)

A

B

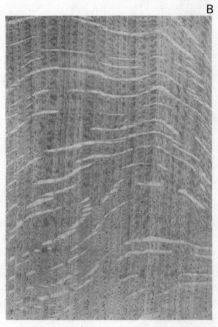

surfaces, producing the figure variously known as the flower or silver grain of oak (Fig. 101A). Seen from this aspect the ray tissue shows up well because it appears lighter in colour than the remainder of the wood. Since extensively truly radial surfaces are virtually impossible to obtain unless the wood is cleft (as used to be done for some purposes), rather than sawn or sliced, the silver grain is usually seen in short somewhat irregular patches, superimposed on the figure produced by the pore rings. A similar effect is seen in the so-called silky oaks (*Grevillea robusta* and *Cardwellia sublimis*), though these trees are not related to the true oaks, but are members of the Proteaceae.

Large rays will also, of course, give rise to figure on tangential surfaces (Fig. 101C), though in this view rays appear as fusiform flecks, which in oak are darker in colour than the background. Both radial and tangential aspects of the rays are also well shown by beech, as for instance in the legs of beech furniture and in some mallet heads, though since the rays do not exceed a few millimetres in height, the figure is on a very much smaller scale than in oak. The multiseriate rays are however very numerous and appear darker in colour than the axial elements.

Between the nearly radial and the truly tangential directions there is of course a range of intermediate orientations of wood surfaces. Where these surfaces display a decorative form of figure they are mostly seen

C

Fig. 101. European oak (*Quercus* sp.). *A*, an almost radial surface; the large rays, which show up on this face lighter than the other tissues, (compare the tangential surface in *C*) form the 'flower' or 'silver grain' of oak. (About 1/2 natural size). *B*, a surface which is also almost radial, but is oblique to the axial direction, so that the rays show only a fraction of their full height; their undulating appearance is due to slight local irregularities in the grain. (About 1/2 natural size). *C*, a tangential surface, showing the large rays, which in this view appear darker than the other tissues. Axial vessel lines can be seen in obliquely orientated zones. These are parts of the U- or V-shaped zones, which would have been more clearly recognizable on a larger specimen. (Scale in cm).

as veneers, nowadays often of minimal thickness. Nevertheless the student will find it useful to remember that a veneer is not to be regarded as one might a printed pattern; it is, on the contrary, a section through a piece of solid wood, cut in a particular way in order to highlight certain features of its structure and to display them to the best advantage, decoratively and economically. He will find it an interesting and sometimes an exacting exercise, in examining a veneer, to attempt to visualize an explanation of its appearance in terms of the underlying three-dimensional structure of the wood from which it was cut. Veneers of oak, for instance, frequently to be seen, are often neither truly radial nor tangential, nor even parallel to the grain, in their orientation (Fig. 101*B*).

Where rays are storied (see Chapter 5) they may produce a type of figure very different from that associated with large non-storied rays. The regularly aligned tiers of rays, even though the rays themselves are small, may in a polished surface reflect the light in a characteristic fashion, giving rise to the appearance known as ripple figure. This is to be seen for example, in mahogany (*Swietenia* spp.), gum guaiacum (*Guaiacum officinale*) and somewhat more easily, since the rays are larger, in okwen (*Brachystegia* spp.).

Fig. 102. Iroko (*Chlorophora excelsa*). A board cut slightly obliquely, showing figure due to aliform confluent parenchyma. (About 1/3 natural size).

Fig. 103. African mahogany (*Khaya* sp.). *A*, crotch figure (about 1/3 natural size). *B*, swirl figure (about 1/8 natural size).

Axial parenchyma, especially when present in quantity, may also contribute to figure. For example, iroko (*Chlorophora* spp.) has a high proportion of parenchyma, which on transverse surfaces can be seen to be predominantly paratracheal, often confluent or banded. On plain-sawn surfaces these irregular bands of parenchyma show up conspicuously as U– or V–shaped areas, lighter in colour than the background, and somewhat irregularly zig-zag in form along their length; the general effect is not unlike partridge-breast figure, though on a coarser scale. The parenchyma is less conspicuous, though still readily visible, on quarter-sawn surfaces (Fig. 102).

Among hardwoods especially there are also various forms of figure arising from grain patterns that diverge markedly from the straight-grained condition. Certain of these are clearly related to outwardly evident structural features of the tree, for example crotch figure, associated with the departure of major branches from the trunk. Others arise from various types of irregularity in the vascular cambium, and others again from fairly regular rhythmic alternations in the 'grain' of the cambium which are perpetuated in the grain of the wood.

At a crotch some of the fibres on the lower side are likely to be aligned in relatively smooth curves extending from the trunk into the

A

B

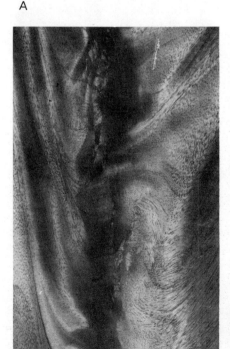
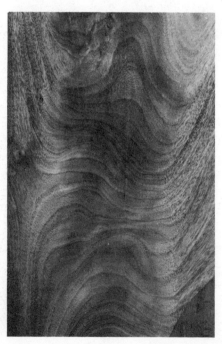

AW–G

branch, whereas on the upper side, where space is more limited and the pressures of the expanding trunk and branch react on each other, the grain may be greatly disturbed, and varied feather-like markings, known as feather crotch, are often found on radial surfaces. Less disturbed regions given rise to smoother curves producing figure known as swirl. The crotch figure of mahogany and walnut is especially prized. Comparable varied forms of figure may be formed near the base of the trunk, at the junctions with the main roots, especially if there are root buttresses (Fig. 103).

Another type of figure involving cambial irregularity, which also has a structural connotation, is that associated with burrs. These are irregular swellings on the trunks or at the bases of trees, arising from the slow growth of clusters of epicormic or adventitious buds which stimulates local expansion of the trunk. Burr walnut is probably the best known example, but burrs may be formed in many other species, and those of a number of others, yew and elm, for instance, besides walnut, are prized for the decorative figure they display on appropriately cut surfaces. The

Fig. 105. European oak (*Quercus* sp.). The surface of the wood of a burr, exposed by removal of the bark (about natural size). The bases of the numerous adventitious shoots forming the burr, and the diversion of the grain around and among them, can be seen.

Fig. 104. An example of figure caused by a burr. (Scale in cm).

figure derives from the numerous very small pin knots which traverse the wood, and the marked irregularity of the grain around and between these knots (Figs. 104 and 105). Burrs often arise in response to injury to the tree, and their formation may be stimulated artificially.

Other forms of figure originate in cambial irregularity not so evidently related to structural features of the tree. The well-known 'bird's-eye' figure, found in some maples (especially *Acer saccharum* and *A. nigrum*) is one of these. It arises in regions of the tree in which there are very numerous and closely but variably spaced indentations in the growth rings, as if the normally smooth contour of the cambium had at some time become locally indented, and the growth-rings of the later-formed wood had then conformed to these indentations. A plain-sawn or rotary-cut surface thus shows these indented areas (the individual 'eyes') as sharply defined patches, a few millimetres in diameter, within which the grain is steeply dimpled in the radial direction, producing a figure of characteristic form. The 'eyes' have an elliptical or horse-shoe-like shape, while in the regions between them the grain follows sinuous

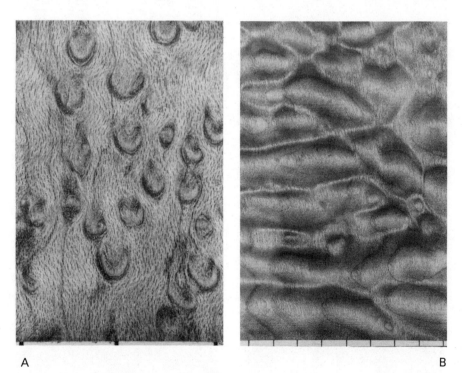

A   B

Fig. 106. *A*, bird's eye maple, and *B*,
quilted maple (*Acer* spp.); see text.
(Scales in cm).

courses in the tangential plane (Fig. 106A). Bird's-eye figure may be locally distributed in the tree, or it may extend throughout the trunk and even into the branches, persisting for many years. The primary cause of the indentations in the cambium is uncertain; they have been attributed to its localized destruction by a fungus. The cambium in these damaged areas is subsequently regenerated, but by the time regeneration has been achieved the resultant indentations in the later growth increments have been initiated, because the surrounding cambium has been displaced outwards by its continuing formation of new wood.

Shallower and more softly contoured depressions in the cambium may give rise to other types of figure. Blister figure may sometimes be produced in ring-porous hardwoods, as it is in softwoods, by the alternation of earlywood and latewood in the irregularly contoured growth increments (Fig. 107A). A somewhat similar figure may also appear in diffuse-porous woods which lack conspicuous growth increments; here it

Fig. 107. Blister figure. *A*, in ash (*Fraxinus* sp.), where it is due to local irregularity in the pore-rings (about 1/2 nature size). *B*, in *Entandrophragma* sp., where it is caused by irregularity in the bands of concentric axial parenchyma (about 2/3 natural size).

A

B

may be caused by local irregularities in bands of confluent parenchyma. These, seen on tangential surfaces, reflect the light differently from the intervening more fibrous areas of the wood (Fig. 107B). Where depressions in the cambium are somewhat elongated transversely they may give rise to undulations in the grain which show up on polished plain-sawn surfaces as a corresponding pattern of varied reflectivity known as quilted figure. This is characteristic of certain maples. (Fig. 106B).

Certain other types of figure derive from more-or-less regular rhythmic changes (as distinct from local irregularities) in the direction of the grain. Thus in some timbers regularly repetitive deviations to the left and right of the axial direction may be seen on a tangential surface, so that the grain follows a sinuous course; the wood is then said to have undulating or wavy grain. The vertical distance between the crests of the undulations on one side or the other of the axial direction — what might be called the wavelength — is usually of the order of a few millimetres, or perhaps up to 1–2 cm. Since the undulations most commonly lie in the tangential direction, if the wood is cleft radially the cleft surfaces so exposed are transversely corrugated, while cleft tangential surfaces are not corrugated. Very occasionally, however, wavy grain may undulate in the radial direction, so that the corrugated cleft surface would then be the tangential or plain-sawn one.

When timber with the more usual form of wavy grain is quarter-sawn or sliced, to produce boards or veneers with radial or near radial surfaces, the axial elements meet these surfaces at various angles in a regularly repeating fashion, in accordance with the undulations of the grain. As a result, these surfaces, when planed and polished, reflect the light differently in different areas, corresponding to the positions of the undulations, so that they show a regular pattern of approximately transverse bands (Figs. 108, 109 and 110). This type of figure is known as fiddle-back figure, because wavy-grained maple (also known as curly maple) is traditionally the preferred wood for the backs of violins. Wavy or undulating grain is frequent in some maples and mahoganies, and has been described in other timbers; an analysis of its structure in ash, sycamore and birch is given by Hejnowicz and Romberger (1973).

A comparable rhythmic type of figure has its origin in alternations of grain direction which occur in a rather different way from those of wavy grain, and also on a much larger scale. It has features in common with spiral grain, referred to on p. 177. But while the figure produced by spiral grain is, except for its oblique orientation, essentially the same as that of straight-grained timber of the same kind, spirality of grain occurs in some trees in a more complex form, in that fairly frequent regular reversals in the direction of the spiral may be seen. Thus the grain of the wood produced over a period of years may have

Fig. 108. Wellingtonia (*Sequoiadendron giganteum*). An almost radial surface, from the butt of the tree, showing fiddle-back figure, the effect of undulating or wavy grain (about 1/2 natural size). Such figure is uncommon in softwoods, but may sometimes be found near the base of the tree. Note also the distinct heartwood.

Fig. 109. An approximately radial surface of a sliced veneer of peroba (*Paratecoma* sp. ?) showing fiddle-back figure. (Scale in cm).

a left-hand or S-spiral, but the direction may then change in later-formed wood to a right-hand or Z-spiral, and after a further interval back again to an S-spiral. Successive reversals follow at intervals of a few years, or perhaps a decade or more (but not annually), so that many alternations may occur in the radius of the trunk of a mature tree. Wood with this type of grain structure is said to have double-spiral or interlocked grain (Fig. 111).

Interlocked grain is well shown on a cleft radial surface, as the alternating zones tend each to split along its own grain, so that a characteristically fluted cleavage is produced. On a smoothed radial surface these zones show up as a series of stripes, in which the vessel lines at the surface may alternate in length because the axial elements of adjacent zones meet the surface at different angles. Moreover when the wood is polished the two sets of stripes reflect the light differently, and produce a pattern of alternating ribbons of light and shade, and the two sets may change their reflectivity, relative to one another, according to the direction of the incident light. (Fig. 112). This effect is known as stripe or ribbon figure; in specimens of the best quality the stripes will be of about equal width.

Stripe figure is particularly well shown by sapele (*Entandrophragma cylindricum*) and utile (*E. utile*). It also occurs, less conspicuously, in the wood of obeche (*Triplochiton scleroxylon*) and ramin (*Gonystylus* spp.), among other tropical trees. It is rare in temperate trees, but has been described in plane (*Platanus hybrida*) and a few others. Wood with stripe figure calls for care in finishing, because whichever way it is planed on a radial face one set of stripes will be smoothed satisfactorily while those of the alternating set will tend to 'pick up'.

Wavy grain and interlocked grain thus have in common the feature of rhythmic alternation in the direction of the grain, though this takes

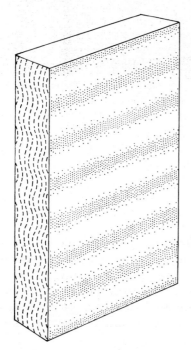

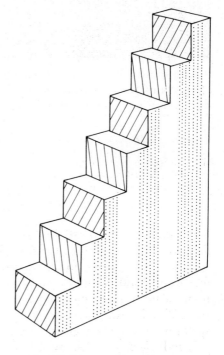

Fig. 110. Diagram of a radially sawn board, showing how undulating grain, visible on the tangential edge of the board, gives rise to fiddle-back figure on the radial face.

Fig. 111. Diagram illustrating interlocked grain, and the resultant stripe figure, in a radially sawn board. The tangential edge of the board has been visualized as cut in a step-wise pattern, to show how the stripes of the figure correspond to the alternations of grain.

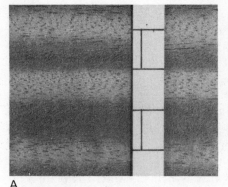
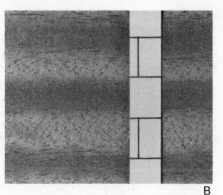

A   B

Fig. 112. *Guarea* sp. A radial surface showing stripe figure, due to interlocked grain. *A*, a small area illuminated from the right-hand side, and *B*, the same area, illuminated from the left-hand side; note the interchange of the light and dark stripes. The stripe effect arises from the fact that because the axial elements in successive zones of the wood meet the surface at different angles, they reflect the light differently. (The scale is in cm).

different forms in the two types. In wavy grain the alternations occur at short distances *axially*, fairly uniformly across the growth increments, throughout a considerable radial distance in the tree, and are not conspicuously subject to change with time; they remain at approximately the same level (though creeping slowly upwards) in many successive growth increments. In contrast, the conspicuous feature of interlocked grain is that the changes of slope are seen to occur in *radial* succession, at fairly regular intervals of a few years, producing successive zones of wood in which the grain slopes in opposite senses alternately. Within any one of these zones, however, the grain direction appears to be a stable one throughout a considerable distance. In sapele for instance, veneered surfaces showing regular parallel stripe figure over a distance of 2 m. or so are commonly to be seen, and Hejnowicz and Zagórska-Marek (1974) refer to the occurrence, among quarter-sawn boards, of lengths of uniform grain pattern exceeding 3 m. Nevertheless the presence of irregularities indicates that this uniformity cannot be assumed to extend throughout the trunk of the tree (in sapele up to 30 m. or more) and Krawczyszyn and Romberger (1980) discount this possibility.

It is interesting also to note that both types of alternation of grain may occur together, giving rise to roe figure. This is formed when wood with interlocked grain contains also the regular short-wavelength undulations of wavy grain.

The analysis of wavy grain by Hejnowicz and Romberger (1973) and of interlocked grain in *Platanus* spp. by Krawczyszyn (1972) and in tupelo (*Nyssa sylvatica*) by Krawczyszyn and Romberger (1980) show moreover that wavy grain and interlocked grain may be described in terms of certain common features suggesting a basis of understanding and an underlying mechanism common to both of them.

In wavy grain, as we have seen, the 'waves' are short, and considered in their radial aspect, move slowly upwards in successive growth increments. Along a radius, therefore, at any given transverse level, changing angles of grain and alternations of S- and Z- directions thus exist, which might be regarded as being comparable with those of ribbon figure, but of very much smaller dimensions. In the interlocked grain of *Platanus*, studied in a number of series of peeled veneers, it was found that the interlocking, observable along a radius at given level, was also in fact produced by undulations of grain, in S- and Z- grained regions, visible in a given tangential surface, which also move upwards as the distance from the pith increases.

In the ribbon figure of tupelo, if a given growth increment is followed upwards in the trunk from the base of the tree, the slope of its grain is found to change slowly with height, from S to Z and back again, over distances of a few metres; the alternating zones of the ribbon figure do not extend unchanged throughout the height of the trunk. They show longitudinal 'waves', basically similar to those of wavy grain, but differing from these in being of much greater 'wavelength', a matter of metres, rather than the centimetres of the 'waves' of *Platanus* or the millimetres of those of wavy grain. Oscillations of this nature occur in all the zones of the interlocked grain, so that an approximate regularity of alternation of grain inclination, considered radially, is maintained at various levels in the trunk. In tupelo, however, upward movement of the grain undulations seems not to be a significant feature.

These complex wavelike patterns in the grain must, of course, have their origin in the cambial zone, which poses the question as to how the 'grain' of the vascular cambium itself comes to have these rhythmically varying orientations. Here it is necessary to refer the reader back to Chapter 3, and the manner of the multiplicative or anticlinal division of cambial cells.

In non-storied cambia such a division of a fusiform cell takes place by a pseudo-transverse wall, which by the unequal growth of the walls of the two daughter cells, comes eventually to lie in the radial longitudinal plane. At the same time the intrusive tip-growth of these cells, which prior to the pseudo-transverse division were one above the other, results in their coming to lie substantially side by side (Fig. 11, p. 36). In this diagram the inclination of the pseudo-transverse division is shown as sloping upwards from left to right, but equally it might have been inclined in the opposite sense, i.e. upwards from right to left, and this difference, influencing as it does the direction of the intrusive growth of the daughter cells, seems to be a factor in the origin and maintenance of spiral grain (Hejnowicz, 1961; Bannan, 1966).

The implication of this apparent effect of the sense of the slope of cambial divisions on the sense of that of spiral grain might well seem to be that in the cambium of straight-grained timber the two opposing directions of the pseudo-transverse wall occur at random in equal numbers. It turns out however that their distribution is not individually random, but that instead there is a mosaic of areas in the cambium, within each of which one or the other direction predominates; these areas have been termed domains by Hejnowicz (1964). Domains vary in size, and are not fixed in position or time; their boundaries may migrate, so that any specific group of cambial cells may at one time be in one domain and later in another. It is not of course the cells themselves which migrate, but the nature of their behaviour in the course of division which changes.

This concept of domains, variable in size and moving within the cambial surface, is not an easy one to visualize; it may perhaps be illustrated by analogy with the behaviour of the plants in a barley field, as may sometimes be seen in windy weather. The plants tend to lean slightly one way or another according to the direction of the wind, and if this is variable, and gusting in strength, it has the effect that the field, as seen from a little distance, shows fleeting patterns of areas of differently leaning plants, patterns which appear to pass across it according to the vagaries of the wind. Though the plants are fixed, the patterns change and move, and similarly in a cambium, a pattern of areas of the 'lean' of pseudotransverse walls – i.e. the domains – moves slowly over its surface, even though the individual cambial cells are stationary.

Bannan (1966) showed that in softwoods there is a general conformity between the slope, S-type or Z-type, of spiral grain, and the pre-dominance and persistence of the one or the other of the directions of orientation of the pseudo-transverse divisions in the cambium. He concluded, however, that though the orientation of these divisions is an important factor in the induction of spiral grain, it is not the only factor; he considered that spiral grain cannot be attributed to any one single cause. Other changes in the cambial zone, leading to a change in the angle of the grain have been described by Savidge and Farrar (1984). In this work an accelerated change of grain angle was induced experimentally by girdling trees and leaving oblique (45°) "bridges" of undamaged tissue across the girdled regions. As these bridges grew in thickness the grain within the new wood changed from the initial axial direction to a 45° inclination (i.e. parallel to the angle of the bridge) within a period of about 50 days.

Nevertheless the concept of this relationship, limited though its scope may prove to be, is suggestive of a line of approach to the study of alternating grain patterns in hardwoods. In this context, however, hardwoods present an additional problem of a different kind. In soft-woods, as we have seen, owing to the uniformity of the wood and the limited intrusive growth which takes place in the maturation of the axial elements, the structural pattern of the cambium, as it existed and functioned at any previous time and place in the formation of the wood, can be reliably inferred from tangential sections of the wood itself; cambial domains can thus be identified. In hardwoods, however, because of the greater diversity of their constituent elements and the much greater and more variable extent to which these undergo intrusive growth, cambial patterns are not preserved in the wood as they are in softwoods. If alternations of grain in hardwoods are to be referred to alternations of cambial orientation, therefore, other evidence bearing on the past history of the latter had to be found.

Two types of such evidence have been described and made use of in relation to this problem. Hejnowicz and Krawczyszyn (1969) observed that in a number of temperate hardwood species the terminal layer (alone) of the wood of the outermost growth increment does preserve the pattern of the cambium still adjacent to it. In this layer, the last to differentiate in the growing season, intrusive growth was found not to occur, the only changes in cell shape which take place being those associated with transverse divisions within fusiform initials leading to the formation of strand parenchyma. From this observation these authors concluded that the terminal layer of the wood elements of any growth increment (they referred to this layer as TLX) may be considered as a record of cambial structure at the time of its formation, i.e. the end of the growing season. Thus certain aspects of cambial structure and behaviour may be assessed, albeit only at yearly intervals, but enabling long-term changes to be identified. This method was used by Krawczyszyn (1971) in a study of *Platanus* wood, in the course of which evidence of a second type came to light, of a very different kind. This derives from the ways in which the rays undergo splitting and fusion (see below). Both methods were also used by Hejnowicz and Romberger (1973) in a study of wavy grain and the relationship of the undulations of the grain to the presence of S- and Z-domains in the cambium.

The involvement of ray patterns in the identification of cambial domains arises from the fact that new rays are not formed solely as a result of the conversion of a fusiform initial in the cambium into a group of ray initials, but, especially in woods in which the rays are mostly multiseriate, they are more usually formed by the splitting of existing rays. This splitting is brought about by the intrusive growth of a fusiform initial into a group of ray initials, or sometimes by the conversion of some members of a group of ray initials into fusiform initials. The split so formed is oblique and may have an S- or Z-orientation. Similarly, when rays fuse to form a larger ray, as for instance as a result of the loss of a fusiform initial from the cambium, the line of fusion may also be orientated in the one direction or the other. Moreover, the areas of predominantly S- and Z-orientations of these changes have been found to be in conformity with the S- and Z-domains of the cambium, as inferred from the directions of its pseudo-transverse divisions. They may thus be used as more readily observable indicators of the extent of these domains. A particularly striking example, in the first annual growth increment in *Platanus hybrida*, was described and illustrated by Krawczyszyn (1973). However, in alternating grain systems the observed cambial domains cannot be wholly co-extensive with the domains of grain direction in the wood recently differentiated from them. It will be clear, for instance, that when an S-domain in the cambium has given rise to similarly orientated wood, movement of the domain pattern, resulting in a swing to Z-orientation in the cambium, must precede the appearance of a corresponding swing in the direction of the grain in the wood. For a period, therefore, the cambium and the recent wood must be expected to be 'out of step' in their directions of cellular orientation (Hejnowicz and Romberger, 1973).

In trees with storied wood structure the origin of interlocked grain presents a further problem. In storied cambia the multiplicative divisions of the cambial cells are radially longitudinal from their initiation; they do not begin as pseudo-transverse divisions which are then subsequently re-orientated. Thus the origin of cambial domains (if that term may be used in this context) cannot be referred to initial differences of orientation of that type of division, and the well-developed interlocked grain and consequent ribbon figure characteristic of such timbers as sapele (*Entandrophragma cylindricum*) and utile (*E. utile*) must have other pre-disposing causes. Hejnowicz and Zagórska-Marek (1974) and Zagórska-Marek (1984) have described a mechanism based upon a limited capacity of the storied cambial cells for localized intrusive growth. This operates in such a way that the tips of these cells (as seen in tangential sections) develop new tapering apices laterally displaced from the existing ones, which have the effect of introducing a lateral shift (in the tangential plane) in the interdigitation of the cells of one storey with those of the stories above and below. The cells thus become inclined and hence the grain of their derivatives follows similarly. Such shifts, alternating in their directions at intervals of a few years, would thus produce interlocked grain. In this way, as in the wood produced by non-storied cambia, the reversals of grain direction can be attributed to rhythmic changes in the behaviour of the cambium. It is interesting to note, in this connection, as Krawczyszyn and Romberger (1979) have reported, that the mean length of vessel elements and parenchyma strands in sapele and utile undergo cyclical changes as the slope of the grain changes from the S-direction to the Z-direction and back again. Their length is at a maximum in the regions of maximal inclination of the grain, and minimal where the grain is in the intermediate truly axial state. These changes of element length are thus to be explained quantitatively as arising from a constant axial height of the tiers of cells of the storied cambium, modified by the slope of the grain; clearly if the storey height is to be held constant, where the cells are tilted they must be longer than where they are truly axially aligned. The changes in their length, which may also be involved in the mechanism of their inclination, serve also as a means of maintaining a constant storey height within the system of fluctuating grain direction.

The origins of the range of cyclic grain patterns thus present many problems as yet unsolved, problems of interest both to timber technologists in relation to figure and to botanists as manifestations of biological rhythms of varied periodicity. Their further study in great depth is however likely to be a most laborious matter. Nevertheless the various types of figure to which they may give rise, and their interrelationships may now be recognized. They are discussed concisely by Hejnowicz and Romberger (1979).

In summary, although in some instances figure may be due to irregular pigmentation, more usually its causes are of a structural nature; the best display of their effects at a surface thus calls for the cutting of that surface in the most appropriate plane. The study of figure reveals the effects of underlying three-dimensional cellular patterns on surface features and although, in relation to certain types of figure, it may not be known how their underlying structures have arisen, the relationship between these structures and their resultant surface effects are fairly clear.

8

Variability of Wood

By the variability of wood we mean the range of appearance, anatomy and chemical and physical properties to be found within the wood of trees of a given species, or in that of an individual tree. Although reaction wood (see Chapter 9) falls within this definition, its occurrence and specialized forms, coupled with the wide-ranging nature of the problems it presents and studies which have been made of them, call for separate treatment.

Variability is a different matter from the diversity of structure which distinguishes, to a greater or lesser degree, the wood of different kinds of trees, even though, as the previous pages so often show, it is frequently necessary, in considering these distinctions, to refer to their variability. Almost any description of wood must be couched in terms which admit of some variation, variation which affects wood structure at all levels of its organization. It thus extends from features such as the presence or absence of knots or resin canals, down through forms of cross-field pitting to matters such as the orientation of microfibrils or the percentage of lignin in cell walls.

In a rather different context it has often been said that no two pieces of wood, even if cut from the same tree, are exactly alike, and although this view of the matter is hardly susceptible of formal proof, it puts the matter in a nutshell; the range of grain, texture and figure seems to be truly infinite (see Chapter 7). This variability contributes in no small measure to the attractiveness of wood in its more decorative functions, for instance in articles of domestic use and ornament, in furniture and panelling; the popularity of imitation 'wood-grain' plastic finishes may be seen as oblique testimony to the aesthetic value of the varied figure of real wood.

At the same time the inherent variability of wood has other consequences of a very different kind. It presents many problems to those concerned in the conversion and utilization of timber as a structural material, because it extends also to the mechanical properties of wood, its density and the various parameters of its strength, which relate to its constructional use in situations where it may be subject to wear or heavy loads. Even when much of the natural variability (such as that due to knots, cracks and irregularities of grain) has been excluded, as in laboratory tests of small clear specimens, there still remains a considerable residue of variation; this is evident, for instance, in the tables of strength properties of timbers compiled by Lavers (1969). It is due to variation in the size and shape of wood cells and in the thickness and chemical composition of their walls. In short, variability is characteristic of wood, to a degree which would be unacceptable in man-made structural materials, and which adds greatly to the difficulties of the design of wood structures.

The variability of wood derives from its origin as a product of the growth of a living tree. Growth is an extremely complex process, subject in its rate, and the form it takes, to a multiplicity of influences, both internal and external, so that all species of organisms show some degree of variation. But the growth of the wood of a tree is not a short-term process, completed like the growth of micro-organisms in a few hours or days, or of many crop plants in a single growing season, but extends over a period of scores or even hundreds of years. In consequence the effects of month-to-month or year-to-year variation in any of the factors affecting it during any part of this extended life-span, may be found within a single individual. Effects such as those of weather, soil conditions, competition with other trees and sylvicultural management may all leave their record in the wood. More casual influences may also derive from accidents such as the fall of branches, damage from the fall of nearby trees, fire, frost, the activities of pests and so on. The age of the tree itself is also a factor in the rate and pattern of its growth, and therefore exerts a continuing influence on the nature of the wood it produces. Differences between the wood of individual trees of the same species will of course arise from causes similar to those influencing the growth of any one tree, but in addition there may be other intrinsic differences between them, such as those of genetic or ecotypic origin. In consequence, two individuals may react differently in their growth, even to similar environmental circumstances, so that the differences between trees, in the properties of their timber, are generally additional to, and greater than, those to be found within one individual. This is of course the rationale of the selection of tree seed from one provenance in preference to another, and the value and potential of tree breeding and selection as a means of increasing the quantity and improving the quality of the timber produced.

Although much of the variability of wood may be attributed with confidence to the varying conditions under which the wood has been formed, some variability is inherent in tree structure in a way substantially independent of external circumstances. It is to this which we now turn our attention.

In general, timbers are described by reference to their structure as it is found in well-grown trunks, which are, of course, the principal sources of wood. The wood of branches and roots tends however to differ from that of trunk wood, and the formal diagnostic features of the anatomy of the latter may not always be recognizable in them (Patel, 1965). In general, branch wood is commonly denser and closer-textured than trunk wood (as is evident, for instance, in knots), and has smaller elements; it also usually includes some proportion of reaction wood. Root wood, on the other hand, has been found to be generally more open in texture than trunk wood, with wider tracheids or vessels (as the case may be): see Bannan (1941), Jane (1970), Patel (1971), Manwiller (1972) and Vurdu and Bensend (1979). However, the observations of Bannan and Bindra (1970b) on white spruce (*Picea glauca*), establishing marked differences between sinker roots and surface roots in the mean lengths of their tracheids, point to significant anatomical variability within root systems. Cutler (1976) has also shown, in more general terms, that the probable extent of root wood variability is greater than is usually appreciated. The increasing use of wood fibre products and particle boards, to which branch wood (and also root wood, if it can be economically extracted) can contribute, lends added interest to observations of their structural characteristics. Manwiller estimated that in the Southern pines of America, stump wood and root wood together are equivalent in bulk to about a quarter of the merchantable timber of the tree.

Within the wood of the trunk itself there is also a range of structure, associated especially with systematic variation in the mean length of tracheids (in softwoods) or fibres (in hardwoods). This was first explored by Sanio (1872) in *Pinus sylvestris*; some of Sanio's data are reproduced in the accompanying table. Sanio concluded (*inter alia*) that at any one level in the trunk the (mean) tracheid length increases throughout the earlier growth increments until a certain length is reached, but from then onwards it remains constant in subsequent growth. Furthermore the (mean) length of the tracheids in any one growth increment increases from the base of the tree upwards, to a certain height, and then decreases. There were also observations on branch wood and root wood, showing comparable trends, which we need not consider.

Since this pioneer work numerous investigators have reported data of a broadly similar nature, and Sanio's conclusions have, in general terms, been substantially confirmed, both for softwoods and hardwoods;

the literature has been reviewed by Spurr and Hyvarinen (1954) and Dinwoodie (1961). However, variations in the pattern described by Sanio clearly occur (Bannan, 1960; Jane, 1970) and some of these are discussed by Bannan (1967a) and Philipson *et al.* (1971). The time taken to achieve maximum cell length at a given height in the trunk

Table II   Mean length of latewood tracheids in the trunk of
a 110 year-old Scots pine.
(data of Sanio, 1872, after de Bary, 1884).

Position in tree	Number of growth ring (from pith)	Mean tracheid length (mm)
Near top	1	0.78
Disc with 21 rings	14	1.74
	18	2.21
	20	2.91
	21	2.82
In the crown	1	0.80
Disc with 35 rings	15	2.60
	17	2.74
	20	2.82
	35	2.78
Trunk	1	0.95
36ft from ground	17	2.74
Disc with 72 rings	19	3.13
	31	3.69
	37	3.87
	40	4.04
	46	4.21
	72	4.21
Near ground	1	–
Disc with 105 rings	20	1.87
	29	2.48
	30	2.60
	31	2.65
	60	2.65
	80	2.69
	105	2.65

may vary considerably, even among individuals of the same species. In addition, after an apparent maximum mean length has been achieved, it is not necessarily maintained at a constant level, as Sanio described, but further changes may take place. There may be a continuing but much slower increase, or marked fluctuation, or, after an approximately constant length has been reached and maintained over a long period, a final decline may supervene as the tree passes into senescence. In softwoods, because the amount of intrusive tip-growth of the differentiating tracheids is small, this variability in tracheid length may be largely interpreted in terms of the occurrence and effects of pseudo-transverse divisions in the cambium (see Chapter 3). Mean cell length is greatly influenced by the frequency of these divisions, which also varies, and which, over an important part of its range of variation, bears an inverse relationship to the growth rate. In the main period of growth of the tree this results in a negative correlation between the rate of wood formation and the mean tracheid length, so that marked fluctuations in the width of the growth rings, such as may be caused environmentally, are accompanied by inverse variations in the tracheid length; the narrower increments have the longer tracheids. However, this does not hold for very narrow increments; the tracheid length reaches a maximum in increments of about 1–2 mm, and in narrower ones tends to fall again; this is because in the formation of these very narrow rings pseudotransverse divisions in the cambium become more frequent instead of less so. Since narrow growth increments, 0.5 mm or less in width, are characteristic of the senescent phase of growth, these relationships offer an explanation of the decline in tracheid length sometimes found in the outer parts of old trunks. In general terms, therefore, it can be said that variation in mean tracheid length at a given level in the trunk arises from changes in the balance of activity in the cambium, as between the rate of occurrence of pseudotransverse divisions on the one hand and the rate of production of new wood cells on the other. It must be added however, that there are some patterns of variation in mean tracheid length which have been described that cannot be interpreted in these terms, and other factors must be involved in them (Bannan, 1960, 1967b; Bannan and Bindra, 1970b).

In hardwoods there occur varied long-term trends in fibre length broadly similar to those which have been found in softwoods, but they arise rather differently. The evidence bearing on pseudotransverse divisions in the cells of (non-storied) hardwood cambia is very limited compared with that for softwoods (Chapter 3), so that though these divisions might be expected to influence in some degree the mean length of cambial cells and thus that of their derivative fibres, the extent of this influence must be in doubt. A much more important factor in fibre length seems to be the degree of intrusive tip-growth which ensues in the course of fibre differentiation. In hardwoods, in contrast to softwoods, this may be very considerable; fibres may be up to some 4-6 times longer than the cambial initials from which they have arisen, and variation in this factor seems likely to be the main cause of variation in fibre length. Nevertheless the end results are rather similar to those reported for softwoods (Jane, 1970).

Hardwoods with storied cambia present another picture, since pseudotransverse divisions do not occur in these cambia; their multiplicative divisions are truly radially longitudinal from the beginning. As a result, the mean length of these cambial cells, which is represented in the wood in the lengths of vessel elements and axial parenchyma strands, remains unchanged throughout the life of the tree – we need not consider, in the present context, the small cyclical changes which occur in it in the formation of interlocked grain (p. 197).

In spite of the constant (and relatively short) length of the cambial cells, the mean lengths of derivative fibres may be up to several times greater than that of the cambial cells. The maximum length may be achieved as early as the second growth increment, with no further continuing upward trend, as was shown by Chalk *et al.* (1955) in muninga (*Pterocarpus angolensis*) and danta (*Nesogordonia papaverifera*). In robinia, however, in contrast, mean fibre length shows a continuing increase in the first 20–40 years of the life of the tree, in a way similar to that characteristic of non-storied woods, eventually reaching a length about six times that of the cambial cells (Hejnowicz and Hejnowicz, 1959; Rao, 1959). In trees such as these, with storied cambia, increasing fibre length must be wholly due to the intrusive tip-growth of these cells during their differentiation.

The wood of the early years of the growth of the trunk of a tree, besides being characterized by relatively short cells, exhibits also other differences from the wood of later growth. The growth increments are commonly wider, and in softwoods may contain less abundant and less well differentiated latewood. In hardwoods the relative proportions and patterns of distribution of the various types of wood cell may differ from those characteristic of later growth; for instance, in ring-porous trees a pore ring may not be formed in their early years (Jane, 1970). Wood with these characteristics is known as juvenile wood or core wood (in distinction from the later-formed mature wood), and may not be reliably usable in the identification of an unknown timber. The period of formation of juvenile wood is variable; it may extend for as long as the first 15–25 growth increments, grading then into mature wood; the change is not an abrupt one. Compared with mature wood the density of juvenile wood is lower, so its strength properties are inferior (Lavers, 1969), and since its fibres are shorter than those of mature wood the microfibrillar helices in their cell walls will tend to be flatter (Chapter 6), so tending also to bring about a lower modulus of elasticity (Cowdrey and Preston, 1965, 1966; Cave, 1968). In some trees juvenile wood is thus unable to sustain the axial compressive loads imposed upon it by the growth stresses which develop progressively in growing trunks (Chapter 6), and in mature specimens these may prove sufficient to

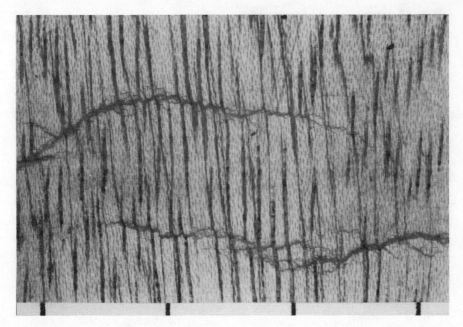

Fig. 113. A piece of utile (*Entandrophragma utile*) containing brittleheart. The irregular dark lines lying across the grain are regions of serious compression failure of the fibres. (The scale is in cm).

cause its partial breakdown. This gives rise to the defect termed brittleheart (also known as spongy heart and punky heart), a condition of the juvenile wood of some tropical trees. Brittleheart tends when bent to yield with a short brash fracture, resembling that of rotten wood, and when sawn across the fibres are broken rather than cut by the saw. The wood may have a somewhat 'carroty' character; it is structurally unreliable and thus unsuitable for use in load-bearing situations. Brittleheart may be recognized on planed surfaces by the presence of fine, somewhat irregular lines extending across the grain, approximately at right-angles to it, which are visible to the unaided eye (Fig. 113); these are lines of weakness and probable lines of further failure under load. Brittleheart tends to develop especially in certain tropical trees which grow vigorously to a large size, such as African mahogany, obeche, agba and seraya among others, (Dinwoodie, 1970); the extent of its occurrence in *Eucalyptus robusta* has been described by Skolmen (1973). Brittleheart can be detected, at an early stage in its development, in the form of microscopic slip-planes and compression failures in the walls of individual fibre cells (see Chapter 6).

Internal growth stresses, besides causing brittleheart, may also be a cause (though not the only one) of other forms of timber breakdown, in particular, splits which radiate from the centre of the trunk (star shakes) and circular splits following the contour of growth increments (ring shakes). These may sometimes develop in the course of the conversion of a trunk with high internal stresses, which are relieved, as it is cut up, by dimensional changes within the wood.

Sanio's measurements of tracheid length in Scots pine, quoted above, refer specifically to the latewood, suggesting perhaps that elsewhere in the growth ring they might be different. This is in fact so; it is well-established that at a given level in the trunk there are systematic fluctuations in tracheid length within each growth increment. In hardwoods also, there are similar seasonal variations in the mean fibre length. Among the timbers which have been studied in this respect it has been found that commonly the shortest tracheids or fibres occur in the earlywood; the mean length increases during the growing period to a maximum at or about the end of the season's growth, and then falls steeply to the low level characteristic of the earlywood of the following year (Bissett and Dadswell, 1950, and Fig. 114). Other patterns of

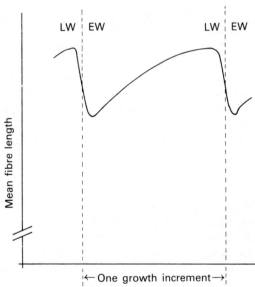

Fig. 114. A generalized diagram showing a common pattern of seasonal variation in fibre length. EW, earlywood; LW, latewood; see text.

LW ¦ EW   LW ¦ EW

Mean fibre length

¦← One growth increment →¦

cyclic change also occur; in some hardwoods the maximum fibre length is reached in the middle of the growth increment, rather than at its end. Another notable exception to the general statement made above was found by Dinwoodie (1963), in an extensive study of Sitka spruce wood drawn from trees of a wide range of age and provenance. In this species the minimum mean tracheid length coincides with the transition from earlywood to latewood, from which there is a steep rise to the maximum at the end of the season's growth. A similar cycle, in which the minimum mean fibre length occurs about the middle of the growth increment, was also found, in *Eucalyptus regnans*, by Bissett and Dadswell (1949). The observed range of variation in mean fibre length extends up to about 20% in softwoods, and up to nearly 200% in hardwoods, though the latter figure appears to be exceptional; most of the observations fall in the range 15–80%. In hardwoods without distinct growth rings, cyclic changes in mean fibre length are very small, 5% or less.

The seasonal cyclic variation in the mean length of softwood tracheids is attributable to the uneven seasonal timing of pseudotransverse divisions in the cambium. In the species in which these occur predominantly at or near the end of the growing season (Bannan, 1960, 1967a) a greater than average proportion of the elements of the earlywood of the following year will be derivatives of cambial cells which have recently undergone pseudo-transverse division, and will therefore be of less than average length; hence the minimum mean tracheid length occurring at this time. As the season advances however, and these cambial cells gradually extend to their full length, the mean length of their derivatives will also increase. The frequencies of pseudo-transverse divisions reported by Bannan (1970) would seem to be sufficient to account in this way for the magnitude of the seasonal fluctuations in tracheid length which have been observed. In Sitka spruce, where the minimum mean tracheid length is delayed until about the middle of the growth increment, it seems likely that this is a consequence of the timing of the pseudo-transverse divisions being less well synchronised than Bannan found in some other softwoods.

The limited evidence bearing on the occurrence of pseudo-transverse divisions in the cambia of hardwoods suggests that they may also tend mostly to occur late in the growing season (Evert, 1961, 1963), and might be expected therefore to exert a cyclic influence on fibre length. However, some at least of the seasonal variation of fibre length in hardwoods which have been reported is too large to have arisen entirely in this way; it must derive also, at least in part, and probably to a major extent, from cyclic seasonal variation in the tip-growth of the fibres. It is noteworthy, in this respect, that seasonal fluctuations in fibre length may also occur in timbers with storied cambia (Chalk *et al.*, 1955; Hejnowicz and Hejnowicz, 1959; Rao, 1959). The minimum fibre length has been found to occur in the earlywood, increasing by some 50–200% to a maximum in the middle of latewood, and then declining steeply at the end of the growing season.

In short, therefore, wide variation in fibre length may develop as a consequence of variation either in the length of cambial initials, or in the extent of the tip-growth of the fibres in the course of their differentiation. These varied patterns of systematic variation in fibre length are not of course evident to the unaided eye; indeed the establishment of their existence has called for a great deal of repetitive and rigorous microscopic study. Though principally perhaps of botanical rather than technological interest, as examples of the many 'gradients' of structure to be found in plants, attention must nonetheless be given to them by those concerned with the quality of wood. Fibre length is an important parameter in the assessment of wood quality, so that, if valid comparisons and choices are to be made among trees, the nature of the variability to which fibre length is liable, within each individual, cannot be ignored.

Another type of inherent variability of the wood within an individual tree is however, in most instances, identifiable by visual inspection; this is the change from sapwood to heartwood. The usually darker heartwood stands out more or less clearly; in some species in which it is not pigmented it may be revealed by chemical tests (Stalker, 1971; Cummins, 1972; Behr, 1974). Tests of this kind have been devised because even though the heartwood may not be immediately visibly distinct from the sapwood, it may be more desirable commercially, on account, for instance, of its lower water content or lesser susceptibility to decay.

The development of sapwood into heartwood, which takes place in a relatively narrow transitional zone, perhaps only the width of one or two growth increments, involves a number of co-ordinated changes (Chattaway, 1952). In softwoods the bordered (inter-tracheid) pits become aspirated, as described in Chapter 4; Harris (1954), working with *Pinus radiata*, has shown how the proportion of aspirated pits increases as the sapwood tracheids become older and pass into the heartwood. Aspiration of the pits of hardwood vessels has also been reported (Thomas, 1972), though how widespread this may be seems to be an open question. The storage starch of axial and ray parenchyma is mobilized and disappears as (presumably) it is utilized as a substrate in the synthesis of the considerable variety of other extraneous substances characteristic of heartwood (see Chapter 6). As the protoplasts of the parenchyma cells break down and disappear, these substances become deposited on the cell walls and in the pit cavities of the wood cells, or even in their lumens; Fengel (1970) has described these changes as they appear at the electron-microscopical level. Among the products of these varied syntheses, resins and gums commonly form plugs in tracheids (Fig. 17) or vessels, and a variety of other materials, besides causing a general darkening of the wood, encrust pit membranes and impregnate the sub-microscopic spaces in cell walls (Hillis, 1968a, 1971). Not only do these spaces become blocked,but some encrusting substances tend also to make the cell wall surfaces hydrophobic (Bailey and Preston, 1969). The general effect of these changes is thus greatly to reduce the permeability of the wood to water, and the heartwood, together with the inner sapwood, in which these changes begin, is no longer concerned in the upward transport of water to the leaves. In many softwoods the heartwood becomes markedly drier than the sapwood, and levels of heartwood moisture content not greatly above the fibre saturation point have been recorded. Hardwoods are more variable in this respect; the moisture content of the heartwood in the standing tree may be much the same as in the sapwood, or in some tree species, as for example in the hickories (*Carya* spp.), it may be markedly higher (Smith and Goebel, 1952; Kozlowski, 1971).

Logs with moist heartwood are of course heavier than in the air-dry state, and tend to sink in water, which led to the adoption in forestry practice in Burma of ensuring the partial drying of teak logs by girdling the trees a few years before their intended felling. The girdling or ringing of a tree, in the usual sense of these terms, refers to the removal of all the tissues external to the wood from a complete band around the base of the trunk. This cuts off the root system from the downward flow of nutrients in the phloem, and results in the slow death of the whole tree. However, if the girdling is not done very carefully, remnants of the cambium left on the surface of the wood may regenerate sufficiently to heal the wound to some extent, and in part, at least, to restore a phloem connection across it; the girdling will then prove ineffective. In the girdling of teak, therefore, a more reliable practice, of cutting deeper into the trunk and removing a band of the sapwood as well as of the bark, was adopted. In still standing but dying trees, which have been treated in this way, the heartwood dries out, with the result that when they are felled the logs can be transported by flotation down a river. The wood of such trees was in effect being partially seasoned as it stood, in an uncontrolled way, and in consequence may be abnormally prone to develop heartshakes (Noel, 1970).

The loss of starch from heartwood renders it less attractive to fungi and insects, and furthermore some of its newly synthesized extractives are toxic to decay organisms, and are largely responsible for its enhanced durability. For example, the resistance to decay of the heartwood of oak and sweet chestnut is attributable to the high tannin content of these timbers (which may reach 9%), and the durability of Western red cedar (*Thuja plicata*) is due to a group of substances known as thujaplicins. These are very potent anti-fungal agents; tested in the laboratory against wood-rotting fungi growing in culture they have been found to be inhibitory at concentrations of 0.001–0.002%. In these tests they were about one hundred times more effective than phenol, and nearly as good as sodium pentachlorphenate, a commercial wood preservative (Rennerfelt, 1948; Roff and Whittaker, 1959). In situations in which the wood is subject to long-continued leaching by rain-water the thujaplicins may however be eventually leached out, and rot may then supervene (Johnson and Cserjesi, 1980). The work of Yatagai and Takahashi (1980), concerned with 70 species of tropical timbers of South-East Asia, also emphasizes, in a more general way, the import-ance of extractives in decay resistance. They found a broadly inverse relationship between the total concentrations of extractives in the heart-woods of the various timbers, and the rates at which, in laboratory tests, samples of sawdust prepared from them were consumed by wood-rotting fungi.

In many hardwoods the synthesis of extractives associated with heart-wood formation is accompanied by further growth of a specialized kind. In the transition zone between sapwood and heartwood, living cells of axial and ray parenchyma which are adjacent to a vessel may grow out through the intervening pits into the vessel cavity, forming structures known as tyloses (singular, tylosis). In their early growth these are thin-walled, rounded, bladder-like extensions of the parenchyma cells, (Fig. 115), but as they continue to enlarge within the vessel they press against

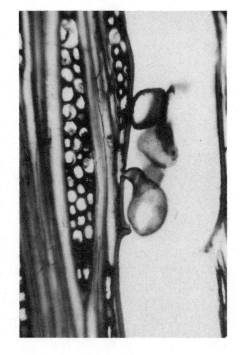

Fig. 115. Queensland walnut (*Endiandra palmerstonii*). T.L.S. × 200. Incompletely formed tyloses arising from ray parenchyma. The rim of a perforation plate can be seen just below the lower tylosis.

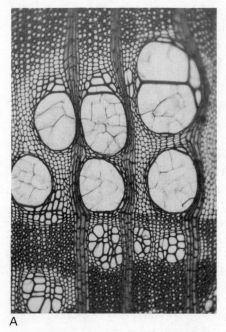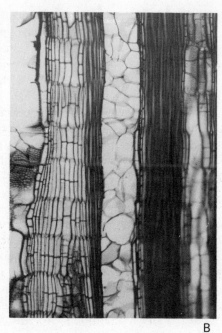

A

B

Fig. 116. Robinia (*Robinia pseudoacacia*). Heartwood, *A*, T.S., *B*, R.L.S., × 65. The vessels are filled with thin-walled tyloses. Note also in *B* the storied strands of axial parenchyma. Strands of one, two and four cells can be seen.

each other and become mutually compressed into irregular more or less prismatic shapes (Fig. 116). From each parent parenchyma cell the nucleus may pass through the pit aperture into a tylosis, pit-pairs are formed in the double walls between the protoplasts of contiguous tyloses, and the walls become thickened and lignified. In some species the thickening may be very marked, so that the tyloses resemble stone cells. Thus the vessel cavity may become filled with a close-packed, apparently parenchymatous or sclerotic mass of cells, blocking it completely. In this way tyloses contribute to the general reduction of permeability of the heartwood, and confer added resistance to the spread of fungal hyphae; resistance to decay is thus enhanced. Some trees which do not regularly exhibit tyloses will produce them locally in response to mechanical damage or severe fungal infection, and of the timbers listed as 'very durable' by the Forest Products Research Laboratory (1969b) nearly half have tyloses, while among the 'perishable' timbers the proportion is only about one-seventh.

The fact that some tree species regularly have tyloses, while others do not, has been linked with differences in the size of their vessel-to-ray pitting. Chattaway (1949), in a survey of some 1100 genera, concluded that tyloses are formed only in timbers in which these pits are relatively large, of diameter greater than 8–10μm, while in timbers in which the pits are smaller than this tyloses are not formed, but resinous or gummy materials are secreted into the vessel cavities. Chattaway also concluded that, among the timbers she studied, tyloses grow only from ray parenchyma cells and only very rarely indeed from axial parenchyma. She was probably mistaken in this; both types of parenchyma are commonly involved in tylosis formation (Esau, 1965a). In vessels which are packed with fully-grown, mature tyloses it is extremely difficult, if not impossible, in ordinary wood sections, to determine where the tyloses have originated. Critical observation of the positions of rays in relation to a vessel may however indicate fairly clearly that some at least of the tyloses in the vessel cannot have originated from ray cells, and must therefore have grown from xylem parenchyma (see also Fig. 117A).

The formation of a tylosis, as it is seen by ordinary light microscopy, may seem to involve the growth in area of the pit membrane lying between the protoplast of a ray or axial parenchyma cell and the cavity of an adjacent vessel, so that the membrane expands into the vessel cavity under the influence of the turgor pressure of the parenchyma cell on its other side. Tylosis formation used to be described in these terms, but electron microscopy has revealed a more complex situation.

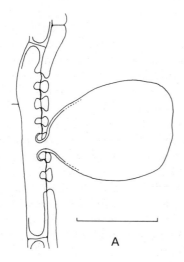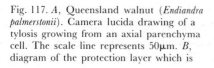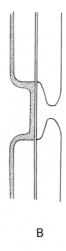

A   B

Fig. 117. A, Queensland walnut (*Endiandra palmerstonii*). Camera lucida drawing of a tylosis growing from an axial parenchyma cell. The scale line represents 50μm. B, diagram of the protection layer which is laid down in ray and axial parenchyma cells prior to tylosis formation. Note the simple pit in the parenchyma cell (left) and the bordered pit in the vessel (right).

In parenchyma cells adjacent to vessels there is an extra layer in the cell wall, deposited on its inner side, next to the protoplast, which has been termed the protection (or protective) layer (Schmid, 1965). This layer overlies the pit membranes (in regions of the cell wall away from the pits it may be less well developed) and it is from this layer that the tylosis develops (Fig. 117B). Traumatic tyloses may be experimentally induced in the sapwood of oaks by bringing cut logs into the laboratory in the growing season (when tyloses may appear in a matter of hours) and the course of this tylosis growth has been studied in *Quercus alba* by Meyer (1967) and Meyer and Côté (1968), and in *Q. rubra* by Murmanis (1975). The pit membrane becomes degraded and ruptured as the protective layer pushes through it and expands to form the tylosis, so that the wall of the latter is an extension of the inner protective layer of the parenchyma cell, not of the original pit membrane. An interesting point arises here in that while both of these species readily produce traumatic tyloses in this way, in *Q. alba*, like other white oaks, abundant tyloses are normally present in the heartwood, but in *Q. rubra*, a red oak, if they are present at all, they are normally no more than sparse. Tylosis development in *Eucalyptus* spp. follows an essentially similar course, with the added feature that the pits in *Eucalyptus* are vestured, and in a pit in which a tylosis is to grow the vestures are first dissolved and disappear. In sclerotic tyloses their walls are multi-layered and each layer comprises numerous finer lamellae of microfibrils (Foster, 1967).

The effective blocking of vessels by tyloses may be readily demonstrated in oak wood by attempting to blow into water through straight-grained sticks of the air-dry heartwood. These may conveniently be 30–50 cm in length and about a square centimetre in cross-section. In the case of *Q. alba* and other white oaks (these include the English species) air will not pass through the wood. In contrast, if the wood is *Q. rubra* or another of the red oaks, bubbles of air will appear at the immersed end. Dry ashwood similarly allows the passage of an air stream, as it does not contain tyloses, or if these are present they are only poorly developed.

Although tyloses are typically to be found in vessel cavities, they may also be formed in other situations. They have been reported in the fibre tracheids of members of the Magnoliaceae (Gottwald, 1972), and also in tracheids of certain *Pinus* spp. Here they have been found growing from ray parenchyma, in a traumatic response to chemical injury inflicted on the trees to encourage the production of resin (Peters, 1974). Structures of similar origin to tyloses, known as tylosoids, sometimes develop from parenchyma cells into intercellular spaces, as is well-known in the resin canals of some conifers. Tylosoids have also been reported in resin canals of red meranti (*Shorea* spp.) (Bamber,

1976).

Blockage of vessels by tyloses is made use of in the choice of wood for the manufacture of barrels which are required to be water-tight, that is, for 'tight cooperage'. Although beer barrels, once ubiquitous, have now been largely replaced by aluminium containers, wooden barrels are still used for the maturing of wines and spirits. These barrels are commonly made of oak, but one of the white oaks must be used. The red oaks, lacking well-developed tyloses, are unsuitable for tight cooperage on account of their greater porosity.

The various characteristic features of heartwood, which reduce its permeability to air and moisture – the aspiration of pits, impregnation of cell walls, incrustation of pit membranes and the formation of tyloses or gum plugs in vessels – are of course correspondingly limiting in relation to the penetrability of the wood by preservatives. In timbers of which the heartwood is exceptionally durable this may be a matter of no great significance, but most of the wood in use in situations in which it is exposed to degradation by decay or insect attack requires artificial preservation, and problems of penetrability are a major factor in achieving this. The preservation of timber is a complex and highly technical matter, both in the choice of the preservative and the manner of its application; see for instance Findlay (1962, 1975), Hunt and Garratt (1967) and Kollmann and Côte (1968).

Turning now to variation in wood which is primarily a result of environmental influences, the principal feature is of course variation in the growth rate of the tree, and especially in the width of the annual growth increments. Within a growth increment the basic features of earlywood and latewood are, in the main, inherently characteristic of the kind of tree, but variation in the growth rate may give rise to variation in the relative proportions of earlywood and latewood, and also in the diameter of their cells and in the thickness of their cell walls. Altogether, therefore, environmental influences are likely to lead to variation not only in the quantity of wood produced, but also in its quality, in such respects as its density, strength and texture.

The physiology of environmentally induced variation in wood formation is very complex; although it has been very extensively studied it is nevertheless still incompletely understood. The difficulties of these investigations are many, but conspicuous among them is the dependence of cambial activity and wood cell differentiation on the growth and well-being, in the widest terms, of the crown of the tree. This results in the susceptibility of wood formation to a great range of environmental influences, which are liable to interact in various ways, so that their effects tend to defy analysis. Accounts of these problems have been given by Kozlowski (1971), Kramer and Kozlowski (1979) and Denne and Dodd (1981), among others. The complexities are exemplified in a simple way in the following paragraphs.

As we have indicated briefly in Chapter 2, increment variation may be largely interpreted in terms of the effects of water stress to which the tree is subject; that is, basically, the degree to which its living cells may be less than fully turgid, and the length of time for which this condition prevails. Water stress is essentially a consequence of an excess of the transpirational loss of water from the leaves (dependent on the evaporating power of the atmosphere and the degree of stomatal opening) over the uptake of water by the roots (limited perhaps by the spread of the root system, competition with the roots of nearby trees, and the available water in the surrounding soil). Water stress, though seemingly a simple concept, may thus be dependent on a great variety of factors – sunshine, temperature, wind-speed, atmospheric humidity, rain-fall, soil structure and drainage – which has the consequence that water stress may be generated by a variety of causes. Moreover these causes may operate for varied periods of time, and so interact in different ways at different times in the growing season. In summer a diurnal cycle in which some degree of water stress develops during the day, but from which more or less complete recovery is made at night, is a commonplace and normal circumstance; when however the water deficit is not made good in this way, but extends and deepens over a longer period, it may become a critical factor in wood formation. Water stress in the leaves may restrict stomatal opening and so reduce the rate of photosynthesis, which provides the food substances necessary for the growth of wood, and this generally reduced level of physiological activity may also curtail the production and downward transport of the growth-regulatory substances which have a function in the maintenance and control of cambial activity and in the differentiation of its products, as for instance in the transition from earlywood to latewood formation. Water stress may also act directly on the cambial zone itself, to reduce the capacity of its cells for enlargement and cell division, or to interrupt or even to terminate its activity and force it into abnormally early dormancy.

The effects of water stress may thus operate in diverse ways; they may even, through their influence on winter bud formation, carry over from one growing season to the succeeding one. In addition the various factors of the environment which contribute to water stress may also have their own more individual influences on wood formation in circumstances in which water stress is not a factor. Temperature, for instance, affects the whole physiology of plants, so that an unusually warm spring may bring forward the beginning of cambial activity, while an unusually warm summer may be contributory to the water stress that curtails it. Again, wind affects trees and their wood in ways not related solely to rates of transpiration, and a light, extremely freely draining soil may be deficient in mineral nutrients as well as being a poor source of moisture. Competition between trees too, though in some circumstances relating to the limited water supply available to their roots, is also largely a consequence of the mutual shading of their crowns, inducing suppression of buds, reduced extension growth and a lower level of photosynthetic activity.

The consequential effects on the wood may be illustrated by reference to plantation trees, growing in an even-aged stand. In their early years, while they are small, they are far enough apart, in relation to their size, to be largely unaffected by their neighbours, and make rapid growth. As they grow, however, they increase in size and spread, and mutual shading tends to have an increasing influence, resulting in a continuing check to photosynthetic activity and wood formation, and hence in narrower growth increments. If the plantation is then thinned, and especially if fertilizer is applied at that stage, the remaining trees will be largely released from their mutual competition and much wider growth increments are likely to follow. Spurr (1979) illustrates an example of this kind of response. In a stand of trees of mixed age the larger, dominant trees may virtually completely suppress the growth of smaller trees, so that growth increments in their wood, which have been initiated in their crowns, may fail to extend downwards to the lower part of their trunks.

In ring-porous hardwoods, such as oak and ash, the effect of slow growth falls largely on the latewood. The earlywood is comparatively little affected, but the latewood may be greatly curtailed; this will often be an effect of summer water stress. The narrow growth increments of such slow-grown wood thus contain a relatively high proportion of early wood, with its large thin-walled vessels, and a relatively low proportion of the mainly thick-walled, fibrous latewood (Figs. 118 and 119). It thus contains less wood substance per unit volume, and is less dense than the wood of faster-grown trees and therefore less strong. At the same time it is more easily worked, so that slow-grown oak may be preferable for highly detailed cabinet work, while that of fast-grown trees is more suited to constructional uses. There are, however, limits to this generalization relating density to growth rate, in that very fast-grown oak may have abnormally thin-walled or only slightly lignified latewood, and so may be of lower than usual density and strength. The maximum strength of oak wood has been estimated as being developed in timber with 6 to 16 rings per 25 mm; slow-grown oak, in contrast, may have up to about 40 rings per 25 mm. Similar considerations apply to ash, in which the strongest timber has 6–10 rings per 25 mm, though wider limits of 4-25 rings per 25 mm have been regarded as being generally acceptable (B.R.E. (PRL), 1972a). In diffuse-porous hardwoods there is no corresponding well-defined relationship between

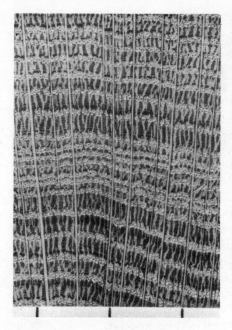

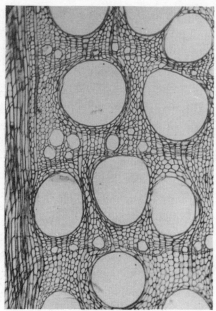

Fig. 118. A transverse surface of European oak (*Quercus* sp.). The considerable variation in the growth rate, shown by variation in the width of the growth increments, can be seen to be due entirely to variation in the amount of latewood. (The scale is in cm).

Fig. 119. Very slow-grown oak (*Quercus* sp.), T.S., × 65. Parts of four growth increments are shown; the latewood zones especially are exremely narrow.

the rate of growth and the density and strength of the timber.

Softwoods differ markedly from ring-porous hardwoods in their structural responses to variation in growth rate; over the major part of the range, the wider the growth increments the higher tends to be the proportion of earlywood. This is a result, under conditions favourable to fast growth, of a delayed transition to the formation of latewood. For this reason fast-grown timber is in general, less dense than slow-grown; furthermore, as we have already seen (p. 202), its tracheids tend to be shorter, and therefore (p. 157) are likely to have flatter microfibrillar helices in their cell walls. All these factors tend to lower its quality.

Differences of this kind may also develop as between the opposite sides of a trunk, the growth rings being wider and the elements being shorter on the sunny side of the tree, i.e. on the South side in the Northern hemisphere and the North side in the Southern hemisphere (Liese and Dadswell, 1959). Similar differences, as between the East and West sides of trees, have been attributed to the influence of pre-vailing Westerly winds, giving rise to wider rings and shorter elements on the East sides (Bannan and Bindra, 1970a).

The usual inverse relationship which has been found in softwoods, between ring width and density, which is characteristic of the greater part of these ranges of variability, does not however hold for very narrow growth rings. In such rings the density of the wood tends to fall, rather than to rise further, so that a maximum value is attained at some intermediate rate of growth. In a number of softwood species which have been studied, this corresponds to a ring width in the region of about 1–2 mm (Kollmann and Côté, 1968), which is the basis for the preference, in softwood to be used for structural purposes, for ring widths falling in the range of 6–20 per 25 mm. A minimum proportion of latewood in the growth rings may also be specified, since the cor-relation between density and proportion of latewood is closer than between density and ring width.

Another kind of variation in wood structure associated with dif-ferences in growth rate concerns the development of rays. In fast-grown timber the rays tend to become more numerous, wider, or higher, than in slow-grown wood; there are marked increases in the total number of ray cells per unit tangential area of the wood. Varying differences of this nature have been described, both in softwoods (Bannan, 1954; Gregory and Romberger, 1975) and in hardwoods (White and Robards, 1966; Carmi et al., 1972; Gregory, 1977). As White and Robards point out, these differences urge caution in the use of numerical data pertaining to the rays for the purpose of timber identification.

In contrast with these variations in wood structure which are broadly related to its growth physiology, environmental influences which cause damage to the tree may induce less generalized effects on the wood, of a traumatic and accidental nature.

In softwoods, as we have seen (Chapter 4), resin canals of traumatic origin may be formed in the timber of a number of genera which do not otherwise develop them, as in *Abies, Cedrus* and *Sequoia* (Fig. 120A) or as an additional feature, often of characteristic form and distribution, in those that do, such as *Pinus* and *Pseudotsuga*. It may be added here, in parenthesis, that traumatically increased resin secretion is not solely a matter of the activity of the epithelia of resin canals. The use of paraquat (an extremely toxic herbicide) as a stimulus to resin pro-duction in American Southern pines, induces a large increase in the resin content of the wood, which comes principally from ray paren-chyma (Roberts and Peters, 1977; Miniutti, 1977).

Under natural conditions, in *Pseudotsuga* and *Pinus*, severe damage to the tree, probably usually caused by wind, leads to the development of internal shakes or cracks in the wood, which often follow the contours

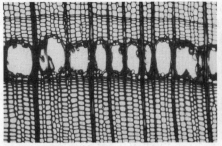

A   B

Fig. 120. Traumatic ducts; *A, Cedrus* sp.,
T.S. × 41, showing a tangential row of
traumatic resin canals; *B, Lovoa
trichilioides*, T.S. × 41, showing a
tangential row of gum ducts. These are
generally considered to be traumatic,
though they are of very frequent
occurrence in the timber.

of a growth ring (ring shakes). Resinous substances may accumulate in these spaces, which are then known as pitch pockets; these may occasionally reach a large size. The use of this distinctive term for them emphasizes the fact that their contents are chemically different from the normal resin of the resin canals. An analogous situation is to be found in some *Eucalyptus* spp. in which internal shakes become filled with a red or reddish-brown secretion known as kino, again quite different from the extractives present in undamaged wood (Hillis, 1971).

In many other hardwoods comparable variation occurs in the production of gummy or resinous extractives, which are often of traumatic origin. For example, in some other *Eucalyptus* spp. tangential lines of cavities or pockets, which contain gums or resins, may be seen in transverse sections of the wood; they are known as gum galls. Their arrangement thus recalls that of traumatic resin canals in a number of softwoods. In agba (*Gossweilerodendron balsamiferum*) the gum ducts which are normally present in the wood may be accompanied by accumulations of gum in cracks in the timber, and in African walnut (*Lovoa trichilioides*) gum galls are almost always present. They are, however, variable in number, and are usually considered to be traumatic in origin. They appear in transverse sections as tangential lines of cavities with dark-coloured contents, and because their arrangement thus tends to follow that of the growth rings, they show on the longitudinal surfaces of converted timber in patterns similar to those of the growth ring figure. They thus contribute an additional decorative feature to the wood (Fig. 120*B*).

In many other timbers, such as species of *Dipterocarpus* and *Shorea* and other genera of the Dipterocarpaceae, internal shakes become filled with pale-coloured chalk-like material (mainly calcium phosphate and carbonate), and similarly in iroko (*Chlorophora excelsa* and *C. regia*) large

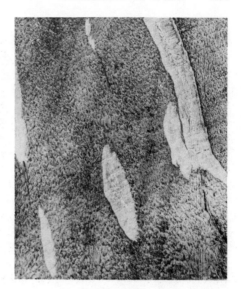

Fig. 121. Iroko (*Chlorophora excelsa*); A sawn surface, showing cavities filled with 'stone'. About 1/3 natural size.

accumulations of 'stone' may be formed. Such deposits markedly affect the workability of the timber, and may blunt or damage tools (Fig. 121).

A different type of traumatically induced variation arises from localized damage to the cambium, such as may result from insect or fungal attack. Bird's eye figure (p. 187), though of uncertain origin, may well be a consequence of injury of this kind. Another leads to the formation in the wood of what are termed pith-flecks, though these (it need hardly perhaps be emphasized) have no connection with the pith of the tree; they are parenchymatous masses produced in response to attack by beetles of the genus *Agromyza*. The females lay their eggs in the bark, and the larvae, feeding in the cambial zone, produce numerous cavities in it, which are mainly axially orientated. These cavities subsequently become filled with parenchyma, which is produced by ray tissue proliferating into them, and, as the stem continues to thicken, the masses of parenchyma so formed, dark in colour and large enough to be visible to the unaided eye, become embedded in the wood. When the timber is converted they appear on longitudinal surfaces as dark streaks and on transverse surfaces as more or less elliptical patches. They are not uncommon in butt logs of some even-textured hardwoods, for example alder, birch and some species of maple.

More generalized injury to the cambium, especially in softwoods, may arise from freezing during exceptionally cold winters. Resumption of growth after frost damage of this kind is marked initially by the formation of a narrow ring of abnormal wood, containing mis-shapen

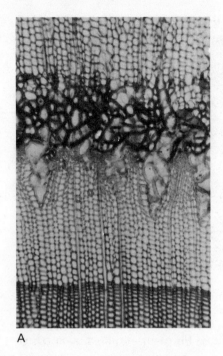

A

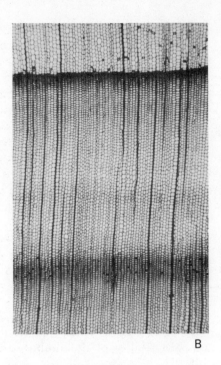

B

Fig. 122. A, *Chamaecyparis* sp., T.S. × 85, showing a frost ring. Wood formation generally has been temporarily disorganized; some of the ray cells are distorted and enlarged. Note the normal growth-ring boundary lower down in the figure.

B, *Thuja plicata*, T.S. × 33, showing a false growth ring near the bottom of the figure, which may be compared with a normal growth-ring boundary higher up. The scattered cells with dark contents are resin cells (i.e. axial parenchyma).

tracheids and ray cells and an unusually high proportion of paren- chyma, termed a frost-ring (Glock *et al.*, 1960; Glerum and Farrar, 1966). This remains as a permanent feature of the wood and a marker of the occurrence of a severe winter (Fig. 122A). A less damaging temporary check in the growth rate during the growing season, caused for instance by drought, may lead to the premature temporary formation of tracheids somewhat resembling those of the latewood. The production of mid-season tracheids may then be resumed before the normal tran- sition to latewood supervenes, so that a false growth ring is formed (Fig. 122B).

In this chapter we have drawn attention to certain major types of variation in the anatomy of wood which have been widely studied, and which, together with the specialized forms of variation characteristic of reaction wood (see Chapter 9), emphasize how diverse are the causes and nature of variation itself. It is convenient to attribute some aspects of it to inherent characteristics of the tree, and others to environmental influences, as we have done, but of course this distinction is not entirely valid; genetic and environmental factors interact in their ultimate effects.

The long-term trends of variation (best known in relation to soft-woods) which can only be described in terms of mean values (as for instance of fibre length, and its relationships to growth rate and mic-rofibril angle) are blurred by what might be termed a general back-ground of narrower-band variation of an apparently unsystematic and random nature. While short-lived fluctuations in environmental influ-ences must play a part in this, it seems likely that a lot of it may well be truly random and accidental in nature, having its origins in the manner in which the cambial cylinder increases in girth and gives rise to increasing numbers of wood cells. At the principal stages in these processes — in the occurrence of pseudotransverse divisions (indi-vidually scattered but much more numerous than is necessary); in the initiation and termination of similarly scattered (and ultimately mostly redundant) files of wood cells, and in the influence of these events on the space available to adjacent surviving cells — there can hardly be other than a significant random and probably competitive element. The apparently endless variety of the shapes and inter-relationships of wood cells, the sort of small-scale variation that is familiar to every wood microscopist, points in this direction. In short, the observed variability of wood, though attributable in broad terms to genetic and environ-mental factors, is in part a product also of the accidents of internal competition in the survival and growth of its constituent elements.

9

Reaction Wood: its Structure, Properties and Functions

Reaction wood is the term applied to certain types of 'abnormal' wood which are characteristically present in branches and leaning trunks (B.R.E. (PRL), 1972b). The description 'abnormal', though a convenient one, is not wholly appropriate, because the presence of reaction wood in these positions is entirely normal. Such wood is abnormal only in the sense that it differs markedly, in its anatomical structure and chemical and physical properties, from the wood of well-grown vertical trunks, which, by convention, is regarded as the norm. Since its properties are inferior, from the timber-user's point of view, to those of normal wood, its presence in timber is regarded as a defect, but this view of it should not obscure the fact that botanically it has an important natural function in the life of the tree. It influences, by its action, the orientation of the trunk and branches, and so, in general terms, has a regulatory effect on the form of the tree.

A branch or leaning trunk may be considered, in simple terms, as a beam supported at one end. It thus tends to droop under its own weight, a tendency which puts the lower side under compression and the upper side in tension; a saw cut made into a branch from the upper side tends to gape as the saw bites deeper into the wood, while one made into the lower side tends to close up, and the saw soon binds. In short, it may be said that a branch or leaning trunk has an (upper) tension side and a (lower) compression side.

Softwoods and hardwoods differ fundamentally in the nature of the reaction wood which they produce and in the positions in which it is formed. In softwoods (conifers) it is usually found on the compression side, and in hardwoods (dicotyledons) on the tension side; thus these two contrasting types of reaction wood are known as compression wood and tension wood respectively. These terms are used, however, to

222

describe wood showing certain characteristic features of structure; they do not mean that either compression or tension, as such, is necessarily a prime cause of the formation of these structural variations. At the same time, compression wood, on the lower side of a leaning trunk, is commonly found to be under compression, and its action may be considered, in simple terms, as tending to 'push' the trunk into a more vertical state. Correspondingly, tension wood, on the upper side, is commonly under tension, and its action may be visualized as tending to 'pull' the trunk more nearly vertical.

The literature relating to the formation and structure of compression wood has been extensively reviewed by Westing (1965, 1968), and that relating to tension wood by Hughes (1965). Shorter accounts of both types of reaction wood, written from rather different points of view, have been given by White (1965), Robards (1969), Scurfield (1973) and Wilson and Archer (1977). Marked production of reaction wood of both kinds involves variation from the normal throughout the sequential processes of the initiation, growth and differentiation of wood cells. Firstly, cambial activity is enhanced so that significantly more cells are produced, and secondly, these cells, considered individually, differentiate into mature forms which are recognizably and characteristically different from those of normal wood. The differences are, however, not necessarily sharply defined; a continuous range of form and structure, between normal wood and well-developed reaction wood, can often be seen. Nevertheless, reaction wood, if distinct at all, can be identified in a log, or in converted timber, without reference to knowledge of the position in the tree in which it grew.

The first of the two aspects of reaction wood formation, its production by increased cell division in the cambial zone, has the consequence that when it occurs in softwoods the growth increments are much wider on the lower side of the trunk or branch, and the pith, the morphological centre, appears displaced upwards. Correspondingly, in hardwoods

Fig. 123. Diagrams of cross-sections of branches, showing the usual form of eccentric growth associated with the formation of reaction wood, *A*, in a softwood; compression wood forms on the lower side. *B*, in a hardwood; tension wood forms on the upper side.

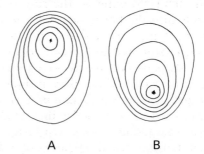

A   B

tension wood formation leads to wider growth increments on the upper side (see Fig. 123). The degree of eccentricity so produced may be very variable, according to the rate or duration of reaction wood formation: in mild cases it may not be very noticeable. A well-developed example is illustrated in Fig. 124, which shows a transverse slice of a branch of yew (*Taxus baccata*) with marked compression wood formation. This specimen shows some 28 growth rings, and although the total width of the wood, measured downwards from the pith, is nearly twice that measured upwards, the numbers of growth increments which can be counted along these two radii are (within the unavoidable uncertainties of such comparisons) substantially the same.

Well-developed compression wood, as in this specimen, can usually be recognized at sight on the end-grain surface of a log by eccentricity

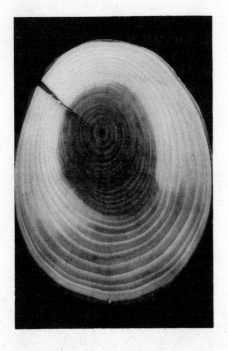

Fig. 124. A transverse slice of a branch of yew (*Taxus baccata*) with compression wood, about natural size. The eccentric growth is brought about by the wider growth rings on the lower side, where the darker colour is due to the pigmented thicker walls of the compression wood tracheids. The dark central zone of the slice is heartwood, which in yew is a warm brown colour.

of this kind, coupled with the presence, in the lower, enlarged sector, of a characteristic reddish brown pigmentation. On account of this feature compression wood was at one time referred to as red wood, in French as bois rouge, and in German as Rotholz; measurement of the pigmented area, as seen in a transverse section, has been used as a rapid method of estimation of the amount of compression wood present. In addition, the proportion of latewood in the growth rings of this region appears greater than normal, though this appearance arises more from a greater thickening of the tracheid walls than from the reduced tracheid diameter characteristic of normal latewood. As might be expected, in relation to the enhanced radial growth of compression wood, its rays may be more numerous or taller than normal (see p. 217), but their basic structure remains unchanged (Timell, 1972a).

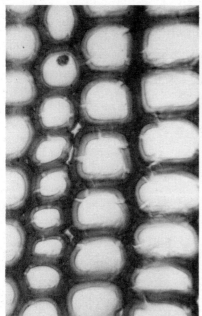

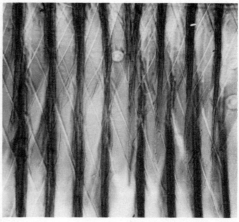

B

A

Fig. 125. Compression wood of spruce (*Picea*, sp.). *A*, T.S. × 450; showing the intercellular spaces and the grooves which are confined to the S_2 layer of the tracheid walls. *B*, R.L.S. × 250; the grooves in the S_2 layer can be seen to follow helical courses.

The characteristic features of strongly differentiated compression wood grade off in intensity upwards in a section of a leaning trunk or branch, through what is termed side wood, into the more or less normal wood of the upper side. Under closer study side wood may show, in lesser degree, some of the features of compression wood; there is a good deal of variation in this respect. The wood of the upper side of the trunk or branch is sometimes, in emphasis of its position, referred to as 'opposite wood' and it may not be entirely normal in its structure (Timell, 1973).

Individual tracheids of well-developed compression wood have a number of characteristic features, and are recognizable by ordinary light microscopy of transverse and longitudinal sections. In transverse sections they appear rounded in shape, and hence with intercellular spaces among them; in this they contrast clearly with the close-fitting angular tracheids of normal wood. Their walls are usually abnormally thick, and show radial grooves in their inner surfaces (Fig. 125*A*). These may not always be as clearly visible as they are in this figure, but are generally well shown in longitudinal sections, where they appear in walls seen in face-view as conspicuous parallel striations on their inner surfaces (Fig. 125*B*), obliquely aligned, commonly at an angle of some 40–45° to the cell axis, and so forming helices around the cell. The relationship between the transverse and longitudinal views of them is shown in the scanning electron-micrograph of Fig. 126*A*, and the grooves are shown at a higher magnification in Fig. 126*B*. These

Fig. 126. *A*. An oblique scanning electron microscope view of a compression wood tracheid in *Pinus sylvestris*, as seen at a transverse surface (× ca. 1500). In this particular specimen the grooves in the tracheid wall are much narrower than those shown in Fig. 125; though they were clearly visible by ordinary light microscopy in longitudinal sections, they were barely detectable in transverse sections. Note the 'normal' tracheid in the lower right-hand part of the figure, showing a trace of an S_3 layer, and no grooves. The very numerous parallel scratches across the surface of the wood are knife marks. *B*. A transmission electron-micrograph of a carbon replica of the inner surface of the wall of a compression wood tracheid of yellow pine (*Pinus strobus*), showing the helical ribs and grooves characteristic of the S_2 layer (× ca. 2500).

A   B

grooves, which extend only partly through the total thickness of the secondary wall, are present in wood taken fresh from the tree, and so are not an artefact of drying (Wardrop and Davies, 1964). In the compression wood region of a trunk or branch virtually all the tracheids will show these features, though it is not unusual for the tracheids of the extreme latewood to be normal in form (but see Timell, 1972b).

In weakly developed compression wood it may be found that the tracheids are rounded in section, but that the grooves in their walls are altogether lacking. Even when they are present, however, as in well-differentiated compression wood, and are clearly visible in a longitudinal section, they may not be detectable with certainty in a transverse section unless it is very thin; this is because they lie very obliquely to the plane of the section. The wider ones may be identifiable, but the majority commonly appear as no more than faintly defined striations lying radially across the inner part of the cell wall, rather than as obvious grooves in it. However, if the section is viewed under the high power of the microscope while the fine adjustment is turned first one way and then the other, a characteristic optical effect will be seen. The ill-defined striation-like images of the grooves in the cell wall will appear to move in unison around the cell in one direction or the other as the plane of sharp focus (i.e. of optical section) is raised or lowered; at different levels vertically it intersects the grooves in different positions laterally. This 'rotating wheel effect' (as it has been termed), once it has been seen and understood, will be recognized as one aspect of the grooved structure of compression wood tracheids. In longitudinal sections the grooves may, at first sight, be deceptively reminiscent of spiral thickening, such as occurs in the normal tracheids of *Psèudotsuga* and *Taxus*, but from which careful observation should enable a clear distinction to be made.

A further difference between compression wood and normal wood, simple in concept though less readily ascertainable, is that compression wood tracheids are, on average, shorter than normal tracheids of the same growth ring; the difference may be up to 20% or so (Büsgen and Münch, 1929; Dadswell and Wardrop, 1949; Wardrop and Dadswell, 1950, 1952; Shelbourne and Ritchie, 1968). Associated with the microscopically visible differences from normal wood there are also differences in chemical composition; compression wood contains some 30–40% more lignin than normal wood, and some 20–25% less cellulose. There are also differences in the chemistry of its hemicelluloses (Timell, 1982).

More specialized studies of the anatomy of compression wood tracheids, by the methods of polarization microscopy and electron microscopy, reveal further differences from normal wood. Firstly, these methods show that the innermost layer of the normal secondary wall, the S_3 layer (see Chapter 6) is absent from compression wood (Fig.

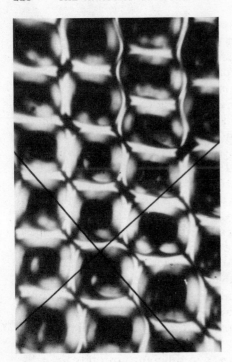

Fig. 127. Compression wood of cypress (*Cupressus* sp.). T.S., polarizing microscope, × 600. Note the rounded form of the tracheids and the absence of a S_3 layer. The thick S_2 layer appears less bright than the S_1 layer; an indication of the difference in their microfibrillar orientation (see Chapter 6).

127). Secondly, they show that the helical grooving is in the inner part of the S_2, and confirm the expectation that the orientation of this grooving parallels that of the microfibrils in this layer. Thus the abnormally thick walls of compression wood tracheids are formed in spite of the absence of the S_3 layer; S_1 and S_2, and more especially S_1, are conspicuously thicker than normal. Both are heavily lignified at maturity, especially the outer part of the S_2. It is relevant here also, in relation to the absence of S_3, to note that in *Taxus*, which develops spiral thickenings on the inner surfaces of its cell walls, in normal wood these are flat spirals, nearly transverse in their orientation, and so corresponding to the microfibrillar spirals of S_3; in contrast, in compression wood, they are more steeply orientated, following the microfibrillar orientation in S_2 (Patel, 1963; Timell, 1978). *Taxus* compression wood (like that of *Araucaria*, *Agathis* and *Ginkgo*), is also unusual in that it does not show the multiple helical checking in this layer, as is generally found in compression wood in other species. *Pseudotsuga*, which like *Taxus*, has spiral thickenings in its normal wood, behaves differently; in severe compression wood these thickenings fail to develop, but the usual helical grooves are formed (Timell, 1978).

Among the features in which compression wood tracheids may differ from those of normal wood it will be noted that not only are they, on average, shorter, but also that their microfibrillar angle, some 40–45° (measured from the axial direction), is greater than normal. This combination recalls the statistical relationship between tracheid length (L) and microfibril angle (Θ) established by Preston for normal wood; $L = A + B.\ cot\ \Theta$ (see Chapter 6). It is of some interest therefore that in *Pinus radiata* Wardrop and Dadswell (1950) found that the constants of this type of relationship between tracheid length and microfibril angle, calculated from their measurements of the tracheids of normal wood, were also applicable to those of compression wood. This means that the less steep microfibrillar orientation characteristic of compression wood is not to be considered in isolation, but is to be regarded as a concomitant of compression wood tracheids being shorter on the average than those of normal wood of comparable position in the tree. Moreover, this difference, in its turn, relates to the enhanced radial growth rate of compression wood (see Chapter 3).

Studies of the development of compression wood in *Pinus radiata* and *Actinostrobus pyramidalis* by Wardrop and Davies (1964) and in *Abies balsamea* by Côté et al. (1968) and Timell (1979) show that the rounded form of the tracheids, as they are seen in transverse sections, and the intercellular spaces between them, develop quite early in their differentiation, at their primary wall stage, before the secondary wall has been laid down. Deposition of the holocellulose framework of the latter follows in the normal way as far as the S_1 and the outer part of the S_2, when small spiral checks or grooves become evident in the S_2, and in the completion of this layer the ridges between these grooves grow independently, at least to some extent. Lignification then follows, most strongly in the outer unfissured part of the S_2. It is clear therefore that the mature form of the S_2 does not arise simply by the deep splitting of an initially smooth and uniformly thick structure, but in part, at least, it grows in its grooved form. Neither is lignification involved in groove formation; it follows later. It is clear also that the former practice, of referring to the discontinuities in the S_2 as checks, is inappropriate and should be abandoned; they are better described as grooves or cavities, and recent authors have adopted these terms for them.

From the utilitarian point of view, as distinct from the purely botanical aspects, the presence of compression wood in timber is a major defect. Compression wood tends to be denser and inconveniently harder than normal wood, properties which derive from its thicker cell walls and greater lignin content. Though these features may confer an enhanced compressive strength, compression wood tends also to be brittle, and its tensile and elastic properties tend to be inferior to those of normal wood. These differences probably derive from the higher mean microfibrillar angles (i.e. flatter microfibrillar helices) of its tracheid walls (Cowdrey and Preston, 1965, 1966; Cave, 1968), coupled with its low cellulose content. Its chemical and physical properties (high lignin content and short tracheids) reduce its suitability even for the manufacture of wood pulp.

Above all however, its shrinkage behaviour during drying is anomalous. Whereas, in normal wood, longitudinal shrinkage is very small, of the order of 0.1 – 0.2%, in compression wood it is much greater, commonly reaching 2%; much higher values, up to 20%, are on record. At the same time the transverse shrinkage may be less than that of normal wood. It follows therefore that if a board happens to contain both compression wood and normal wood, it will tend in seasoning to undergo different degrees of shrinkage in these anatomically different regions, resulting in the development of abnormally high internal stresses. These in turn will lead to abnormally severe warping, and checks and cracks are likely to be more frequent or more extensive. In severe cases actual splitting of the board will occur.

This anomalous shrinkage behaviour is attributable in the main to the high mean microfibrillar angles chracteristic of compression wood tracheids. In juvenile core wood (see Chapter 8), where similar high microfibrillar angles occur, similar anomalous shrinkage properties are associated with them. In compression wood, however, some other structural feature may also be involved (Harris and Meylan, 1965; Meylan, 1968).

Tension wood in dicotyledons, like compression wood in conifers, is commonly associated with enhanced activity in the cambial zone. It differs from normal wood, however, in entirely different ways. Visually it is much less obvious than compression wood; while in some species the practised eye may detect it on an end-grain surface by means of its slight difference from normal in reflectance or sheen, this is by no means generally so. On longitudinal saw-cuts its presence is often revealed by a characteristic woolly or furry surface to which it gives rise. An extreme case, in *Ocotea rubra*, was described and illustrated by Jutte (1956); here the surface of the wood could be brushed up like hair. Côté and Day (1965) illustrate another example, in *Swietenia mahagoni*.

Anatomically, tension wood is closer-textured than normal wood. It tends to have fewer vessels, of smaller diameter than usual, and a greater proportion of fibres, which may be abnormally thick-walled. Its important diagnostic feature, however, is the presence of gelatinous fibres, also known as tension-wood fibres (the terms are synonymous). These are fibres in which the inner part of the secondary wall is characteristically unlignified, or shows only very slight lignification,

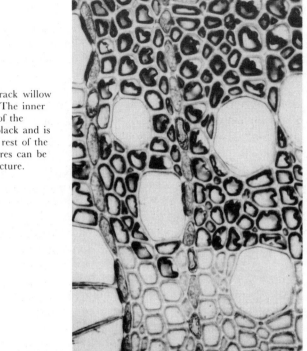

Fig. 128. Tension wood of crack willow (*Salix fragilis*), T.S., × 400. The inner layer (G-layer) of the walls of the gelatinous fibres is stained black and is in places detached from the rest of the wall. Some normal wood fibres can be seen in the bottom of the picture.

and which, in unstained sections, has a somewhat swollen or gelatinous appearance. It is known as the G-layer, or sometimes as S_g, an extension of the terminology, S_1, S_2, and S_3, which is applied to the three principal layers of the secondary wall of the normal fibre cell (see Chapter 6). Another usage is of forms such as $S_2(G)$, meaning, in this instance, that the G-layer replaces (not follows) the normal S_2. The G-layer seems to be only rather weakly attached to the earlier-formed layers of the cell wall, and in the sectioning process it is readily pulled away from them by the dragging action of the knife; it is thus commonly seen in a more or less distorted form, as in Fig. 128. Gelatinous fibres are fairly readily recognizable by ordinary microscopic methods; commonplace staining procedures, such as the use of phloroglucinol and hydrochloric acid, or safranin and light green (or better, lignin pink and chlorazol black E, as recommended by Robards and Purvis, 1964) serve to emphasize the unlignified G-layer, and thus to distinguish these fibres from those of normal wood. They may be seen in transverse sections in patches of very variable extent, ranging from small groups scattered among predominantly normal fibres, to dense bands occupying the major part of the width of a growth ring.

The more searching methods of polarization- and electron-microscopy, and X-ray diffraction, reveal further details of gelatinous fibre structure and its variability. The development of the G–layer may begin at different stages in the differentiation of the fibre cell, so that it may follow the deposition of the S_1 layer, and so replace the S_2 and the S_3, or it may be delayed until after the S_2, thus replacing the S_3 alone. Less frequently it may be later still, following the formation of the full complement, S_1, S_2, and S_3, of the normal secondary wall (Wardrop and Dadswell, 1955; Robards, 1967). Presumably this variation reflects the varied stages in their differentiation which the fibres had achieved when the stimulus to the production of the G-layer (whatever this may be) reached them. Thus, unlike compression wood tracheids, which can be recognized in sections early in their development by their shape and intercellular spaces, tension wood fibres become fully distinctive only as their differentiation approaches completion.

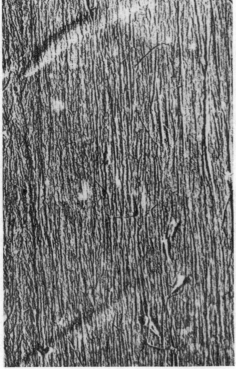

Fig. 129. An electron-micrograph of a replica prepared from a G-layer of the tension wood of *Salix*; × ca. 20000. The microfibrils are axially aligned.

Fig. 130. Fibres of European beech (*Fagus sylvatica*); T.S.. polarizing microscope, × ca. 650. *A*, from normal wood, *B*, from tension wood. In *A* the S_1, S_2 and S_3 layers of the fibre walls can be distinguished. In *B*, though the S_1 layer is distinct, the S_2 and S_3 layers are lacking, and the G-layer can be seen only where it has been displaced from its axial orientation during the preparation of the section.

The G-layer itself differs in its ultrastructure from all other parts of wood cell walls. X-ray diffraction and electron miscroscopy confirm the evidence of polarization microscopy in showing that its microfibrils are axially orientated, or very nearly so (Wardrop and Dadswell, 1955; Wardrop, 1964b; Robards, 1967) (Fig. 129). This has the consequence that in transverse sections the G-layer is barely if at all visible by polarization microscopy (Fig. 130), because the direction of view of its microfibrils is then along their length. Electron microscopy also shows its microfibrils to be less closely packed than those of the other secondary wall layers, so that its structure is of a more open nature. Its convoluted appearance in transverse sections, frequently shown in electron micrographs, may however be an artefact (Robards, 1967; Mia, 1968). Staining reactions and analyses show that chemically it consists almost entirely of cellulose with no more than a small proportion of other carbohydrates. The work of Norberg and Meier (1966) is of particular interest in this context, in that they were able, by the use of ultra-sonic vibration, to detach the fragments of G-layer from sections of the tension wood of aspen (*Populus tremula*) and so to examine them separately. These were found to have an unusually high value of optical birefringence (0.064), which is indicative of an exceptionally highly ordered

A   B

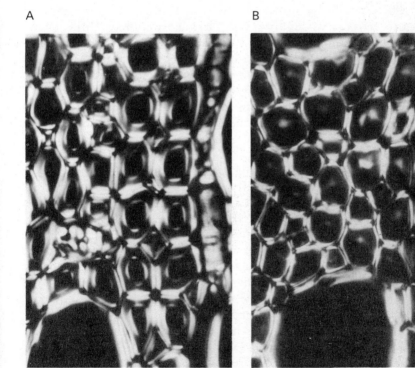

crystalline cellulose structure. Moreover their hydrolysis gave rise to a mixture of sugars, of which 98.5% was glucose, together with 1.5% of xylose. This again is consistent with a structure consisting almost wholly of cellulose microfibrils.

Mean fibre length in tension wood has been reported by different investigators as being greater, less than, or no different from that of normal wood. This diversity of opinion has probably arisen, at least in part, from the use of different procedures in the selection of the sample of normal wood with which the comparison is to be made. The proportion of tension wood present, its position in the tree and the variability of wall structure of its individual fibres may also have some bearing on the matter. Tension wood also differs from normal in its physical properties. Shrinkage on drying is much higher than normal, commonly reaching 1% longitudinally; this is attributed by Boyd (1977a) to the unusually thin S_2 layer of its gelatinous fibres (often this is absent altogether), coupled with the large microfibrillar angle of the S_1. But since gelatinous fibres rarely make up more than 50% of the total wood of the tension wood zone, the potentially large longitudinal shrinkage to be expected from these features of their structure is restrained by that of the normal wood around them. The G-layer alone undergoes no significant longitudinal shrinkage on drying (Norberg and Meier, 1966), but being rather loosely attached to the outer parts of the mature tension wood fibre wall, it may well have little or no influence in restraining the shrinkage of the fibre as a whole. The tangential shrinkage of tension wood is also greater than normal, and may lead to the development, during drying, of fine multiple checking in the wood which is termed honeycombing. It may also give rise, in a radially sawn board, to longitudinal strip-like zones of excessive shrinkage, a consequence of the collapse of bands of gelatinous fibres in the timber. The board thus develops a corrugated surface, an effect which is known as washboarding.

In its strength properties, as might be expected, tension wood also differs from normal. Though its tensile strength, especially when seasoned, may be equal to or greater than that of normal wood, its strength in compression is low, a consequence probably of its low lignin content. Somewhat unexpectedly, perhaps, slip planes and minute compression failures are frequent in tension wood, except in those regions of it which have been most recently formed. They are probably related to its action in the growing tree (see p. 249). Tension wood may also be unsuitable even for the manufacture of paper pulp, as was described for a short-rotation variety of poplar, by Parham *et al.* (1977). They found that owing to the presence of the G-layer the tension wood fibres did not collapse and flatten in the paper-making process, like those of normal wood, so that pulp prepared from them tended to form bulky, porous and poorly-bonded paper.

It is clear, therefore, on the grounds of the shrinkage, strength and working properties of tension wood, that its presence must tend to degrade the quality of the timber in which it occurs. Nevertheless, in the small proportions in which tension wood is frequently found, its various effects on the properties of the wood as a whole may often be only of relatively minor importance.

In outlining the structure and properties of compression wood and tension wood in the foregoing pages we have considered them as variant structural forms of normal wood, which, in relation to the commercial uses of timber, are to be regarded as defects. In this approach we have thus entirely passed over the more fundamental botanical aspects of their initiation, growth and function in the living tree. Considered from this point of view compression wood and tension wood are not simply two disparate modified forms of wood structure; they are alternative anatomical reactions, by softwoods and hardwoods respectively, to similar external circumstances, which in the growing trees lead by different mechanisms to essentially the same final effects, i.e., to changes in the orientation of the trunk or branches.

Most investigators are agreed – though Boyd (1976a and b, 1977b) has recently rejected this view (see p. 244) – that in the main the formation of reaction wood of both kinds is a response to a gravitational stimulus. In the trunks of trees this arises from a deviation in their attitude from the truly vertical direction. In this matter trees are remarkably sensitive; in *Pinus* spp. deflections of the order of $2 - 3°$ have been estimated as sufficient to initiate compression wood formation (Westing, 1965), and for tension wood formation in willow (*Salix fragilis*), Robards (1966) estimated the minimum as 'a degree or so'. However, the grounds for this statement are not wholly clear. An example of the sensitivity of compression wood formation in spruce in a tree with a slightly sinuous trunk, is well-illustrated by Büsgen and Münch (1929). In the branches of trees, however, as distinct from their trunks, the circumstances relating to reaction wood formation appear to be more complex; their behaviour is thus considered separately (see p. 241).

The concept of the prime importance of gravity as the controlling influence, rather than the physical forces of longitudinal compression or tension as such (which, however Boyd (*loc. cit.*) has considered anew to be the operative factors), developed in the light of experiments such as those first carried out by Ewart and Mason-Jones (1906), which have since been repeated by numerous other investigators (see for instance, Sinnott, 1952; Westing, 1965; Wilson & Archer, 1977). In one kind of these experiments the vertical leading shoots of young conifers (softwood trees) were bent and tied in vertical loops at the beginning of the growing season, so that the tissues on the inner side of the loop were put under compression and those on the outer side under tension. Yet it was found subsequently that compression wood had developed along the outer (tension) side of the lower half of the loop and along the inner (compression) side of the upper half; see Fig. 131. It was thus formed on the lower side of both upper and lower halves of the loop, so matching its usual position on the lower side of branches and leaning trunks, irrespective of the imposed compression and tension of the experimental procedure. Jaccard (1938), Robards (1965) and others have since carried out similar experiments and made similar observations on the distribution of tension wood in dicotyledonous (hardwood) trees; this was always formed along the upper sides of both upper and lower halves of the loop, again matching its usual positions in the tree.

Fig. 131. Diagrams illustrating the formation of reaction wood (shaded) in growing stems bent into vertical loops; *A*, compression wood in a softwood; *B*, tension wood in a hardwood.

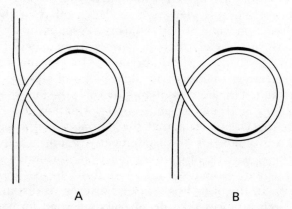

A   B

Ewart and Mason-Jones' findings were confirmed and extended by White (1907), who showed, *inter alia*, that young softwood seedlings of various species kept horizontal, but firmly supported mechanically to eliminate bending stress, still formed compression wood. She rotated potted seedlings of *Cupressus sempervirens* (now called *Sequoia sempervirens*) on a clinostat, and found that if grown for a month while rotating at a rate of one revolution in four hours they formed a complete cylinder of slightly differentiated compression wood round the stem, but while rotated at a rate of one revolution in two minutes none was formed: she considered that a minimal period of gravitational stimulus of one to two hours was sufficient for the initiation of a response. The response itself would not of course appear in that time, but would take a matter of some days to develop. Further evidence for the role of gravity in compression wood formation emerged also from an experiment with white pine (*Pinus strobus*) by Burns (1920). Plants (growing in pots) were placed with their stems horizontal and bent at right angles, but still in the horizontal plane. They produced compression wood along their lower sides, unaffected by the lateral compression and tension imposed by the bend (Fig. 132). Wardrop (1964b) has reported conceptually related experiments with *Tristania conferta*, an Australian hardwood. Here tension wood was formed on the upper sides of horizontally bent stems, but not if they were rotated on a clinostat. The successful substitution of centrifugal force for gravity in the initiation of reaction wood (Jaccard, 1939, 1940), comparable to the way in which it can

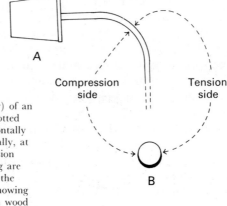

Fig. 132. *A*, a diagram (plan view) of an experiment of Burns (1920). A potted white pine has been grown horizontally with its shoot bent, also horizontally, at right angles, so that the compression and tension set up by the bending are lateral. *B*, a transverse section of the stem in the region of the bend, showing that the formation of compression wood (shaded) is nevertheless on the lower side.

be used to induce apical geotropic curvature, also added weight to the concept of the essentially gravitational nature of the natural stimulus to the formation of reaction wood.

It might be expected therefore that the amount or proportion of reaction wood in a leaning stem would be related to its angular displacement from the vertical, and Burns (1920) considered this to be so in seedlings of pine and spruce; other workers have since greatly extended the evidence on this point. In standing trees, however, the expected relationship may be obscured by variation in the amount of reaction wood present which is not apparently related to the degree of lean; see, for instance, the work of Kaeiser (1955) and Berlyn (1961) on *Populus*, Arganbright and Bensend (1968) on *Acer*, Cano-capri and Burkart (1974) on *Quercus* and Barger and Ffolliott (1976) on *Pinus*. The production of reaction wood is clearly influenced by the prevailing rate of growth, and hence by other factors which bear on this, for instance by the 'release' of the trees remaining after the thinning of a stand, or in the approaching senescence of old trees. It must also be borne in mind, in relation to studies of reaction wood in the trunks of standing trees, that reaction wood, after it has been formed, remains as a permanent feature of the trunk, whereas the deviation from the vertical which initiated its formation may well have been corrected, or at least modified, by its presence and action. Thus correlations between lean and the amount of reaction wood present seem likely to become progressively weaker with time. This was well shown by Spurr and Friend (1941), who found that the death of the main shoot apex in *Pinus strobus*, caused by a weevil, followed by the re-orientation of a lateral branch to replace the lost apex, may lead to the growth of an outwardly almost straight vertical new trunk. This however still contained the compression wood concerned in the re-orientation of the branch, sufficient in its extent to render the wood of the new trunk seriously defective in the commercial sense. Other instances have been described by Mergan (1958) and Hejnowicz (1967) in their studies of the initially drooping extension growth of the leading shoots of certain conifers, and the subsequent erection of the new growth to the vertical. This is brought about by the formation and action of compression wood in the young leader, so that this compression wood remains in the core of the trunk as a permanent record of its earlier non-vertical state.

The relationship between deviation from the vertical and production of tension wood was explored experimentally in crack willow (*Salix fragilis*), in such a way as to avoid this kind of complication, by Robards (1966). He grew rooted cuttings in a framework, throughout an experimental period of $6\frac{1}{2}$ months, so that groups of them were supported and constrained in their growth, at each of certain angles, which ranged from the normal vertical direction through 180° to the completely inverted position; subsequently he estimated the degree of eccentricity of their overall xylem development during the experiment, and the extent of their production of tension wood fibres.

Some of Robards' findings are represented graphically in Fig. 133. He recorded the eccentricity in terms of the ratio of the thickness of the increment of wood produced on the upper side of a leaning shoot to that produced on the lower side, expressed on a percentage basis; if there was no eccentricity this ratio would therefore be 100. In the Figure, however, the eccentricity was graphed as its logarithm, so that (since log 100 = 2) the figure 2 at the bottom left-hand side of the graph corresponds to equal, non-eccentric wood formation. The scale of the percentage of tension wood formation, on the right-hand side of the Figure, refers to the radial thickness of the zone of tension wood produced on the upper side of a leaning shoot, calculated as a percentage of the thickness of the wood produced on both the upper and lower sides, added together. Each point on the graphs in the Figure represents the mean of 10 measurements of the xylem of 8–10 shoots, made at intervals along their length, i.e. 80–100 measurements in all.

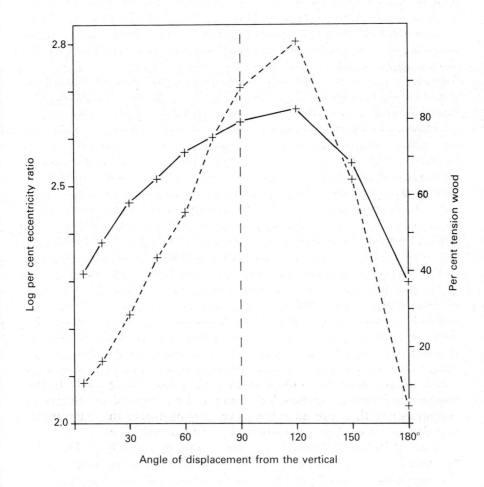

Fig. 133. Crack willow (*Salix fragilis*). The production of tension wood in shoots in relation to their displacement from the vertical (see text). – + – – – + – – – + – The log, percentage eccentricity of the stem. + —— + —— + The radial dimension of the zone of tension wood, expressed as a percentage of the year's total xylem diameter. Note that both the graphs peak at 120.° Redrawn from Robards (1966).

It is clear from the graphs that both the eccentricity of wood formation and the production of tension wood were strongly and progressively influenced by deviation from the vertical, though in slightly different ways; in shoots grown within a few degrees of the upright or upside-down position the xylem may contain 35–40% of tension wood fibres, even though its eccentricity remains relatively small.

The two graphs are however alike in recording maximum responses in shoots grown at an angle of 120° to the vertical. According to simple theory (the sine law, propounded by Sachs about a century ago) the maximum stimulus to reaction wood formation would be expected to be experienced by shoots grown horizontally, that is at a deviation of 90° from the vertical (sine 90° = 1, the maximum value that the sine of an angle can have). This apparent discrepancy is a point of some interest, because it recalls other types of plant response to gravity, for example the orthogeotropic behaviour of certain root tips, which, it is well established, show a maximum sensitivity to geotropic stimulation at angles between 120° and 135° to the vertical.

It has long been hypothesized (Haberlandt, 1914) that the perception of the gravitational field by plant apices depends on the behaviour of specialized amyloplasts (starch grains) in certain of their cells. These grains differ from those of ordinary storage starch in being mobile, and are known to fall towards the physically lower side of the cell in which they occur. Thus if the plant member is tilted they change their position within the cell, relative to its other parts, according to its changed orientation with respect to gravity. It is therefore postulated that this sedimentation movement signals to the root or shoot (as the case may be) an indication of this orientation, and so initiates a geotropic response. The grains are thus visualized as acting, in a general sense, like the statoliths in the statocysts of animals, and are referred to as statolithic starch grains. There is a good deal of experimental evidence in support of this theory; see for instance the discussions by Audus (1962, 1969, 1979) and Volkman and Sievers (1979). In any case there seems to be no substantial alternative to a mechanism of this kind.

On the assumption of a statolithic mechanism Audus (1964) put forward a plausible explanation of the occurrence of the maximum effective geotropic stimulus in a root tip at a deviation from the vertical of about 120°. This explanation need not concern us in detail, but it is relevant to the production of reaction wood insofar that Robards interpreted his finding of the maximum response in *Salix* at 120° as indicating that the graviperception mechanism which initiates reaction wood formation, like that believed, for good reaons, to be operative in the geotropic responses of plant apices, is a statolithic one. Its location and *modus operandi* are, however, still unknown, though since reaction wood may be produced, to an axially localized extent, virtually anywhere along the length of a growing main stem in the regions where this happens to be non-vertical, the capability of graviperception must be very generally distributed. The sensory mechanism seems likely to be in or very near the cambial zone, though if it is, the widespread occurrence of spiral grain in the trunks of trees (Kozlowski, 1971) must be recognized as an additional complication in its operation. There is another problem here too. When a leaning trunk is re-orientated by a reaction wood, it may often, in its curvature, overshoot the truly vertical direction; the initial production of reaction wood on one side, which brought about its erection, is then followed by reaction wood formation on the opposite side, so tending to correct the overshoot. However, Archer and Wilson (1973) found, in their experiments with *Pinus strobus*, that the shift of compression wood formation from one side of the trunk to the other occurred *before* the trunk had reached the vertical state; it seems therefore that the possibility of an overshoot was being antici- pated, a matter which might reasonably be regarded as being beyond the control capability of a simple statolithic system. In any case, no statolithic mechanism relating to reaction wood has been identified anatomically, so that although the hypothesis of its presence and action is, on various counts, a reasonable and attractive one, and has been widely accepted in various forms, the structural evidence for its existence is virtually nil. The indication of possibly statolithic starch grains in the cortex of one-year shoots of *Populus robusta*, reported by Leach & Wareing (1967), can hardly be regarded as representative in this respect.

We now turn to some consideration of the formation and function of reaction wood in branches. As we have already noted, compression wood in softwoods is usually produced on the lower side of branches, and tension wood in hardwoods on the upper side, positions which parallel those in which they are commonly found in leaning trunks. In spite of this similarity, however, the circumstances of the presence of reaction wood in trunks and branches are really rather different. In a leaning trunk the function of reaction wood is clearly to deflect it towards the truly vertical, and the nearer a trunk approximates to the vertical state the less is its tendency to produce reaction wood. Though a large proportion of trunks – perhaps all of them – contain some reaction wood, it may nevertheless be reasonably postulated that, ideally, a trunk which had never, during its lifetime, been deflected from the truly vertical by weather, site conditions or accident of growth, would contain no reaction wood whatever. In branches, however, the presence of reaction wood is the usual and expected condition, and moreover it does not normally deflect them into a vertical position. Its function and action in branches, compared with its function and action in trunks, is thus at first sight different, and as other evidence shows, also more complex.

This evidence derives from various sources, and especially from experiments in which branches of trees are bent upwards and constrained in attitudes nearer to the vertical than their natural ones. Work of this kind has been described by Sinnott (1952), who experimented with *Pinus strobus*, and who outlined and discussed earlier work – notably that by Hartmann (1942) – on other species. In general, if a branch of a softwood is forced upward into a markedly more vertical position than normal, it produces compression wood on its upper side. Correspondingly, as Wardrop (1956, 1964b) and others have shown for certain hardwoods, branches tied up into steeper attitudes produce tension wood on their lower sides. These observations suggest, as the basis of an explanatory hypothesis, that somewhere between the normally observed angle of a branch (at which of course, it has reaction wood in the normal position) and a steeper, experimentally imposed angle, sufficient to give rise to reaction wood in the opposite, 'crossed-over' position, there might be expected to be an intermediate angle, at which reaction wood would not be formed at all. This is the 'characteristic angle' of Sinnott (1952) and the 'equilibrium position' (EP) of Wilson and Archer (1977), and we may visualize that in branches reaction wood is formed in response to their deflection from the charac-

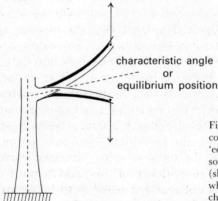

characteristic angle
or
equilibrium position

Fig. 134. Diagram illustrating the concept of the 'characteristic angle' or 'equilibrium position' of a branch of a softwood (see text). Compression wood (shaded) is formed on the upper side when the branch is displaced above the characteristic angle and on the lower side when displaced below it.

teristic angle, and not, as in trunks, from the vertical direction (Fig. 134). This in turn suggests that branches, like trunks, may have graviperceptive mechanisms, but that these differ from those of trunks in that their zero-response positions are offset from the vertical, so that they sense deviations from the characteristic angle rather than from the truly vertical direction. Thus when branches are bent upwards, reaction wood formation is initiated which will tend to bend them down, back towards this angle. Under natural circumstances, on the other hand, the maintenance of branches at or near the characteristic angle must be visualized as complicated by the natural plasticity of wood, especially in the green state, and its capacity for 'creep' (see Chapter 6). A growing branch, with its annually increasing burden of foliage, and often also of fruit, will tend progressively to bend downwards, under its own weight, and its continued production of reaction wood can thus be seen as the appropriate response necessary to maintain it at or near the characteristic angle (Sinnott, 1952); the characteristic angle might be expected to be slightly above the normally observed angle (Wilson and Archer, 1977). The sagging of the branches of old trees down to ground level seems likely to be a consequence of a change with age in their characteristic angle, or perhaps, more simply, a result of their slow growth and their failure to produce sufficient reaction wood adequately to counteract their plastic deformation.

Although branches thus behave as if they have their own systems of graviperception mechanisms, to which they can respond individually, nevertheless the characteristic branch angle is a feature of the tree as a whole, and must, fundamentally, be genetically determined. It may however become modified in response to damage to the tree. For instance, in a conifer, if the trunk is decapitated, young lateral branches tend to bend upwards from below, by the production of additional compression wood on their lower sides, and one of them (or sometimes more than one) will become vertical, so replacing the missing apex of the trunk. Thus what was initially a lateral branch ultimately becomes a main trunk, a change which results from changes not only in its production of reaction wood, but also in the geotropic response of its apical meristem. The loss or removal of a branch may also result in adjacent branches, at the same level, producing reaction wood laterally and thus bending sideways to fill the gap. Clearly, sequences such as these are not localized responses of individual branches acting independently, but are evidence of the involvement of internal correlative action in the tree. In the light of evidence of this kind Sinnott (1952) emphasized that the production of reaction wood is to be regarded as regulatory of tree form, rather than simply as a response to gravity, and this must of course, be especially true of the lateral re-orientation of branches. The role of reaction wood in relation to the architecture of trees has also been described and discussed, for dicotyledons, by Fisher and Stevenson (1981). Nevertheless this aspect of its action does not significantly diminish the major role of gravity in setting the pattern of tree form to which this regulatory function relates, nor does it dispose of the problem of what the mechanism may be, in the individual leader or branch, which senses whether it is or is not at an attitude appropriate to the innate pattern.

Reaction wood is also known to occur in the roots of some trees, and apparently not in others in which it has been sought (Patel, 1964; Höster and Liese, 1966). What its function in roots may be, seems in general terms problematical; conceivably perhaps, in a wind-rocked tree, its action might contribute to the recovery of a more firmly rooted state. However, a uniquely functional example of tension wood in roots has been described by Zimmermann *et al.* (1968) in the aerial roots of *Ficus benjamina*. These roots are initially pendulous from the tree; later, after their tips have become firmly rooted in the soil, they thicken, producing tension wood all round until they are some 10 mm in thickness. In so doing they shorten markedly, and so become taut and rigid – rooted into a container of soil, they will lift it off the ground – thereafter they produce normal wood. Their tension wood fibres are identical in structure with those of the upper sides of the branches. In this instance therefore, reaction wood is formed, and performs a function, apparently independently of gravitational relationships The immediate stimulus involved here in its induction is not known, but seems likely to be of an internal regulatory nature, rather than one of direct gravitational influence.

While, in the more usual manifestations of reaction wood formation and activity, gravity has generally be considered to be the stimulus involved, Boyd (1976a and b, 1977b) has rejected this view. He has restated and enlarged upon an alterative view of long standing, that the true stimulus is the bending stress which inevitably develops within a non-vertical trunk or branch. In support of this view he has proposed alternative interpretations of the results of a number of published experiments, (which had generally been considered to establish the inductive action of orientation in relation to gravity) in such a way as to emphasize that the possible effects of bending stress had not been excluded.

Opinions clearly differ on some of these matters, and Wilson and Archer (1977), in their review of the induction problem, considered in general terms that the evidence points to gravity, rather than stress, as the inductive stimulus. They accepted, however, that stress may be operative in some instances, the evidence being insufficient to exclude it. These authors also remarked on another factor impinging on this question, in that there is a good deal of evidence indicative of the presence of tension wood in vertical stems. It is thus important to know, at least for some species, how far, if at all, gelatinous fibres may be a normal constituent of the wood of truly vertical stems. The results of Robards' (1966) experiment (see Fig. 133) are suggestive in this context. Stems which were held nominally vertical, but which in the course of the experiment acquired a lean of 5° from the vertical, were found to have a mean content of tension wood of 38%; this is nearly half of the mean maximum observed (82% at 120°), a considerable divergence from expectation on the basis of the sine law. Whether similar shoots held accurately vertical, would or would not have developed any tension wood, is of course not known, and would call for a very demanding higher order of experimental precision to establish.

In the formation of reaction wood in stems, where the initiating stimulus seems most probably to be gravitational, there is nevertheless a very considerable hiatus in our physiological understanding of the sequence of events between the initial stimulus, considered in terms of its possible control of the sedimentation of some kind of particle in a hypothetical statolithic mechanism, and the final production and differentiation of reaction wood, a hiatus which it is at present impossible to bridge. However, there is a good deal of evidence involving auxin (β-indolyl acetic acid, or IAA) in the intermediate stages. Auxin is of course well-known to be concerned in the geotropic curvature of plant apices, and also in the general regulation of cambial activity (see Chapter 3), so its involvement in the formation of reaction wood is perhaps only to be expected. It is well established (Wershing and Bailey, 1942; Onaka, 1949; Nečessaný, 1958 and other investigators) that the application of auxin to erect softwood stems induces compression wood formation. It has also been found that the normal formation of tension wood in certain hardwood stems can be suppressed by the application of auxin (Nečessaný, 1958; Cronshaw and Morey, 1968) and can be induced by the use of 2–3–5 tri-iodo-benzoic acid (TIBA), (Cronshaw and Morey, 1965; Kennedy and Farrar, 1965). The significance of this is that TIBA is a recognized anti-auxin, a substance known in other aspects of growth physiology to counter the effects of auxin. In the present context the induction of tension wood formation by applied TIBA can in its turn be suppressed by the application also of auxin (Morey and Cronshaw, 1968). Thus the general picture emerges that supra-normal auxin concentrations tend to the formation of compression wood, while sub-normal auxin activity is conducive to tension wood production. There is also some evidence that tension wood formation is associated with transverse gradients of auxin concentration, rather than specifically with sub-normal levels (Casperson, 1965; Blum, 1971). However, the finding of a higher auxin level in the lower sides of branches, in both a softwood and a hardwood (Nečessaný, 1958 and others) is in harmony with the experimental evidence on the effects of auxin activity outlined above. Thus it seems highly probable that the initial gravitational stimulus may induce either a synthesis or a redistribution of auxin as an essential step towards the production of reaction wood. Such induced variation in auxin concentration must presumably be locally superposed on the general downward movement of auxin from the buds which is necessary for the maintenance of cambial activity. It is perhaps for this reason that compression wood production tends sometimes to spread downwards slightly, from a branch into a trunk, or from a leaning part of a trunk into a vertical part. Auxin levels tend to fall towards the end of the growing season, which may explain why compression wood often fails to develop in the terminal zones of growth rings (see p. 227). While other growth-regulating substances besides auxin, especially gibberellic acid and cytokinins, are known to be involved in cambial activity, they seem not to be concerned, at least not directly, in the differentiation of the specific cell forms of reaction wood.

The *modus operandi* of auxin in this matter, as indeed in its other roles in plant development, presents many unanswered problems. Reaction wood formation involves, as we have seen, variation from the 'normal' in cell number, cell shape, cell wall morphology and chemical structure – that is to say variation at every stage in the growth of wood from cambial division to final differentiation of mature cells.

Accepting however, as indeed at present we must, our ignorance in these matters, and going on further to enquire how it comes about that reaction wood functions in re-orientating leaning trunks and branches, we meet another set of problems to which again there are only incomplete answers.

It is generally considered that the mechanical effects of reaction wood are generated, for the main part at least, in its varied processes of maturation. Thus it may be visualized that compression wood tracheids, as they differentiate from their thin-walled state as newly-formed cambial derivatives, into their mature form, exert a longitudinal extensive force; this force, acting on the lower side of a leaning shoot, tends to 'push' it into a more nearly vertical position. Nevertheless, since compression wood tracheids differ from those of normal wood even in their primary wall stage, it cannot be entirely excluded that some extension force might be generated prior to secondary wall formation, as indeed Frey-Wyssling (1952, 1976) has long maintained. Their distorted cell tips (Wardrop, 1965b; Yoshizawa *et al.*, 1985) and apparent failure to inter-digitate smoothly by intrusive growth, are perhaps suggestive of some action of this kind; so too is the consistently higher osmotic pressure of the cambial zone of the lower side, compared with that of the upper, reported by Jaccard and Frey-Wyssling (1934) and Jaccard, (1934). However, Boyd (1973) has calculated that turgor effects, as proposed by Frey-Wyssling, would be quite inadequate to be effective. On the other hand, since wood cells normally tend to contract in length as they come to maturity, cell extension at this late stage in their differentiation is difficult to visualize. It has been attributed in compression wood to the unusually high lignin content, (Wardrop, 1965b; Boyd, 1973 and 1985); there is evidence that the deposition of lignin tends to swell the cell wall matrix, and reason to believe that this swelling, occurring to an exceptional degree, in tracheids with the relatively flat microfibrillar helices characteristic of compression wood, would bring about an increase in their length. These postulated inter-relationships thus visualize the circumstances of the expansion of compression wood as approximately to the converse of those considered to be responsible for its abnormal shrinkage on drying, where the loss of cell wall water, in causing shrinkage of the matrix, leads to unusually great longitudinal contraction (see p. 230).

Tension wood fibres, in contrast, acting as they usually do on the upper side of a leaning trunk, apparently produce their effect by under-going unusually large longitudinal contraction as they differentiate, so exerting a tensile force and tending to 'pull' the trunk into a more upright stance. Unlike the tracheids of compression wood they are not conspicuously different from their counterparts in normal wood until relatively late in their differentiation; their distinct form becomes evi-dent only with the deposition of the G-layer. Yet this layer is apparently not strongly attached to the remainder of the cell wall, and comprising a very high proportion of virtually axial microfibrils, seems singularly ill-adapted to the generation of an abnormally large or abnormally long-lasting contractile force. The origin of this force in tension wood thus remains unexplained (Wilson, 1981).

The uncertainties surrounding the generation of the regulatory forces of reaction wood do not, however, reflect on the very real existence of these forces. The isolation of samples of reaction wood from leaning trunks results in its expansion (compression wood) or contraction (ten-sion wood), as was shown by Hejowicz (1967), or, more precisely, in the growth-strain studies referred to below. The examples quoted by Westing (1965), of the slow righting of leaning conifers over periods of many years, exemplify very strikingly the effectiveness of compression wood in this process. The instance of tension wood formation and action in *Ficus* roots (Zimmermann *et al.*, 1968), referred to above, though unrepresentative, nevertheless has a more general interest, in that it demonstrates most clearly, in an intact plant member, the reality of the contractile force that tension wood can develop.

Some experiments on *Eucalyptus* shoots, reported by Wardrop (1956, 1964b), show the role of cambial activity in forming tension wood and so generating such forces. Shoots placed horizontally normally tend to re-erect themselves, but fail to do so if the bark (i.e. the tissue external to the wood, including the cambium) is stripped off along their upper sides; its removal only from their lower sides does not inhibit re-erection. Another related experiment of his has wider implications. Here the apical parts of young trees were constrained into horizontal positions as indicated in Fig. 135A; the tie-wire had a spring balance incorporated

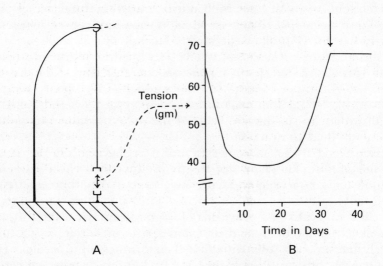

Fig. 135. Diagram illustrating an experiment showing the generation of longitudinal force by tension wood (redrawn, after Wardrop, 1964b). On the left is represented a sapling held in a bent position by a tie-wire connected to a spring balance. On the right the changing tension in the wire, shown by the balance, is recorded graphically over a period of six weeks (see text).

in it so that the tension in the wire could be monitored. The results of one such experiment, with a tree of *Liquidambar styraciflua*, are shown in Fig. 135*B*. Initially, for about 8 days, the tension in the wire fell significantly; this can be attributed to plastic 'creep', and consequent strain relaxation, in the wood (see Chapter 6). Then, as the cambium of the horizontal part of the stem began to produce tension wood along its upper side, the tension in the tie-wire recovered, and after 32 days had reached its original level. Shortly afterwards, at the point in time indicated by the arrow, the tree was defoliated and disbudded, and the stem was artificially weighted to simulate the weight of the parts removed. As the subsequent horizontal portion of the graph shows, further increase in the tension in the tie-wire was inhibited. The reason is, of course, that the removal of the buds and leaves had cut off the normal supply of growth-regulating substances necessary for continued cambial activity (see Chapter 3), so that tension wood formation had ceased. This experiment thus emphasizes that the contractile force of tension wood is generated in its formation and maturation. Westing (1965) refers briefly to similar experiments with softwood trees, showing similar initial strain relaxation, and subsequent recovery of the restraining force, as compression wood developed.

Though the forces generated in reaction wood may be visualized in simple terms, as we have already indicated as 'pushing' or 'pulling' a leaning trunk into a more vertical position, these forces do not, in reality, act in isolation, because there are considerable growth stresses 'built-in' to timber quite apart from those generated by reaction wood (see Chapter 6). In vertical trunks these are characteristically symmetrical about the axis of the trunk and are hence in equilibrium laterally; what reaction wood does in leaning trunks is to introduce an element of asymmetry into this complex of growth stresses, so that it is the net effect of this asymmetry of forces which gives rise to their curvature (Wilson and Archer, 1977). Examples of such asymmetry of growth stresses in growing trees have been described by Boyd and Foster (1974) in *Pinus radiata*, by Trénard and Guéneau (1975) and Saurat and Guéneau (1976) in beech, and by Boyd (1977a) in *Pinus radiata* and *Eucalyptus* spp. In these investigations the trunks were sampled at various points around their circumference, and superficial longitudinal growth stresses (or strains) correlated with the presence of reaction wood. In observations of this nature on standing trees it is of course not clear how far the strains may have given rise to the tension wood, or *vice versa*. The findings of Saurat and Guéneau (1976) introduce a further complication, in that even on the lower side of leaning trunks the strains in the surface wood were tensional, and tension wood was present.

The effects of growth stresses in righting a leaning trunk will of course be moderated by the weight of the trunk and its branches, its angle to the vertical, and the elasticity and plasticity of the existing wood, all of which will be subject to change as the tree grows and the righting process advances. Furthermore, as reaction wood formation continues, the mechanical properties of the older reaction wood itself (properties in respect of which it will differ from normal wood) must also be a factor. For instance, the contractile effects of tension wood differentiation must be expected to impose a compressive force on adjacent, slightly older, tension wood, and it is noteworthy in this respect that Wardrop (1956) and Côté and Day (1965) have reported the occurrence of slip planes (i.e. microscopic compression failures) in all but the most recent tension wood. Correspondingly, tension failures occur in compression wood (Westing, 1965). Thus the mechanical aspects of the bending of a leaning trunk into a more vertical stance, considered in any detail, present extremely complex problems (Archer and Wilson, 1973; Wilson and Archer, 1977).

In concluding this chapter, therefore, it may be said that in general terms the structure of reaction wood, and the reasons for the deleterious effects of its presence in commercial timber, are reasonably well understood; so too broadly, are its functions in the living tree and the importance of gravity as its principal initiating influence. Nevertheless there are still wide gaps in our knowledge and understanding of the mechanism of its initiation in relation to gravity, and the correlative influences within the trees which are also involved. Its mode of action, and the origin of the mechanical forces which it generates, are also far from being understood. The study of reaction wood, which began in the last century in response to what then seemed to be a limited problem in timber technology, has since expanded and developed into wider fields of botanical, biochemical and biophysical study, presenting problems to which there are still no wholly satisfactory solutions.

10

The Identification of Timbers

The identification of an unknown specimen of a timber, insofar that it may be possible at all, aims at naming the kind of tree from which it had been cut. Ideally this would extend to the botanical species, but frequently the timbers of the various species of a genus are too much alike for this to be possible, and the identification will not extend further than to the genus at large, or in some instances to a group of species within the genus.

Any identification of a wood sample is based wholly or principally on the systematic use of its anatomical structure. Among hardwoods it suffices for many practical purposes to refer to those features which may be seen under low magnification (as with a hand-lens) on clean-cut transverse and longitudinal surfaces. Among softwoods however, microscopic examination of sections will usually be necessary, though in the light of experience it is possible to recognize some more outwardly characteristic timbers by their grosser features. In addition to anatomical characters, the density, hardness, colour, smell and even taste of the wood may supply further clues to its identity. The colour of wood is however, variable, (notably of course as between sapwood and heartwood) and the perception and description of smell and taste are very personal matters, which, moreover, cannot be wholly satisfactorily recorded for use by others. They are thus only of limited application in the general characterization of a timber, though the recognition by an individual observer of a certain smell or taste of a given timber may prove to him, even if not to others, to be a useful adjunct to other information relating to it.

The characteristic smell of a timber, if it has one, is strongest in the green freshly sawn wood, as is shown, for instance, by elm. In general the smell fades as the timber is dried, though it may sometimes be

251

partially restored by warmth or slight moistening. When a characteristic smell is recorded for a timber, it refers to the wood in the dry state, because the smell of wood which has been exposed to moist conditions for a long period may be largely due to fermentative action on its surfaces by micro-organisms, rather than to some component (a volatile extractive) of the wood itself. It is also possible for a timber with no marked smell of its own to pick one up from a strong external source.

The smell or taste of a timber, considered as a product of its content of extraneous substances, is an indicator, even if a very subjective one, of some unknown but characteristic feature of the chemical composition of the timber. This suggests, therefore, that if more objective chemical tests could be devised, which identify (or even merely indicate the presence of) some unique or unusual chemical property of a timber, they might usefully contribute to its identification. Information of this kind might be especially valuable in instances where the timber cannot be fully identified on anatomical grounds alone.

This situation is well exemplified by the timbers of the several hundred species of the Australian genus *Eucalyptus*. Thus jarrah (*E. marginata*) and karri (*E. diversicolor*) are not reliably distinguishable (if at all) by anatomical means, but Dadswell and Burnell (1932) found that if thin splinters of the heartwood of these timbers are burnt *in still air* (this is important) the residues after burning are quite different. Jarrah burns to leave a black charcoal, while karri burns to a white ash. This so-called 'burning-splinter' test reveals a difference between the two timbers which must lie in their content of extraneous substances, even though the basic nature of this difference remains unknown. This test has also been applied to other Australian timbers (Dadswell and Eckersley, 1935), and other chemical tests have also been devised to distinguish certain other *Eucalyptus* species; Dadswell (1931) described simple chemical tests to separate a number of those with light-coloured heartwoods, while Cohen (1935) applied similar tests to some of the dark-coloured species. In some instances the chemical nature of the differences, as for example, between different types of tannins, were identified. Cohen (1933) also devised a chemical test to distinguish the timbers of two Australian species of *Araucaria*, hoop pine (*A. cunninghamii*) and bunya pine (*A. bidwillii*), which are also very similar anatomically.

The range of extraneous substances known to be present in timbers is extremely wide (as is indicated briefly in Chapter 6), and has been the subject of very numerous chemical investigations. These are beyond the scope of this book, but it is nevertheless appropriate to refer to the work of Bevan *et al.* (1965) who studied the extractives in the wood of 20 African species of the family Meliaceae, by reference to several hundred specimens of them. This family includes the American as well as the African mahoganies, and a number of other genera of dark-coloured outwardly somewhat similar timbers. The specimens were extracted with light petroleum, and the extracts were examined by thin-layer chromatography to separate their component extractives. It was found that each species contained an individual mixture of extractives, giving characteristic chromatographic patterns, so that they could be recognized and identified in this way. For example, among the African mahoganies (*Khaya* spp.), the wood of *K. anthotheca* could be distinguished from that of the other species, a distinction that cannot be made on anatomical grounds alone.

The recognition in this way of the chemical differences between members of a group of taxonomically related timbers is thus clearly a fairly complex matter; though interesting and potentially valuable it calls for appropriate laboratory facilities, and is hardly of 'practical' utility, as for instance in a saw-mill. However, a much simpler test, enabling a petroleum extract of *K. anthotheca* to be distinguished from those of other *Khaya* spp., was devised by Morgan and Orsler (1967). Particular value attaches to the identification of wood from this species, since its sawdust is a cause of dermatitis among wood-workers. This is believed to be due to its content of anthothecol.

Another group of rapid chemical and physical tests, for the identification of members of a group of ten African 'mahogany-like' timbers, which are commonly used for veneers, has been devised by Steiger (1972); he also gives a design for a punched-card key (see below) based upon these tests. The characters used in the key include such matters as the colour of water- and alkali-extracts of the wood, their reactions with ferric chloride, the presence in them of foam-producing substances, the way the wood burns and the presence and nature of crystals in the ash. However, the scheme calls for one test to be applied to the bark as well as to the wood, so that the key is not wholly applicable to veneers as such.

Tests of this nature, designed to distinguish similar timbers, must, as in these instances, be relatively easy and simple to perform if they are to be of every-day practical value. They may then be useful even though the timbers to be distinguished are also recognizable anatomically, as indeed the majority of Steiger's veneer timbers are, at least in the log. A comparable situation relating to softwoods has been described by Kutscha *et al.* (1978), who found a simple test to separate Eastern Canadian spruce (*Picea* spp., mainly *P. glauca*) from balsam fir (*Abies balsamea*). These timbers are often sold in mixed lots, even though they differ in their strength properties, optimum drying times, shrinkage potential and gluing properties. *Picea* and *Abies* are, of course, anatomically distinguishable (Chapter 4), but in a saw-mill a simple chemical test is easier and quicker than a microscopical examination. The test makes use of bromo-phenol blue, a pH indicator, which gives different colour reactions with the timbers of the two genera. Kutscha *et al.* also give references to a number of other published tests which have been used to separate various softwoods.

A seemingly similar test was proposed by Stearns (1950) to distinguish the timbers of red and white oaks. This test is however basically an oxidation/reduction test, which gives different colour reactions with the two groups of timbers. It involves the use of benzidine, which is nowadays recognized as being carcinogenic, so that its continued use cannot be recommended; compare the work of Stalker (1971) and Cummins (1972).

Trees, like other plants, may differ in their absorption of mineral substances, and may differ also in the quantities of these substances which are present in their wood. Aluminium is a normal constituent of plant ash (it has in some instances been considered to be an essential micro-nutrient) but as Kukachka and Miller (1980) showed by examination of the wood of some 3000 genera from 250 families, the amounts of aluminium present in wood are generally very small. Among the genera they examined, however, those of the family Vochysiaceae (and certain others) were found to have conspicuously high levels of aluminium in their wood; in certain species of *Vochysia*, which furnish the timber known as quaruba of Central and South America, aluminium was found to be present in amounts exceeding 2% of the total ash content of the wood. A simple 'spot' test for aluminium, easily and quickly applicable to wood, if it proved positive, was thus found at once to narrow down the possible range of identity of an unidentified timber specimen.

Whatever features may be used in the identification of wood, however, this process may be considered fundamentally as having two aspects. Firstly there is the collection, collation, assessment and presentation in an appropriate form of the many details of structure (and other properties) which may be useful in characterizing individual timbers and in distinguishing one from another. Then, assuming that this necessary preliminary work has been done, there is secondly the problem of effective access to this very extensive body of knowledge by would-be users of it. The student is likely to be concerned only with the second of these, but he should nevertheless be aware, in general terms, of the problems of the first.

These call for expertise of various kinds, of foresters and botanists of diverse specialisms. For instance, in a hitherto unworked and probably only partly known forest area, not all the trees may be fully named botanically, and the identification of individual species, coupled with the sampling of their timbers, will be a necessary step in the establishment of authenticated correlations of particular kinds of wood with particular botanical species. In principle this may seem to be a relatively simple matter, but in practice the problems multiply. In a mixed tropical forest there may be hundreds of species, some perhaps new to science, and many of which bear their leaves, flowers and fruits (on which their botanical identification depends) at great heights above the ground. Thus logs of different species may be mis-named, or may be grouped in mixed batches, and uncertainties of identification may be perpetuated.

Assuming, however, that there are authenticated specimens available, it is desirable that a selection of them should be examined, from different sources, so that some assessment can be made of the variability of the timber; which of its features are most consistently present (and so most likely to be useful in its identification) and which are so variable as to be usable only with caution. The recognition of what are often referred to as 'good' characters – i.e. those which are reliably diagnostic – is an important matter, and one which is achieved only in the light of experience. In broad terms, these characters are of a qualitative morphological or anatomical nature, such as are discussed in Chapters 4 and 5; quantitative numerical and dimensional data tend to be so subject to variation as to be of limited diagnostic value. The amount of work involved, in the aggregate, in the compilation of a body of knowledge of these matters, which may be reliably used for the identification of the wood of members of a major group of trees, is very large indeed. The student who, for instance, makes use of Phillips' 'Identification of Softwoods' (1948), or 'Identification of Hardwoods' by Brazier and Franklin (1961) cannot but be deeply impressed by the range of work previous investigators cited by these authors as the background to their works, and which they have collated, assessed and integrated with their own expertise.

The use of the very extensive literature of wood anatomy as an immediate source of information for the purposes of wood identification clearly presents major problems. Descriptions and illustrations of wood structure are too numerous and too dispersed to be searched effectively for those that might fit an unknown wood, and collections of wood specimens and microscope slides, such as are assembled in timber laboratories, present comparable problems. Systematic guidelines to identification, such as the works cited above, are necessary, systems in which the information specifically required for this purpose has been selected, assembled and presented in a form in which it can be searched in a logical manner. Such systems of recording and presenting data in this way and for this purpose are termed 'keys'. A key may be designed to include the timbers of a particular area, or those of a particular taxonomic group.

Various types of key have been proposed for the identification of wood, but only two need concern us here; the dichotomous type of key, broadly similar to those used in floras for the identification of genera and species, and the multiple-entry punched-card type of key. The latter is the more useful pattern for timber identification, but nevertheless the dichotomous type of key works adequately where the number of timbers to be considered is not too large; it has been used, for instance, by Brazier and Franklin, (1961), Jane (1970) and Core, Côté and Day (1979). It is also an instructive form of key, and will be considered first.

The dichotomous type of key is so called because it consists of a numbered series of paired statements describing contrasting features of wood structure briefly and precisely, and at the first and subsequent steps in the key the user is required to decide which of the two paired alternative descriptions best fits his unknown specimen. His decision having been made, the number following the description he has chosen indicates to which step in the key he should then proceed, where he makes another choice and is directed accordingly to a further pair of alternatives; repetition of this process should eventually lead to the name of the unknown specimen. A name having thus been arrived at, its accuracy must then be tested by comparison of the unknown with a known specimen of the same name, or with an authoritative description relating to it. Reference to photomicrographs of authenticated specimens, such as those prepared by the Building Research Establishment (1978), may also be useful.

The satisfactory operation of a key in relation to a particular timber depends on a number of factors. The first is, of course, that the designer of the key should have had that timber in mind among those which the key was intended to identify. Clearly, if the information relating to a timber has not been written into a key, it cannot be extracted from it. Secondly, and in a more general sense, the quality of a key – its accuracy and workability – depends on the knowledge and skill of the designer of it. He must of course make use of 'good' characters, but must at the same time make allowance for the natural variability of the timbers. The characters used must also be such as to be conveyed precisely in a few words. It is in fact no easy matter to make an effective dichotomous key to more than a few timbers, as it requires the designer to have in mind the important features of all of them, to sort these into contrasting alternatives suited to the dichotomous treatment, and to put the various stages of the key into the best order. Thirdly, there is the competence of the user of the key. While this need not aspire to the level of that of the designer of the key, it does call for a good fundamental understanding of the diversity of the anatomy of wood, the ability to recognize its significant detail as it may appear in hand specimens and microscope sections, and a working knowledge of the specialized terminology used to describe it.

A short example of a simple dichotomous key to separate eight common hardwood timbers (oak, ash, sweet chestnut, elm, European beech, birch, alder and poplar) is given below. This is based largely on features of these timbers which are discernible with a hand-lens, and mainly also on those visible on transverse surfaces. References to vessel arrangement apply to its appearance in this view, and the term 'oblique' used in this context means a direction which is neither truly radial nor tangential. To the novice some features used in the key may call for microscopical confirmation, but as he or she becomes more familiar with the timbers they will probably find that a hand-lens examination will suffice to recall to the memory the nature of the structures in doubt. The small selection of timbers included in this key is of course an arbitrary one, and an attempt to enter the key with a timber not in the list would prove abortive or misleading; specimens of willow and plane, for instance, would in the first instance be mis-identified, probably as poplar and beech respectively. Although these errors would come to light when the unknowns were compared with known specimens of these timbers (or with descriptions of them, as in Chapter 5) the unknown specimens would of course still remain unidentified.

Key to eight European hardwoods

1	Wood ring-porous	2
1	Wood diffuse-porous	5
2	Rays variable in width, at least some very wide	3
2	Rays all fine	4
3	Latewood vessels very small, in flame-like arrangement	oak
3	Latewood vessels in conspicuous undulating tangential bands	elm
4	Latewood vessels few, scattered, singly or in pairs, surrounded by a "halo" of parenchyma	ash
4	Latewood vessels in oblique lines	sweet chestnut
5	Rays variable in width, at least some very wide	6
5	Rays all fine	7
6	Wide rays noded; numerous and conspicuous on tangential surfaces, up to 3–4 mm high; vessels scattered, mostly single	beech
6	Rays not noded; wide rays (aggregate rays) very high, up to 3–4 cm, irregularly spaced; vessels mostly in radial chains	alder
7	Vessels small, singly or in radial groups of 2–4; texture fine; cut surface lustrous	birch
7	Vessels small, very numerous, mostly in oblique or festoon-like groups, some in short radial lines; texture open; cut surface woolly	poplar

In general, for the identification of softwood timbers, reference must be made to their microscopic features. The specimen key which follows illustrates the use of these features in separating the timbers of the commoner genera to be seen in Britain, i.e. *Pinus, Picea, Abies, Larix, Cedrus, Taxus, Pseudotsuga, Tsuga, Araucaria, Thuja* and *Juniperus*. It also distinguishes the timbers of the three principal groups of species of *Pinus*. *Thuja* here is represented by *T. plicata* (Western red cedar), often used for greenhouse construction, and *Juniperus* by the pencil cedars.

Key to some common softwoods

1	Ray tracheids always present	2
1	Ray tracheids normally absent	9
2	Resin canals always present	3
2	Resin canals normally absent	8
3	Resin canals with thin-walled epithelial cells, often appearing torn in sections	4
3	Resin canals with thick-walled epithelial cells	6
4	Ray tracheids dentate	5
4	Ray tracheids smooth	*Pinus* (soft pine group)
5	Cross-field pits large, 1, rarely 2, window-like	*Pinus* (Scots pine or red deal group)
5	Cross-field pits 3–6, pinoid	*Pinus* (pitch pine group)
6	Spiral thickening normally abundant esp. in early wood; uniseriate rays low, av. 8 cells; fusiform rays without "tails"	*Pseudotsuga*
6	Spiral thickening rarely present; uniseriate rays high, often >20 cells; fusiform rays with "tails"	7
7	Transition from earlywood to well-defined latewood abrupt; radial resin canals showing 9–12 epithelial cells in TLS; "tails" of fusiform rays markedly unequal, ratio of their cell numbers usually in the range 2:1 to 3:1	*Larix*
7	Transition from earlywood to ill-defined latewood gradual; radial resin canals showing 7–9 epithelial cells in TLS; "tails" of fusiform rays more nearly equal, ratio of their cell numbers usually in the range 1.5:1 to 2:1	*Picea*
8	Tori of bordered pits with scalloped margins; cross-field pits piceoid, cupressoid and taxodioid; rays high, sometimes >40 cells	*Cedrus*

8	Tori of bordered pits with transverse bars extending across pit membranes; cross-field pits cupressoid; rays low, rarely >16 cells	*Tsuga*

9	Axial tracheids with abundant spiral thickening	*Taxus*
9	Axial tracheids without spiral thickening	10

10	Multiseriate pitting frequent in axial tracheids	11
10	Multiseriate pitting infrequent or absent	12

11	Multiseriate pitting of axial tracheids alternate, up to 3–4 rows; cross-field pits cupressoid	*Araucaria*
11	Multiseriate pitting of axial tracheids opposite, at most in 2 rows; cross-field pits mostly taxodioid, but also cupressoid	*Thuja plicata*

12	Rays high, sometimes >30 cells; horizontal walls of ray cells well-pitted	*Abies*
12	Rays low, rarely >12 cells; horizontal walls of ray cells with few pits	13

13	Little contrast between earlywood and latewood; cross-field pits mostly cupressoid, but may be taxodioid; intercellular spaces among tracheids frequent	*Juniperus*
13	Narrow bands of latewood sharply distinct from earlywood; cross-field pits mostly taxodioid, but may be cupressoid	*Thuja plicata*

This key, like the previous one, would lead the user astray if he attempted to identify a timber which had not been considered in the construction of the key; the wood of *Sequoia*, for example, would probably appear, not wholly satisfactorily, to be that of *Thuja*. This error would be revealed by detailed reference to Chapter 4.

Three other points concerning the key also call for comment. Firstly, the reader will have noted the somewhat unsatisfactory nature of the features used to separate *Larix* and *Picea* (¶7 of the key). The numerical characteristics used are not clearly distinct, but overlap in their ranges, and moreover, it may be added, even within these ranges the data are not wholly reliable. Apart from the nature of their earlywood to latewood transition, and the more pronounced latewood of *Larix* (Fig. 19), these two timbers are indeed very much alike in their microscopic features. Seen in the log, however, the pigmented heartwood of *Larix*, in contrast with the pale heartwood of *Picea*, affords an additional difference between them.

Secondly, it will also have been noted that *Thuja* appears twice in the key, at ¶'s 11 and 13, so that there are two routes to its identification. This is an example of a device often used in dichotomous keys, to take account of the variability of the genera or species which are to be distinguished; in this instance the variability is in the occurrence of biseriate pitting. This feature, though always present in *Thuja*, may sometimes be so sparsely distributed as to be easily overlooked in a small section, and provision has thus been made for this contingency.

Thirdly, in looking for the intercellular spaces characteristic of *Juniperus*, the student must take care not to be misled by the presence of compression wood, which has similar spaces and may occur in any softwood (see Chapter 9). If this is suspected the 'rotating wheel effect' might be looked for in a transverse section, and confirmation sought in examination of a longitudinal section. The characteristic grooving of the tracheid walls, if present, would clearly identify compression wood.

It is a very worthwhile exercise in the study of wood anatomy, calling for good observation and critical thought, for the student to construct his own key to a small number of timbers, or perhaps to attempt to extend the keys given here so that they might take into account one or two extra genera. He will then appreciate more fully the special difficulties inherent in the construction of these keys.

A multiple-entry, punched-card type of key for timbers was devised in the Forest Products Research Laboratory in 1936, for the identification of hardwoods (Clarke, 1938). A key of this type, based on characters of the wood which are discernible by hand-lens, was published later (F.R.P.L., 1952), and one using microscopic characters followed (Brazier and Franklin, 1961). This type of key was applied also to softwoods by Phillips (1941, and in an amended form, 1948). In later years many other keys of a similar type have been designed by other workers for a variety of more specialized purposes. It is unfortunate that the Brazier and Franklin key, the hardwood key most useful to students, has been out of print for some years; although the preparation of a second edition was announced by the Building Research Establishment in 1978, its publication is still awaited.

Punched-card keys make use of perforated cards in which the (numbered) perforations are arranged along the edges of the cards. The cards also have one corner cut off obliquely, so that they can readily be stacked all the same way round. Each card in the key represents one timber and bears its name, and each perforation represents an anatomical feature or some other attribute of the wood, and an indication in broad terms of its geographical origin. The selection of these features for use in the key, so that they may be relevant to all the timbers it is

Fig. 136. An example of a punched card for use with the Brazier and Franklin microscope key for the identification of hardwoods. This card has been clipped to record the data for *Ulmus procera*.

FAMILY:- Ulmaceae

NAME:- Ulmus procera Salisb.

NOTES:- also some other Ulmus spp.

F.P.R.L. Microscope Key to Hardwoods

A B C D E F G H

J K L M N O P Q

a b c d e f g h

j k l m n o p q

VESSELS

1 EXCLUSIVELY SOLITARY
2 RAD. MULTIPLES PREDOM.
3 RAD./OBLIQUE ARRANGEMENT
4 TANGENTIAL ARRANGEMENT
5 *Pore Clusters*
6 PERFS. SIMPLE
7 MULT. PERF. PLATES
8 PLATES WITH > 20 BARS
9 SPIRALS
10 PITS MINUTE
11 PITS OPPOSITE OR SCAL.
12 *Pits Vestured*
13 *Vessels Absent*
14 *Tyloses Abundant*
15 *Tyloses Sclerosed*
16 *Gum or Deposits*
17 *Mean T.D. < 50μ*
18 *Mean T.D. < 100μ*
19 *Mean T.D > 200μ*

Axial Canals

20 NORMAL
21 NORMAL, TANG. LINES
22 *Traumatic*

FIBRES, etc.

23 SEPTATE
24 THICK-WALLED
25 FIBRE-TRACHEIDS
26 *Tracheids Present*
27

RAYS

28 COMMONLY > 1 MM. HIGH
29 EXCLUSIVELY 1 - SERIATE
30 COMMONLY 4-10-SERIATE
31 COMMONLY > 10-SERIATE
32 AGGREGATE RAYS
33 HOMOGENEOUS
34 HETEROGENEOUS TYPE I
35 HETEROGENEOUS TYPE II
36 HETEROGENEOUS TYPE III
37 2- or 3-SER. PARTS NARROW
38 TILE CELLS; D. or PT. TYPE
39 *Sheath Cells*
40 CANALS OR LATEX TUBES
41 STORIED
42 PITS→VESSELS LARGE, ROUND
43 PITS→VES. LARGE, GASH-LIKE
44 PITS→VESSELS SMALL

PARENCHYMA

45 RARE OR ABSENT
46 TERMINAL OR INITIAL
47 PREDOM. APOTRACHEAL
48 *Diffuse*
49 DIFFUSE-IN-AGGREGATES
50 PREDOM. PARATRACHEAL
51 SCANTY PARATRACHEAL
52 VASICENTRIC
53 ALIFORM OR CONFLUENT
54 BANDED
55 BANDS 1 - SERIATE
56 BANDS ≮ 4-SERIATE
57 FUSIFORM CELLS COMMON

Other Features

58 INCLUDED PHLOEM
59 AXIAL ELEMENTS STORIED
60 OIL OR MUCILAGE CELLS

CRYSTALS, etc.

61 *Rhomboidal in Rays, Pa., Fib.*
62 *Rhomboidal in Chambered Cells*
63 *Rhomboidal in Idioblasts*
64 *Silica in Rays, Pa., Fib., Ves.*
65 *Raphides or Druses*
66 *Elongated, etc., Sand*

PHYSICAL PROPERTIES

67 DISTINCTIVE ODOUR
68 DISTINCTIVE COLOUR
69 WHITE
70 YELLOW OR BROWN
71 REDDISH
72 SPEC. GRAV. < O.5
73 SPEC. GRAV. > 1.0

GEOGRAPHICAL REGIONS

74 EUROPE TO JAPAN, ETC.
75 INDIA, ETC.
76 MALAYA, ETC.
77 AUSTRALIA, NEW ZEALAND
78 TROP. AFRICA & MASC. IS.
79 SOUTH AFRICA
80 NORTH AMERICA
81 TROP. AMERICA, W. INDIES
82 TEMP. SOUTH AMERICA

GROWTH RINGS

83
84 *Distinct and Regular*
85 RING-POROUS
86 INTERMED-RING-POROUS
87
88

proposed to include in the key, and effective in relation to their separation, is of course a matter calling for wide knowledge and experienced judgement. For the F.P.R.L. hardwood keys, relating to nearly 400 timbers, 8in x 5in cards and 86 features were used (Fig. 136). Phillips' softwood key, however, used only 53 features, (most of which are, of course, quite different from those appropriate to hardwoods) recorded on 5in x 3in cards.

For all the timbers in such keys, and for all the identificatory features that they have, the corresponding perforations in the cards are clipped through to the edge of the card (with a clipper similar to that used by railway ticket inspectors) so that they become notches rather than perforations. If a feature is present in a timber, but is not well developed, the notch is, in addition, marked with ink. If, in the course of the natural variation of a timber, a given feature may or may not be present, then two cards must be prepared for that timber, one clipped and one left unclipped at the corresponding perforation. A timber variable in two independent features thus calls for four cards, and one variable in three needs eight cards, and so on. The number of cards in the key thus generally exceeds the number of timbers to which they refer.

The published versions of these keys do not include the actual clipped cards, but extend only so far as to describe the characters used in the key, to list the numbers of the perforations which refer respectively to these characters, and to give detailed instructions, for all the timbers in the key, as to which perforations are to be clipped. The actual clipping is left to the would-be owner of a copy of the key, who is thus required to take an essential and demanding part in its construction.

In the use of a punched-card key the cards are accurately stacked on edge (in any order), the unknown timber is examined and any of its features which appear in the key are noted. It might, for instances, first be seen to be ring-porous. If so, a knitting needle would be inserted into the perforation for ring-porous, so as to pass right through the stack, and the stack would be gently shaken. All the cards for ring-porous timbers, having been clipped at this perforation, would thus fail to be retained by the needle, and would fall out of the stack. They would then be restacked and treated in the same way with respect to a second feature, and the process would be repeated until eventually only one card fell out. This card (on the assumption that the unknown timber was among those represented in the key) would bear the name of the timber.

There are a number of advantages of punched-card keys over other kinds. Firstly the features used to sort the cards may be taken in any order, so that should an unknown specimen show very conspicuous or unusual features, these may be used in the early stages of card selection, with a resultant saving of time. Secondly, if the features used in the key have been well chosen in the first place, the key can be extended to include new timbers simply by adding extra cards, without the necessity for alteration of those already existing. Obviously there must be limits in this; it would clearly be impracticable to attempt to put hardwoods and softwoods in the same key, and among hardwoods alone the number of cards could well become inconveniently large. Thirdly, since each punched card carries a brief résumé of the principal distinctive characteristics of the timber to which it refers, when a card for an unknown specimen has been finally selected by the use of the key, the presumptive identity of the specimen can be checked against all the features recorded on the card, not merely those which happened to have been used in the selection process. Although the entries on the cards may thus themselves serve substantially to confirm an identification, it is always possible that the unknown specimen may be one of a timber not considered by the constructor of the key. For this reason (among others) reference to more extensive information bearing on the identification may sometimes prove to be necessary, so that keys are normally accompanied by references to the primary sources of the data used in their construction. Reference to data on wood anatomy of this kind has been facilitated by Gregory (1980), who has produced an annotated bibliography of more than 450 works (post 1900), relating to wood structure and identification. The works cited deal with the structure of timbers of very varied groups, defined in taxonomic or geographical terms, as for example the timbers of a genus or family, or those grown in a particular country or imported into it. The bibliography also includes references to keys, to lists of characters for the preparation of punched cards, and to works containing photographs which may be useful in timber identification.

The multiple-entry punched-card type of key has proved, for major purposes, to be the most useful type, and in recent years has been shown to promise further development. Since each card bears what is in effect a number code for its corresponding timber, the recording and sorting of these codes are amenable to the application of computer techniques, and Miller (1980) has described and discussed a computer programme adapted for this work. The data for 4700 entries in the 'Oxford Card' multiple-entry key, which had been recorded by Chalk in the course of the preparation of the sections on wood structure in the 'Anatomy of Dicotyledons' (Metcalfe and Chalk, 1950), have also been computerized (Pearson and Wheeler, 1981), and a list of standard characters suitable for computerized hardwood identification has been prepared by the International Association of Wood Anatomists (1981).

The use of computer techniques thus introduces new methods of storage and search of the great range of data bearing on wood structure which now exists, and of absorbing additions to it in the future. But the computer can operate only within the limitations of the information supplied to it; a successful search for the identity of an unknown timber must depend not only on the quality of the anatomical data stored in the computer, but equally, on the quality of the data pertaining to the unknown specimen which is presented to the computer in the course of the search.

The knowledge and skill of wood anatomists, in the observation and interpretation of wood structure, will thus be no less indispensable to the future identification of wood by computer than they are at present by the use of the older methods.

Appendix

In this appendix we list firstly the common names, with their botanical equivalents, of the timbers referred to in the text. Wherever possible the common name used is that to be found in the British Standard 881 & 589: 1974, Nomenclature of Commercial Timbers. Secondly we list the botanical names with their equivalent common names. Since the lists refer only to timbers mentioned in the text they are not exhaustive. More comprehensive lists can be found in Howard, (1948), Beekman (1964), Corkhill, (1979) and Boutelje, (1980).

Common names with their botanical equivalents

Softwoods

cedar
Atlantic	*Cedrus atlantica* (Endl.) Carr.
atlas	*C. atlantica* (Endl.) Carr.
deodar	*C. deodara* (Roxb.) Loud.
Japanese	*Cryptomeria japonica* (L. f.) D. Don
of Lebanon	*Cedrus libani* A. Rich.
Port Orford	*Chamaecyparis lawsoniana* (A. Murr.) Parl.
pencil, East African	*Juniperus procera* Hochst. ex A. Rich.
pencil, Virginian	*J. virginiana* L.
western red	*Thuja plicata* D. Don
white	*T. occidentalis* L.
yellow	*Chamaecyparis nootkatensis* (D. Don) Spach

cypress
bald	*Taxodium distichum* (L.) Rich.
Monterey	*Cupressus macrocarpa* Gord.

southern	*Taxodium distichum* (L.) Rich.
swamp	*T. distichum* (L.) Rich.
fir	
balsam	*Abies balsamea* (L.) Mill.
Colorado	*A. concolor* Lindl. & Gordon
Douglas	*Pseudotsuga menziesii* (Mirb.) Franco
grand	*Abies grandis* (Dougl.) Lindl.
silver	*A. alba* Mill.
hemlock	
eastern	*Tsuga canadensis* (L.) Carr.
western	*T. heterophylla* (Rof.) Sarg.
kauri	
East Indian	*Agathis dammara* (A.B. Lamb.) L.C. Rich.
Fijian	*A. vitiensis* (Seem.) Drake
New Zealand	*A. australis* (D. Don) Salisb.
Queensland	*A. microstachya* J.F. Bail. f. & C.T. White.
	A. palmerstonii F. Muell.
	A. robusta (C. Moore ex F. Muell.) F.M. Bail.
larch, European	*Larix decidua* Mill.
manio	*Podocarpus salignus* D. Don, and *P. nubigenus* Lindl.
matai	*P. spicatus* R. Br.
monkey puzzle	*Araucaria araucana* K. Koch
nutmeg, Californian	*Torreya californica* Torr. = *Tumion californicum* (Torr.) Greene
pine	
Austrian	*Pinus nigra* Arnold
Canadian red	*P. resinosa* Ait.
bunya	*Araucaria bidwillii* Hook.
celery-top	*Phyllocladus rhomboidalis* Rich.
Chile	*Araucaria araucana* (Molina) K. Koch
cow's tail	*Cephalotaxus* sp.
cypress, white	*Callitris glauca* R. Br.
hoop	*Araucaria cunninghamii* Ait. ex D. Don
huon	*Dacrydium franklinii* Hook. f.
jack	*Pinus banksiana* Lamb.
kauri	*Agathis australis* (D. Don) Salisb.
lodgepole	*Pinus contorta* Dougl.
Norfolk Island	*Araucaria excelsa* R. Br.
Parana	*A. angustifolia* (Bert) O. Ktze.
pitch, American	*Pinus palustris* Mill. and *P. elliottii* Engelm.
Caribbean	*P. caribaea* Morelet

radiata	*Pinus radiata* D. Don
Scots	*P. sylvestris* L.
western white	*P. monticola* Dougl., ex D. Don
yellow	*P. strobus* L.
podo	*Podocarpus gracilior* Pilg.
	P. milanjianus Rendle
	P. usambarensis Pilg.
redwood	*Pinus sylvestris* L.
Californian	*Sequoia sempervirens* (D. Don) Endl.
rimu	*Dacrydium cupressinum* Soland.
sempilor	*Dacrydium elatum* (Roxb.) Wall.
sequoia	*Sequoia sempervirens* (D. Don) Endl.
spruce	
Eastern Canadian	*Picea* spp., mainly *P. glauca* (Moench) Voss
Norway	*P. abies* (L.) Karst.
Sitka	*P. sitchensis* (Borg.) Carr.
West Himalayan	*P. smithiana* (Wallich) Boissier
western white	*P. glauca* (Moench) Voss
totara	*Podocarpus totara* D. Don ex Lamb. and *P. hallii* T. Kirk
wellingtonia	*Sequoiadendron giganteum* (Lindl.) Buch. = *Sequoia gigantea* (Lindl.) Decne.
whitewood	
in part	*Abies alba* Mill.
in part	*Picea abies* (L.) Karst.
yew	*Taxus baccata* L.

Hardwoods

afara (=limba)	*Terminalia superba* Engl. & Diels
afrormosia	*Pericopsis elata* van Meeuwen
agba	*Gossweilerodendron balsamiferum* (Verm.) Harms.
alder	
common	*Alnus glutinosa* (L.) Gaertn.
grey	*A. incana* Moench
alstonia	*Alstonia congensis* Engl. *A. boonei* De Wild.
apopo	
(= African walnut)	*Lovoa trichilioides* Harms.
apple	*Malus sylvestris* Mill.
ash	
American	*Fraxinus nigra* Marsh.

European	*F. excelsior* L.
Japanese	*F. mandshurica* Rupr.
mountain	*Eucalyptus regnans* F. Muell.
Victorian	
(= Tasmanian oak):	*E. regnans* F. Muell.
aspen, European	*Populus tremula* L.
balsa	*Ochroma pyramidalis* Urb.
	(= *O. lagopus* Sw.)
basralocus	*Dicorynia guianensis* Amsh.
	(= *D. paraensis* Benth.)
basswood	*Tilia americana* L.
beech	
American	*Fagus grandifolia* Ehrh.
European	*F. sylvatica* L.
Japanese	*F. crenata* Bl.
silver	*Nothofagus menziesii* Oerst.
beeches, 'southern'	*Nothofagus* spp.
bibolo	
(= African walnut)	*Lovoa trichilioides* Harms.
birch, European	*Betula pendula* Roth.
	(= *B. verrucosa* Ehrh.)
	B. pubescens Ehrh.
blackbean	*Castanospermum australe*
	A. Cunn. & Fraser ex Hook.
bombax, West African	*Bombax spp.*
boxwood, European	*Buxus sempervirens* L.
brush box	*Tristania conferta* R. Br.
canarium, Malayan	*Canarium* sp.
cedar	
South American	*Cedrela fissilis* Vell.
celtis, African	*Celtis* spp.
	including *C. zenkeri* Engl.
	and *C. soyauxii* Engl.
cherry	
American	*Prunus serotina* Ehrh.
European	*P. avium* L.
chestnut	
American	*Castanea dentata* Borkh.
horse	*Aesculus hippocastanum* L.
sweet	*Castanea sativa* Mill.
cocuswood	*Brya ebenus* DC.
cottonwood	
eastern	*Populus deltoides* Bartr. ex Marsh.
danta	*Nesogordonia papaverifera* Capuron

ebony	*Diospyros* spp.
ekki	*Lophira alata* Banks ex Gaertn. f.
elm, English	*Ulmus procera* Salisb.
eng	*Dipterocarpus tuberculatus* Roxb.
gaboon	*Aucoumea klaineana* Pierre
grevillea	
(= African silky oak)	*Grevillea robusta* A. Cunn.
hackberry	*Celtis occidentalis* L.
hawthorn	*Crataegus laevigata* (Poiret) DC. and *C. monogyna* Jacq.
hazel	*Corylus avellana* L.
hickory	*Carya glabra* (Mill.) Sweet and *C. ovata* (Mill.) K. Koch
holly	*Ilex aquifolium* L.
hornbeam	*Carpinus betulus* L.
horsechestnut	
European	*Aesculus hippocastanum* L.
hububalli	*Loxopterygium sagotti* Hook. f.
idigbo	*Terminalia ivorensis* A. Chev.
iroko	*Chlorophora excelsa* B. & H.f. and *C. regia* A. Chev.
jarrah	*Eucalyptus marginata* Donn. ex Sm.
jelutong	*Dyera costulata* Hook. f.
kapur	*Dryobalanops* spp.
Malaysian	*D. aromatica* Gaertn. f.
karri	*Eucalyptus diversicolor* F. Muell.
keruing	*Dipterocarpus* spp.
kokko	*Albizzia lebbeck* Benth.
krabak	*Anisoptera* spp.
laburnum	*Laburnum anagyroides* Medic.
lauan	
(Philippines)	*Shorea* spp.
white	*Parashorea* spp.
laurel, Chilean	*Laurelia sempervirens* (R. & Pav.) Tul. (= *L. aromatica* Juss.)
lignum vitae	*Guaiacum officinale* L.
lilac	*Syringa vulgaris* L.
limba (= afara)	*Terminalia superba* Engl. & Diels
lime	
European	*Tilia vulgaris* Hayne
Japanese	*T. japonica* Simpk.
small-leaved	*T. cordata* Mill.
logwood	*Haematoxylon campechianum* L.

louro, red	*Ocotea rubra* Mez
madrona	*Arbutus menziesii* Pursh.
magnolia	*Magnolia grandiflora* L. and
	M. virginiana L.
mahogany	
African	*Khaya* spp., mainly *K. ivorensis* A. Chev.
American	*Swietenia* spp.
	S. macrophylla King. and
	S. mahagoni Jacq.
Cuban (U.K.)	*S. mahagoni* Jacq.
mansonia	*Mansonia altissima* A. Chev.
maple, rock	*Acer nigrum* Mich. f. and
	A. saccharum Marsh.
meranti	*Shorea* spp.
mersawa	*Anisoptera* spp.
mora	*Mora excelsa* Benth.
muhuhu	*Brachylaena hutchinsii* Hutch.
muninga	*Pterocarpus angolensis* DC.
myrtle, Tasmanian	*Nothofagus cunninghamii* (Hook.) Oerst.
Oak	
American red	*Quercus rubra* L. emend. Du Roi
	(and other spp.)
American white	*Q. alba* L. (and other spp.)
cork	*Q. suber* L.
European, (common,	
pedunculate):	*Q. robur* L.
European, (sessile)	*Q. petraea* (Matt.) Liebl.
evergreen = holm	*Q. ilex* L.
silky, African	
(= grevillea)	*Grevillea robusta* A. Cunn.
silky, Australian:	*Cardwellia sublimis* F. Muell.
Tasmanian	*Eucalyptus regnans* F. Muell.
	(and other spp.)
obeche (=wawa):	*Triplochiton scleroxylon* K. Schum.
ogea	*Daniellia ogea* (Harms.) Rolfe ex Holl.
	D. thurifera Bennett
okwen	*Brachystegia* spp. including
	B. eurycoma Harms.
	B. leonensis Hutch. & Burtt Davy.
	B. nigerica Hoyle & Burtt Davy
opepe	*Nauclea diderrichii* (De Wild. & Th. Dur)
	Merr.
	(= *Sarcocephalus diderrichii* De Wild. & Th.
	Dur.)

osier, common	*Salix viminalis* L.
pear	*Pyrus communis* L.
pecan	*Carya pecan* Engl. & Graebn.
peroba	*Paratecoma* sp.
plane	
European:	*Platanus hybrida* Brot. =
(in U.K., = London)	*P. acerifolia* Willd.
poplar	
white	*Populus alba* L.
grey	*P. canescens* Sm.
Canadian	*P. balsamifera* L.
quaruba	*Vochysia* spp.
ramin	*Gonystylus* spp., mainly
	G. macrophyllum (Miq.) Airy-Shaw
	(= *G. bancanus* Baill.)
rauli	*Nothofagus procera* (Poepp. & Endl.) Oerst.
red gum, American	*Liquidambar styraciflua* L.
robinia	*Robinia pseudoacacia* L.
rosewood, Indian	*Dalbergia latifolia* Roxb.
sapele	*Entandrophragma cylindricum* Sprague
sassafras	*Sassafras officinale* Nees et Eberm.
satiné	*Brosimum paraense* Hub.
sepetir, swamp	*Pseudosindora palustris* Sym.
seraya	*Shorea* spp.
sida	
(=African walnut)	*Lovoa trichilioides* Harms.
spotted gum	*Eucalyptus maculata* Hook.
sterculia	
brown	*Sterculia rhinopetala* K. Schum.
yellow	*S. oblonga* Mast.
stringy barks	*Eucalyptus* spp. including
	E. acmenioides Schau.
	E. carnea (R.T. Bak.) L. Johnson
sugi	*Cryptomeria japonica* (L. f.) D. Don
sycamore	*Acer pseudoplatanus* L.
teak	*Tectona grandis* L.f.
tulip tree (U.K.)	*Liriodendron tulipifera* L.
(= Amer. whitewood)	
tepa	*Laurelia serrata* Ph.
tupelo	*Nyssa sylvatica* Marsh.
	(and other spp.)

utile	*Entandrophragma utile* Sprague
walnut	
African	*Lovoa trichilioides* Harms.
	(= *L. klaineana* Pierre ex Sprague)
American	*Juglans nigra* L.
European	*J. regia* L.
Nigerian	*Lovoa trichilioides* Harms.
Queensland	*Endiandra palmerstonii* (F.M. Bail.)
	C. T. White & W. D. Francis
wawa (=obeche)	*Triplochiton scleroxylon* K. Schum.
whitebeam	*Sorbus aria* Crantz.
whitewood, American	*Liriodendron tulipifera* L.
willow	
cricket-bat	*Salix alba* cv. *calvar* G. Mayer
	(= *S. alba* var. *coerulea* Sm.)
white or crack	*S. fragilis* L.
common osier	*S. viminalis* L.
zebrano	*Microberlinia* sp.

Botanical names with their common names

Softwoods

Abies alba Mill	whitewood (in part), silver fir
A. balsamea (L.) Mill.	balsam fir
A. concolor Lindl. & Gord.	Colorado fir
A. grandis (Dougl.) Lindl.	grand fir
Actinostrobus pyramidalis Miquel.	
Agathis australis (D. Don) Salisb.	New Zealand kauri, kauri pine
A. dammara (A.B. Lamb.) L.C. Rich.	East Indian kauri
A. microstachysa J.F. Bail. f. &	
C.T. White	Queensland kauri
A. palmerstonii F. Muell.:	Queensland kauri

A. robusta (C. Moore ex F. Muell.) F.M. Bail.	Queensland kauri
A. vitiensis (Seem.) Drake	Fijian kauri
Araucaria angustifolia (Bert.) O. Ktze.	Parana pine
A. araucana (Molina) K. Koch	Chile pine
A. bidwillii Hook.	bunya pine
A. cunninghamii Ait. ex D. Don:	hoop pine
A. excelsa R. Br.	Norfolk Island pine
Callitris spp.	cypress pines
C. glauca R. Br.	white cypress pine
Cedrus atlantica (Endl.) Carr.	Atlas or atlantic cedar
C. deodara (Roxb.) Loud.	deodar
C. libani A. Rich	cedar of Lebanon
Cephalotaxus spp.:	cow's tail pines
Chamaecyparis lawsoniana (A. Murr.) Parl.	Port Orford cedar
C. nootkatensis (D. Don) Spach:	yellow cedar
Cryptomeria japonica (L. f.) D. Don	sugi, Japanese cedar (U.K.)
Cupressus macrocarpa Gord.	Monterey cypress
Dacrydium cupressinum Soland.	rimu
D. elatum (Roxb.) Wall.	sempilor
D. franklinii Hook. f.	huon pine
Juniperus procera Hochst, ex A. Rich.	East African pencil cedar
J. virginiana L.	Virginian pencil cedar
Larix decidua Mill	European larch
Phyllocladus rhomboidalis Rich	celery-top pine
Picea abies (L.) Karst.	whitewood (in part), Norway spruce
P. glauca (Moench) Voss	western white spruce
P. sitchensis (Borg.) Carr.	Sitka spruce
P. smithiana (Wallich) Bossier	West Himalayan spruce
Pinus banksiana Lamb.	jack pine
P. caribaea Morelet	Caribbean pitch pine
P. contorta Dougl.	lodgepole pine
P. elliottii Engelm.	American pitch pine (in part)
P. monticola Dougl. ex D. Don:	western white pine
P. nigra Arnold	Austrian pine
P. palustris Mill.	American pitch pine (in part)
P. radiata D. Don	radiata pine
P. resinosa Ait.	Canadian red pine
P. strobus L.	yellow pine
P. sylvestris L.	redwood, Scots pine
Podocarpus gracilior Pilg.	podo
P. hallii T. Kirk	totara
P. milanjianus Rendle	podo

P. nubigenus Lindl.	manio
P. salignus D. Don	manio
P. spicatus R. Br.	matai
P. totara D. Don ex Lamb.	totara
P. usambarensis Pilg.	podo
Pseudotsuga menziesii (Mirb.) Franco	Douglas fir
Sequoia sempervirens (D. Don) Endl.	Sequoia, California redwood
Sequoiadendron gigantum (Lindl.) Buch. (= *Sequoia gigantea* (Lindl.) Decne.)	wellingtonia
Taxodium distichum (L.) Rich.	southern cypress, swamp cypress, bald cypress
Taxus baccata L.	yew
Thuja occidentalis L.	white cedar
T. plicata D. Don	western red cedar
Torreya californica Torrey (= *Tumion californicum* (Torr.) Greene)	Californian nutmeg
Tsuga canadensis (L.) Carr.	eastern hemlock
T. heterophylla (Rof.) Sarg.	western hemlock

Hardwoods

Acer spp.	maples
A. nigrum Michx. f.	rock maple
A. pseudoplatanus L.	sycamore
A. saccharum Marsh.	rock maple
Aesculus hippocastanum L.	European horsechestnut
Albizzia falcata	
A. lebbeck Benth.	kokko
Alnus glutinosa (L.) Gaertn.	common alder
A. incana Moench	grey alder
Alstonia boonei De Wild.	alstonia
A. congensis Engl.	alstonia
Anisoptera spp.	mersawa, krabak etc.
Antrocaryon spp.	
Arbutus menziesii Pursh.	madrona
Aucoumea klaineana Pierre	gaboon
Betula spp.	birches
B. pendula Roth. and	
B. pubescens Ehrh.	European birch
Bombax buonopozense P. Beauv.	West African bombax
Brachylaena hutchinsii Hutch.	muhuhu
Brachystegia spp., including	okwen
B. eurycoma Harms.	

B. leonensis Hutch. & Burtt Davy
B. nigerica Hoyle & A.P.D. Jones
Brosimum paraense Hub.   satiné
Brya ebenus D.C.   cocuswood
Buxus sempervirens L.   European boxwood
Canarium spp.   canarium
Cardwellia sublimis F. Muell.   Australian silky oak
Carpinus betulus L.   hornbeam
Carya glabra (Mill.) Sweet.   hickory
C. illinoensis K. Koch
(= *C. pecan* Engl. & Graeb.)   pecan
C. ovata (Mill.) K. Koch   hickory
Castanea dentata Borkh.   American chestnut
C. sativa Mill.   sweet chestnut
Castanospermum australe
   A. Cunn. & Fraser ex Hook.   blackbean
Cedrela fissilis Vell.   South American cedar
Celtis occidentalis L.   hackberry
C. soyauxii Engl.
C. zenkeri Engl.
and other spp.   African celtis
Chlorophora excelsa (Welw.) B. & H.f.   iroko
C. regis A. Chev.   iroko
Corylus avellana L.   hazel
Crataegus laevigata (Poiret) DC.   hawthorn
C. monogyna Jacq.   hawthorn
Dalbergia latifolia Roxb.   Indian rosewood
Daniellia ogea (Harms) Rolfe ex Holl.   ogea
D. thurifera Bennett   ogea
Dicorynia guianensis Amsh.
(= *D. paraensis* Benth.)   basralocus
Diospyros spp.   ebonies
Dipterocarpus tuberculatus Roxb.   eng
Dryobalanops spp.   kapur
D. aromatica Gaertn. f.   Malaysian kapur
Durio sp.
Dyera costulata Hook. f.   jelutong
Endiandra palmerstonii(F.M. Bail.)
   C.T. White & W.D. Francis   Queensland Walnut
Entandrophragma cylindricum   sapele
   (Sprague) Sprague
E. utile (Dawe & Sprague) Sprague   utile
Eucalyptus acmenoides Schau.   stringy bark
E. carnea (R.T. Bak.) L. Johnson   stringy bark

E. camaldulensis Dehn.	red gum
E. diversicolor F. Muell.	karri
E. maculata Hook.	spotted gum
E. marginata Donn. ex Sm.	jarrah
E. regnans F. Muell.	Tasmanian oak
Fagus spp.	beeches
F. crenata Bl.	Japanese beech
F. grandifolia Ehrh.	American beech
F. sylvatica L.	European beech
Fraxinus spp.	ashes
F. excelsior L.	European ash
F. mandshurica Rupr.	Japanese ash
F. nigra Marsh.	American ash
Gonystylus macrophyllum (Miq.) Airy-Shaw	ramin
Gossweilerodendron balsamiferum (Verm.) Harms.	agba
Grevillea robusta A. Cunn.	grevillea, African silky oak
Guaiacum officinale L.	lignum vitae
Haematoxylon campechianum L.	logwood
Hoheria angustifolia Raoul.	
Ilex aquifolium L.	holly
Juglans nigra L.	American walnut
J. regia L.	European walnut
Khaya ivorensis A. Chev.	African mahogany
K. anthotheca C. DC.	African mahogany
Laburnum anagyroides Medic.	laburnum
Laurelia sempervirens (R. & Pav.) Tul. (= *L. aromatica* Juss.)	Chilean laurel
L. serrata Ph.	tepa
Liquidambar styraciflua L.	American red gum
Liriodendron tulipifera L.	American whitewood
Lophira alata Banks ex Gaertn. f.	ekki
Lovoa trichilioides Harms. (= *L. klaineana* Pierre ex Sprague)	African walnut
Loxopterygium sagotti Hook. f.	hububalli
Magnolia grandiflora L.	magnolia
M. virginiana L.	magnolia
Malus sylvestris Mill.	apple
Mansonia altissima A. Chev.	mansonia
Mora excelsa Benth.	mora
Nauclea diderrichii (De Wild. et Th. Dur.) Merr. (= *Sarcocephalus diderrichii* De Wild. & Th. Dur.)	opepe

Nesogordonia papaverifera Capuron	danta
Nothofagus spp.	'southern beech'
N. cunninghamii (Hook.) Oerst.	Tasmanian myrtle
N. menziessii Oerst.	silver beech
N. procera (Poepp. & Endl.) Oerst.	rauli
Nyssa sylvatica Marsh.	tupelo
Ochroma pyramidalis Urb.	
(= *O. lagopus* Sw.)	balsa
Ocotea rubra Mez	red louro
Parashorea spp.	lauan, meranti, seraya
Pericopsis elata van Meeuwen	afrormosia
(= *Afrormorsia elata* Harms.)	
Platanus hybrida Mill.	European plane
(= *P. acerifolia* Willd.)	London plane (U.K.)
Populus spp.	poplars
P. alba L.	white poplar
P. balsamifera L.	Canadian poplar
P. canescens Sm.	grey poplar
P. deltoides Bartr. ex Marsh.	eastern cottonwood
P. robusta Schneid	black poplar
P. tremula L.	European aspen
Prunus avium L.	European cherry
P. serotina Ehrh.	American cherry
Pseudosindora palustris Sym.	swamp sepetir
Pterocarpus angolensis DC	muninga
Pterospermum spp.	
Pterygota kamerunensis	
Pyrus communis L.	pear
Quercus spp.	oaks
Q. alba L.	American white oak
Q. ilex L.	holm oak
Q. petraea (Matt.) Liebl.	European oak; =
(= *Q. sessiliflora* Salisb.)	sessile oak or
	durmast oak (U.K.)
Q. robur L.	European oak; =
(= *Q. pedunculata* Ehrh.)	pedunculate oak (U.K.)
Q. rubra L. emend. Du Roi	American red oak
(= *Q. borealis* Michx. f.)	
Q. suber L.	cork oak
Robinia pseudoacacia L.	robinia
Salix spp.	willows
S. alba cv. *calvar* G. Mayer	
(= *S. alba* var. *coerulea* Sm.)	cricket-bat willow
S. fragilis L.	white willow; crack willow
S. viminalis L.	common osier

Sassafras	sassafras
S. officinale Nees et Eberm.	
Shorea spp.	lauan, meranti, seraya
S. gysbertsiana	
Sorbus aria Crantz	whitebeam
Sterculia oblonga Mast.	yellow sterculia
S. rhinopetala K. Schum.	brown sterculia
Swietenia macrophylla King	American mahogany
S. mahagoni Jacq.	American mahogany; Cuban mahogany (U.K.)
Syringa vulgaris L.	lilac
Tectona grandis L. f.	teak
Terminalia ivorensis A. Chev.	idigbo
T. superba Engl. & Diels	afara, limba
Tilia spp.	limes
T. americana L.	basswood
T. cordata Mill	small-leaved lime
T. japonica Simpk.	Japanese lime
T. vulgaris Hayne	European lime
Triplochiton scleroxylon K. Schum.	obeche, wawa
Tristania conferta R. Br.	brush box
Ulmus procera Salisb.	English elm
Vochysia spp.	quaruba
Wrightia tomentosa	

Literature Cited

Publications of the Forest Products Research Laboratory, Princes Risborough, Buckinghamshire, England, are listed under F.P.R.L. Publications of the F.P.R.L. since its designation as the Princes Risborough Laboratory of the Building Research Establishment are listed under B.R.E. (PRL). Publications from this Laboratory by named authors are listed also under their names. The International Association of Wood Anatomists is abbreviated as I.A.W.A.

ADLER, E. (1977). Lignin chemistry, past, present and future. *Wood Sci. Technol.* **11**, 169–218.

ALVIM, P. DE T. (1964). Tree growth periodicity in tropical climates. *In* ZIMMERMANN, M. H.(*Ed.*), 1964.

AMOBI, C. C. (1974). Periodicity of wood formation in twigs of some tropical trees in Nigeria. *Ann. Bot.* **38**, 931–6.

ARCHER, R. R. and WILSON, B. P. (1973). Mechanics of compression wood response, II. On the location, action and distribution of compression wood formation. *Pl. Physiol.* **51**, 777–82.

ARGANBRIGHT, D. G. and BENSEND, D. W. (1968). Relationship of gelatinous fibre development to tree lean in soft maple. *Wood Sci.* **1**, 37–40.

ARTSCHWAGER, E. (1950). The time factor in the differentiation of secondary xylem and phloem in pecan. *Amer. J. Bot.* **37**, 15–24.

AUDUS, L. J. (1962). The mechanism of the perception of gravity by plants. Soc. Exp. Biol., *Symp. No. 16*, 197–226.

—— (1964). Geotropism and the modified sine rule: an interpretation based on the amyloplast statolith theory. *Physiol. plant.* **17**, 737–45.

—— (1969). Geotropism. *In* WILKINS, M. B. (*Ed.*), 1969.

279

——(1979). Plant geosensors. *J. Exp. Bot.* **30**, 1051–73.

BAAS, P. (1982). (*Ed.*). New perspectives in wood anatomy. The Hague, Martinus/Junk.

BAAS, P., BOLTON, A. J. and CATLING, D. M. (1976). (*Eds.*). Wood structure in biological and technological research. Leiden, University Press.

BAILEY, I. W. (1913). The preservative treatment of wood. II. The structure of pit membranes in the tracheids of conifers and their relation to the penetration of gases, liquids and finely divided solids into green and seasoned wood. *For. Quart.* **11**, 12–20.

—— (1920). The formation of the cell plate in higher plants. *Proc. Nat. Acad. Sci. USA.* **6**, 197–200.

—— (1923). The cambium and its derivative tissues. IV. The increase in girth of the cambium. *Amer. J. Bot.* **10**, 499–509.

—— (1936). The problem of differentiating and classifying tracheids, fibre tracheids and libriform fibres. *Trop. Woods* **45**, 18–23.

—— (1954). Contributions to plant anatomy. Waltham, Mass., Chronica Botanica.

—— and KERR, T. (1935). The visible structure of the secondary wall and its significance in physical and chemical investigations of tracheary cells and fibres. *J. Arnold Arb.* **16**, 273–300.

—— and VESTAL, M. R. (1937). The significance of certain wood-destroying fungi in the study of the enzymatic hydrolysis of cellulose. *J. Arnold Arb.* **18**, 196–205.

BAILEY, P. J. and PRESTON, R. D. (1969). Some aspects of softwood permeability: structural studies with Douglas fir sapwood and heartwood. *Holzforsch.* **23**, 113–9.

BAILLIE, M. G. L. (1982). Tree-ring dating and archaeology. London, Croom Helm.

BAMBER, R. K. (1976). Tylosoids in the resin canals of the heartwood of some species of *Shorea*. *Holzforsch.* **30**, 59–62.

BANNAN, M. W. (1934). Origin and cellular character of xylem rays in gymnosperms. *Bot. Gaz.* **96**, 260–81.

—— (1941). Variability in wood structure in roots of native Ontario conifers. *Bull. Torrey Bot. Club* **68**, 173–94.

—— (1950). The frequency of anticlinal divisions in fusiform cambial cells of *Chamaecyparis*. *Amer. J. Bot.* **37**, 511–9.

—— (1954). Ring width, tracheid size and ray volume in stem wood of *Thuja occidentalis*. *Can. J. Bot.* **32**, 466–79.

—— (1955). The vascular cambium and radial growth in *Thuja occidentalis*. *Can. J. Bot.* **33**, 113–38.

—— (1960). Ontogenetic trends in conifer cambium with respect to frequency of anticlinal divisions and cell length. *Can. J. Bot.* **38**, 795–802.

—— (1966). Spiral grain and anticlinal divisions in the cambium of conifers. *Can. J. Bot.* **44**, 1515–38.

—— (1967a). Anticlinal divisions and cell length in conifer cambium. *For. Prod. J.* **17**, (6), 63–9.

—— (1967b). Sequential changes in rate of anticlinal division, cambial cell length and ring width in the growth of coniferous trees. *Can. J. Bot.* **45**, 1359–69.

—— (1968). Anticlinal divisions and the organization of conifer cambium. *Bot. Gaz.* **129**, 107–113.

—— (1970). A survey of cell length and frequency of multiplicative divisions in the cambium of conifers. *Can. J. Bot.* **48**, 1585–9.

—— and BINDRA, M. (1970a). The influence of wind on ring width and cell length in conifer stems. *Can. J. Bot.* **48**, 255–9.

—— (1970b). Variations in cell length and frequency of anticlinal divisions in the vascular cambium throughout a white spruce tree. *Can. J. Bot.* **48**, 1363–71.

BARBER, N. F. and MEYLAN, B. A. (1964). The anisotropic shrinkage of wood. *Holzforsch.* **18**, 146–56.

BAREFOOT, A. C. and HANKINS, F. W. (1982). Identification of modern and tertiary woods. Oxford, Clarendon Press.

BARGER, R. L. and FFOLLIOTT, P. F. (1976). Factors affecting occurrence of compression wood in individual ponderosa pine trees. *Wood Sci.* **8**, 201–8.

BARGHOORN, E. S. JR. (1940). The ontogenetic development and phylogenetic specialization in the xylem of dicotyledons. *Amer. J. Bot.* **27**, 918–28.

BARNETT, J. R. (1977). Tracheid differentiation in *Pinus radiata*. *Wood Sci. Technol.* **11**, 83–92.

—— (1981a). Secondary xylem cell development. *In* BARNETT, J. R. (*Ed.*), 1981b.

—— (1981b). (*Ed.*). Xylem cell development. Tunbridge Wells, Kent, Castle House Publications.

BARTHOLIN, T. (1979). The *Picea – Larix* problem. *I.A.W.A. Bull.* 1979(1), 7–10.

DE BARY, A. (1884). Comparative anatomy of the phanerogams and ferns. Engl. trans. Oxford, Clarendon Press.

BAUCH, J. and BERNDT, H. (1973). Variability of the chemical composition of pit membranes in the bordered pits of gymnosperms. *Wood Sci. Technol.* **7**, 6–19.

——, LIESE, W. and SCHULTZE, R. (1972). The morphological variability of the bordered pit membranes in gymnosperms. *Wood Sci. Technol.* **6**, 165–84.

BEEKMAN, W. B. (1964). (*Ed.*), Elsevier's wood dictionary in seven languages, vol. 1. Amsterdam, Elsevier Publications.

BEHR, E. A. (1974). Distinguishing heartwood in northern white cedar. *Wood Sci.* **6**, 394–5.

BERLYN, G. P. (1961). Factors affecting the incidence of reaction tissue in *Populus deltoides* Bartr. *Iowa St. J. Sci.* **35**, 367–424.

BEVAN, C. W. L., EKONG, D. E. U. and TAYLOR, D. A. H. (1965). Extractives from West African species of the Meliaceae. *Nature, London.* **206**, 1323–5.

BISSETT, I. J. W. and DADSWELL, H. E. (1949). The variation of fibre length within one tree of *Eucalyptus regnans* F.v.M. *Austral. For.* **13**, 86–96.

—— (1950). The variation in cell length within one growth ring of certain angiosperms and gymnosperms. *Austral. For.* **14**, 17–29.

BLACK, T. M. (1963). Some features of the timber anatomy of *Pinus contorta* Loudon and *P. banksiana* Lambert, *J. Inst. Wood Sci. No. 11*, 57–65.

BLUM, W. (1971). Uber die experimentelle Beeinflussung der Reaktionsholzbildung bei Fichten und Pappeln. *Ber. Schweiz, bot. Ges.* **80**, 225–51.

BOSSHARD, H. H. and HUG, U. E. (1980). The anastomoses of the resin canal system in *Picea abies* (L.) Karst., *Larix decidua* Mill. and *Pinus sylvestris* L. *Holz als Roh-u. Werkstoff*, **38**, 325–8.

BOUTELJE, J. B. (1962). The relationship of structure to transverse anisotropy in wood with reference to shrinkage. *Holzforsch.* **16**, 33–46.

—— (1980). Encyclopedia of world timbers. Stockholm, Swedish For. Prod. Res. Lab.

BOYD, J. D. (1950a). Tree growth stresses. I. Growth stress evaluation. *Austral, J. Sci. Res.* **B, 3**, 270–93.

—— (1950b). Tree growth stresses. II. The development of shakes and other visual features in timber. *Austral. J. Appl. Sci.* **1**, 296–312.

—— (1973). Compression wood force generation and functional mechanics. *New Zeal. J. For. Sci.* **3**, 240–58.

—— (1976a and b). Basic cause of differentiation of tension wood and compression wood, Pts. I. and II. *Drevársky Výskum* **21**, 57–66 and 133–44.

—— (1977a). Relationship between fibre morphology and shrinkage of wood. *Wood Sci. Technol.* **11**, 3–22.

—— (1977b). Basic cause of differentiation of tension wood and compression wood. *Austral. For. Res.* **7**, 121–43.

—— (1985). The key factor in growth stress generation in trees— lignification or crystallisation. *I.A.W.A. Bull.* n.s. **6**, 139–50.

—— and FOSTER, R. C. (1974). Tracheid anatomy changes in response to changing structural requirements of the tree. *Wood Sci. Technol.* **8**, 91–105.

BRAUN, H. J. (1959). Die Vernetzung der Gefässe bei *Populus*. *Ztschr. f. Bot.* **47**, 421–34.

—— (1961). The organization of the hydrosystem in the stemwood of trees and shrubs. *I.A.W.A. Bull.* 1961(2), 2–9.

—— (1970). Funktionelle Histologie der sekundären Sprossachse; I, das Holz. Handbuch der Pflanzenanatomie, 2 Aufl. Spezielle Teil 9, i. Berlin, Borntraeger.

BRAZIER, J. D. and FRANKLIN, G. L. (1961). Identification of hardwoods; a microscope key. *F.P.R.L. Bull. No. 46.* London, H.M.S.O.

B.R.E. (PRL) (1972a), Selecting ash by inspection. *Tech. Note No. 54.*

—— (1972b). Reaction wood (tension wood and compression wood). *Tech. Note No. 57.*

—— (1972c). Handbook of hardwoods, 2nd ed., (revised FARMER, R. H.). London, H.M.S.O.

—— (1977). A handbook of softwoods, 2nd ed. London, H.M.S.O.

—— (1978). Photomicrographs of world woods. London, H.M.S.O.

BRITISH STANDARDS INSTITUTION. (1974). Nomenclature of commercial timbers, including sources of supply. B.S. 881 and 589. London.

BROWN, R. M. JR. and MONTEZINOS, D. (1976). Cellulose microfibrils: visualization of biosynthetic and orienting complexes in association with the plasma membrane. *Proc. Nat. Acad. Sci. USA.* **73**, 143–8.

——, WILLISON, J. H. M. and RICHARDSON, C. L. (1976). Cellulose biosynthesis in *Acetobacter xylinum*; visualization of the site of synthesis and direct measurement of the *in vivo* process. *Proc. Nat. Acad. Sci. USA.* **73**, 4565–9.

BURGGRAAF, P. D. (1972). Some observations on the course of the vessels in the wood of *Fraxinus excelsior* L. *Acta bot. Néerl.* **21**, 32–47.

BURNS, G. P. (1920). Eccentric growth and the formation of redwood in the main stem of conifers. *Vt. Agr. Sta. Bull.* **219**, 1–16.

BÜSGEN, H. and MÜNCH, E. (1929), The structure and life of forest trees. (Engl. trans. Thomson, T.). London, Chapman and Hall.

BUTTERFIELD, B. G. (1976). The ontogeny of the vascular cambium in *Hoheria angustifolia* Raoul. *New Phyt.* **77**, 409–20.

—— and MEYLAN, B. A. (1972). Scalariform perforation plate development in *Laurelia novaezelandiae* A. Cunn., a scanning electron microscope study. *Austral. J. Bot.* **20**, 253–9.

—— (1979). Observations on trabeculae in New Zealand hardwoods. *Wood Sci. Technol.* **13**, 59–65.

—— (1980). Three-dimensional structure of wood (2nd ed). London, Chapman and Hall.

—— (1982). Cell wall hydrolysis in the tracheary elements of secondary xylem. *In* BAAS, P. (*Ed.*), 1982.

CANO-CAPRI, J. and BURKART, L. F. (1974). Distribution of gelatinous fibres as related to lean in southern red oak (*Quercus falcata* Michx.). *Wood Sci.* **7**, 135–6.

CARMI, A., SACHS, T. and FAHN, A. (1972). The relation of ray spacing to cambial growth. *New Phyt.* **71**, 349–53.

CASPERSON, G. (1965). Über endogene Faktoren der Reaktions-holzbildung. I Mitteilung. Wuchstoffapplikation an Kastan-ienepikotylen. *Planta* **64**, 225–40.

CATESSON, A. M. (1974). Cambial cells. *In* ROBARDS, A. W. (*Ed.*), 1974.

CAVE, I. D. (1968). The anisotropic elasticity of the plant cell wall. *Wood Sci. Technol.* **2**, 268–78.

—— (1969). The longitudinal Young's modulus of *Pinus radiata* wood. *Wood Sci. Technol.* **3**, 40–8.

CHAFE, S. C. (1979). Growth stress in trees. *Austral. For. Res.* **9**, 203–23.

CHALK, L. (1970). Short fibres with clearly defined intrusive growth, with special reference to *Fraxinus*. In ROBSON, N. K. B., CUTLER, D. F. and GREGORY, M. (*Eds.*), 1970.

—— MARSTRAND, E. B. and WALSH, J. P. DE C. (1955). Fibre length in storied hardwoods. *Acta bot. Néerl.* **4**, 339–47.

CHATTAWAY, M. M. (1933). Tile cells in the rays of the Malvales. *New Phyt.* **32**, 261–73.

—— (1949). The development of tyloses and the secretion of gum in heartwood formation. *Austral. J. Sci. Res.* **B, 2**, 227–41.

——(1952). The sapwood–heartwood transition. *Austral. For.* **16**, 25–34.

CLARKE, S. H. (1938). A multiple-entry perforated-card key with special reference to the identification of hardwoods. *New Phyt.* **37**, 369–74.

CLOWES, F. A. L. and JUNIPER, B. E. (1968). Plant cells. Oxford, Blackwell.

COHEN, W. E. (1933), A simple chemical test for separating the woods of hoop pine (*Araucaria cunninghamii*) and bunya pine (*Araucaria bidwillii*). *J. C.S.I.R. Austral.* **6**, 126–7.

—— (1935). The identification of wood by chemical means. Pt. 2. Alkalinity of ash and some simple tests for the identification of the coloured woods of the genus *Eucalyptus*. *C.S.I.R. Austral. Pamph. No. 53.*

COMSTOCK, G. L. and CÔTÉ, W. A. JR. (1968). Factors affecting permeability and pit aspiration in coniferous wood. *Wood Sci. Technol.* **2**, 279–91.

CORE, H. A., CÔTÉ, W. A. and DAY, A. C. (1979). Wood structure and identification (2nd ed). Syracuse, N. Y., University Press.

CORKHILL, T. (1979). A glossary of wood. London, Stobart & Son.

CÔTÉ, W. A. JR. (1965) (*Ed.*). Cellular ultrastructure of woody plants. Syracuse, N. Y., University Press.

CÔTÉ, W. A. JR. and DAY, A. C. (1965). Anatomy and ultrastructure of reaction wood. *In* CÔTÉ, W. A. Jr. (*Ed.*) 1965.

—— KUTSCHA, N. P. and TIMELL, T. E. (1968). Studies on compression wood, VIII. Formation of cavities in compression wood tracheids of *Abies balsamea* (L.) Mill. *Holzforsch.* **22**, 138–44.

COWDREY, D. R. and PRESTON, R. D. (1965). The mechanical properties of plant cell walls: helical structure and Young's modulus of air-dried xylem in *Picea sitchensis. In* CÔTÉ, W. A. Jr. (*Ed.*), 1965.

—— (1966). Elasticity and microfibrillar angle in the wood of sitka spruce. *Proc. Roy. Soc. Lond.***B, 166**, 245–72.

CRITCHFIELD, W. B. (1960). Leaf dimorphism in *Populus trichocarpa. Amer. J. Bot.* **47**, 699–711.

—— (1970). Shoot growth and heterophylly in *Ginkgo biloba. Bot. Gaz.* **131**, 150–62.

CRONSHAW, J. (1965). Cytoplasmic fine structure and cell wall development in differentiating xylem elements. *In* CÔTÉ, W. A. Jr. (*Ed.*), 1965.

—— and MOREY, P. R. (1965). Induction of tension wood by 2, 3, 5-tri-iodo-benzoic acid. *Nature, London* **205**, 816–8.

—— (1968). The effect of plant growth substances on the development of tension wood in horizontally inclined stems of *Acer rubrum* seedlings. *Protoplasma,* **65**, 375–91.

—— and WARDROP, A. B. (1964). The organization of cytoplasm in differentiating xylem. *Austral. J. Bot.* **12**, 15–23.

CUMMINS, N. H. O. (1972). Heartwood differentiation in *Pinus* spp. – a modified azo dye test. *New Zeal. J. For. Sci.* **2**, 188–91.

CUTLER, D. F. (1976). Variation in root-wood anatomy. *In* BAAS, P. BOLTON, A. J. and CATLING, D. M. (*Eds.*), 1976.

CUTTER, E. G. (1978). Plant anatomy, Pt. I Cells and tissues, (2nd ed). London, Arnold.

DADSWELL, H. E. (1931). The identification of wood by chemical means, Pt. I. *C.S.I.R. Austral. Pamph. No. 20.*

—— *and* BURNELL,, M. (1932). Method for the identification of the coloured woods of the genus *Eucalyptus. C.S.I.R. Austral. Bull. No. 67.*

—— and ECKERSLEY, A. M. (1935). The identification of the principal commercial Australian timbers other than *Eucalyptus. C.S.I.R. Austral. Bull. No. 90.*

—— and WARDROP, A. B. (1949). What is reaction wood? *Austral. For.* **13**, 22–33.

DENNE, M. P. and DODD, R. S. (1981). The environmental control of xylem differentiation. *In* BARNETT, J. R. (*Ed.*), 1981b.

—— and WILSON, J. E. (1977). Some quantitative effects of indole acetic acid on the wood production and tracheid dimensions of *Picea. Planta* **134**, 223–8.

DESCH, H. E. (1981). Timber, its structure, properties and utilization. (6th ed., revised DINWOODIE, J. M.). London, Macmillan.

DETIENNE, P. and MARIAUX, A. (1977). Nature et periodicité des cernes dans le bois rouge de méliacées. *Bois et forêts des tropiques* No. 175, 52–61. (Seen only in *For. Abstr.* **39**, 382, 1978).

DINWOODIE, J. M. (1961). Tracheid and fibre length in timber – a review of literature. *Forestry* **34**, 125–44.

—— (1963). Variation in tracheid length in *Picea sitchensis* Carr. *F.P.R.L. Spec. Rep. 16.*

—— (1966a). Growth stresses in timber – a review of literature. *Forestry* **39**, 162–70.

—— (1966b). Induction of cell wall dislocations (slip planes) during the preparation of microscope sections of wood. *Nature, Lond.* **212**, 525–7.

——(1968). Failure in timber. Pt. I. Microscopic changes in cell wall structure associated with compression failure. *J. Inst. Wood Sci.* **4**, 37–53.

—— (1970). Brittleheart. *F.P.R.L., Timberlab News* No. 6.

—— (1975). Timber, a review of the structure – mechanical property relationship. *J. Micros.* **104**, 3–32.

—— (1978). Failure in timber. Pt. 3. The effect of longitudinal compression on some mechanical properties. *Wood Sci. Technol.* **12**, 271–85.

—— (1981). Timber, its nature and behaviour. Wokingham, England, van Nostrand and Rheinhold.

DUNNING, C. E. (1968), Cell wall morphology of long-leaf pine latewood. *Wood Sci.* **1**, 65–76.

ERIKSSON, Ö., GORING, D. A. I. and LINDGREN, B. O. (1980). Structural studies on the chemical bonds between lignins and carbohydrates in spruce wood. *Wood Sci. Technol.* **14**, 267–79.

ESAU, K. (1965a). Plant anatomy (2nd ed). New York, Wiley and Sons.

—— (1965b). Vascular differentiation in plants. New York, Holt, Rinehart and Winston.

EVERT, R. F. (1961). Some aspects of cambial development in *Pyrus communis*. *Amer. J. Bot.* **48**, 479–88.

—— (1963). The cambium and seasonal development of the phloem in *Pyrus malus*. *Amer. J. Bot.* **50**, 149–59.

—— and DESHPANDE, B. P. (1970). An ultrastructural study of cell division in the cambium. *Amer. J. Bot.* **57**, 942–51.

EWART, A. J. and MASON-JONES, A. J. (1906). The formation of redwood in conifers. *Ann. Bot.* **20**, 201–4.

FAHN, A. and ARNON, N. (1963). The living wood fibres of *Tamarix aphylla* and the changes occurring in them in the transition from sapwood to heartwood. *New Phyt.* **62**, 99–104.

—— and LESHEM, B. (1963). Wood fibres with living protoplasts. *New Phyt.* **62**, 91–8.

FARMER, R. H. (1972). Handbook of hardwoods. 2nd ed. London, H.M.S.O.

FENGEL, D. (1970),. Ultrastructural changes during aging of wood cells. *Wood Sci. Technol.* **4**, 176–88.

FERGUS, B. J. and GORING, D. A. I. (1970). The distribution of lignin in birch wood as determined by ultraviolet microscopy. *Holzforsch.* **24**, 118–24.

——, PROCTER, A. R., SCOTT, J. A. N. and GORING, D. A. I. (1969). The distribution of lignin in spruce wood as determined by ultraviolet microscopy. *Wood Sci. Technol.* **3**, 117–38.

FINDLAY, G. W. D. and LEVY, J. F. (1970). Wood anatomy in three dimensions. *In* ROBSON, N. K. B. *et al.* (*Eds.*), 1970.

FINDLAY, W. P. K. (1962). The preservation of timber. London, A. and C. Black.

—— (1975). Timber: properties and uses. London, Granada Publications.

FISHER, J. B. and STEVENSON, J. W. (1981). Occurrence of reaction wood in branches of dicotyledons and its role in tree architecture. *Bot. Gaz.* **142**, 82–95.

FOSTER, R. C. (1967). Fine structure of tyloses in three species of Myrtaceae. *Austral. J. Bot.* **15**, 25–34.

F.P.R.L. (1948). Identification of softwoods. *Bull.* No. 22. London, H.M.S.O.

—— (1952). Identification of hardwoods; a lens key. *Bull.* No. 25. London, H.M.S.O.

—— (1961). Identification of hardwoods; a microscope key. *Bull.* No. 46. London, H.M.S.O.

—— (1963). Variation in tracheid length in *Picea sitchensis* Carr. *Spec. rep.* No. 16.

—— (1969a). The strength properties of timbers. *Bull.* No. 50 (2nd ed.). London, H.M.S.O.

—— (1969b). The natural durability classification of timber. *Tech. Note* No. 40. London, H.M.S.O.

—— (1970). Wood-bending handbook. London, H.M.S.O.

FREI, E. and PRESTON, R. D. (1961). Cell wall organization and wall growth in the filamentous algae *Cladophora* and *Chaetomorpha*. I. The basic structure and its formation. *Proc. Roy. Soc. Lond.* **B, 154**, 70–94.

FREY-WYSSLING, A. (1952). Wachstumsleistungen des pflanzlichen Zytoplasmas. *Ber. Schweiz. bot. Ges.* **62**, 583–91.

—— (1976). The plant cell wall (Encyclopaedia of Plant Anatomy, Vol. 3, Pt. 4) (3rd ed). Berlin, Borntraeger.

FRITSS, H. C. (1976). Tree rings and climate. New York, Acad. Press.

GIDDINGS, T. H. JR., BROWER, D. L. and STAEHELIN, L. A. (1980). Visualization of particle complexes in the plasma membrane of *Micrasterias denticulata* associated with the formation of cellulose fibrils in primary and secondary walls. *J. Cell Biol.* **84**, 327–39.

GLERUM, C. and FARRAR, J. L. (1966). Frost-ring formation in the stems of some coniferous species. *Can. J. Bot.* **44**, 879–86.

GLOCK, W. S., STUDHALTER, R. A. and AGERTER, S. R. (1960). Classification and multiplicity of growth layers in the branches of trees at the extreme lower forest border. *Smithson. misc. Coll.* **140**, (1), Publ. 4421.

GOTTWALD, H. P. J. (1972). Tyloses in fibre tracheids. *Wood Sci. Technol.* **6**, 121–7.

GREENIDGE, K. N. H. (1952). An approach to the study of vessel length in hardwood species. *Amer. J. Bot.* **39**, 570–4.

GREGORY, M. (1980). Wood identification: an annotated bibliography. *I.A.W.A. Bull.* n.s. **1**, 3–41.

GREGORY, R. A. (1977). Cambial activity and ray cell abundance in *Acer saccharum. Can. J. Bot.* **55**, 2559–64.

—— and ROMBERGER, J. A. (1975). Cambial activity and height of uniseriate rays in conifers. *Bot. Gaz.* **136**, 246–53.

GREGORY, S. C. and PETTY, J. A. (1973). Valve action in bordered pits of conifers. *J. Exp. Bot.* **24**, 763–77.

HABERLANDT, G. (1914). Physiological plant anatomy. London, Macmillan.

HARADA, H. (1965a). Ultrastructure and organization of gymnosperm cell walls. *In* CÔTÉ, W. A. Jr. (*Ed.*), 1965.

—— (1965b). Ultrastructure of angiosperm vessesl and ray parenchyma. *In* CÔTÉ, W. A. Jr. (*Ed.*), 1965.

—— and CÔTÉ, W. A. JR. (1967). Cell wall organization in the pit border region of softwood tracheids. *Holzforsch.* **21**, 81–5.

HARRIS, J. M. (1954). Heartwood formation in *Pinus radiata* D. Don. *New Phyt.* **53**, 517–24.

—— (1981). Spiral grain formation. *In* BARNETT, J. R. (*Ed.*), 1981b.

—— and MEYLAN, B. A. (1965). The influence of microfibril angle on longitudinal and tangential shrinkage in *Pinus radiata. Holzforsch.* **19**, 144–53.

HARTMANN, F. (1942). Das statische Wuchsgesetz bei Nadel- und Laubbaumen. Vienna, Springer-Verlag. (Original not seen; see also *For. Abstr.* **11**, Abs. No. 2813).

HAUPT, W. and FEINLEIB, M. E. (1979) (*Eds.*). Encyclopaedia of plant physiology, new series. Berlin, Springer-Verlag.

HEJNOWICZ, A. and HEJNOWICZ, Z. (1959). Variations of length in vessel members and fibres in the trunk of *Robinia pseudoacacia. Acta Soc. Bot. Pol.* **28**, 453–60.

HEJNOWICZ, Z. (1961). Anticlinal division, intrusive growth and loss of fusiform initials in non-storied cambium. *Acta Soc. Bot. Pol.* **30**, 729–48.

—— (1964). Orientation of the partition in pseudo-transverse divisions in cambia of some conifers. *Can. J. Bot.* **42**, 1685–91.

—— (1967). Some observations on the mechanism of orientation movements of woody stems. *Amer. J. Bot.* **54**, 684–9.

——— (1980). Tensional stress in the cambium and its developmental significance. *Amer. J. Bot.* **67**, 1–5.

——— and KRAWCZYSZYN, J. (1969). Orientated morphogenetic phenomena in cambium of broad-leaved trees. *Acta Soc. Bot. Pol.* **38**, 547–60.

——— and ROMBERGER, J. A. (1973). Migrating cambial domains and the origin of wavy grain in xylem of broad-leaved trees. *Amer. J. Bot.* **60**, 209–22.

——— (1979). The common basis of wood grain figures is the systematically changing orientation of cambial fusiform cells. *Wood Sci. Technol.* **13**, 89–96.

HEJNOWICZ, Z. and ZAGÓRSKA-MAREK, B. (1974). Mechanism of changes in grain inclination in wood produced by storeyed cambium. *Acta Soc. Bot. Pol.* **43**, 381–98.

HERTH, W. (1985). Plasma membrane rosettes involved in localized wall thickening during xylem vessel formation of *Lepidium sativum* L. *Planta* **164**, 12–21.

HILLIS, W. E. (1962) (*Ed.*). Wood extractives and their significance in the pulp and paper industries. New York, Acad. Press.

——— (1968a). Chemical aspects of heartwood formation. *Wood Sci. Technol.* **2**, 241–59.

——— (1968b). Heartwood formation and its influence on utilization. *Wood Sci. Technol.* **2**, 260–7.

——— (1971). Distribution, properties and formation of some wood extractives. *Wood Sci. Technol.* **5**, 272–89.

HÖSTER, H.-R. and LIESE, W. (1966). Über das Vorkommen von Reaktionsgewebe in wurzeln und Asten der Dikotyledonen. *Holzforsch.* **20**, 80–90.

HOWARD, A. L. (1948). A manual of the timbers of the world, (3rd ed.). London, MacMillan.

HOWARD, E. T. (1971). Bark structure of Southern pines. *Wood Sci.* **3**, 134–48.

——— and MANWILLER, F. G. (1969). Anatomical characteristics of Southern pine stem wood. *Wood Sci.* **2**, 77–86.

HOWES, F. N. (1974). A dictionary of useful and everyday plants and their common names. Cambridge, University Press.

HUGHES, J. F. (1965). Tension wood: a review of the literature. *For. Abstr.* **26**, 1–9 and 179–86.

HUNT, G. M. and GARRATT, G. A. (1967). Wood preservation, (2nd ed.). London, McGraw-Hill.

I.A.W.A. (1964). Multilingual glossary of terms used in wood anatomy. Winterthur, Switzerland, Koncordia.

——— (1981). Standard list of characters suitable for computerized hardwood identification. *I.A.W.A. Bull.* n.s. **2**, 99–105.

ISEBRANDS, J. G. and PARHAM, R. A. (1974). Tension wood anatomy of short rotation *Populus* spp. before and after Kraft pulping. *Wood Sci.* **6**, 256–65.

JACCARD, P. (1934). Über Versuche zur Bestimmung der Zellsaftkonzentration in der Kambialzone bei exzentrischem Dickenwachstum. II. *Jb. wiss. Bot.* **81**, 35–58.

—— (1938). Exzentrisches Dickenwachstum and anatomisch-histologische Differenzierung des Holzes. *Ber. Schweiz. bot. Ges.* **48**, 491–537.

—— (1939). Tropisme et bois de réaction provoqués par la force centrifuge. *Ber. Schweiz. bot. Ges.* **49**, 135–48.

—— (1940). Tropisme et bois de reaction provoqués par la force centrifuge chez le feuillus. *Bot. Schweiz. bot. Ges.* **50**, 279–84.

—— and FREY-WYSSLING, A. (1934). Über Versuche zur Bestimmung der Zellsaftkonzentration in der Kambialzone bei exzentrischem Dickenwachstum. I. *Jb. wiss. Bot.* **79**, 655–80.

JACOBS, M. R. (1945). The growth stresses of woody stems. *Commonw. Bur. For. Austral. Bull.* No. 28.

JANE, F. W. (1956). The structure of wood. London, A. and C. Black.

—— (1970). The structure of wood, (2nd ed., revised WILSON, K. and WHITE, D. J. B.). London, A. and C. Black.

JOHNSON, E. L. and CSERJESI, A. J. (1980). Weathering effect on thujaplicin concentration in western red cedar shakes. *For. Prod. J.* **30**, (6) 52–3.

JUTTE, S. M. (1956). Tension wood in wane. (*Ocotea rubra* Mez.). *Holzforsch.* **10**, 33–5.

—— and LEVY, J. F. (1971). Scanning reflection electron microscopy in studies of wood structure and its degradation. *I.A.W.A. Bull.* 1971(1), 3–13.

—— and SPIT, B. J. (1963). The submicroscopic structure of bordered pits in the radial walls of tracheids in parana pine, kauri and European spruce. *Holzforsch.* **17**, 168–78.

KAEISER, M. (1955). Frequency and distribution of gelatinous fibres in Eastern cottonwood. *Amer. J. Bot.* **42**, 331–4.

KEITH, C. T. (1971). The anatomy of compression failure in relation to creep-inducing stresses. *Wood Sci.* **4**, 71–82.

—— and CÔTÉ, W. A. JR. (1968). Microscopic characterization of slip lines and compression failures in wood cell walls. *For. Prod. J.* **18**, (3), 67–74.

KENNEDY, R. W. and FARRAR, J. L. (1965). Induction of tension wood with the anti-auxin 2-3-5 tri-iodo-benzoic acid. *Nature*, (*Lond.*) **208**, 406–7.

KOLLMANN, F. F. P. and CÔTÉ, W. A. JR. (1968). Principles of wood science and technology, I. solid wood. New York, Springer-Verlag.

—— KUENZI, E. W. and STAMM, A. J. (1975). Principles of wood science and technology. II. Wood-based materials. New York, Springer-Verlag.

KOZLOWSKI, T. T. (1964). Shoot growth in woody plants. *Bot. Rev.* **30**, 335–92.

—— (1971). Growth and development of trees (2 vols). New York, Acad. Press.

KRAMER, P. J. and KOZLOWSKI, T. T. (1979). Physiology of woody plants. London, Acad. Press.

KRATZL, K. (1965). Lignin – its biochemistry and structure. *In* CÔTÉ, W. A. JR. (*Ed.*), 1965.

KRAWCZYSZYN, J. (1971). Unidirectional splitting and uniting of rays in the cambium of *Platanus* accompanying the formation of interlocked grain in wood. *Acta Soc. Bot. Pol.* **40**, 57–79.

—— (1972). Movement of the cambial domain pattern and mechanism of formation of interlocked grain in *Platanus*. *Acta Soc. Bot. Pol.* **41**, 443–61.

—— (1973). Domain pattern in the cambium of young *Platanus* stems. *Acta Soc. Bot. Pol.* **42**, 637–48.

—— and ROMBERGER, J. A. (1979). Cyclical cell length changes in wood in relation to storied structure and interlocked grain. *Can. J. Bot.* **57**, 787–94.

—— (1980). Interlocked grain, cambial domains, endogenous rhythms and time relations, with emphasis on *Nyssa sylvatica*. *Amer. J. Bot.* **67**, 228–36.

KRIBS, D. A. (1968). Commercial foreign woods on the American market. New York, Dover Publications (a revised reprint of the first edition of 1950).

KUČERA, L. (1975). Die dreidimensionale Strukturanalyse des Holzes, 2 Mitteilung: Das Gefäss/Strahl-Netz bei der Buche (*Fagus sylvatica* L.). *Holz a. Roh- u. Werkst.* **33**, 276–82.

—— and BARISKA, M. (1982). On the fracture morphology in wood. Part I. An SEM study of deformation in wood of spruce and aspen under ultimate axial compression loads. *Wood Sci. Technol.* **16**, 241–59.

KUKACHKA, B. F. and MILLER, R. B. (1980). A chemical spot test for aluminium and its value in wood identification. *I.A.W.A. Bull.* n.s. **1**, 104–9.

KUTSCHA, N. P., LOMERSON, J. T. and DYER, M. V. (1978). Separation of eastern spruce and balsam fir by chemical methods. *Wood Sci. Technol.* **12**, 293–308.

LAMING, P. R. (1974). On intercellular spaces in the xylem ray parenchyma of *Picea abies*. *Acta Bot. Néerl.* **23**, 217–33.

LARSON, P. R. and ISEBRANDS, J. G. (1974). Anatomy of the primary/
secondary transition zone in stems of *Populus deltoides*. *Wood Sci.
Technol*. **8**, 11–26.

LAVERS, G. M. (1969). The strength properties of timbers. *F.P.R.L.
Bull*. No. 50 (2nd ed.).

LEACH, R. W. A. and WAREING, P. F. (1967). Distribution of auxin in
horizontal woody stems in relation to gravimorphism. *Nature, London*
214, 1025–7.

LEVY, J. F. (1965). The soft-rot fungi: their mode of action and significance in the degradation of wood. *Adv. Bot. Res*. **2**, 323–57.

LIESE, W. (1965a). The warty layer. *In* CÔTÉ, W. A. JR. (*Ed*.), 1965.

—— (1965b). The fine structure of bordered pits in softwoods. *In* CÔTÉ,
W. A. Jr. (*Ed*.), 1965.

—— and DADSWELL, H. E. (1959). Über den Einfluss der Him-
melsrichtung auf die Länge von Holzfasern und Tracheiden. *Holz als
Roh- u. Werkst*. **17**, 421–7.

MAHMOOD, A. (1968). Cell grouping and primary wall generations in
the cambial zone, xylem and phloem in *Pinus*. *Austral, J. Bot*. **16**,
177–95.

MANWILLER, F. G. (1972). Tracheid dimensions in root-wood of Southern pine. *Wood Sci*. **5**, 122–4.

MARK, R. E. (1976). Cell wall mechanics of tracheids. Newhaven,
Conn., Yale University Press.

MARTS, R. O. (1955). Some structural details of Douglas fir pit membranes by phase contrast. *For. Prod. J*. **5**, 381–2.

McELHANNEY, T. A. *et al*. (1935). Canadian woods, their properties
and uses. Ottawa.

McINTOSH, D. C. (1955a). Effect of rays on radial shrinkage of beech.
For. Prod. J. **5**, 67–71.

—— (1955b). Shrinkage of red oak and beech. *For. Prod. J*. **7**, 355–8.

—— (1957). Transverse shrinkage of red oak and beech. *For. Prod. J*.
7, 114–20.

MERGAN, F. (1958). Distribution of reaction wood in Eastern hemlock
as a function of its terminal growth. *For. Sci*. **4**, 98–109.

METCALFE, C. R. and CHALK, L. (1950). Anatomy of the dicotyledons,
2 vols. Oxford, Clarendon Press.

—— (1983). Anatomy of the dicotyledons (2nd ed.), Vol. II. Wood
structure, etc. Oxford, Clarendon Press.

MEYER, R. W. (1967). Tylosis development in white oak. *For. Prod. J*.
17, (12), 50–6.

—— and CÔTÉ, W. A. JR. (1968). Formation of the protective layer
and its role in tylosis development. *Wood Sci. Technol*. **2**, 84–94.

MEYLAN, B. A. (1968). Cause of high longitudinal shrinkage in wood.
For. Prod. J. **18**, (4), 75–8.

—— and BUTTERFIELD, B. G. (1972). Three-dimensional structure of wood. London, Chapman and Hall.

—— (1978). Helical orientation of microfibrils in tracheids, fibres and vessels. *Wood Sci. Technol.* **12**, 219–22.

—— (1981). Perforation plate differentiation in the vessels of hardwoods. *In* BARNETT, J. R. (*Ed.*), 1981b.

—— and PROBINE, M. C. (1969). Microfibril angle as a parameter in timber assessment. *For. Prod. J.* **19**, (4), 30–3.

MIA, A. J. (1968). Organization of tension wood fibres with special reference to the G-layer in *Populus tremuloides* Michx. *Wood Sci.* **1**, 105–15.

MILES, A. (1978). Photomicrographs of world woods. London, H.M.S.O.

MILLER, R. B. (1980). Wood identification via computer. *I.A.W.A. Bull.* n.s. **1**, 154–60.

MINIUTTI, V. P. (1977). Microscopic observations of paraquat induced light wood in slash pine. *Wood Sci.* **9**, 113–7.

MITCHELL, A. (1974). A field guide to the trees of Britain and Northern Europe. London, Collins.

MOREY, P. R. and CRONSHAW, J. (1968). Developmental changes in the secondary xylem of *Acer rubrum* induced by various auxins and 2, 3, 5-tri-iodobenzoic acid. *Protoplasma* **65**, 287–313.

MORGAN, J. W. W. and ORSLER, R. J. (1967). A simple test to distinguish *Khaya anthotheca* from *K. ivorensis* and *K. grandifoliolia. J. Inst. Wood Sci.* **18**, 61–4.

MUELLER, S. C. and BROWN, R. M. JR. (1980). Evidence for an intramembrane component associated with a cellulose microfibril-synthesizing complex in higher plants. *J. Cell Biol.* **84**, 315–26.

—— (1982). The control of cellulose microfibril deposition in the cell wall of higher plants, Pts. I and II. *Planta* **154**, 489–500 and 501–15.

MURMANIS, L. (1970). Locating the initial in the vascular cambium of *Pinus strobus* L. by electron microscopy. *Wood Sci. Technol.* **4**, 1–14.

—— (1975). Formation of tyloses in felled *Quercus rubra* L. *Wood Sci. Technol.* **9**, 3–14.

—— (1977). Development of vascular cambium into secondary tissues of *Quercus rubra* L. *Ann. Bot.* **41**, 617–20.

—— (1978). Breakdown of end walls in differentiating vessels of *Quercus rubra* L. *Ann. Bot.* **42**, 679–82.

—— and SACHS, I. B. (1969). Seasonal development of secondary xylem in *Pinus strobus. Wood Sci. Technol.* **3**, 177–93.

NANKO, H. and CÔTÉ, W. A. (1980). Bark structure of hardwoods grown on southern pine sites. Syracuse, New York, Syracuse University Press.

NEČESSANÝ, V. (1958). Effect of β-indole acetic acid on the formation of reaction wood. *Phyton* **11**, 117–27.

NELMES, B. J., PRESTON, R. D. and ASHWORTH, D. (1973). A possible function of microtubules suggested by their abnormal distribution in rubbery wood. *J. Cell Sci.* **13**, 741–51.

NICHOLSON, J. E. (1971). A rapid method for estimating longitudinal growth stresses in logs. *Wood Sci. Technol.* **5**, 40–8.

NOEL, A. R. A. (1970). The girdled tree. *Bot. Rev.* **36**, 162–95.

NORBERG, P. H. and MEIER, H. (1966). Physical and chemical properties of the gelatinous layer in tension wood fibres of aspen (*Populus tremula* L.). *Holzforsch.* **20**, 174–8.

NORTHCOTE, D. H. and PICKETT-HEAPS, J. D. (1966). A function of the Golgi apparatus in polysaccharide synthesis and transport in the root-cap cells of wheat. *Biochem J.* **98**, 159–67.

NOSKOWIAK, A. S. (1963). Spiral grain in trees. A review. *For. Prod. J.* **13**, 266–75.

O'BRIEN, T. P. (1981). The primary xylem. *In* BARNETT, J. R. (*Ed.*), 1981b.

ONAKA, F. (1949). Studies in compression and tension wood, (original in Japanese). English summary. *For. Abstr.* **11**, Abs. No. 2815.

PARAMESWARAN, N. and LIESE, W. (1969). On the formation and fine structure of septate wood fibres of *Ribes sanguineum*. *Wood Sci. Technol.* **3**, 272–86.

—— and RICHTER, H.-G. (1984). The ultrastructure of crystalliferous cells in some Lecythidaceae with a discussion of their terminology. *I.A.W.A. Bull.* n.s. **5**, 229–36.

PARHAM, R. A., ROBINSON, K. W. and ISEBRANDS, J. G. (1977). Effects of tension wood on Kraft paper from a short rotation hardwood (*Populus* 'Tristis' No. 1). *Wood Sci. Technol.* **11**, 291–303.

PARKE, R. V. (1959). Growth periodicity and the shoot tip of *Abies concolor*. *Amer. J. Bot.* **46**, 110–8.

PATEL, R. N. (1963). Spiral thickening in normal and compression wood. *Nature, London* **198**, 1225–6.

—— (1964). On the occurrence of gelatinous fibres with special reference to root wood. *J. Inst. Wood Sci.* **12**, 67–80.

—— (1965). A comparison of the anatomy of the secondary xylem in roots and stems. *Holzforsch.* **19**, 72–9.

—— (1971). Anatomy of the stem and root wood of *Pinus radiata* D. Don. *New Zeal. J. For. Sci.* **1**, 37–49.

PEARSON, R. G. and WHEELER, E. A. (1981). Computer identification of hardwood species. *I.A.W.A. Bull.* n.s. **2**, 37–40.

PETERS, W. J. (1974). Tylosis formation in *Pinus* tracheids. *Bot. Gaz.* **135**, 126–31.

PETTY, J. A. (1972). The aspiration of bordered pits in conifer wood. *Proc. Roy. Soc. Lond.* **B 181**, 395–406.

PHILIPSON, W. R., WARD, J. M. and BUTTERFIELD, B. G. (1971). The vascular cambium, its development and activity. London, Chapman and Hall.

PHILLIPS, E. W. J. (1941). The identification of coniferous woods by their microscopic structrue. *J. Linn. Soc. (Bot.)* **52**, 259–320.

—— (1948). Identification of softwoods. *F.P.R.L. Bull.* No. 22. London, H.M.S.O.

PHILLIPS, I. D. J. (1976). The cambium. *In* YEOMAN, M. M. (*Ed.*), 1976.

PHILLIPS, R. (1978). Trees in Britain, Europe and North America. London, Pan Books.

PICKETT-HEAPS, J. D. (1974). Plant microtubules. *In* ROBARDS, A. W. (*Ed.*), 1974.

PRESTON, R. D. (1934). The organization of the cell wall of the conifer tracheid. *Phil. Trans. Roy. Soc. Lond.* **B 224**, 131–74.

—— (1952). The molecular architecture of plant cell walls. London, Chapman and Hall.

—— (1964). Structural and mechanical aspects of plant cell walls with particular reference to synthesis and growth. *In* ZIMMERMANN, M. H. (*Ed.*), 1964.

—— (1974). The physical biology of plant cell walls. London, Chapman and Hall.

—— (1979). Polysaccharide conformation and cell wall function. *Ann. Rev. Plant Physiol.* **30**, 55–78.

PRIESTLEY, J. H. (1930). Studies in the physiology of cambial activity. II. The concept of sliding growth. *New Phyt.* **29**, 96–140.

—— SCOTT, L. I. and MALINS, M. E. (1933). A new method of studying cambial activity. *Proc. Leeds Phil. Soc.* **2**, 365–74.

PURITCH, G. S. (1971). Water permeability of grand fir (*Abies grandis* (Doug.) Lindl.) in relation to infestation by the balsam woolly aphid, *Adelges piceae* Ratz. *J. Exp. bot.* **22**, 936–45.

RAO, B. S. (1959). Variation in structure of the secondary xylem in individual dicotyledonous trees. Ph.D. thesis, University of London.

RENNERFELT, E. (1948). Investigations of thujaplicin, a fungicidal substance in the heartwood of *Thuja plicata* D. Don. *Physiol. Plant.* **1**, 245–54.

RICHARDS, P. W. (1952). The tropical rain forest. Cambridge, University Press.

ROBARDS, A. W. (1965). Tension wood and eccentric growth in crack willow (*Salix fragilis* L.). *Ann. Bot.* n.s. **29**, 419–31.

—— (1966). The application of the modified sine rule to tension wood production and eccentric growth in the stem of crack willow (*Salix fragilis* L.). *Ann. Bot.* n.s. **30**, 513–23.

—— (1967). The xylem fibres of *Salix fragilis* L. *J. Roy. Micros. Soc.* **87**, 329–52.

—— (1968). On the ultrastructure of differentiating secondary xylem in willow. *Protoplasma* **65**, 449–64.

—— (1969). The effect of gravity on the formation of wood. *Sci. Prog. (Oxf.)* **57**, 513–32.

—— (1970). Electron microscopy and plant ultrastructure. London, McGraw-Hill.

—— (1974) (*Ed.*). Dynamic aspects of plant ultrastructure. London, McGraw-Hill.

—— and KIDWAI, P. (1969). A comparative study of the ultrastructure of resting and active cambium in *Salix fragilis* L. *Planta* **84**, 239–49.

—— (1972). Microtubules and microfibrils in xylem fibres during primary cell wall formation. *Cytobiologie* **6**, 1–21.

—— and PURVIS, M. (1964). Chlorazol black E as a stain for tension wood. *Stain Technol.* **39**, 309–15.

ROBERTS, D. R. and PETERS, W. J. (1977). Chemically inducing light wood formation in Southern pines. *For. Prod. J.* **27**, (6), 28–30.

ROBSON, N. K. B., CUTLER, D. F. and GREGORY, M. (1970) (*Eds.*). New research in plant anatomy. London, Acad. Press.

ROELOFSEN, P. A. (1958). Cell wall structure as related to surface growth. *Acta Bot. Néerl.* **7**, 77–89.

—— (1959). The plant cell wall. Encyclopaedia of plant anatomy, Vol. III, Pt. 4. Berlin, Borntraeger.

ROFF, J. W. and WHITTAKER, E. I. (1959). Toxicity tests of a new tropolone, β-thujaplicinol, occurring in Western red cedar. *Can. J. Bot.* **37**, 1132–4.

SAURAT, J. and GUÉNEAU, P. (1976). Growth stresses in beech. *Wood Sci. Technol.* **10**, 111–23.

SAUTER, J. J., ITEN, W. and ZIMMERMANN, M. H. (1973). Studies on the release of sugar into the vessels of sugar maple (*Acer saccharum*). *Can. J. Bot.* **51**, 1–8.

SAVIDGE, R. A. and FARRAR, J. L. (1984). Cellular adjustments in the vascular cambium leading to spiral grain formation in conifers. *Can. J. Bot.* **62**, 2872–9.

SCHMID, R. (1965). The fine structure of pits in hardwoods. *In* CÔTÉ, W. A. JR. (*Ed.*), 1965.

—— and MACHADO, R. D. (1964). Zur Entstehung und fein Struktur skulpturierter Hoftüpfel bei Leguminosen. *Planta* **60**, 612–26.

SCHNIEWIND, A. P. (1959). Transverse anisotropy of wood. *For. Prod. J.* **9**, 350–9.

SCHOLANDER, P. F. (1958). The rise of sap in lianas. *In* THIMANN, K. V. (*Ed.*), 1958.

SCHWANKL, A. (1956). Bark (*trans. and ed.*, EDLIN, H. L.). London, Thames and Hudson.

SCURFIELD, G. (1973). Reaction wood, its structure and function. *Science* **179**, 647–55.

SHELBOURNE, C. J. A. and RITCHIE, K. S. (1968). Relationships between degree of compression wood development and specific gravity and tracheid characters in loblolly pine (*Pinus taeda* L.). *Holzforsch.* **22**, 185–90.

SINNOTT, E. W. (1952). Reaction wood and the regulation of tree form. *Amer. J. Bot.* **39**, 69–78.

—— and BLOCH, R. (1939). Changes in intercellular arrangements during the growth and differentiation of living plant tissues. *Amer. J. Bot.* **26**, 625–34.

SKENE, D. S. (1969). A three-dimensional reconstruction of the wood of *Eucalyptus maculata* Hook. *Holzforsch.* **23**, 33–7.

—— and BALODIS, V. (1968). A study of vessel length in *Eucalyptus obliqua* L'Hérit. *J. Exp. Bot.* **19**, 825–30.

SKOLMEN, R. G. (1973). Characteristics and amount of brittleheart in Hawaii-grown robusta eucalyptus. *Wood Sci.* **6**, 22–9.

SMITH, W. R. and GOEBEL, N. B. (1952). The moisture content of green hickory. *J. For.* **50**, 616–8.

SPACKMAN, W. and SWAMY, B. G. L. (1949). The nature and occurrence of septate fibres in dicotyledons. *Amer. J. Bot.* **36**, 804.

SPURR, S. H. (1979). Sylviculture. *Sci. Amer.* **240**, (2) 62–75.

—— and FRIEND, R. B. (1941). Compression wood in weevilled Northern white pine. *J. For.* **39**, 1005–6.

—— and HYVÄRINEN, M. J. (1954). Wood fibre length as related to position in tree and growth. *Bot. Rev.* **20**, 561–75.

STALKER, I. N. (1971). A safer test for distinguishing heartwood and sapwood in pines. *J. Inst. Wood Sci.* **5**, 21–4.

STAMM, A. J. (1971). Review of nine methods for determining the fibre saturation points of wood and wood products. *Wood Sci.* **4**, 115–28.

STEARNS, T. L. (1950). Distinguishing red oak from white oak by chemical colour reaction. *Southn. Lumberm.* **184**, 50.

STEIGER, A. (1972). Schnellbestimmung eineger afrikanischer Furnierholzer mit einfachen physikalischen und chemischen Methoden. *Holztechnol.* **13**, 175–9.

STEVENS, W. C. and TURNER, N. (1970). Wood-bending handbook. London, H.M.S.O.

SÜSS, H. and MÜLLER-STOLL, W. R. (1969). Über das Faserwachstum, seine Beziehungen zum jahresperiodischen Dickenwachstum und die Faseruberlappung bei einegen Laubhölzern. *Holzforsch.* **23**, 145–51.

THIMANN, K. V. (1958) (*Ed.*). The physiology of forest trees. New York, Ronald Press.

THOMAS, R. J. (1972). Bordered pit aspiration in angiosperms. *Wood and Fibre*, **3**, 236–7.

—— and KRINGSTAD, K. P. (1971). The role of hydrogen bonding in pit aspiration. *Holzforsch.* **25**, 143–9.

—— (1972). A note on hydrogen bonding and pit aspiration. *Wood Sci.* **5**, 63–4.

TIMELL, T. E. (1965). Wood and bark polysaccharides. *In* CÔTÉ, W. A. Jr. (*Ed.*), 1965.

—— (1967). Recent progress in the chemistry of wood hemicelluloses. *Wood Sci. Technol.* **1**, 45–70.

—— (1972a). Beobachtungen an Holzstrahlen im Druckholz. *Holz als Roh- u. Werkstoff* **30**, 267–73.

—— (1972b). Nature of the last-formed tracheids in compression wood. *I.A.W.A. Bull.* 1972(4), 10–19.

—— (1973). Studies in opposite wood in conifers. *Wood Sci. Technol.* **7**, 1–5, 79–91 and 163–72.

—— (1978). Helical thickenings and helical cavities in normal and compression wood of *Taxus baccata*. *Wood Sci. Technol.* **12**, 1–15.

—— (1979). Formation of compression wood in balsam fir (*Abies balsamea*), II. Ultrastructure of the differentiating xylem. *Holzforsch.* **33**, 181–91.

—— (1982). Recent progress in the chemistry and topochemistry of compression wood. *Wood Sci. Technol.* **16**, 83–122.

TRÉNARD, Y. and GUÉNEAU, P. (1975). Relations entre constraintes de croissance longitudinales et bois de tension dans le hêtre (*Fagus sylvatica* L.). *Holzforsch.* **29**, 217–23.

VAN VLIET, G. J. C. M. (1978). Vestured pits of Combretaceae and allied families. *Acta Bot. Néerl.* **27**, 273–85.

VOLKMAN, D. and SIEVERS, A. (1979). Graviperception in multicellular organisms. *In* HAUPT, W. and Feinleib, M. E. (*Eds.*), **7**, 573–600.

VURDU, H. and BENSEND, D. W. (1979). Specific gravity and fibre length in European black alder roots, stems and branches. *Wood Sci.* **12**, 103–5.

WAISEL, Y., NOAH, I. and FAHN, A. (1966). Cambial activity in *Eucalyptus camaldulensis* Dehn. II. The production of xylem and phloem elements. *New Phyt.* **65**, 319–24.

WARDROP, A. B. (1956). The nature of reaction wood. V. The distribution and formation of tension wood in some species of *Eucalyptus*. *Austral. J. Bot.* **4**, 152–66.

—— (1964a). The structure and formation of the cell wall in xylem. *In* ZIMMERMANN, M. H. (*Ed.*), 1964.

—— (1964b). The reaction anatomy of arborescent angiosperms. *In* ZIMMERMANN, M. H. (*Ed.*), 1964.

—— (1965a). Cellular differentiation in xylem. *In* CÔTÉ, W. A. JR. (*Ed.*), 1965.

—— (1965b). The formation and function of reaction wood. *In* CÔTÉ, W. A. JR. (*Ed.*), 1965.

—— (1981). Lignification and xylogenesis. *In* BARNETT, J. R. (*Ed.*), 1981b.

—— and DADSWELL, H. E. (1950). The nature of reaction wood. II. The cell wall organization of compression wood tracheids. *Austral. J. Sci. Res.* **B, 3**, 1–13.

—— (1952). The nature of reaction wood. III. Cell division and cell wall formation in conifer stems. *Austral. J. Sci. Res.* **B, 5**, 385–98.

—— (1955). The nature of reaction wood. IV. Variations in cell wall organization of tension wood fibres. *Austral. J. Bot.* **3**, 177–89.

—— (1957). Variations in the cell wall organization of tracheids and fibres. *Holzforsch.* **11**, 33–41.

—— and DAVIES, G. W. (1964). The nature of reaction wood. VIII. The structure and differentiation of compression wood. *Austral. J. Bot.* **12**, 24–38.

—— and HARADA, H. (1965). The formation and structure of the cell wall in fibres and tracheids. *J. Exp. Bot.* **16**, 356–71.

—— and PRESTON, R. D. (1947). Organization of the cell walls of tracheids and fibres. *Nature, London* **160**, 911–13.

—— (1951). The submicroscopic organization of the cell wall in conifer tracheids and wood fibres. *J. Exp. Bot.* **2**, 20–30.

WAREING, P. F. (1969). Germination and dormancy. *In* WILKINS, M. B. (*Ed.*), 1969.

—— and PHILLIPS, I. D. J. (1981). Growth and differentiation in plants (3rd ed). Oxford, Pergamon Press.

WENHAM, M. W. and CUSICK, F. (1975). The growth of secondary wood fibres. *New Phyt.* **74**, 247–61.

WERSHING, H. F. and BAILEY, I. W. (1942). Seedlings as experimental material in the study of 'redwood' in conifers. *J. For.* **40**, 411–4.

WESTING, A. H. (1965). Formation and function of compression wood in gymnosperms. *Bot. Rev.* **31**, 381–480.

—— (1968). Formation and function of compression wood in gymnosperms. II. *Bot. Rev.* **34**, 51–78.

WHITE, D. J. B. (1965). The anatomy of reaction tissues in plants. *Viewpoints in Biology* **4**, 54–82.

—— and ROBARDS, A. W. (1966). Some effects of radial growth rate upon the rays of certain ring-porous hardwoods. *J. Inst. Wood Sci.* No. 17, 45–52.

WHITE, J. (1907). The formation of redwood in conifers. *Proc. Roy. Soc. Victoria* n.s. **20**, 107–24.

WHITMORE, T. C. (1975). Tropical rain forests of the Far East. Oxford, Clarendon Press.

WILKINS, M. B. (1969) (*Ed.*). Physiology of plant growth and development. London, McGraw-Hill.

WILLIS, J. C. (1931). A dictionary of flowering plants and ferns (6th ed.). Cambridge, University Press.

—— (1973). A dictionary of flowering plants and ferns (8th ed., revised AIRY-SHAW, H. K.). Cambridge, University Press.

WILSON, B. F. (1963). Increase in cell wall surface area during enlargement of cambial derivatives in *Abies concolor*. *Amer. J. Bot.* **50**, 95–102.

—— (1964). A model for cell production by the cambium of conifers. *In* ZIMMERMANN, M. H. (*Ed.*), 1964.

—— (1981). The development of growth strains and stresses in reaction wood. *In* BARNETT, J. R. (*Ed.*), 1981b.

—— and ARCHER, R. R. (1977). Reaction wood: induction and mechanical action. *Ann. Rev. Pl. Physiol.* **28**, 23–43.

WODZICKI, T. J. and BROWN, C. L. (1973). Cellular differentiation of the cambium in the Pinaceae. *Bot. Gaz.* **134**, 139–46.

YATAGAI, M. and TAKAHASHI, T. (1980). Tropical wood extractives' effects on durability, paint curing time and pulp sheet resin spotting. *Wood Sci.* **12**, 176–82.

YEOMAN, M. M. (1976) (*Ed.*). Cell division in higher plants. London, Acad. Press.

YLINEN, A. and JUMPPANEN, P. (1967). Theory of the shrinkage of wood. *Wood Sci. Technol.* **1**, 241–52.

YOSHIZAWA, N., MATSUMOTO, S. and TOSHINAGA, I. (1985). Morphological features of tracheid tips associated with compression wood formation in *Larix leptolepis* Gord. *I.A.W.A. Bull.* n.s. **6**, 245–53.

ZAGÓRSKA-MAREK, B. (1984). Pseudo-transverse divisions and intrusive elongation of fusiform initials in the storeyed cambium of *Tilia*. *Can. J. Bot.* **62**, 20–7.

ZIMMERMANN, M. H. (1964) (*Ed.*). The formation of wood in forest trees. New York, Acad. Press.

—— (1983). Xylem structure and the ascent of sap. New York, Springer-Verlag.

—— and BROWN, C. L. (1971). Trees, structure and function. New York, Springer-Verlag.

—— and JEJE, A. A. (1981). Vessel length distribution in stems of some American woody plants. *Can. J. Bot.* **59**, 1882–92.

—— and TOMLINSON, P. B. (1967). Method for the analysis of the course of vessels. *I.A.W.A. Bull.* 1967(1), 2–6.

——, WARDROP, A. B. AND TOMLINSON, P. B. (1968). Tension wood in aerial roots of *Ficus benjamina* L. *Wood Sci. Technol.* **2**, 95–104.

Index

In general, timbers are indexed only by reference to their botanical names.

Page numbers in heavy type refer to illustrations.

For the timbers listed on pp. 73 and 128, of which the identification is discussed at some length, references to those of their characteristics which are most significant in their identification are indicated by the phrase 'chars. of'.

chemical tests in, 252 *et seq.*
computerisation of, 263
fundamental problems of, 254, 255
keys for, 255 *et seq.*
variability as a factor in, 255
Ilex aquifolium, 91
chars. of, 128, **136**, **141**
spiral thickening of fibres, 100
interfascicular cambium, 31
internode, meaning of, 22
intrusive growth, 31
in cambial cells, 31, 32, 40
in fibres, **41**, 98, 206
iroko, figure of, **184**
'stone' in, **219**
isolation cells, 124

jarrah and karri,
separation of, 252
Juglans,
axial parenchyma of, **109**
pigmentation of, **180**
semi-ring-porous structure, 106
Juniperus, chars. of, 79, 80, **81**, **82**
juvenile wood, 203

karri and jarrah,
separation of, 252
keys, dichotomous, 255 *et seq.*
specimens of, 257–259
keys, perforated card, 260 *et seq.*
specimen card, **261**
Khaya, 95, 112, 121, 253
kino, 218
knots, **17** *et seq.*
arris, 17
dead, **18**
live, **18**
loose, **18**
pin, 20
round, 17
spike, 17
splay, 17
tight, **18**

Laburnum, 95, 96
Lammas shoots, 28
Larix, chars. of,
71, **72**, 73, 74, **75**, 76
cf. Picea 74–76
latewood, 12
latex, traces, 105
tubes, 105, **110**, **123**

Laurelia, 96
marginal ray cells, **124**
leaf primordia, 25
lenticels, 43
lignin, 144, 147, **148**
compounds with hemicelluloses, 148
ligno-cellulose, 148
Liquidambar, 95, 119
Liriodendron, 91, chars. of, **136**
terminal parenchyma of, 112, **113**
log, cut surfaces of a, **14**
transverse 11, **14**
radial longitudinal, 15
tangential longitudinal, 15
Lovoa trichilioides, 104
axial parenchyma of, **111**
pigmentation of, 179
gum ducts in, **218**

maceration of wood,
fibres in, **41**
methods of, 68
tracheids in, 68, **69**, 70
Magnolia, 92, 112, 124
scalariform pitting in, **94**, 95
mahoganies, chemical
tests for, 252, 253
mahogany, African,
crotch and swirl figure in, **185**, 186
maples, figure in,
bird's-eye, **187**
quilted, **187**
margo, 56
meristems, meristematic, 11
metaphloem, 30
metaxylem, 29
micelles, 147
microfibrils, 148, 149, **158**
formation of, 166 *et seq.*
micron (μm), 143
middle lamella, **51**
lignification of, 162, 163
mucilage cells (in rays), 121
multiplicative divisions, **36** *et seq.*

names of trees, 3 *et seq.*
nanometre, 143
nodular end walls, 61, **62**

oaks,
chemical tests for, 254
diffuse-porous, 106
European, 129, **130**, **131**